BANK RESOLUTION
AND CRISIS MANAGEMENT

BANK RESOLUTION AND CRISIS MANAGEMENT

Law and Practice

Simon Gleeson
Randall Guynn

OXFORD

UNIVERSITY PRESS

OXFORD

UNIVERSITY PRESS

Great Clarendon Street, Oxford, OX2 6DP,
United Kingdom

Oxford University Press is a department of the University of Oxford.
It furthers the University's objective of excellence in research, scholarship,
and education by publishing worldwide. Oxford is a registered trade mark of
Oxford University Press in the UK and in certain other countries

© Oxford University Press 2016

The moral rights of the authors have been asserted

First Edition published in 2016

Impression: 1

Published in the United States of America by Oxford University Press
198 Madison Avenue, New York, NY 10016, United States of America

British Library Cataloguing in Publication Data
Data available

Library of Congress Control Number: 2016933791

ISBN 978–0–19–969801–1

Printed and bound by
CPI Group (UK) Ltd, Croydon, CR0 4YY

CONTENTS—SUMMARY

CONTENTS

TABLE OF CASES

TABLE OF LEGISLATION

ABBREVIATIONS

AMV	asset management vehicle
BA	Banking Act 2009
BCBS	Basel Committee on Banking Supervision
BHC	bank holding company
BIO	Bail-in Order
BRRD	Bank Recovery and Resolution Directive
CCAR	Comprehensive Capital Analysis and Review
CCP	central clearing counterparty
CET1	common equity Tier 1
CIWUD	Credit Institutions Winding-up Directive
CMG	Crisis Management Group
CoCos	contingent convertible debt securities
CRD	Capital Requirements Directive
CRR	Capital Requirements Regulation
DGS	deposit guarantee scheme
DIP	debtor-in-possession
DRI	direct recapitalization instrument
D-SIB	domestic systemically important banking group
EBA	European Banking Authority
ECB	European Central Bank
ECHR	European Convention on Human Rights
ECJ	European Court of Justice
EEA	European Economic Area
EFSF	European Financial Stability Facility
EFTA	European Free Trade Association
EME	emerging markets economy
EMIR	European Market Infrastructure Regulation
ESA	European Supervisory Authority
ESM	European Stability Mechanism
EU	European Union
FBO	foreign banking organization
FCA	Financial Conduct Authority
FDIA	Federal Deposit Insurance Act
FDIC	Federal Deposit Insurance Corporation
FHFA	Financial Housing Finance Authority
FIBA	Financial Institutions Bankruptcy Act
FINMAR	Financial Stability and Market Confidence Sourcebook
FIRREA	Financial Institutions Reform, Recovery and Enforcement Act
FSB	Financial Stability Board
FSCS	Financial Services Compensation Scheme

FSMA	Financial Services and Markets Act 2000
GDP	gross domestic product
GLAC	gone concern loss absorbing capacity
G-SIB	global systemically important banking group
G-SII	global systemically important institution
HERA	Housing and Economic Recovery Act
holdco	holding company
HQLA	high quality liquid asset
IA	Insolvency Act 1986
IADI	International Association of Deposit Insurers
IDI	insured depository institution
IMF	International Monetary Fund
IPO	initial public offering
ISDA	International Swaps and Derivatives Association
JPMCB	JP Morgan Chase Bank
LLP	limited liability partnership
LTCM	Long-Term Capital Management
LTD	long-term unsecured debt
MAHC	mixed-activity holding company
MOU	Memorandum of Understanding
MPE	multiple point of entry
MREL	minimum requirement for eligible liabilities
NBC	National Bankruptcy Conference
NCA	national competent authority
NCWOL	no-creditor-worse-off-than-in-liquidation
NRA	national resolution authority
OCC	Office of the Comptroller of the Currency
P&A	purchase and assumption
PPT	partial property transfer
PRA	Prudential Regulation Authority
QFC	qualified financial contract
RCH	Recognized Clearing House
repo	repurchase agreement
RIE	Recognized Investment Exchange
RWA	risk-weighted asset
SAR	special administration regime
SEC	Securities and Exchange Commission
SIFI	systemically important financial institution
SIFMA	Securities Industry and Financial Markets Association
SIPA	Securities Investor Protection Act
SIPC	Securities Investor Protection Corporation
SLHC	savings and loan holding company
SME	small to medium-sized enterprise
SPE	single point of entry
SRB	Single Resolution Board
SREP	supervisory review and evaluation process
SRM	Single Resolution Regime, Mechanism
SRMR	Single Resolution Mechanism Regulation

SRR	Special Resolution Regime
SSM	Single Supervisory Mechanism
SSMR	Single Supervisory Mechanism Regulation
TARP	Troubled Asset Relief Program
TBTF	too big to fail
TCH	The Clearing House Association
TLAC	total loss absorbing capacity
TLGP	Temporary Liquidity Guarantee Program
TPRRA	Taxpayer Protection and Responsible Resolution Act
UNCITRAL	United Nations Commission on International Trade Law

PART I

ELEMENTS OF BANK RESOLUTION REGIMES

1

INTRODUCTION

A. Why do we Resolve Banks?

Banks are *unlike* commercial companies in many ways. A fundamental difference is **1.01** that whereas commercial companies produce widgets, banks produce money and credit, which we will refer to as financial widgets. Moreover, it is a fundamental fact of their business that banks generally cannot continue to produce their financial widgets whilst insolvent.[1] In ordinary corporate insolvency practice, it is entirely practical to allow an insolvent business to continue to produce its widgets—be they commodities like corn, manufactured goods like cars, or services like air travel. This is the basis for insolvency regimes like Chapter 11 of the US Bankruptcy Code, UK Administration, and many other corporate reorganization regimes around the world. The essence of these approaches is that an insolvent commercial company can continue to pay commercial creditors of the firm—who are therefore prepared to continue to trade with it—whilst postponing payments to financial creditors. The plan of reorganization can even allow the claims of financial creditors to be permanently written down (after equity has been) or converted into equity interests in the firm as the final act of the insolvency proceeding. Treating the claims of financial creditors as subordinate to the claims of commercial creditors is justified on the ground that it results in more value for the financial creditors than shutting down the firm and liquidating its assets. Thus the firm can remain open and continue to produce its widgets whilst insolvent.

The reason banks generally cannot continue to produce their most important widgets **1.02** whilst insolvent is that their most important widgets are a certain type of financial liability that is widely accepted as money for payments in the broader economy.[2]

---

[1] Indeed, they typically cannot do so merely if enough of the consumers of their money-like widgets fear the banks may be insolvent or if the banks cannot convert their illiquid assets into liquid assets, except at a steep discount to face value.

[2] Douglas W Diamond and Philip H Dybvig, 'Bank Runs, Deposit Insurance, and Liquidity', 91 J Pol Econ (1983) 401, 405 ('demand deposits are a vehicle through which banks fulfill their role of turning illiquid assets into liquid assets'); Gary B Gorton, *Misunderstanding Financial Crises: Why We Don't See Them Coming* (2012) 5–6 ('The output of a car company is cars. The output of a consulting

As a result, the distinction between commercial creditors and financial creditors is not a meaningful one for banks. This was more obvious hundreds of years ago than it is today. For instance, modern banking emerged in Lombardy during the thirteenth century when Italian commodity merchants figured out how to offer book-entry claims or bills of exchange (i.e. paper money) representing interests in gold, silver, and other commodity money held in custody that could be used to make payments to strangers over long distances more cheaply and safely than making them by physical delivery of commodity money. Widespread bank lending developed along with fractional-reserve banking, which emerged when the Italian merchant-bankers learned that they only needed to hold a reserve equal to a fraction of the commodity money represented by the outstanding amount of book-entry claims and bills of exchange issued by them in order to satisfy the expected flow of withdrawal requests for commodity money. The Italian bankers brought modern banking to England, setting up shop along Lombard Street, near where the Bank of England now stands. English goldsmiths continued the tradition of issuing receipts or notes representing interests in commodity money during the latter half of the seventeenth century, and the Bank of England started to do so when it was chartered in 1694. Banks were chartered in the United States during the eighteenth and nineteenth centuries primarily to create a supply of paper money (i.e. bank notes) because there was not enough gold, silver, or other useful forms of commodity money to satisfy the demands of ordinary commerce. Today, the most common form of money-like claims produced by banks are demand deposits, which are claims against banks that can be transferred by cheque or electronic transfer to pay for goods and services in the wider economy.

1.03   Because the most important output of banks are certain types of financial liabilities that function as money, the distinction between commercial creditors and financial creditors is not a meaningful one for banks. Indeed, a key difference between a commercial firm and a bank is that a bank has no such division—almost all of its creditors are by definition financial creditors. For a bank, 'failure' and 'immediate cessation of business' have in the past been synonymous terms.

1.04   Of course, demand deposits and other money-like instruments are not the only financial widgets produced by banks. They also produce a variety of other financial services that are essential to the economy as a whole. Examples of these other critical operations include: making loans and other extensions of credit; clearing and settling financial transactions; retail and corporate banking; borrowing and lending between financial institutions; market-making in certain securities; and custody and financial brokerage services. Some of these services will survive the insolvency of the bank—borrowers, for example, are generally unaffected by the failure of their lender—but most will not. Thus the cumulative impact on the economy of the failure of a bank which provides multiples service is likely to be great.

1.05   Bank resolution regimes were developed because banks have in the past not been able to be liquidated or reorganized under traditional insolvency laws without risking a collapse in bank asset values and runs on demand deposits and other money-like liabilities throughout the banking system. Such runs can lead to a severe contrac-tion in the supply of money and credit throughout the financial system, resulting in substantial harm to the wider economy in the form of reduced output, increased unemployment and social unrest. Indeed, Milton Friedman and Anna Schwartz blamed the failure and liquidation of nearly 10,000 small US banks during the 1930s for what they called The Great Contraction in the supply of money (and credit), resulting in or deepening the Great Depression.[3] Dealing with insolvent banks by shutting them down and liquidating their assets is like dealing with an insolvent power company by shutting it down and selling off its turbines. In both cases, the residual value of the firm is likely to be minimized rather than maximized since going concern values are almost certainly greater than liquidation values. Just like allowing the production of electricity to be shut down, moreover, allowing the production of money and credit and other critical operations to be shut down can result in substantial harm to the wider economy.

This, however, takes us back to the major distinction between banks and other types **1.06** of companies. When an ordinary company becomes insolvent, the mechanism which is applied is to divide its financial and commercial creditors. Commercial creditors (such as suppliers) continue to be paid; payments to financial creditors are suspended. This permits the business to continue in operation throughout the insolvency. The object of this approach is for the business to be reorganized or sold as a going concern, thereby maximizing recoveries and limiting the loss. A neces-sary part of this approach, however, is that creditors be capable of being divided in this way—a business which is not capable of paying its ordinary commercial debts must close. The problem with a bank is that the distinction between commercial creditors and financial creditors is not a meaningful one—for any business whose output includes producing money-like financial liabilities, its commercial creditors are effectively a subset of its financial creditors.

B. Operating Liabilities/Capital Structure Liabilities

Bank resolution regimes seek to address this issue by dividing financial liabilities **1.07** into two classes: operating liabilities and capital structure liabilities. Operating liabilities include demand deposits, client money balances, short-term money market exposures, financial contract liabilities arising from risk-mitigating hedges, and certain exposures to financial infrastructures. Capital structure liabilities include regulatory capital, long-term unsecured debt (e.g. with an original maturity of one year or more), and deposit insurance funds. In all cases, the objective of the resolution is to

---

company is advice. The output of a shipping company is transportation services. The output of a bank is debt…that people and companies find useful for transactions').

[3] Milton Friedman and Anna Jacobson Schwartz, *A Monetary History of the United States, 1867– 1960* (1963), ch 7.

permit operating liabilities to be paid whilst capital structure liabilities are written down or otherwise absorb losses.[4]

C. Resolution an Optional Process

1.08   It should be noted that resolution is always an optional process. Governments or designated authorities may choose to invoke special resolution regimes, may choose not to do so and to let ordinary insolvency processes take their course, or may choose a variety of other options. It is not necessary to show—and it cannot be shown—that all failing institutions will in all cases be subject to resolution. The requirement is to show that all institutions are capable of being resolved.

D. Resolution under Traditional Insolvency Laws

1.09   Certain US global systemically important banking groups (US G-SIBs) have developed resolution strategies under the traditional US insolvency laws. For example, most of them submitted 2015 resolution plans under Title I of the Dodd–Frank Wall Street Reform and Consumer Protection Act (Dodd–Frank Act) that included single-point-of-entry (SPE) resolution strategies under the existing Chapter 11 of the US Bankruptcy Code.[5] This has not involved any amendments to Chapter 11 to subordinate capital structure liabilities to operating liabilities. Instead, the US G-SIBs have taken advantage of their holding company structures. They have restructured their liabilities so that their operating liabilities are segregated at the operating subsidiary level and a substantial layer of capital structure liabilities are segregated at the top-tier holding company. This results in the parent's capital structure liabilities being structurally subordinate to the group's operating liabilities. This in turn allows the top-tier parent of a US G-SIB to file a voluntary petition under Chapter 11 and do a quick transfer of all of its assets, including its ownership interests in operating subsidiaries, to a debt-free bridge holding company under section 363 of the US Bankruptcy Code and impose all of the group's losses on the parent's capital structure liabilities. The parent's capital structure liabilities are left behind in its bankruptcy estate and are subject to suspension, write-downs, and otherwise absorbing losses. The operating subsidiaries are recapitalized by the

---

[4] Art 44(2) BRRD provides a longer list of protected exposures.
[5] Federal Deposit Insurance Corporation (FDIC), Title I and IDI Resolution Plans, available at: <https://www.fdic.gov/regulations/reform/resplans/> (accessed 26 October 2015) (Bank of America, Citigroup, Goldman Sachs, JP Morgan Chase, Morgan Stanley, State Street). An SPE strategy is a resolution strategy whereby only the top-tier parent of a banking group (ie, the single point of entry) is put into insolvency or resolution proceedings, and the group's operating subsidiaries remain open and operating. The operating subsidiaries may remain that way, be sold to third parties, or be wound down in an orderly manner outside of their own insolvency proceedings.

parent immediately before it files the Chapter 11 petition, and remain open and operating (in some cases pursuant to capital contribution agreements secured by the parent's assets). As a result, the group's bank subsidiaries continue to be able to pay and produce new money-like liabilities and continue their other critical operations, whilst their parent is insolvent. The holders of the parent's capital structure liabilities bear all of the group's losses.

The United States is also considering amendments to its traditional insolvency **1.10** regime to add a special resolution regime for financial firms, generally referred to as a proposed Chapter 14 for the US Bankruptcy Code.[6] These proposed amendments to the US Bankruptcy Code would include a new priority scheme that would subordinate a financial firm's capital structure liabilities to its operating liabilities.

E. Solving the Problem of 'Too Big to Fail'

The approach to resolution outlined above provides the most promising solution **1.11** to the 'too-big-to-fail' (TBTF) problem. There are two reasons why it might be unacceptable to allow a large bank to fail. One of these is the credit loss which would be inflicted on the holders of demand deposits and other short-term creditors of the bank—losses which might result in runs on banks, contagion and cascading insolvencies of banks throughout the financial system, which could result in a severe contraction in the stock of money and credit, which would cause severe collateral damage to the real economy in the form of reduced economic output, increased unemployment, and social unrest. However, for most large banks the more significant consideration is that disruption of the services provided by banks to the real economy could have more damaging effects on that economy even than a sharp contraction of credit. This could occur because, as noted above, banks are the gatekeepers of the payment system, and access to the payment system is essential for any commercial actor—indeed, it is arguable that (in developed countries at least) access to an efficient payment system is essential for any form of meaningful economic participation in society. Suspending part of the payment system for any extended period of time would interrupt commercial activity even more drastically than credit losses arising out of deposits. Also, since access to payment services generally necessitates the maintenance of some form of deposit with the bank concerned, these impacts would be cumulative rather than alternative. The primary

---

[6] Financial Institutions Bankruptcy Act of 2015, HR 2947, 114th Cong, 1st Sess (2015); Taxpayer Protection and Responsible Resolution Act, S 1840, 114th Cong, 1st Sess (2015). See also Thomas H Jackson, 'Bankruptcy Code Chapter 14: A Proposal' in Kenneth E Scott and John B Taylor (eds) *Bankruptcy Not Bailout: A Special Chapter 14* (Hoover Institution 2012); Thomas H Jackson, 'Building on Bankruptcy: A Revised Chapter 14 for Recapitalisation, Reorganisation, or Liquidation of Large Financial Institutions' in Kenneth E Scott, Thomas H Jackson, and John B. Taylor (eds) *Making Failure Feasible: How Bankruptcy Reform Can End 'Too Big to Fail'* (Hoover Institution 2015).

policy objective of bank resolution is therefore to avoid such damage to the systems which underpin the economy.

1.12 Focusing on this objective helps to illuminate the issue of what it is exactly that we are trying to avoid. When we say that an institution is TBTF, what we generally mean is that suspending its business whilst its assets are liquidated would injure the economy by more than the cost of bailing out the institution concerned at taxpayer expense. However, the problem that we are trying to solve here is not the fact that the institution or its investor would incur losses, but the fact that sudden termination of its business would impose systemic damage. If it can be demonstrated that mechanisms exist whereby an institution can be restored to solvency without such sudden termination and without any government bailout, then the institution is not TBTF. Thus no institution is TBTF where, for any forecastable loss:

(a) the institution could be restored to solvency without requiring any government capital injections, and

(b) such restoration could be effected without suspending the institution's production of demand deposits or other money-like instruments or other critical operations that are essential to the broader economy.

The argument presented in this book is that such a mechanism has been developed, and could be applied to all existing institutions.

2

BANK RESOLUTION TECHNIQUES

It is clear that there is no single mechanism for resolving all types of banks—all **2.01** resolution authorities look at their powers as a 'toolkit', with the determination of the appropriate tool for the job being made on a case-by-case basis.

This raises the question of whether the tools which currently exist cover all **2.02** potential cases, or whether there remain lacunae in coverage. We know that certain institutions—for example relatively small US community, mid-size, or even regional banks—can be resolved, because the Federal Deposit Insurance Corporation (FDIC) has a long, successful track record of doing so. We know that the new single-point-of-entry (SPE) resolution model works for certain US global systemically important banking groups (US G-SIBs), and so on. However, the question that we have to ask is whether the suite of tools that we have covers the whole universe of banks and banking groups. In order to demonstrate the coverage of these methods it is necessary to consider a hierarchy of approaches to bank failure. This is broadly as follows:

1. restructuring of the business, involving asset and business sales, and recapitalization through raising new equity;
2. sale of all or a majority of the business by the purchase of assets and the assumption of liabilities (i.e. a purchase and assumption transaction) or otherwise;
3. write-down (after equity has been written down) or conversion to equity of subordinated or senior debt;[1]
4. liquidation;
5. state aid.[2]

---

[1] At this stage we are indifferent as to whether this is achieved by bail-in or by the use of structural tools.

[2] It is important to distinguish 'state aid' such as capital injections to insolvent companies from the provision of state secured liquidity on commercial terms to solvent companies in difficulties. The provision of secured liquidity includes lender of last resort financing by central banks. Government or central bank action of the latter kind is unproblematic provided that it does not constitute a disguised commitment of taxpayer funds to support the solvency of the institution concerned. In technical terms, such transactions are covered by the 'Market Economy Investor Principle', which is the test applied by competition authorities to determine whether a transaction contains elements of state aid.

2.03   The first two stages may involve the use of a number of resolution tools. These tools have the effect in practice of moving assets around the group to be resolved, and are in practice no more than preliminary steps to the process of resolution. Their primary usefulness is the creation of separate pools to which separate tools may be applied—thus, for example, a transfer of certain assets and liabilities to a bridge bank may enable that bridge bank to be sold as a going concern, thereby enabling bail-in of the remaining capital instruments. It is also true that these tools may be applied to have the effect of a resolution tool—thus, a transfer to a bridge bank leaving some creditors behind in the transferor entity may have the effect of bailing in those creditors—but for these purposes we concentrate on the economic effect rather than the legal name of these tools.

2.04   It is also important to be clear-eyed about the state—and option. There may be many reasons—not all of them economic—which might drive a state to rescue an institution. It should be pointed out that this is by no means a specific characteristic of banks—similar government intervention has been practised in many jurisdictions with firms ranging from car manufacturers to steelworks, and from shipbuilders to coal mines. The aim of designers of bank resolution architectures is to ensure that at all times government has an option not to intervene, not to prevent government from ever intervening.

2.05   Finally, in this context, real-world experience in the context of car manufacturers and steelworks has been that formal procedures, once rendered credible, are rarely used. The normal state of resolution for a business in the commercial world is a restructuring in which creditors voluntarily agree to a variation in their rights in order to optimize the prospects of the business continuing in existence and thus being able to repay a larger proportion of the amounts owed to them than would otherwise be the case. This is likely to be the position in the banking industry of the future. In order for a negotiated settlement to be successful, it is essential that the alternative to settlement be both unattractive and plausible. Creditors of banks in 2008 had no incentive to negotiate, and could reasonably await bail-out, because governments had no credible alternative course of action. This explains the apparent paradox that, provided resolution is plausible in theory, it will not be needed in practice, and to the extent that it is not plausible in theory, it will have to be demonstrated in practice.

A. Types of Banks

2.06   In conceptual terms banks can be divided into the following classes.

Small deposit-taking institutions

2.07   In general the primary safeguard for depositors in institutions of this kind is the deposit guarantee scheme (DGS). Banks of this kind can be left to fail and their depositors can be left to their recourse to the DGS without systemic damage. It may frequently be the case that some commitment of DGS resources to recapitalization (sometimes referred to as DGS bail-in) may produce a lower cost to the DGS itself than allowing the institution to fail and paying claims, but either approach is effective for this purpose.

Larger deposit-taking institutions with little or no long-term wholesale funding

These institutions are in general too big for the relevant DGS to cover, and do not **2.08** have long-term wholesale market creditors who can be bailed in without destabilizing the banking system. In such cases, resolution is managed through writing down the uninsured and unpreferred component of the deposit base. It is in respect of these institutions that the gone concern loss absorbing capacity (GLAC) tool is of most relevance, since it forces such institutions to maintain a minimum level of long-term non-deposit funding.

Wholesale institutions with little or no deposit funding

These institutions are those which it is envisaged will be resolved through what **2.09** could be described as a 'classical' restructuring or bail-in of their wholesale funding. The problem is likely to be a determination of which wholesale obligations can be bailed in without disturbing or destroying the commercial basis of the institution.

Large institutions with substantial wholesale and deposit funding bases

In these cases the primary issue is to ensure that the allocation of losses does **2.10** not result in runs that could destabilize the financial system. In such cases, it is important to ensure that long-term unsecured senior creditors are structurally, contractually, or legally subordinate to short-term unsecured senior creditors, and that senior creditors otherwise are treated equally, and in particular that long-term senior funding depositors are bailed in along with other long-term wholesale unsecured creditors.

B. Implementation

It is one thing to say that we have a complete set of techniques in isolation, but **2.11** another to say that they can be implemented in practice, and the argument is sometimes advanced that no matter how plausible bank resolution plans may seem in theory, political realities mean that they can never be implemented in practice. This argument is based on the assumption that internationally active banks can only be resolved with the active cooperation of multiple governments and resolution authorities around the world.

2.12 Although it is true that international resolution is likely to require multiple activities by multiple regulators, and it is certainly true that coordination between public sector entities would enhance the efficiency of resolution, it is not true that the lack of such cooperation would be a complete bar to resolution. At its simplest, where a single point of entry approach to resolution is employed, the only resolution activities which are required are those which take place at the group holding company level. Any subsidiary below that holding company which requires recapitalization will undergo a solvent restructuring involving the creation of new equity by the holding company. The aim of this structure is precisely to ensure that resolution is only required in respect of one entity in one country—all other group members should remain solvent and trading throughout the process. The only request which the resolution authority in the home country needs to make of resolution authorities in other countries should be that they do not take positive steps to interfere with the resolution process. It does not seem unreasonable for this level of cooperation to be expected.

2.13 It is true that a classical single point of entry approach requires a particular corporate structure, and not all systemically important banking groups have that structure. This has led to the further objection that since making all banking groups conform to the SPE corporate structure would be onerous or—in some cases—arguably impossible, the idea that global resolution for groups that do not already reflect this structure is fatally flawed.

2.14 This is incorrect, but in order to understand why it is necessary to begin with the understanding that the SPE approach is simply one way of achieving a policy outcome. The policy outcome which the SPE approach delivers is to pre-designate a minimum value of long-term unsecured creditors of the institution (whether by statute or otherwise[3]) as being those creditors whose claims will be written down (or off) in order to recapitalize the entity before any losses are imposed on any other creditors. In an SPE structure, this designation is effected by specifying creditors of the holding company as having this status. However, this is clearly not the only way of achieving that aim. Provided that the creditors concerned are easily and unambiguously identifiable, it is immaterial for this purpose whether they are creditors of any specific group company. What matters is that the terms of the instruments that they hold make clear, either explicitly, as with contingent convertible debt securities (CoCos), which convert into equity upon the occurrence of a specified trigger event such as a capital shortfall, or by necessary implication of the relevant applicable law, that

---

[3] For example, senior unsecured debt issued at holding company level by an institution whose presumptive path to resolution was by single point of entry at the holding company level.

they will be written down in order to recapitalize the bank before any excluded liabilities are written down, or alternatively, that they will be written down before any excluded liabilities are written down under the applicable statutory priority scheme. In principle it is easier for all concerned if the holding company is resolved and the bank subsidiary is untouched, but there is no strong reason why the designation approach should not produce the same result for the same value of designated debt.

Given this, it should be clear that size is pretty much irrelevant to resolvability— **2.15** larger institutions need more 'bail-in-able' debt; smaller institutions need less or can rely on the relevant deposit insurance scheme, but that is about it. The possibility of resolution is independent of the size of the institution requiring resolution.

It may therefore be asked how concern about the potential for failure of system- **2.16** ically important institutions became sidetracked onto the issue of 'size'? The answer is almost certainly that 'size' in this context has become confused with complexity. Larger institutions are generally observed to do more things in more places than smaller institutions, and one of the things which became clear during the crisis was that liquidation or a traditional insolvency approach—in which the institution to be resolved is separated into its different business lines and those lines are dealt with separately—becomes impracticable beyond a certain size of institution. Furthermore, the Lehman Brothers case showed that liquidation, without regard to ongoing business, is potentially destructive of value and gives rise to unfair inequalities of treatment of claimants when the business is broken up along legal entity and jurisdictional lines. This is not because separating out a large institution is impracticable per se—any institution can be dealt with in this way given sufficient time—but because in order to effect a resolution of a service provider, one of the key drivers is to avoid interruption of service. An extended closure of the institution concerned pending the completion of this analysis is not a practical approach to resolution.[4] It is therefore the case that certain institutions can be said to be unresolveable *using a traditional insolvency approach under pre-crisis law in most countries (i.e. not in accordance with the Financial Stability Board's Key Attributes for Effective Resolution Regimes).* However, it is precisely in response to this discovery that alternative approaches have been developed which are not dependent on an insolvency-based approach, and can be applied at the group level. It is precisely this possibility of group level application which means that the technique can be applied to any firm, regardless of its size.

This is not, of course, to underplay the importance of complexity. As noted above, **2.17** a prerequisite for resolution is that resolution authorities should be able to get their

---

[4] There are, of course, many things that can be done to facilitate this; in particular, through living wills and other approaches, which to some extent 'pre-pack' the institution for resolution. However, the efficacy of such approaches can never be undoubted, since their effectiveness depends to some extent on the regulator being able to predict the part of the bank's business which will suffer the shock concerned.

arms easily and quickly around the problem to be solved, and in particular to be able to establish reasonably accurately the size of the problem which needs to be solved. This is likely to require continuing work on the part of banks and resolution authorities (acting individually and through crisis management groups), and has not yet been delivered. However, there seems little doubt that it can be and will be, as mandated by the Financial Stability Board (FSB) and G20.

2.18 There is no mechanical rule which can be applied to say with certainty which firms should be resolved, and which may be safely left to fail in a traditional insolvency proceeding. The question of whether any particular institution need to be resolved is determined by the condition of the economy—and the market—at the relevant time. The exemplar for this is the situation in the United Kingdom in 2008, when the UK government was forced—at the height of the crisis—to guarantee the obligations of London Scottish Bank, which at that time had around £250m of deposits. The rationale for this decision was the fear that at that particular point the collapse of any UK bank, no matter how small, might set off a devastating run on the UK banking system as a whole. This startling demonstration of the fact that at the height of a crisis the classes of 'too-big-to-fail' and 'too-small-to-notice' might overlap was a reminder that any deposit-taking institution might, in certain circumstances, require resolution.

2.19 One of the most important issues with resolution is its impact on the entitlements of participants in the resolved entity. The best starting point for this analysis is to remember that the difference between creditors and equity investors is that equity investors are entitled to everything that is left after the creditors have been paid. Thus, a measure which reduces the claims of creditors by £1 therefore increases the net assets to which equity holders are entitled by £1. Where the value of equity pre-resolution has been reduced to zero, it is a simple matter to say that if creditor's claims are written down, creditors should receive all the new equity created by the write-down of their claims. However, real life is rarely this tidy.

2.20 It is vitally important in considering bank failure to remember that 'failure' in the context of a bank has an entirely different meaning from the term 'failure' in the context of a normal firm. A normal firm may continue trading for as long as it has £1 of positive asset value and a reasonable expectation that that value will grow rather than shrink. A bank, by contrast, must close its doors—or more accurately, will be closed by its regulator—as soon as its capital falls below the mandated value set by its regulator or it is likely to run out of a sufficient amount of cash or other liquid assets to satisfy its obligations as they come due. Thus, *a failed bank is almost necessarily still solvent*, at least in the sense that an insolvency practitioner would understand the term. This, in turn, means that the failed bank is likely to have a significantly positive net asset value, and in turn that its equity may still have a significantly positive value.

This raises the fascinating question of the value of such equity. Equity in a bank **2.21** which is no longer considered viable by its regulator exists in a kind of Schrodinger state, as can be seen in the rescue of Bear Stearns by J.P. Morgan. Although shares of Bear had a book value of US$84 per share immediately prior to its failure, J.P. Morgan initially agreed to pay just US$2 per share, on the basis that had it not been prepared to guarantee the obligations of Bear Stearns, the almost inevitable outcome would have been liquidation, in which it was assumed that the resulting outcome for shareholders would have been complete wipeout.

There is an interesting discussion of this point in *Starr International Company, Inc* **2.22** *v United States*.[5] At the point at which the Federal Reserve advanced its rescue loan to AIG, it was common ground that had the loan not been advanced, the firm would have become insolvent, but because of the making of the loan, it did not do so. However, part of the terms of the loan were that then existing equity holders were diluted by the issuance of new equity to the US Treasury equal to 79.9 per cent of the equity of AIG on a fully diluted basis. The US Federal Court of Claims recently held—inter alia—that the issuance of new equity was unauthorized and amounted to an illegal exaction by the US Treasury, but that the US government was not required to compensate the equity holders for any lost value resulting from the unauthorized dilution, because their equity would, but for the Federal Reserve intervention, have been valueless.

The truth of this proposition can in turn be tested by considering the outcome of **2.23** the Lehman Brothers administration in the United Kingdom. Upon the failure of Lehman Brothers, it was widely expected that creditors of the UK firm would lose out badly, and claims on the entity traded as low as 30 per cent of their face value. However, the final announcement by the administrators confirms that the eventual payout to creditors was 110 per cent of the face value of their claims (the reason that the payment was more than 100 per cent was that claims in UK insolvency attract interest at what is currently a penal rate (8 per cent simple interest per annum)), and this in turn ensures that there is very unlikely to be any surplus for shareholders). However, the key point here is that creditors were paid in full with a surplus, and the expectation that equity claimants could be disregarded was demonstrated to be—at least—oversimplistic.

Finally, we note that it must be conceded that not all banks can be resolved. The **2.24** issue here is that in order to resolve a bank using normal resolution techniques, it is necessary to have a reasonably clear picture of the current state of the bank and a clear pathway towards solvency. Put simply, you can't know how to fill a potential hole if you can form no reasonable estimate at all of the size of the hole.[6] Recent

---

[5] No 11-779C (US Fed Ct Claims 15 June 2015).
[6] This fact pattern is most commonly encountered in institutions which have suffered significant fraud or systems failure.

experience has taught us that in some cases the quality of the assets of a failed institution is so bad and its capitalization and liquidity position so poor that it is practically impossible to create a worst-case scenario. Without such a scenario, credible resolution is impossible. However, such institutions pose a relatively simple problem. A firm which is not capable of being recapitalized and reorganized through resolution has truly failed, in that the continuation of its business, no matter how desirable, is no longer possible. It must fail and be liquidated in the ordinary fashion—the question is simply one of who pays for that failure. Provided that the answer to this question is that the loss falls on the capital holders, the relevant DGS and uninsured creditors, there is no reason to conclude that impossibility of resolution has any very significant consequences.

C. Bank Groups

2.25 Much of the discussion about bank resolution is predicated on the basis of the simplifying assumption that a bank is a single entity. In economic terms this may be correct, but in legal terms it is clearly not. Most banks, and all systemically important banks, operate as groups of legal entities. In legal terms, groups do not exist—it is only the companies which comprise the group which can enter into contracts, incur liabilities, or fail. This is not, however, the way that economists (or people generally) see the world. Businesses are generally thought of as single undertakings—'Ford' or 'BP' are unitary concepts. Thus for a lawyer it makes perfect sense to talk of a group being partially insolvent, in that some of its components are insolvent whilst others are not. For non-lawyers, however, the concept is almost meaningless—it is like speaking of a human being as being partly dead.

2.26 However, in the same way that it is possible in emergencies to preserve the life of a living organism by removing dead parts, it is possible in emergencies to preserve the franchise value of parts of bank groups by allowing other parts to become insolvent. To press the analogy slightly further, the question of whether this is possible or not rather depends on the functions of the parts being amputated. There are some parts of a group whose removal can be accomplished without damaging the business of the group as a whole, but there are others whose removal entails the immediate and automatic extinction of the entire organism. It is by no means always crystal clear which is which.

2.27 There is therefore no automatic answer to the question 'What are we trying to resolve—the group or the bank?'—the only meaningful answer is 'It depends'. Consequently, it is necessary to think about bank resolution tools not only in the context of individual legal entities, but also in the context of how those tools could be applied to bank subsidiaries within a group, to parent companies of banks, and potentially to non-bank subsidiaries of banks. This is a difficult piece of analysis. To complicate matters further, bank groups are by no means uniform, and different bank managements have different strategies as to how the economic activity of the bank should be reflected in the legal structure of the group.

Finally as regards groups, one of the key differences in the use of these tools is that **2.28** the distinction between unitary and 'archipelago' banks—that is, between banks whose business is conducted as a single entity versus those banks whose structure is deliberately divided into multiple separable banks—is not relevant to the practicability or otherwise of resolution.[7] The resolution of an archipelago bank will in general be done as a series of separate resolutions of the troubled subsidiaries concerned (i.e. multiple points of entry), with at least some banking subsidiaries escaping resolution altogether. However, once this allocation has been made, the resolution of the subsidiaries concerned will proceed along the same lines as the resolution of a unitary bank group. The difference here is simply where within the group the resolution action is taken. The topic of resolution at the group level is considered in greater detail in Chapter 3 of this work.

D. Resolution as an Invasion of Private Rights

One of the most controversial things about bank resolution is the fact that, viewed **2.29** from one perspective, it is a gross interference with the rights of private individuals. Any process in which administrative action, unsanctioned by the court, may deprive owners of lawfully acquired property rights, is necessarily legally problematic. This issue is explicitly addressed in the recitals to the Bank Recovery and Resolution Directive (BRRD) says (recital 9):

> [T]he power of the authorities to transfer the shares or all or part of the assets of an institution to a private purchaser without the consent of shareholders affects the property rights of shareholders.

Further, any intervention in a solvent business is a violation of the freedom to **2.30** conduct a business as guaranteed by Article 16 of the Charter of Fundamental Rights.[8] However, the BRRD states (recital 17) that the limitation of that fundamental right is 'necessary in order to strengthen the business of institutions and

---

[7] We would emphasize here that these are ideals rather than descriptions of actual institutions. Unitary banks will have at least some operating subsidiaries, and unitary groups are likely to be found within archipelago banks. Thus these are conceptual poles between which bank group structures are located.

[8] Charter of Fundamental Rights of the European Union 2010/C 83/02. This codified a wide number of 'fundamental rights', and is given legal effect in the European Union through Art 6(1) of the Treaty of European Union. It is not to be confused with the European Convention on Human Rights (ECHR). The Charter is an EU document, is part of EU law, and is subject to the ultimate interpretation of the European Court of Justice (ECJ). It only applies in relation to EU law, but all EU law—including the BRRD—must be interpreted in member states in accordance with it. It is commonly but incorrectly believed that the United Kingdom and Poland have an 'opt-out' from this Charter through Protocol 30.

avoid institutions growing excessively or taking excessive risks without being able to tackle setbacks and losses and restore their capital base', and 'it requires preventative action to the extent that it is necessary to address the deficiencies and therefore it complies with Article 52 of the Charter of Fundamental Rights'.

2.31 Although these concerns are expressed in the context of EU law, the fundamental issues are serious constitutional and human rights law issues in almost all countries. The international position is exhaustively surveyed in an International Bar Association report[9] which reviewed the position in the G20 countries, and concluded that:

> All jurisdictions have confirmed that any constitutional/human rights protection which do accrue to investors in shares or bonds, or contractual counterparties, can be limited under the laws of their jurisdiction if the limitation is imposed in the public interest. In many cases, there are requirements that limitations will be proportionate to the public interest at stake, imposed by statute (rather than by regulation or through the exercise of an administrative discretion) and/or that some form of compensation is attributed.

2.32 Finally, one of the key elements of the resolution planning process is the idea that resolution authorities should be able to require changes to the structure and organization of institutions and their groups. This can conflict with Article 16 of the Charter of Fundamental Rights, the right to conduct business. As a result, authorities' discretion in this direction should be restricted to what is necessary to ensure resolvability.

2.33 Ironically, the United States may be one of the countries in which the conflict between insolvency laws and individual economic rights is almost never debated today. This lack of any serious debate is almost certainly a result of two historical factors. First, the US Constitution expressly authorizes the US Congress to enact bankruptcy laws,[10] which has always been seen as the authority to create reasonable exceptions to any contractual or other property rights in the event of insolvency. Second, the United States engaged in a vigorous debate over the conflict between economic rights and economic regulation during the Great Depression, and the proponents of a broad power to engage in economic regulation won the day, with the *Lochner* line of cases, which had granted constitutional protection to economic rights, being overruled and widely discredited.[11] While the US Constitution clearly imposes some limits on the bankruptcy power of Congress to interfere with settled

---

[9] Lisa Curran and Jaap Willeumier, *Report of the International Bar Association in connection with Legal Issues arising in relation to Proposals for Bank 'Bail-In' Measures*, Submitted on behalf of the Financial Crisis Task Force of the Legal Practice Division; 29 November 2010.

[10] US Const, Art I, § 8, cl 4.

[11] Starting with *Lochner v New York*, 198 US 45 (1905), the US Supreme Court struck down a series of state and federal laws such as zoning laws and labour laws, because they amounted to economic regulation that interfered with what the Supreme Court characterized as the fundamental right to the freedom of contract. During the early years of the Great Depression, the Supreme Court

contractual and property rights, it is not clear what those limits are and they have not been very protective since the *Lochner* line of cases were discredited.

The most serious debate over the scope of the federal bankruptcy power to interfere **2.34** with economic rights is reflected in litigation over the original terms of the AIG rescue and the unilateral change in the original terms of the rescue of Fannie Mae and Freddie Mac. The plaintiffs in AIG challenged the power of the US Treasury to acquire equity in AIG as part of the government's compensation for the Federal Reserve's rescue of that firm. While the plaintiffs nominally won in the Federal Court of Claims, the court refused to award them any damages on the ground that AIG would have been forced into bankruptcy and the entire value of the plaintiffs' shares would have been wiped out without the rescue. The plaintiffs in the Fannie Mae and Freddie Mac litigation have challenged the power of the US Treasury and the Financial Housing Finance Authority (FHFA) to unilaterally amend the terms of the original deal between the US Treasury and Fannie Mae and Freddie Mac, to implement the so-called net worth sweep, which gave the US government the exclusive right to all of the future net worth of Fannie Mae and Freddie Mac.

The situation that is most likely to give rise to a serious claim for compensation **2.35** under the Takings Clause of the US Constitution is one in which a bank is placed into an FDIC receivership before it is balance-sheet insolvent and the FDIC substantially undervalues the bank based on fire-sale prices, distributes that deflated value to the most senior claimants, and wipes out the equity and other junior claims. If the equity or other junior claimants can show that the FDIC substantially undervalued the bank or its assets and distributed a windfall to a third-party purchaser or the senior claimants, the junior claimants should have a strong argument that the FDIC effectively 'took' a portion of their property rights without giving the junior claimants just compensation as required by the Takings Clause. The solution to this problem would be for the FDIC to preserve the relative priority of the junior claims, just in case the bank or its assets turn out to be worth more than the FDIC's

---

struck down one federal law after another that the Roosevelt Administration had championed as part of its New Deal. This conflict between the judicial branch and the legislative and executive branches of government incensed President Roosevelt, who announced his so-called court-packing plan to increase the size of the Supreme Court from nine to fifteen justices. The plan was controversial because it was widely viewed as a way to manipulate the outcome of Supreme Court decisions. But since the US Constitution did not specify the number of justices on the Supreme Court, it appeared to be something the President had the raw power to do. President Roosevelt abandoned his controversial plan when one of the justices, who had appeared to have supplied the critical fifth vote in a series of five-to-four decisions striking down New Deal legislation based on the *Lochner* line of cases appeared to switch his position and supply the critical fifth vote in a series of five-to-four decisions upholding the constitutionality of subsequent New Deal legislation. This apparent switch in voting has been called the 'switch in time that saved nine'. The *Lochner* line of cases were overruled and repudiated on the ground that they had no basis in the text or history of the US Constitution—i.e. that the pre-New Deal Court had invented the constitutional right to the freedom of contract out of thin air. Almost no one defends *Lochner* today. Moreover, the repudiation of the *Lochner* line of cases led the Supreme Court to cut back on the economic rights that are clearly protected by the text of the

valuation based on fire-sale prices, by giving the junior claimants warrants or other participation interests allowing them to participate in any unexpected upside.[12]

E. Deposit Insurance in Resolution

2.36 It is sometimes argued that bank resolution is unnecessary, since the objective which it seeks to secure—continuation of services to bank users—is already secured through depositor protection measures such as deposit insurance and depositor preference. In some respects this is clearly wrong, since depositor preference in many countries (in particular the EU) does not extend to anything other than retail and small corporate depositors measures, and deposit protection fund coverage is limited in value. However, even for retail depositors, falling back on a deposit guarantee is a poor alternative to continuation of service. This was dramatically illustrated in the United Kingdom in the aftermath of the failure of Northern Rock, as retail depositors discovered that the fact that they would get their deposit back eventually was not going to help them to pay the rent or buy groceries that week (or, at that time, for many weeks to come).

2.37 This means that bank resolution and depositor protection measures must coexist—they are not alternatives. It is therefore necessary to consider the interaction of the two regimes.

2.38 In general, depositors are protected up to specified limits by deposit guarantee schemes (DGSs), which have the effect of passing any loss that would otherwise be suffered by such depositors through to the other banks in the relevant banking system. The fact that a DGS distributes losses within a system makes clear why such schemes are irrelevant in a systemic crisis—claims on a DGS are valueless if all of the contributories are unable to contribute.[13] However, in the event of institutional

---

US Constitution by construing them very narrowly. For example, the Contracts Clause in the US Constitution expressly protects contracts against interference by state governments. The Supreme Court, which for more than a hundred years had applied the Contracts Clause against economic regulation by the Federal government through the due process clause of the Fifth Amendment to the US Constitution, started limiting the Contracts Clause to State regulation only. It even started upholding state regulation that interfered with contracts as long as the regulation had what it called a 'rational basis'. Although the Takings Clause in the Fifth Amendment to the US Constitution expressly applies against the Federal government, the US Supreme Court has come very close to saying that any Federal economic regulation survives a challenge under the Takings Clause if it does not amount to a total taking and there is a rational basis for such regulation.

[12] See Douglas G Baird and Donald S Bernstein, 'Absolute Priority, Valuation Uncertainty and the Reorganization Bargain' 115 Yale L Journal 1930 (2005) (arguing that competing creditors often agree to a relative priority rule to resolve disputes about valuation in US bankruptcy proceedings when asset values are highly uncertain).

[13] This elides the difficult question as to whether government is properly viewed as a contributory to a national DGS. However, if government is the sole remaining contributor to a DGS, then the process becomes identical to government bail-out and the use of the DGS becomes nominal.

failure within a basically sound system, the DGS is the primary protection for depositors within that system.

The fact that calls on a DGS are allocated to other banks in the relevant system **2.39** also provides (in theory at least) an economic incentive for banks to monitor each other's risktaking, and gives a strong interest in the efficient resolution of the failed bank in a way which minimizes losses to insured depositors, and therefore to them.

It is therefore important to all systemic participants that the involvement of the **2.40** DGS in a bank resolution is structured so that the resources of the DGS are deployed in a way which minimizes losses to its contributors. This means that the DGS should not be restricted only to bearing losses after failure, but should be able to deploy its resources—cooperatively with other parties—to reduce the magnitude of the losses actually suffered. This is sometimes referred to as 'bailing in the DGS', but this concept is unhelpful, since it implies voluntary assumption of losses by the DGS. In a classical DGS rescue, the DGS expends a small amount of money voluntarily in order to avoid the risk of suffering a greater loss at a later stage.

A further element to be addressed is the fact that in general immediate funding **2.41** for a DGS is provided by the relevant government. All DGSs are either explicitly or implicitly guaranteed by their governments, on the basis that no government would in practice allow the DGS in its territory to collapse (although, as was seen in the *Iceland* case, a government may well be prepared to cut loose overseas depositors in its banks in order to rescue its domestic system[14]). Thus where a DGS is called upon for any commitment, the immediate source of the credit exposure behind that commitment is the relevant government, even if the ultimate cost is charged back to the DGS members over a somewhat longer timescale. This point has been used to argue that involvement of the DGS in bank resolution is in fact nothing more than a disguised form of government bail-out, since in the immediate response to the crisis it is the government's credit which is committed. It is argued that since this approach is in principle no different from a direct commitment of taxpayer's funds accompanied by the imposition of a tax on the banks over a subsequent period (as has been the case in, for example, the United Kingdom), the two are identical.

It should be noted as a preliminary point that this argument is equally applic- **2.42** able to pre-funded and post-funded schemes. Although in pre-funded schemes it is possible that very small institutions may be resolved using only the funding already in existence, pre-funded schemes do not in general hold sufficient funds

---

[14] The facts are set out in the decision of the European Free Trade Association (EFTA) Court on the matter; *Case E-16/11—EFTA Surveillance Authority v Iceland.*

to meet even a significant fraction of the deposits held by a G-SIB or D-SIB.[15] A pre-funded scheme is simply a scheme where the scheme operator has sufficient funds in its pocket to cover some level of expected loss—for any level above that, its recourse to its sponsoring government is the same as that for an unfunded scheme.

2.43 There are a number of important distinctions which can be made between DGS bail-in and government bail-out. However, the most important is simply that the costs incurred by a DGS should ultimately fall back on the other members of the financial system concerned.[16] There is an element of intertemporal allocation here, in that the aim of the government intervention is generally to transfer the liability from the system during the crisis, when it is weak and less able to absorb the losses, to the same system post-crisis, when it will have recovered and will be more able to absorb the losses. However, assuming that the system remains in being, there is never any issue of the exposure incurred by government falling anywhere other than on the system participants concerned in proportion to their liability to contribute to the scheme—a liability which bears no other resemblance to a tax. Put simply, in order to argue that a DGS bail-in constitutes taxpayer assistance, it is necessary to argue that DGS contribution levies are taxes—a proposition which would, at the very least, sound strange to any competent government statistician or administrative court.

2.44 Cross-border issues with DGSs are notoriously difficult. The current trend is towards requiring at least retail (and therefore insured) deposit-taking to be conducted within local subsidiaries in each country—an approach which has the merit of ensuring that each local banking subsidiary is part of the local DGS. However, where deposits are taken through a cross-border branch network the problem swiftly becomes intractable—the Icesave experience in the United Kingdom[17] dramatically illustrated the fact that a foreign DGS is ultimately backstopped by the sovereign of the jurisdiction in which the bank concerned is established, and if that sovereign is unable or unwilling to finance the compensation of foreign depositors, this creates a gap which will—in practice—need to be filled by the banks or government of the host jurisdiction. The structuring of DGSs as regards cross-border deposit-taking remains an unresolved issue.

---

[15] A G-SIB is a global systemically important banking group (i.e. a group with cross-border operations) and a D-SIB is a domestic systemically important banking group (i.e. a group that is systemic within a particular domestic economy).

[16] Assuming that there are sufficient institutions left in the system able to absorb those costs. Where this is not the case, as was seen in Iceland, the cost will ultimately be borne by the government and distributed through general taxation.

[17] LandsBanki, an Icelandic bank, had accepted deposits through branches in the UK and the Netherlands under the name 'Icesave'. When it collapsed in 2008, the Icelandic deposit protection scheme was already effectively exhausted. The Icelandic Government chose to guarantee deposits made with Icelandic branches of the bank, but not those made with the United Kingdom or Dutch branches. See n 14 above for citation of the subsequent litigation.

F. Deposit Guarantee Schemes and Systemic Crises

The final point to make in this context is that DGSs are tools created to absorb **2.45** losses from a single bank failure where that failure occurs within a solvent banking system. In a systemic crisis, a DGS may well turn from being part of the solution to being part of the problem, and in particular may become a channel for the transmission of systemic risk. The point is clearly made in the BCBS/IADI *Core Principles for Effective Deposit Insurance Systems*:

> A deposit insurance system is not intended to deal, by itself, with systemically significant bank failures or a 'systemic crisis'. In such cases all financial system safety-net participants must work together effectively. In addition, the costs of dealing with systemic failures should not be borne solely by the deposit insurance system, but dealt with through other means such as by the state. (p. 3)

This point is also picked up in the *Iceland* decision. In defending discrimination **2.46** by the Icelandic authorities against non-Icelandic depositors under the Icelandic depositor protection arrangements, the court said that 'EEA [European Economic Area] states enjoy a wide margin of discretion in making fundamental choices of economic policy in the specific event of a systemic crisis'. Put simply, not only are DGSs not designed to be used in the event of systemic crises, but it may be unwise to count on their being available in the event of such crises. This was, of course, equally visible during the Cyprus crisis—once all of the banks in a particular country are in trouble, recourse to the DGS of that country ceases to be a relevant consideration.

G. Depositor Preference

Increased focus on the role of the DGS in resolution, and on the possible function **2.47** of a DGS as a transmitter of financial vulnerability within the banking system, has resulted in increased interest in depositor preference.

Depositor preference means a legal priority in insolvency for depositor creditors of **2.48** a failed bank over claims of all other senior, unsecured creditors (subject perhaps to limited wage and trade claims). Depositor preference has a long history in the United States and other countries, and is generally based on the idea that depositors are the people whom bank regulation seeks to protect, and that therefore in any competition between depositors and others for the assets of the bank, depositors should have preference. However, a number of countries have actively rejected the notion, on the basis that the resulting interference with the rights of other creditors stunts the ability of the institution concerned to do business.

Depositor preference is also sometimes territorial. Thus, for example, in the United **2.49** States, deposits payable in the United States (domestic deposits) are preferred, such that after bank capital the burden of losses incurred by a failed bank falls on the other creditors of the bank, including the holders of deposits payable solely out-side the United States (foreign branch deposits),[18] before it falls on the holders of domestic deposits. The effect of this arrangement in practice has been that the assets of most failed institutions have been insufficient to satisfy the claims of both the holders of domestic deposits and the holders of any claims junior to domestic deposits. For example, based on our review of ten of the largest institutions to fail in the United States in 2008 and 2009, domestic deposits generally accounted for at least 97 per cent of the failed institution's liabilities,[19] and the value of each institution's assets averaged just 65 per cent of total liabilities at the time of failure.[20] Under these conditions, the assets will be insufficient to satisfy the claims on all domestic deposit liabilities; as a result, nothing will be left for general unsecured claims or any other claims junior to domestic deposits.

2.50 Once depositor preference has been established, the structure of a bank is generally likely to change such that any creditor who is not a depositor may seek to become a secured creditor. The fewer the unsecured creditors, the larger the risk to those creditors, and therefore the smaller the pool of unsecured creditors is likely to be. This means that the introduction of depositor preference may result in a greater likelihood that depositors (or the DGS) will have to be bailed-in in the absence of any other bail-in-able senior creditors.

2.51 Ironically, the domestic deposit liabilities of the US G-SIBs (except for Morgan Stanley Bank) accounted for a substantially smaller percentage of their total

---

[18] FDIA, § 11(d)(11), 12 CFR § 1821(d)(11). Three US law firms—Cleary Gottlieb, Davis Polk, and Sullivan & Cromwell—jointly published a paper in which they argued that foreign branch deposits should be ranked equally with domestic deposits for purposes of s. 11(d)(11). Cleary Gottlieb, Davis Polk, and Sullivan & Cromwell, *The Status of Foreign Branch Deposits under the Depositor Preference Rule* (2 January 2013). The FDIC rejected that view, however, based on an opinion by a then acting general counsel of the FDIC in 1994. FDIC, *Deposit Insurance Regulations; Definition of Insured Deposit*, 78 Fed Reg 56583 (13 September 2013); FDIC Advisory Opinion, *'Deposit Liability' for Purposes of National Depositor Preference Includes Only Deposits Payable in the US*, FDIC 94-1 (28 February 1994). According to the FDIC, a foreign branch deposit must be dually payable at both the foreign branch and in the United States to be included in the term 'deposit liability'. 78 Fed Reg (13 September 2013) 56583, 56586.

[19] Our review was based on data contained in each closed institution's call report as of the quarter ended immediately before it was closed. See ANB Financial, NA (closed 9 May 2008) (98 per cent); BankUnited (closed 21 May 2009) (95.5 per cent); Colonial Bank (closed 14 August 2009) (98 per cent); Corus Bank, NA (closed 11 September 2009) (99 per cent); Downey Savings and Loan, FA (closed 21 November 2008) (99.5 per cent); First National Bank of Nevada (Closed 25 July 2008) (95 per cent); Georgian Bank (closed 25 September 2009) (99 per cent); Guaranty Bank (closed 21 August 2009) (98 per cent); Indymac, FSB (closed 11 July 2008) (98 per cent); Silver State Bank (closed 5 September 2008) (95 per cent); Washington Mutual Bank (closed 25 September 2008) (89 per cent).

[20] See ANB Financial, NA (closed 9 May 2008) (79 per cent); BankUnited (closed 21 May 2009) (56 per cent); Colonial Bank (closed 14 August 2009) (76 per cent); Corus Bank, NA (closed 11 September 2009) (65 per cent); Downey Savings and Loan, FA (closed 21 November 2008) (81 per cent); First National Bank of Nevada (closed 25 July 2008) (60 per cent); Georgian Bank (closed 25 September 2009) (49 per cent); Guaranty Bank (closed 21 August 2009) (63 per cent); Indymac, FSB (closed 11 July 2008) (57 per cent); Silver State Bank (closed 5 September 2008) (63 per cent).

liabilities compared to smaller more domestic banks.[21] All of the G-SIBs (except Morgan Stanley Bank) had significant amounts of liabilities that are subordinate to domestic deposit liabilities, including foreign branch deposits, federal funds liabilities, trading liabilities, other borrowed money, subordinated debt, and other liabilities.[22] As a result, the value of the assets of such a bank in receivership is far more likely to be sufficient to satisfy all the claims on domestic deposits, thus resulting in no loss to the US deposit insurance fund and allowing for some distribution to junior claimants.[23]

Territorial depositor preference has sometimes been alleged to be disguised protectionism. This was the allegation which was rejected in the *Iceland* case,[24] but in that case the rejection was based on the fact that the systemic crisis which the Icelandic government faced was so severe that it could not have met its obligations extraterritorially. In the United States, by contrast, territoriality is a matter of course, since all claims on deposits payable in the United States have preference over claims on foreign branch deposits that are payable solely outside the United States (although not foreign branch deposits that are dually payable at the foreign branches and in the United States).[25] There is more or less universal agreement that such structures are destructive and should be avoided. However, this is broadly where the consensus ends. **2.52**

In general, depositor preference comes in two forms: preference up to the insured limit, and unlimited preference.[26] Depositor preference up to the insured limit is, properly viewed, not depositor preference but DGS preference—the depositor will be compensated out of the DGS, and is therefore indifferent to the preference **2.53**

---

[21] Domestic deposits as a percentage of total liabilities were as follows according to the relevant call reports at 30 June 2015: Bank of America, NA, 83 per cent; The Bank of New York Mellon, NA, 52 per cent; Citibank, NA, 37 per cent; Goldman Sachs Bank USA, 78 per cent; J.P. Morgan Chase Bank, NA, 60 per cent; Morgan Stanley Bank, NA: 97 per cent; State Street Bank & Trust, 44 per cent; Wells Fargo Bank, NA, 77 per cent.

[22] Subordinated liabilities were as follows according to the relevant call reports at 30 June 2015: Bank of America, NA, 17 per cent; Bank of New York Mellon, NA, 48 per cent; Citibank, NA, 63 per cent; Goldman Sachs Bank USA, 22 per cent; J.P. Morgan Chase Bank, NA, 40 per cent; Morgan Stanley Bank, NA: 3 per cent; State Street Bank & Trust, 56 per cent; Wells Fargo Bank, NA, 23 per cent.

[23] This conclusion is consistent with the public summaries of the 2015 Title I and insured depository institution (IDI) resolution plans filed by the US G-SIBs, which generally concluded they could be resolved under a severely adverse economic scenario without any loss to the deposit insurance fund. See FDIC, Title I and IDI Resolution Plans, available at: <https://www.fdic.gov/regulations/reform/resplans/> (accessed 14 October 2015).

[24] See n 14 above.

[25] It is interesting to note that this provision was not introduced into US law as a piece of banking policy, but as part of a budget settlement intended to reduce the future notional expenditures of the US government as recognized in its budgeting process.

[26] Financially there is a surprising degree of variation from country to country as to the quantum of total deposits actually covered by insurance—within the G20 the percentage of total deposits actually covered by insurance ranges from 19 per cent (Singapore) to 79 per cent (the United States)—see the FSB Thematic Review on Deposit Insurance Systems of 8 February 2012, Table 5 at p. 48.

position, whereas the contributories to the DGS will get the benefit of the preference through their subrogated claim against the failed institution.

2.54 Unlimited depositor preference is generally confined to certain classes of depositors (e.g. it is unusual for deposits placed by financial institutions to receive this
preference). However, protected types of depositors include individuals, small- to
medium-sized enterprises (SMEs), pension funds, and charities.

2.55 The United States, in particular, has an unlimited depositor preference regime
which covers (broadly) all deposits payable in the United States (but not foreign
branch deposits payable solely outside the United States). This has the immense
advantage of avoiding the necessity for 'line-drawing' for protected classes. The
FDIC believes that this unlimited depositor preference has facilitated US bank
resolutions, since it means that entire deposit books can be easily and rapidly dealt
with provided that the total assets of the institution in resolution exceed the value
of the deposit book. However, an object-lesson in the dangers of this approach was
given in the collapse of the Cypriot banks, which were almost exclusively deposit-
funded, in that once the value of the deposit book falls below the asset value (plus
the resources of the DGS), the allocation of pain amongst depositors involves an
emergency triage of depositors into classes who are to be more or less affected by the
loss, and such emergency triage is both politically painful and, almost by definition,
unjust in certain cases.

H. Depositor Preference and 'No Creditor Worse Off than in Liquidation'

2.56 The introduction of depositor preference significantly changes the dynamics of
bank resolution. This is because by changing the position on liquidation, depositor
preference automatically changes the extent to which the creditor concerned
can be bailed in without breaching the 'no creditor worse off than in liquidation'
(NCWOL) principle. Thus, where a bank has eighty of assets, eighty of deposit
liabilities, and twenty of other liabilities, the insolvency position will be that the
depositors will make full recovery and the other creditors will receive nothing. This
situation may have advantages—for example, the FDIC experience is that this is
helpful for the conclusion of purchase and assumption (P&A) transactions, since if
the assets exceed the value of preferred deposits by even one cent, it then becomes
possible to transfer all of the preferred deposits to a replacement institution (or a
bridge bank) without contravening the ordinary rule of priority. The converse of
this position is that unsecured creditors other than depositor creditors commonly
receive no recovery at all in FDIC resolutions.

3

BANK RESOLUTION
AND BANK GROUPS

The easiest mental model to use in understanding bank groups is probably the **3.01** Marxist model. Marx regarded society as composed of the 'base'—the forces and relations of production which constitute economic reality—and the 'superstructure'— culture, institutions, and social norms. Base determines superstructure, and a failure to perceive the realities of the base—or a belief that superstructure has any 'real' existence—constitutes false consciousness. Bank groups can usefully be considered using this paradigm. The 'base' comprises the systems and processes which conduct the banks' day-to-day business, whereas the 'superstructure' is the legal construct which sits on top of the base. In analysing the bank itself, a focus on legal structures is a form of false consciousness. In determining whether an entity can continue to function, what matters is not whether the legal entities are solvent on an accounting basis, but whether the underlying systems are continuing to operate. The failure of Lehman Brothers International (Europe) provides a dramatic demonstration of this proposition—when the systems stop working, the institution is finished, and the notional solvency or otherwise of the legal entities is a detail for historians rather than a material fact.

The reason that this is important in the international context is that in most situ- **3.02** ations where banks operate through different national subsidiaries, it is highly likely that their operational, payment, and functional activities will be conducted through bank-wide systems. Even in contexts where bank regulators have required national subsidiarization they have generally not gone so far as to require the maintenance of separate free-standing national operational systems—generally because such a requirement would add substantially to the service costs incurred by national customers. However, in the absence of such a requirement, the question of the possible survivability of the national subsidiary is a function of the continuing existence of the underlying systems. This has a number of consequences. One is that if the architecture of the bank is such that the system concerned is effectively operated by the troubled institution, then the failure of that institution will necessarily cause cessation of operations throughout the group. In order to address this issue without

27

fragmenting operational systems in a way which would create massively increased costs, it is clearly necessary to create some degree of independence for the function concerned. However, any significant reconstruction of bank systems would impose costs which are very significant on banks, and such costs (payable as they are out of profits) would directly impact capital levels and further inhibit banks' ability to produce demand deposits and other forms of money and create extensions of credit. In short, it is by no means clear that any G-SIB break-up would be feasible without requiring in effect a complete reconstruction of the bank itself.[1]

3.03 Lawyers (perhaps justifiably) tend to perceive corporate groups on a legal entity by legal entity basis. However, this is not in general how groups are either managed or resourced. A simplified model of a conventional bank group might be as shown in Figure 3.1.

3.04 The key point here is that each of these layers will be subdivided. Legal structure will be subdivided into individual legal entities, IT infrastructure will be subdivided into different systems, and management structure will be subdivided into business areas. These subdivisions are not necessarily congruent with the subdivisions at other layers.

3.05 Sometimes one or more of these will conjoin. In Figure 3.1, the column on the right is most likely to represent a newly acquired subsidiary, where management, systems and legal structure will all—at the point of acquisition—be discrete. However, over time the process of integration of such business into the parent group is likely to result in any of the three layers being merged—booking may be transferred to a new legal entity, management may be restructured within the wider group, and IT systems may be integrated. None of these processes are generally related to the others—banks do not generally prioritize legal structures when designing management processes or IT systems, or IT functionality when designing trade booking structures.

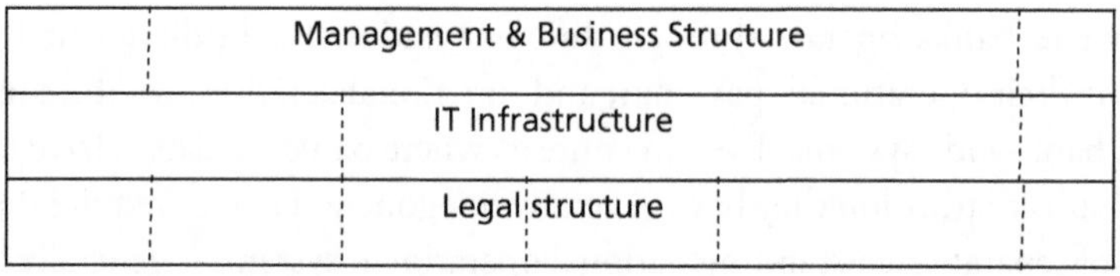

Management & Business Structure		
IT Infrastructure		
Legal structure		

Figure 3.1 Simplified model of a conventional bank group

---

[1] Authorities are beginning to address this issue—see for example the FSB's Consultative Document on 'Guidance on Arrangements to Support Operational Continuity in Resolution' of November 2015 and the Bank of England's consultation paper on 'Ensuring Operational Continuity in Resolution' of 11 December 2015. However, these proposals fall well short of mandating a matching of system structures with legal structures, accepting that such a requirement would be costly and disproportionate.

The effect of all this, however, is to expose as an illusion the idea that because busi-   **3.06**
ness is conducted within a particular legal subsidiary, it is therefore segregated—or
capable of being easily divided from—the other activities of the group. A subsidiary
is, in legal realist terms, simply a few lines in a company registry—the question of
whether a particular business can be separated and easily sold from a group is much
more likely to be determined by its management and control structures than by the
legal substructure of its contracts.

A. Resolution in the Context of Groups

Thus far we have considered the bail-in of a bank. However, most large banks are   **3.07**
members of groups, and it is frequently the case that in a bank group there is an
unregulated bank holding company above the bank.

In the case illustrated in Figure 3.2, if the resolution were to be conducted at   **3.08**
the bank level the effect of the resolution would be to break the group structure
(since the bank would cease to be a subsidiary of the holding company)—and
would be likely to push the holding company into insolvency (since the ability
to liquidate the shares would become deferred and its dividend flow from the
regulated bank would cease). This problem clearly would not arise if the senior
borrowing were primarily at the holding company level. However, practices vary
amongst banks as to whether funding is (a) raised at the holding company level
and downstreamed, (b) raised at the level of the bank itself, or (c) raised at both
levels. Thus it is impossible to make any general assumption as to where in the
group eligible debt will be raised.

This means that the structure of any resolution must be adapted to the specific case   **3.09**
of the bank group concerned. This can be most easily understood by considering
the case of the slightly more complex bank group illustrated in Figure 3.3.

In this case, the group has creditors at multiple levels and within multiple legal
entities.

The starting point for consideration of this situation should be the fact that it is   **3.10**
desirable for both the group and for its regulator that creditors should be clear

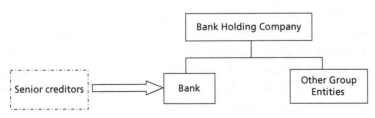

Figure 3.2 Resolution at the bank level

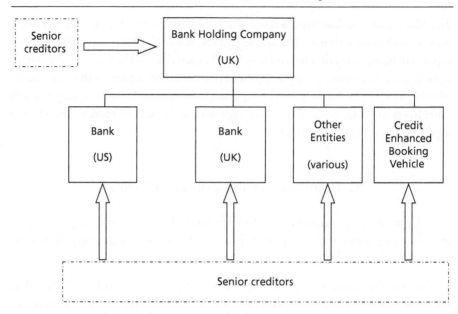

Figure 3.3 Resolution of a more complex bank group

which parts of the group they are exposed to. Creditors of the holding company will clearly consider themselves exposed to the group as a whole, and creditors of the booking vehicle will consider themselves exposed—in credit terms at least—solely to that booking vehicle. However, for the US subsidiary bank, for example, the question of whether that bank would, in difficulty, be able or entitled to call upon the resources of the remainder of the group would have to be determined as part of the living will process.

3.11 What all of this comes down to is nothing more complex than that the resolution structure should reflect the existing structure of the group and the expectations of creditors as to their counterparty exposures. This is neither unreasonable nor overly challenging, and certainly does not represent an insuperable barrier to the establishment of resolution regimes, at least where the bank holding company and the entities issuing eligible debt are incorporated in the same country. The position is more challenging where the group has a more subsidiarized structure containing large entities issuing debt that are not incorporated in the same country as the bank holding company, as the local regulator will not have direct powers over the holding company to implement the resolution. Again, this is not a fundamental objection to the adoption of a resolution approach by regulators for those groups for whom resolution is possible and at present most large banking groups with a bank holding company structure have their bank holding company incorporated in the same jurisdiction as their principal banking entities. It also potentially aligns the interests of regulators in effective resolution planning with the interests of banks in operating integrated legal entities operating internationally through branches rather than subsidiaries.

However, cross-border issues should not mean that it is impossible to implement **3.12** a resolution in a case where the troubled bank or its bank holding company also has troubled foreign subsidiaries. In many cases, the parent will have substantial assets that can be used to recapitalize its subsidiaries and its subsidiaries will have significant intra-group borrowings from their parent bank or bank holding company owing to the downstreaming of funding raised at the parent level. The bail-in of debt at the level of the parent bank or bank holding company should create enough capital to give it the capacity to contribute assets to its subsidiaries or write off or convert into equity loans to its subsidiaries, enabling their recapitalization as part of the overall process, even if the local regulator does not have an effective resolution regime. This may have the result of insulating the creditors of those subsidiaries against losses, at the expense of the parent's creditors, but this will not be unfair or create moral hazard as long as it is known in advance that debt incurred at the parent level is structurally subordinated to debt incurred at the subsidiary level. If it is, market forces will cause the return on debt incurred at the parent level to go up to reflect the greater risk of such debt and the return on debt at the subsidiary level to go down to reflect the lower risk of such debt. In effect, creditors at the subsidiary level will be forced to internalize the cost of their preferred position, thus driving out any moral hazard, and creditors at the parent level will be fully compensated for the additional risk they bear. In addition, if local regulators have a local resolution regime with corresponding powers, there should be ways in which the group's lead regulator and the local regulators can coordinate the exercise of their powers to produce an appropriate result, without the need (outside the European Union) for complex international treaties which could take many years to negotiate.

A resolution of a bank subsidiary within an integrated group would ordinarily **3.13** require external senior creditors of that bank subsidiary to be issued new shares in that subsidiary. However, such issue could result in the subsidiary ceasing to be part of the integrated group; an outcome which might not be practical either for the subsidiary bank or the group. Consequently, if the resolution authority wishes to preserve the integrity of the group, it may arrange for the written-down creditors of the subsidiary to be given new equity in the group parent. The write-down or -off of the eligible debt in the subsidiary would create capital reserves in the subsidiary. The issue of the shares in the holding company does not necessarily require any intermediate step of requiring the subsidiary to issue additional shares or debt to its parent company, but the mechanics would depend on local corporate law sensibilities. There is no reason why this should not be done by statute, and if the bank and the holding company are established in the same jurisdiction, a legislative solution in that jurisdiction should be capable of being crafted.

In the context of groups, it is also important to note that a consistent policy would **3.14** be required as regards debts to the top-tier parent. The question of whether debts to the top-tier parent should be treated differently from any other debt in the context of a resolution is not straightforward. However, it is by no means clear that it is necessary to have a single answer to this question on a global basis—the optimum solution would seem to be that this issue should be addressed between individual banks and their lead regulators as part of the 'living wills' discussion. Again, this may be easier to accomplish in the 'targeted' approach where banks continue to be able to issue senior debt that *is not* eligible for bail-in alongside subordinated debt that *is* eligible for bail-in.

B. Transmission of Capital within Groups

3.15 A further problem potentially arises within groups as regards the transmission of capital. In general, where a member of a group has surplus capital, if another member of the group is in need of capital, a number of mechanisms exist for transferring that capital within the group.

3.16 At its simplest, the transferring entity can use its excess equity to purchase new shares in the transferee entity. However, this is generally not permitted where capital is to be transmitted upwards, since subsidiaries generally cannot buy shares in their own parent. Alternative mechanisms exist—the entity which has excess capital can distribute its excess capital up the chain in the form of dividends until it reaches the parent holding company, at which point the parent holding company can downstream the excess capital to the subsidiary which is short of capital. This is, of course, subject to any restrictions which may be imposed by local corporate law.

3.17 An alternative is the indirect creation of capital by the forgiveness of intra-group debt. This is an effective mechanism (cancellation of debt results in an automatic increase in shareholders' funds), but relies on there being forgivable debt in place, and on the directors of the forgiving company being confident that 'giving away' a company asset is within their powers and duties.[2]

3.18 Another alternative is the capital contribution—a straightforward gift of money or other property from one company to another—although there are sometimes accounting difficulties with having capital contributions recognized as capital.

3.19 In practice, there are a host of tax, accounting, and regulatory rules which can inhibit the use of any of these mechanisms. These rules are difficult enough in one jurisdiction, but rapidly become a major obstacle when transfers between a number of different jurisdictions are involved.

---

[2] It is also possible that such a transfer might be recharacterized by applicable company law as a dividend.

C. Specific Bank Group Structures

Bank groups are protean—not only are they very different one from another, but **3.20** also they may change significantly as the business of the bank changes. As should have been clear from the foregoing, generalization about 'bank groups' are impossible because each large bank group is to some extent unique, and even simple generalizations about 'the holding company' or 'the group' are liable to counterexamples. However, it is to some extent possible to separate bank groups into broad types, and we suggest here a taxonomy which may enable some progress to be made in addressing resolution options.

For the purposes of the examples that follow, we have divided creditors into three **3.21** broad types:

Banking creditors, meaning retail and wholesale depositors and creditors arising out of the provision by the bank of payment and custody services;

Investment business creditors, meaning swap counterparties, trading counterparties, exchanges, clearing systems, and other investment business counterparties (including repurchase agreement (repo) counterparties).

Capital structure creditors, meaning long-term unsecured creditors of the bank, including bondholders and other long-term unsecured finance providers.

In Figure 3.4 we see a more or less 'empty' holding company holding a bank with **3.22** a large balance sheet. Assets not held within the bank itself will generally be held by subsidiaries of the bank. Funding is likely to be raised primarily at the bank level, since any funding raised at the holding company level is structurally subordinated to funding raised at the bank level. However, regulators will require a certain type and amount of financial funding to be raised at the holdco level,

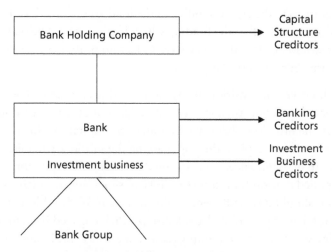

Figure 3.4 The 'bank holdco' model

since this will be the first in the firing line in the event of single-point-of-entry (SPE) resolution at the holdco level. In general derivatives, markets and trading business will all be done out of the bank rather than the holdco, since the bank will be the most creditworthy member of the group and will ensure that counterparties have the lowest risk exposure (and therefore the lowest costs of dealing with it).

3.23   In the context of this institution, two issues arise. One is that it is unlikely that short-term unsecured investment business creditors will be written down through the resolution mechanism, as long as the bank group has sufficient capital structure liabilities to absorb losses and fully recapitalize the bank group. This is because avoiding such write-downs is likely to maximize the residual value of the bank for the benefit of its capital structure financial creditors, reduce the risk of runs that could destabilize the banking system, and allow operations that are critical to the market to be continued—three important policy objectives for the resolution authority. Further, short-term unsecured bank depositors are also unlikely to be written down for similar reasons, as long as the group has sufficient capital structure liabilities to absorb losses.

3.24   Mechanically, resolving the holdco model is in some respects the easiest challenge. If creditors are at the level of the holdco, it is a relatively simple matter to extinguish their claims and issue them with new shares in the holdco. The holdco's assets can then be downstreamed to the bank.

3.25   The position of creditors of the holding company is not, however, as simple as it seems. Orthodox corporate finance would dictate that by becoming creditors of the holdco, they have voluntarily accepted a position where they are structurally subordinated to creditors of the bank. It is therefore highly arguable that such creditors should be written down first before direct creditors of the bank are affected. However, most creditors of holdcos assume that status as a result of diligent enquiry as to the credit standing of the holdco concerned. If the structure of that holdco was that all of the funding which it raised would be downstreamed as equity, it would be clear that they were in fact no more than synthetic equity investors in the relevant subsidiary.

3.26   This is not, however, the position of any bank holding company in real life. Bank regulators have been concerned for many decades about the idea of 'double leverage'—that is, the situation where a parent raises debt capital and downstreams it to its subsidiary as equity capital, thereby enabling the subsidiary to raise more debt on the strength of its enhanced equity capital position. The regulatory tool which is usually applied to prohibit this is consolidated supervision, which requires that a bank group should have sufficient equity at the consolidated level to meet the risks on its total asset portfolio. A bank group which engaged in significant double leveraging would in general simply cease to meet its consolidated capital ratio and be closed down by its regulators. In addition to this, rating agencies generally publish for any rated bank group a 'double leverage ratio' which makes clear to investors the extent to which debt has actually been downstreamed as equity. The upshot of all of this is that a person who becomes a creditor of a holdco in fact does so on the basis that (a) it is highly likely that money attributable to debt financing will be downstreamed as debt and not as equity, and (b) that although the person has no direct controls or covenants to ensure that outcome, she can in general rely on regulators to ensure that it is done, and on rating agencies to tell her if it is not done.

What follows from all of this is that to say that a creditor of a bank holdco has vol- **3.27** untarily accepted the status of a subordinated creditor of the holdco's subsidiaries is in some way wide of the mark. Unless corporate finance law in the jurisdiction of the subsidiary deems intragroup creditors to be subordinated to external creditors,[3] or intragroup creditors contractually agree to be subordinated to external creditors, intragroup creditors are entitled to no worse treatment than the treatment which would be accorded to any other creditor of the subsidiary concerned. This position is illustrated in Figure 3.5.

The senior creditors of the holdco would expect the holdco as internal creditor **3.28** of the bank to be in exactly the same position as the external creditors of the bank. The bank has, in aggregate, 200 creditors; if it fails, those creditors are entitled to be treated pari passu, and the recoveries of the holdco as internal creditor will be no different from those of the external creditors of the bank—if the external bank creditors recover 50 cents on the dollar, the holdco can expect to recover the same on its internal credit to the bank.

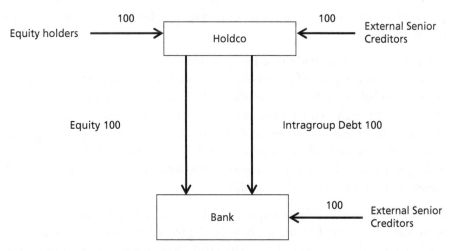

Figure 3.5 Structure of creditors

---

[3] This does happen, but it is rare.

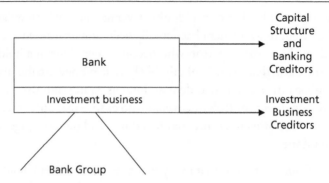

Figure 3.6 The 'big bank' model

3.29 The difference, of course, is that in order to recapitalize the bank subsidiary, it will be necessary for the holdco to downstream assets to the bank, including by forgiving any internal credit to the bank, with the external holdco creditors being written down to the extent the remaining assets of the parent (including its ownership in the recapitalized bank) are insufficient to satisfy all of the claims of the external holdco creditors. There are fundamentally two options here. One is to write down all creditors of the bank equally. This could result in the bank passing outside the holdco group, since the aggregate amount of the claims of the external senior creditors of the bank could be greater than the amount of the holdco's claims on its internal credit to the bank. The other is to discriminate between different creditors—internal and external, bank and group—according to some other plan. The key issue here is that if creditors come to believe that the latter might be the approach taken, it will be extremely difficult for them to value their investments unless the authority concerned is prepared to make a clear statement as to what that plan may be, and to stick to it in practice.

3.30 In Figure 3.6 we see the traditional European bank structure, in which a large bank is itself the top company of the group. Assets not held within the bank itself will generally be held by subsidiaries of the bank. Funding is raised primarily at the bank level, although secured creditors may be creditors of ringfenced subsidiaries. In general, the 'big bank' is likely to do its derivatives, markets, and trading business out of the main legal entity, since this will be the most creditworthy member of the group and will ensure that counterparties have the lowest risk exposure (and therefore the lowest costs of dealing with it).

3.31 In Figure 3.7 we see a holding company which owns a bank and a non-bank investment firm. These activities are likely to be ringfenced by local legislation into a 'bank chain' and a 'non-bank chain', with restrictions on transactions between the two sides of the group below the level of the holding company. In this case, it is more likely that significant capital structure liabilities may have been incurred at

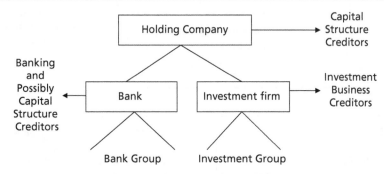

Figure 3.7 The 'bank/non-bank holdco' model

the parent company level, since lenders at that level will have access to a larger asset pool than lenders to the bank. It is possible that significant capital structure liabilities will have been incurred at the bank level. Indeed, it is possible that all three components—the bank, the investment firm, and the holding company—may have incurred capital structure liabilities.

We need to begin with a hypothesis as to where in the group the loss has been **3.32** incurred. For the purposes of this chapter we will assume that the loss has been incurred in the banking part of the group.

At the level of the bank itself, the issues here are no different from the 'big bank' **3.33** model. Considering the position of the investment firm immediately raises the 'dead in parts' problem. It should be remembered that in this context it is highly likely that the bank and the investment firm will share the same branding, the same advertising campaign, and the same IT, processing, and payment systems. As a result, it may well be the case that the survival of the investment firm will be entirely dependent on the survival of the bank. Clearly, if the resolution can be conducted entirely at the group level, that is likely to be the optimal solution.

In Figure 3.8 is a more or less empty holding company that owns a number of **3.34** banks—generally incorporated in different jurisdictions and subject to some degree of restrictions on their interconnection. In this case, it is likely that at least some capital structure liabilities have been incurred at the holding company level, although it is likely that some (but perhaps not all) of the subsidiary banks will also have incurred some external capital structure liabilities.

Resolving the global multi-bank is more interesting than in the previous cases. **3.35** The architecture of the global multi-bank is generally in response to pressures from national regulators who require national businesses to be undertaken by separately capitalized local subsidiaries. Since we have hypothesized that the holding company is 'empty' (i.e. has no economic activity of its own), it must follow that the loss causing the crisis must have been experienced in one or other of the bank subsidiaries. The effect of a write-down of the holdco's capital

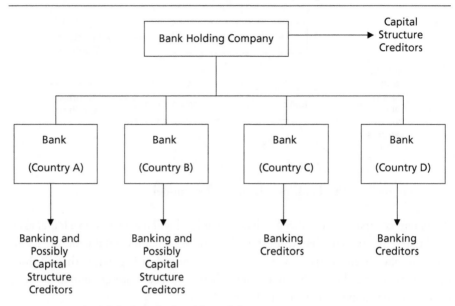

Figure 3.8 The 'global multi-bank' model

structure liabilities is to create new equity at the holdco. The holdco can create new equity at the bank which has suffered the loss by forgiving intra-group debts owed by the bank to the holding company in respect of funding previously received. However, if the holding company has insufficient assets that can be downstreamed (including an insufficient amount of intragroup receivables to forgive) to the troubled subsidiary bank in order to recapitalize the bank, there could *in extremis* arise the possibility of bailing in external capital structure financial creditors of the troubled bank in order to recapitalize the troubled bank. It might even be possible to bail in any external capital structure financial creditors of the sister banks and distribute any of their excess assets to the bank that needs to be recapitalized.

3.36 The permutations in this regard are complex and difficult. Considering the group above, if Bank A gets into trouble and its own capital structure liabilities are insufficient to recapitalize it, should the capital structure creditors of Bank B be called on? If they are, how does the capital get transferred from Bank B to Bank A? What if Bank C (which has no eligible debt) gets into difficulties—should the capital structure creditors of Banks A or B be written down and their excess assets be contributed to Bank C to recapitalize it? To complicate matters further, if the resolution of Bank A results in majority control of Bank A being transferred to the capital structure creditors of Bank A, those creditors may take advantage of their status as the controlling shareholders of Bank A to restrain the new capital thus created from being transferred elsewhere within the group.

3.37 It is clear that these are no more than illustrations of broad classes of group structures, and it should also be clear that in each case the theoretical deployment of exposures would be dependent primarily on the type and volume of funding raised at each legal entity within the group.

D. Branches and Subsidiaries

Much of the discussion about bank regulation and resolution has been con- **3.38**
ducted in the context of a discussion about branches and subsidiaries—in particular, the extent to which resolution authorities may decide to protect their
national economies by requiring overseas banks operating in them to operate
through a domestic subsidiary. The argument, in broad terms, is that branch
status reduces the level of control available to national resolution authorities in
respect of the national businesses. The basis of this approach is articulated in the
International Monetary Fund (IMF) paper on 'Subsidiaries or Branches—Does
One Size Fit All?':[4]

> In the absence of effective international cooperation in [bank resolution], resolution
> of institutions, in the event of a failure within a banking group, may be less costly
> and less destabilizing if these entities are organized as subsidiaries.

This suggests that in general it should be possible for a state to argue that it has a pos- **3.39**
itive public interest in requiring banks to operate through subsidiaries in its jurisdiction because 'healthy subsidiaries that operate independently of the parent may,
in principle, be better able to survive the failure of the parent or other affiliates'.[5]
It is important to emphasize that the IMF position is that such concerns are only
valid whilst there is no substantive progress internationally on satisfactory cross-
border resolution regimes.

It is also important to note that it is generally an error to think about 'subsidiary' **3.40**
status as being a monolithic set of concepts common to all countries. The rules
applicable to foreign branches vary wildly in different jurisdictions, and range from
countries such as India and Brazil, where branches face local capital and liquidity charges identical to those applied to subsidiaries and are required to maintain
boards with local representation, to the countries of the European Union, amongst
whom branching is an absolute right with no interference (in theory) permitted to
the host regulator. Even between these extremes the position varies considerably—
for example, many would expect to find the rules of the United Kingdom and the
United States to be reasonably similar as regards foreign branches, but as Table 3.1
illustrates, the differences remain substantial.

Thus it is important to remember that the regulation of branches is already protean, **3.41**
with no globally established norms for dealing with them.

---

[4] SDN/11/04, 7 March 2011, J Fiechter et al.
[5] Ibid.

Table 3.1 Comparison of current UK and US regulation of bank branches

	Current UK Treatment (non-EU Branches)	Current US Treatment
Level of home state supervision required	No equivalence measure—UK authorities must satisfy themselves that the bank as a whole is compliant with UK capital requirements	US must find that a bank is subject to comprehensive consolidated supervision in its home state before approving a branch application
Requirement for initial branch capital	No	Yes—banks must maintain a 'capital equivalency deposit' with a depositary bank
Requirement for ongoing risk-based capital	No	No
Ongoing liquidity requirement for the branch	Yes—branches must be self-sufficient in liquidity, although there is a power to permit groupwide liquidity management where the group is adequately supervised	Not currently, but proposals to impose liquidity requirements on US branches of non-US banks with combined US assets of $50bn or more
Branch asset requirements	No	New York Department of Financial Services can require a branch to maintain assets (but currently does not, unless the bank of which it is part fails or is in troubled condition)
Central Bank reserve requirements	Yes—cash ratio deposits with the bank of England	Yes—reserve requirements with the Federal Reserve
Restrictions on branch deposit-taking	No	Yes—generally, US branches of non-US banks are not permitted to take retail deposits or FDIC-insured deposits
Restrictions on other activities of the branch	No	Yes—subject to the same restrictions as US banks (including underwriting securities)
Do local requirements apply to the bank as a whole?	No	Yes—bank as a whole will be treated as a bank holding company and subject to restrictions on non-bank activities (including Volcker Rule), with broad exemptions for activities outside the United States
Are the branch's deposits insured under the local scheme?	Yes	No
What are the host authority's powers over the branch in the event of failure?	None—ordinary bankruptcy law will apply. This will change when the RRD is brought into force	US state-licensed branches of foreign banks are subject to special resolution regime of licensing state; US federally licensed branches of foreign banks are subject to the OCC's resolution powers, which are not very clearly defined
Are local assets reserved for local creditors on the [bank's/branch's] failure?	No	Probably, in the case of the branch's failure; it depends on the home country resolution strategy in the case of the bank's failure.

E. Branch vs Subsidiary

There is a commonly held belief amongst some commentators (and politicians) that **3.42**
the position of creditors and authorities, as regards a bank business in a country,
is improved if that business becomes a separately incorporated subsidiary in that
country. As noted above, this is simply wrong. It is incorrect to say that branch or
subsidiary architectures are necessarily superior or inferior to each other—these are
simply legal concepts which trigger particular legislative provisions, and the provisions triggered have compensating advantages and disadvantages in both cases.

The easiest way to address this is to begin with the taxonomy of banks put forward **3.43**
by the Federal Reserve in the discussion section of its notice of proposed rulemaking for enhanced prudential standards applicable to certain large foreign banking
organizations ('FBO proposal').[6] This divides federal branches into aggregators
and net recipients of intercompany funding. An aggregator branch is established
to accumulate deposits (or other forms of finance) in its host jurisdiction and to
remit those deposits to the bank's offices and affiliates outside the host jurisdiction.
One of the reasons given by the Federal Reserve for the FBO proposal was that US
branches of foreign banks have become aggregators, and that their effect is to use
US deposits to fund the accumulation of assets by its non-US affiliates outside the
United States. The concern with aggregators is that in the event of a financial crisis, the assets financed by host country deposits are outside the control of the host
country resolution authority concerned, and if the home authority is not prepared
to remit the assets (or their value) to the host country resolution authority, the host
country authority may be left with an insufficient amount of assets to satisfy all the
claims against the branch. Requiring an aggregator branch to become a subsidiary
may solve this problem if it has the effect of ensuring that the subsidiary has enough
assets to pay its liabilities. However, if the problem to be addressed is simply that
assets *owned* within the jurisdiction are *located* outside the jurisdiction, it seems
completely irrelevant where the legal entity which is the asset owner is located.
Put another way, it should be possible to require any asset owned by a branch to be
returned in the same way and to the same extent that it would be possible to require
an asset owned by a subsidiary to be returned.

---

[6] Federal Reserve System, *Enhanced Prudential Standards and Early Remediation Requirements
for Foreign Banking Organizations and Foreign Nonbank Financial Companies*, 77 Federal Register
(28 December 2012) 76628, 76629–76630. Federal Reserve System, *Total Loss-Absorbing Capacity,
Long-Term Debt, and Clean Holding Company Requirements for Systemically Important U.S. Bank
Holding Companies and Intermediate Holding Companies of Systemically Important Foreign Banking
Organizations*, 80 Federal Register (30 November 2015) 74926–74964. For a visual summary of
the Federal Reserve's proposed rule, see the Davis Polk memo *Federal Reserve's Proposed Rule on Total
Loss-Absorbing Capacity and Eligible Long-Term Debt* (10 November 2015), available at <http://www.
davispolk.com/sites/default/files/2015_11_10_Federal_Reserves_Proposed_Rule_on_TLAC_and_
Eligible_LTD.PDF> (accessed 6 December 2015).

3.44 Net recipient branches are the mirror image of aggregator branches. A net recipient branch exists to make loans and/or originate assets in the host country, deploying funding raised outside it. A net recipient branch is always 'solvent', to the extent that local assets generally exceed local liabilities. However, a net recipient branch is likely to be highly illiquid, since a central model of funding is almost invariably accompanied by centralized liquidity management. It is possible for a net recipient branch to exist in subsidiary form provided that the business is very small relative to that of the parent bank—if it is not, then exposure limits within the subsidiary bank will cap its recourse to group funding. In general, regulators should prefer net recipient branches to be branches, since otherwise limits on intra-group exposures will disrupt the business model.

3.45 Regulators' concerns about net recipient branches are generally focused on the withdrawal of credit issue. If a bank with a net recipient branch comes under stress, it is a fairly safe assumption that the bank will cease to roll over credits in the net recipient branch, repatriating assets to the parent to assuage the stress. Hence the argument that requiring a net recipient branch to subsidiarize will prevent this happening.

3.46 A further issue relates to costs of funds. Assume two countries, A and B. A is solvent, has a strong economy, and therefore relatively lower costs of funds for domestic institutions. B has a weak budgetary position and a declining economy, and therefore higher costs of funds. It makes perfect sense for banks established in A to establish net recipient branches in B, and this development should be beneficial for both A and B—A because it derives an increased return on investment, and B because this will reduce the cost of funds to industry in B. Authorities in B may therefore have reasons to incentivize the establishment of net recipient branches. Conversely, however, the authorities in A may object to their banks behaving in this way, since they will put their assets at increased risk of default or appropriation. This is an example of a situation where the home authority may prefer overseas operations to be done through a subsidiary whilst the host authority would strongly prefer these activities to be done through a branch. However, if we reverse the hypothesis, and assume that banks in B seek to deal with the position by establishing aggregator branches in A, the authorities in A may be unwilling to assent to this unless the business in A is done through a subsidiary.

3.47 The strength and weakness of national supervisors is also an issue. A subsidiary enables a host authority to exercise some greater degree of supervision over the business practices of the entity concerned. However, a more accurate way of looking at this is that a host country regulator who permits an overseas bank to open a branch in its jurisdiction places considerably more faith in the home regulator of that bank than one that requires a subsidiary. Thus, regulators who perceive themselves as 'strong' may be unwilling to permit branches of banks which they perceive as being established in home jurisdictions with 'weak' regulators.

Finally, there is the sovereign issue. Although in theory sovereigns do not stand **3.48** behind their banks, it is unquestionably true that the failure of a sovereign may result in the failure of the banks in that country. Thus a supervisor in a host country needs to assess both the risks inherent in the home country government and the extent to which contagion risk may damage that business. If the home country sovereign is financially weak, the host country authorities are likely to require sub-sidiarization to limit contagion. However, where the home country sovereign is financially strong, the host authority may prefer a branch structure.

Creditors perspective

It is also important to consider this issue from the perspective of a creditor of the **3.49** business concerned. From a creditor's perspective, in most cases their wish would be to deal with a branch. A creditor of a branch may pursue assets belonging to the bank concerned anywhere in the world they can be found, whereas a creditor of a subsidiary is limited to those assets which can be proved to be owned by that subsidiary. Possibly more importantly, where the local business is in difficulties, company law in many jurisdictions places severe limits on the extent to which a parent company can advance funds to a subsidiary which is insolvent and not likely to resume business. Thus if local business is subsidiarized, the parent company concerned may be forced by corporate benefit and other similar rules to refuse to provide additional capital to the subsidiary, leaving creditors of the subsidiary with no recourse to other parts of the group.

Thus far we have simplified this discussion by looking at the two-party situation. **3.50** However, for SIFIs, the three-party situation is almost equally important. This situation arises where a bank incorporated in Country A deals through its branch in Country B with a customer in Country C. Since money is the easiest thing in the world to move across borders given modern technology, this is a pattern which occurs with increasing frequency. In general, arrangements of this kind are unproblematic when the bank is operating through a branch structure—the customer is a customer of the bank. It is generally immaterial both to the customer and to the bank whether the customer deals with an office of the bank in Country A or Country B—the customer's legal rights and remedies are generally the same. With a subsidiaries structure, by contrast, the customer must elect on day one which legal entity to deal with,[7] and the result of that election will determine the customer's rights and remedies.

Finally, a commonly observed phenomenon in the resolution literature has been **3.51** that non-lawyers tend to place too much importance on legal concepts. In law, and for regulatory reporting purposes, there are significant differences between a foreign branch and a foreign subsidiary. However, from a legal realist perspective,

---

[7] Dealing with both conventionally weakens the customer's position, since he loses set-off rights.

both are simply businesses headquartered outside the parent bank's home country conducting business in a host jurisdiction. The host regulator for any branch has always had considerable flexibility as regards some aspects of the regulation of the branch—for example, host regulators control branch liquidity, the appointment of senior staff in the branch, compliance by the branch with local customer protection rules, and a number of other issues, in many cases in the same way in which they would control the activities of a separately incorporated local subsidiary. One way of putting this is that for a large banking branch business, incorporating that branch as a subsidiary would not have a dramatic impact on the day to day activities of the head of compliance of that business.

Liquidity

3.52 It has always been the case that supervisors of bank branches have a degree of control over the liquidity of the branches which they supervise—the general principle of bank regulation is that capital is for home state supervisors but liquidity is for host state supervisors. The logic of this may be open to question—in particular, this arrangement is designed for a world in which branches act exclusively within the boundaries of their host country, and becomes illogical if the branch does a significant amount of cross-border business itself—but it is nonetheless the general rule.

3.53 Requiring fixed liquidity pools on a branch-by-branch basis, however, would rapidly become onerous and reduce efficiency. More importantly, this is a security policy which comes with a heavy price, both in terms of cost to the bank and in terms of restricting the business of the branch. Consequently, regulators were historically prepared to permit arrangements under which the bank, under appropriate supervision, managed its liquidity position centrally.

3.54 It is now clear that the problem with these arrangements was that, as established, they gave little or no thought to the question of how the central pool would be allocated in the case of crisis. The spectre before every host regulator is the outcome of the Lehman collapse, where a 'sweep' arrangement which collected group liquidity into one particular entity had operated on the evening of the day prior to the failure, leaving the entities from which the cash had been swept hopelessly illiquid (and potentially unresolvable) the following business day. It is, however, an error to conclude that the problem was the sweep. The problem was not the sweep, but the fact that no thought had been given on any side to the question of how the funds swept should have been disposed in the event of a crisis. Accepting that this is a problem which needs to be solved, there are simpler, less costly, and more effective tools available to address it than subsidiarization.

3.55 The sensible approach to the problem would be an agreement among resolution authorities as to the disposition of the liquidity pool concerned. If we assume for this purpose that the liquidity pool is managed at the group level under the supervision of the home state supervisor, all that would be necessary to create such an arrangement would be for the members of the group's crisis management group to agree on the relative levels of liquidity which would be allocated to the various subsidiaries and branches, and agree that in the event of the commencement of group resolution, those amounts would be made available on demand to the relevant group businesses. In effect, the host supervisor would determine a liquidity requirement for the hosted business and communicate that requirement to the home supervisor. The home supervisor would then assume the obligation to ensure that the liquidity pool of the group as a whole was at least equal to the sum of the local requirements.

It may be objected that local insolvency laws may make it difficult for authorities **3.56** to make such transfers. However, this is to misunderstand the nature of liquidity management. While liquidity is highly relevant during business as usual, it may be even more relevant at the recovery and resolution stages of managing bank failure. The absence of sufficient liquidity can result in insolvency by forcing a bank to sell assets at fire-sale prices and thus lock-in capital-depleting losses.

Capital

The easiest way to approach this is to consider the role of capital in a subsidiary. **3.57** Begin with a regulator who wants a branch in its jurisdiction to convert to a subsidiary. The most immediate impact is that it will harm the recourse of the creditors of the business, who now have claims only on the local assets owned by the subsidiary and not on the global assets owned by the bank itself. The trade-off is that the subsidiary will have an excess of assets over liabilities (since it is required to maintain capital), and that excess will in theory be available to the host state regulatory authority to discharge local creditors. However, it should be noted that this does not change the position of, or benefit, local creditors, as an equivalent surplus will necessarily be maintained at the global bank level. What the subsidiarization requirement does is to restrict the creditor's claims to a narrower pool of assets under the control of the host state resolution authority, as opposed to a larger pool under the control of the home state authority.

It is therefore the case that when we speak of 'capital' in a subsidiary, what we mean **3.58** is that the subsidiary has more assets than liabilities. It is perfectly possible to do an equivalent analysis for branches, and in other areas of analysis (notably tax law), the concept of 'branch capital' is unproblematic. However, a simple 'assets less liabilities' calculation tends to break down on the fact that although assets of a bank may be attributable to a particular branch, in general liabilities are not, and although it is possible to establish which assets can reasonably be said to be 'assets of the branch', in the absence of complex branch ringfencing provisions in funding arrangements (which would themselves have significant impact on the costs of those arrangements), it is not possible to say that a particular liability is a liability of one branch but not another, unless it is payable solely at a particular branch or branches outside a specified jurisdiction.

3.59 However, what is important in this context is to look at the problem which the host authority is trying to solve in the first place. The primary focus of the host authority is precisely to protect 'local' creditors—that is, local owners of local liabilities. Viewed from this perspective, it is quite easy to identify which creditors are 'branch' creditors—they are those creditors in the jurisdiction concerned who can reasonably look to the resolution and regulatory authorities in that jurisdiction to protect their interests. The paradigm case here would be local retail depositors, but local corporates who bank with the branch and local business who use the branch for payment services would both also fall within that class. The basis of this selection is the local regulator's obligation to protect customers in its jurisdiction, and following this line of argument gives us a plausible approach to identifying local creditors—that is, local creditors for this purpose are those creditors with whom the bank would not be permitted to deal without the authorization which the branch or the subsidiary has been given by the local regulator.

3.60 This would give us a way of addressing local capital requirements, in that it suggests that what the local regulator should require is a surplus of local assets over local liabilities. If the bank has no local liabilities, then the local regulator should be unconcerned; if the bank has more local liabilities than local assets, the local regulator will consider itself exposed and take steps to limit that exposure. A requirement that local assets exceed the claims of local creditors would seem to be effective in this regard.

3.61 A further issue—and one which creates a great deal of difficulty—is that an intelligent local resolution authority might argue that it is no use having local assets if those local assets are capable of being seized by overseas creditors so as to leave local creditors unprotected. This would argue for local ringfencing, which is an almost complete block to resolution. However, this again is to elide two different problems. In a resolution all that is needed is a presumption that local resolution authorities may apply local assets in satisfaction of the claims of local creditors. If this is sufficient for the resolution (using a no-creditor-worse-off-than-in-liquidation yardstick), then the problem is solved. However, in a liquidation, the issue goes away, since equality of treatment of creditors will be the appropriate outcome. The key point here is that in resolution assets are not distributed—the structure of a resolution is to put the entity being resolved in a position that it can continue in business without a cash and asset outflow. Thus a resolution can be conducted on the basis that local assets can be used to support the local business without imperilling the order of distribution of assets on an insolvency.

3.62 The overall effect of these two principles would be to require banks operating in host jurisdictions to increase the amount of their assets in these jurisdictions, to restrict to some extent the use of capital and liquidity resources around the enterprise, to require a greater degree of focus on location of assets and liabilities, and to increase significantly the amount of internal analysis and regulatory consent required for developing new lines of business, opening new business lines, or entering new markets. All of these have the effect of increasing fragility within the institution, since any restriction on the institution's ability to deploy its assets to meet a crisis will increase the chances of the crisis overwhelming the institution.

4

TOTAL LOSS ABSORBING CAPACITY

4.01 In order to resolve a bank, it is necessary to recapitalize it, and unless it is possible to raise new equity from new investors, it will be necessary to effect the recapitalization by reducing the claims of some creditors—the process known as bail-in. Whether this is done through 'bail-in by transfer' or 'bail-in by write-down', the ultimate economic outcome is the same—certain creditors will have their claims reduced or extinguished, and be given equity as compensation for this reduction. If this cannot be done without destabilizing the financial system, the institution cannot be resolved without impacting protected creditors. It is therefore necessary for each systemically important institution to have a sufficient amount of the right kind of liabilities—that is, liabilities that can be written down without destabilizing the financial system in order to make resolution operationally feasible.

4.02 In order to be successful, a resolution must ultimately produce a post-resolution entity which has sufficient capital to be not just solvent but credible. The starting point for most authorities in this regard is that the equity value of a failed institution is likely to be negligible. Thus the working assumption is generally that the minimum required bail-in-able debt for such an institution is likely to be that amount which, when written down or converted to equity, would completely recapitalize the bank concerned. Thus as a rule of thumb minimum bail-in-able debt for a successful bail-in should be roughly equal to what would be expected of a normal bank in normal markets, adjusted downward for any expected reduction in the bank's balance sheet to reflect the losses that are expected to cause the bank to fail and the sale of assets during the resolution process to provide sufficient funding and liquidity for the continuing banking entity (the good bank).

4.03 Bank capital requirements are, of course, a function of the size of the balance sheet, and in this regard a discussion has continued for some time as to whether it is reasonable to assume that the post-crisis balance sheet will be smaller than the pre-crisis balance sheet—the point being, of course, that if the balance sheet is likely to be smaller (as a result of the losses that cause the bank to fail and by asset sales to fund the good bank during the resolution process or otherwise), the amount of going concern capital required to be created by bail-in will be less than the among of going concern capital needed pre-bail-in.

The upshot of all this discussion is that since modern banks tend to operate with **4.04** capital levels very significantly in excess of their regulatory minima, the rule of thumb is that the minimum amount of bail-in-able debt that any bank should maintain should be sufficient to result in the bank having the required amount of regulatory capital implied by its expected balance sheet post-failure.

That minimum can, of course, only be made up of liabilities which could in **4.05** practice be written down without fostering runs or otherwise destabilizing the financial system. In theory, this includes every long-term unsecured liability. However, some resolution authorities believe that long-term unsecured liabilities vary widely amongst themselves in terms of how easy or difficult they are to bail in. Netting rights, calculation difficulties, counterclaims, settlement finality legislation, and the need to preserve commercial relationships all create different types of problems for resolution authorities contemplating bailing in certain types of liabilities. Thus, the aim of the rules is not simply to prescribe the existence of a class of long-term unsecured debt that can be bailed in without destabilizing the financial system, but to prescribe a class of long-term unsecured debt that is structured in such a way that it can be easily and effectively bailed in without undue difficulty.

At this point, a word on terminology may be in order. Capital is generally thought **4.06** of as falling into two broad forms: 'going concern' and 'gone concern'. Going concern capital refers to those claims on the issuer—equity, and very occasionally, limited recourse debt—whose value can be reduced by that issuer whilst remaining solvent. Gone concern capital, by contrast, refers to claims which can be written down, but require some sort of insolvency or other process to be triggered before the reduction can be made. This distinction is not a bright line—modern contingent convertible debt securities (CoCos), for example, which convert from debt to equity on the occurrence of particular trigger events which occur whilst the issuing institution is still solvent, fall somewhere between the two. The sort of loss absorbing capacity that we are talking about in this chapter, however, falls very clearly into the 'gone concern' bucket, and as a result the general term for it is GLAC—'gone concern loss absorbing capacity'. There are currently two proposed rules and one final international standard that relate to loss absorbing capacity—a final international standard produced by the Financial Stability Board (FSB), which is generally known as TLAC (total loss absorbing capacity), a requirement proposed by the European Union in the Bank Recovery and Resolution Directive (BRRD), which is generally known as MREL (minimum requirement for eligible liabilities), and a proposed regulation issued by the Federal Reserve establishing both a minimum TLAC and separate minimum GLAC requirement in the form of a long-term unsecured debt (LTD) requirement.

4.07 The essence of any GLAC requirement is that the issuing entity should have a certain proportion of its liabilities comprised of high-quality, long-dated, unsecured liabilities that can reliably absorb losses in a gone concern situation. The broad outline of the principles here is as follows:

- It must be sufficiently likely that the liability will actually exist when the firm enters resolution. A consensus has developed that this means the debt must have a remaining maturity of at least one year to be counted, since the assessment to be made by the authority is not 'will this be here tomorrow', but 'will this be here at all times within a reasonable planning horizon?'
- The liability must be within the scope of the insolvency or resolution laws of the issuing firm's home jurisdiction and any actions to impose losses on that liability need to be respected by foreign jurisdictions. Any such actions are likely be respected by foreign jurisdictions when the debt securities are governed by the laws of the firm's home jurisdiction. But foreign jurisdictions may be less likely to recognize such actions in the case of debt securities governed by foreign law. Such cross-border recognition will clearly be given when the relevant foreign jurisdiction has a statute that gives effect to the home country's insolvency and resolution proceedings and the conditions for such cross-border recognition are satisfied. Such cross-border recognition may also be given based on long-standing judicial principles of international comity. But it may be necessary for some firms to include contractual recognition clauses in their debt securities governed by foreign law in order to bolster the likelihood of cross-border recognition.
- The amount of claims under any instrument in insolvency or resolution proceedings must be easy to determine in advance, and the instruments need to be operationally straightforward to expose to loss. This is one of the stated reasons for the exclusion of structured notes from certain of the proposed and final GLAC minimum standards.
- Exposing the liability to loss must not be likely to give rise to valid legal challenge or claim for compensation under the no-creditor-worse-off-than-in-liquidation (NCWOL) safeguard. The point here is that if GLAC instruments ranked pari passu with short-term debt and other operating liabilities, on liquidation they would both be required to be written down pro rata. Writing down GLAC whilst leaving those other obligations whole might give rise to claims from holders of GLAC that they would have been better off in liquidation, and should therefore be compensated. There are broadly two solutions to this problem. One is to exclude short-term debt and other operating liabilities from bail-in. The alternative is to require that short-term debt and other operating liabilities be preferred to the claims of non-GLAC, thus solving the NCWOL problem by changing the position of the debt in the creditor priority scheme in insolvency or resolution proceedings.

It should be noted that although this last condition would be satisfied by the issu- **4.08**
ance of Tier 2 subordinated debt, it does not necessarily imply a mandate to issue
Tier 2 subordinated debt. It is entirely possible in law to create debt which ranks
above Tier 2 but below ordinary unsecured creditors.[1]

The BRRD includes a requirement for EU member states to set minimum require- **4.09**
ments for loss absorbency for all banks.[2] The Federal Reserve has published a
notice of proposed rulemaking, proposing an external TLAC and separate external
LTD (GLAC) requirement at the top-tier parent holding company level to facilitate this strategy.

The FSB has also recently finalized[3] a set of minimum international standards to **4.10**
achieve the availability of adequate loss absorbing capacity for global systemically
important banking groups (G-SIBs) in resolution by setting a new minimum
requirement for TLAC. The minimum TLAC requirement is a requirement for
loss absorbing capacity on both a going concern and gone concern basis, incorporating existing Basel III minimum capital requirements and excluding Basel III capital buffers. The FSB paper is expected to be replicated in the EU—the European
Banking Authority (EBA) has said:[4]

> The EBA's work [on MREL] interacts considerably with the work of the Financial
> Stability Board ('FSB') to develop a related global standard on Total Loss Absorbing
> Capacity (TLAC) for globally systemically important banks (G-SIBs). The EBA
> aims to implement the MREL as required by the BRRD, and in a way that is con-
> sistent with the developing international framework, while ensuring proportionality
> in its application to institutions other than G-SIBs.

The FSB has calibrated its minimum TLAC requirement at 18 per cent of risk- **4.11**
weighted assets (RWAs) on a fully phased-in basis (16 per cent initially) and 6.75
per cent of total Basel III exposures (6 per cent initially). The final calibration of the
FSB's Minimum TLAC requirements took into account public comment letters
and the results of a quantitative impact study and market survey.

One of the more interesting issues about the FSB's final TLAC standard is that **4.12**
some of it is expected but not required to be in the form of long-term unsecured
debt. This is, in fact, a considerable departure from the ordinary Basel mechanism. There is nothing in the Basel accords which actually requires capital to be
comprised of anything other than equity—an institution is free to choose to
meet its entire capital requirement with ordinary common equity if it so desires.

---

[1] Although many banks covenant not to do this in their Tier 2 issuance covenants.
[2] BRRD Art 45.
[3] Financial Stability Board, *Principles on Loss-absorbing and Recapitalisation Capacity of G-SIBs in Resolution: Total Loss-absorbing Capacity (TLAC) Term Sheet* 9 November 2015.
[4] *Consultation paper on Draft regulatory technical standards on criteria for determining the minimum requirement for own funds and eligible liabilities under directive 2014/59/EU* EBA/CP/2014/41 of 28 November 2014.

It might therefore have been expected that this would also be true of the FSB's TLAC proposal—after all, if equity is sufficient to meet higher forms of capital requirement, it seems perverse to argue that it is not sufficient to meet lower levels of the same requirement. However, the final FSB standard provides that TLAC in the form of debt capital instruments is expected to constitute at least 33 per cent of the TLAC requirement.

4.13 The logic behind this apparently paradoxical position is that resolution is only necessary in the first place when a firm has insufficient equity. To rely on a pure equity buffer is therefore tantamount to taking the position that resolution will never be required—that is, that an institution which has its entire TLAC requirement composed of equity has so much equity that it simply can never fail. This is not a position which the FSB is prepared to adopt. Thus, no matter how much equity an institution has, it is always required to maintain a debt buffer which can be bailed in if that equity is consumed.

4.14 This distinction highlights the blurring around the edges which the TLAC requirement creates. It is clear that equity is going concern capital—that is, it is capable of absorbing losses whilst the entity concerned continues trading. It is also clear that bail-in-able, TLAC-eligible, long-term unsecured debt is gone concern capital—it is only usable once the firm has been placed in resolution. Alternative Tier 1 and Tier 2 instruments, which fall somewhere between these two, are now best considered as hybrids falling somewhere between going and gone concern capital.

A. Eligibility of Liabilities as TLAC

4.15 As noted above, TLAC should consist only of liabilities that can be effectively written down or converted into equity during resolution of a G-SIB without disrupting the provision of critical functions or giving rise to material risk of successful legal challenge or compensation claims. The FSB has therefore produced a 'term sheet', which sets out the minimum criteria that liabilities must meet to be eligible as TLAC.

B. Public Disclosures

4.16 To enhance the credibility and feasibility of resolution and strengthen market discipline, the FSB principles and term sheet set out disclosure requirements for G-SIBs in regard to the amount, maturity, and composition of TLAC as well as the position of TLAC-eligible liabilities in the creditor hierarchy so that creditors and other counterparties of G-SIBs have clarity about the order in which they will absorb losses in resolution.

C. Regulation of Investors

To reduce the risk of contagion, the FSB term sheet (section 15) proposes rules on **4.17** deductions from G-SIBs' own TLAC or regulatory capital equal to their exposures to TLAC liabilities issued by other G-SIBs. This is supplemented by a proposal from the Basel Committee[5] to the effect that all banks holding TLAC issued by G-SIBs should be required to deduct that holding from Tier 2 capital, subject to certain exceptions.

D. TLAC and Groups

G-SIB groups are comprised of large numbers of legal entities, and applying resolu- **4.18** tion tools to each one is not a practical proposition. The resolution strategy for each G-SIB must therefore involve resolution at the group level, by applying resolution tools to a single parent, or a small number of intermediate parent entities—or, in FSB parlance, resolution entities which serve as the single point or multiple points of entry to resolution. This entity, or these entities, are the entities which will be resolved, and a necessary consequence of this is that these are the entities which must either issue TLAC to external investors, or must have access to that TLAC.

Direct issuance of TLAC by subsidiaries to external investors is generally unat- **4.19** tractive, so the issue which arises is as to how subsidiaries can be 'given access' to TLAC issued by a parent. One way of achieving this is for the resolution entity to downstream the net proceeds or assets purchased with the net proceeds from the TLAC to material subsidiaries in the form of intercompany extensions of credit to the subsidiaries (internal TLAC). This pre-positioned internal TLAC could con- tain provisions that allow any losses suffered at the subsidiary level to be pushed up to the resolution entity—for example, by converting the intragroup debt to equity without placing the subsidiary into resolution, if home and host authorities agree that this is necessary. Since, in a cross-border resolution of a G-SIB, it is in the interests of both home and host resolution authorities that key subsidiaries that are not themselves resolution entities do not formally enter resolution, and instead resolution tools are applied only to resolution entities, this should incentivize coop- eration between home and host and reduce incentives to ringfence assets locally in an uncooperative manner (although requiring pre-positioned internal TLAC is a form of *ex ante* ringfencing).

A crucial consideration of a resolution strategy's effectiveness is the availability **4.20** of sufficient amounts of loss absorbing capacity at the right location(s) within a

---

[5] Basel Committee on Banking Supervision 'Consultative Document on TLAC Holdings', November 2015.

G-SIB's group structure. Depending on the preferred resolution strategy, resolution entities may be the top-tier parent or holding company, intermediate holding companies, or subsidiary operating companies. The resolution entity and any direct or indirect subsidiaries of the resolution entity, which are not themselves resolution entities, form the resolution group. A G-SIB may consist of one or more resolution groups. It may form a single resolution group with the parent company, which may be a holding company or an operating entity, as the sole resolution entity or, alternatively, consist of two or more resolution groups with a corresponding number of resolution entities. A TLAC requirement will apply to each resolution entity within each G-SIB and will be set in relation to the consolidated balance sheet of each resolution group.

4.21 When a resolution entity enters resolution, TLAC issued by the resolution entity and held by external creditors would be written down (after equity) or converted into the equity of the (recapitalized) resolution entity (or a newly established bridge entity) or both. Losses would be absorbed in the first instance by the shareholders and thereafter by the external creditors of the resolution entity according to the applicable creditor hierarchy.

E. Internal TLAC

4.22 A key objective of the FSB's international TLAC standard is to provide home and host authorities with confidence that G-SIBs can be resolved in an orderly manner and thereby diminish any incentives to ringfence assets domestically. A resolution entity should generally act as a source of loss absorbing capacity for its subsidiaries where those subsidiaries are not themselves resolution entities. This can be easily achieved where the parent and the subsidiary are in the same jurisdiction and subject to the same authorities. It becomes more difficult, however, where the two are in different countries. The issue, in a nutshell, is as to how the authorities in a country where a bank subsidiary is established can be given reassurance that in the event of a group-wide problem, assets at the parent level will in fact be downstreamed to recapitalize the local subsidiary.

4.23 The FSB's international standard provides that subsidiaries located outside of their resolution entity's home jurisdiction, that are identified as material, and that are not themselves resolution entities would be subject to an internal TLAC requirement in proportion to the size and risk of the material subsidiaries' exposures, in absence of an agreement to the contrary between home and host authorities. The presence of an adequate amount of internal TLAC should provide host authorities of G-SIB subsidiaries with the comfort that resources will be available through the write-down or conversion of the internal TLAC to recapitalize subsidiaries. The FSB's international standard is that the amount of internal TLAC that should be maintained at material foreign subsidiaries (absent agreement to the contrary between home and host authorities) should be equivalent to 75–90 per cent of the external TLAC requirement that would apply to a resolution entity on a standalone basis. This quantum of internal TLAC was intended to provide sufficient comfort to host authorities that home authorities would use the resolution entity's assets to recapitalize its foreign subsidiaries, including any receivables on any required internal TLAC.

F. FSB TLAC Term Sheet

Paragraphs 4.25–4.80 summarize the term sheet in the FSB's final international **4.24** TLAC standard. The numbered headings below correspond to each of the numbered terms in the term sheet.

1—Objective

The objective of the FSB Minimum TLAC requirement is to ensure that G-SIBs **4.25** have the loss absorbing and recapitalization capacity necessary to help ensure that, in and immediately following a resolution, critical functions can be continued without taxpayers' funds (public funds) or financial stability being put at risk.

2—Covered firms

The final FSB standard currently applies only to G-SIBs. **4.26**

3—Minimum external TLAC requirement

Under the FSB standard, G-SIBs will be required to meet a new requirement for **4.27** Minimum External Total Loss Absorbing Capacity ('Minimum TLAC') alongside minimum regulatory capital requirements.

The Minimum TLAC requirement will be applied to each resolution entity within **4.28** each G-SIB. A resolution entity is the entity or entities to which resolution tools will be applied in accordance with the resolution strategy for the G-SIB. Depending on the resolution strategy, resolution entities may be parent or subsidiary operating companies, or ultimate or intermediate holding companies.

The Minimum TLAC requirement will be set in relation to the consolidated bal- **4.29** ance sheet of each resolution group. The resolution group is the group of entities that includes a single resolution entity and any direct or indirect subsidiaries of the resolution entity which are not themselves resolution entities or subsidiaries of other resolution entities. All subsidiaries form part of a resolution group.

A G-SIB's aggregate Minimum TLAC requirement should be invariant to whether **4.30** it has one or more than one resolution entities.

4—Calibration of minimum external TLAC

4.31 A comprehensive quantitative impact study and cost–benefit analysis was used to inform the determination of the common minimum TLAC requirement for all G-SIBs.

4.32 The common minimum TLAC requirement will be 18 per cent of the resolution group's RWAs on a fully phased-in basis (16 per cent until 1 January 2022). This does not include any applicable regulatory capital buffers, which sit on top of minimum TLAC. Authorities may set requirements above the common minimum G-SIB with a capital conservation buffer of 2.5 per cent and a 1 per cent G-SIB surcharge would therefore need to maintain overall TLAC, including combined capital buffers, of at least 21.5 per cent of the RWAs of the resolution group and a G-SIB with a 2.5 per cent G-SIB surcharge would need to maintain TLAC, including combined capital buffers, of at least 23 per cent of RWAs, assuming that the capital conservation buffer were 2.5 per cent and the applicable countercyclical buffers were set to zero and that no other buffers applied.

4.33 The common minimum TLAC requirement must also be at least 6.75 per cent of the Basel III leverage ratio denominator on a fully phased-in basis (6 per cent until 1 January 2022).

4.34 G-SIBs that are headquartered in emerging markets economies (EMEs) will not be subject to the common minimum TLAC requirement until 1 January 2025 (fully phased-in by 1 January 2028).

5—Additional firm-specific external TLAC requirements

4.35 Authorities which are home to resolution entities, in discussion with Crisis Management Groups (CMGs) and validated through the Resolvability Assessment Process, are free to set a minimum TLAC requirement for any G-SIB resolution entity above the common minimum for any reason, including to implement an orderly resolution, minimize the impact on financial stability, ensure the continuity of critical functions, or avoid exposing taxpayers' funds to loss with a high degree of confidence. The amount and distribution of TLAC within a G-SIB should also be sufficient to facilitate an orderly resolution and incentivize home–host cooperation (see below).

6—Relationship with capital requirements

4.36 Minimum TLAC is an additional requirement to minimum regulatory capital requirements set out in the Basel III framework. Items that count towards satisfying minimum regulatory capital requirements may also count towards satisfying the minimum TLAC requirement subject to the exceptions described in paragraphs 4.37–4.38 (among others).

Only common equity Tier 1 (CET1) in excess of that required to satisfy minimum **4.37** regulatory capital requirements and the common minimum TLAC requirements may count towards regulatory capital buffers.

Regulatory capital instruments issued by entities forming part of a material sub- **4.38** group (as defined below) may count towards common minimum TLAC only to the extent home and host authorities agree that their conversion into equity would not result in a change in control of those entities that would be inconsistent with the agreed upon resolution strategy.

Starting on 1 January 2022, regulatory capital must meet the eligibility external **4.39** criteria for eligible TLAC in order to count as TLAC.

To help ensure that a failed G-SIB has sufficient outstanding long-term debt for **4.40** absorbing losses or effecting a recapitalization in resolution, there is an expectation that the sum of a G-SIB's resolution entity or entities' eligible TLAC in the form of LTD will be equal to or greater than 33 per cent of their common minimum TLAC requirements.

According to the FSB term sheet, a breach, or likely breach, of the common mini- **4.41** mum TLAC requirement should ordinary be treated by supervisory and resolution authorities as seriously as a breach, or likely breach, of minimum regulatory capital requirements.

7—Instruments eligible for inclusion in external TLAC

The core features set out below apply to all instruments that count towards satisfy- **4.42** ing the common minimum TLAC subject to certain exceptions discussed below. Liabilities not included in TLAC remain subject to potential exposure to loss in resolution, in accordance with the applicable resolution law.

Credible *ex ante* commitments to recapitalize a G-SIB in resolution as necessary **4.43** to facilitate an orderly resolution and, in particular, to provide continuity of the firm's critical functions, from those authorities which may be required to contribute both to resolution funding costs (to cover losses and meet recapitalization needs) and temporary resolution funding may count towards a firm's common minimum TLAC, subject to the agreement of the relevant authorities, and so long as there are no legal impediments to so doing, including that there is no requirement that senior creditors are exposed to loss when such a contribution is made, and that there is no particular limit specified in law in respect of the amount which may be contributed. Such commitments must be pre-funded by industry contributions and may account for an amount equivalent to 2.5 per cent RWA towards the resolution entity's minimum RWA TLAC requirement when the common minimum risk-weighted TLAC ratio is 16 per cent and 3.5 per cent when the common minimum risk-weighted TLAC ratio is 18 per cent.

8—Issuer

4.44 External TLAC must be issued and maintained directly by resolution entities except for the following:

(a) CET1 regulatory capital issued by subsidiaries forming part of a resolution entity's resolution group and held by third parties, if treated as CET1 by the applicable Basel Capital rules

(b) regulatory capital instruments issued by cooperative banks or financial institutions related to them that have in place a mutual solidarity scheme that protects their solvency and liquidity

(c) regulatory capital instruments, other than CET1, issued by subsidiaries until 31 December 2021

(d) debt instruments issued by finance subsidiaries issued before 1 January 2022 if consistent with Basel III, provided there is substantial legal certainty that the instruments are loss absorbing, and home and host authorities agree.

4.45 All regulatory capital instruments issued by the resolution entity or resolution entities of a firm and held by third parties are eligible to satisfy the common minimum TLAC requirements.

9—Eligibility criteria

4.46 TLAC-eligible instruments must:

(a) be paid-in

(b) be unsecured

(c) not be subject to set-off or netting rights that would undermine their loss absorbing capacity in resolution

(d) have a remaining contractual maturity of at least one year or be perpetual

(e) not be redeemable by the holder prior to maturity, unless the option is not exercisable for at least one year

(f) not be funded directly by the resolution entity or a related party unless the home and host authority agree.

4.47 In addition, the appropriate authority should ensure that the maturity profile of a G-SIB's TLAC liabilities is adequate to ensure that its TLAC position can be maintained should the G-SIB's access to capital markets be temporarily impaired.

10—Excluded liabilities

4.48 Eligible external TLAC must not include:

(a) insured deposits

(b) sight deposits and short-term deposits (deposits with an original maturity of less than one year)

(c) liabilities arising from derivatives

(d) debt instruments with derivative-linked features such as structured notes

(e) liabilities arising other than through a contract, such as tax liabilities

(f) liabilities which are preferred to normal senior unsecured creditors under the relevant insolvency law

(g) any other liabilities that, under the laws governing the issuing entity, are excluded from bail-in or cannot be written down or converted into equity by the relevant resolution authority without giving rise to a material risk of successful legal challenge or valid compensation claims.

11—Priority

Eligible external TLAC must generally absorb losses prior to excluded liabilities in insolvency or in resolution without giving rise to material risk of successful legal challenge or valid compensation claims; and authorities must ensure that this is transparent to creditors (see sub-section 21 below for requirements for disclosure). In all cases, the means of subordinating eligible external TLAC to excluded liabilities, the risk of successful legal challenge or valid compensation claims, and the transparency of the order in which creditors can expect to bear losses in insolvency or in resolution, is subject to discussion in the CMG and to review in the FSB Resolvability Assessment Process. **4.49**

To ensure that eligible external TLAC absorbs losses as described in the preceding paragraph, it must generally be: **4.50**

(a) contractually subordinated to all excluded liabilities on the balance sheet of the resolution entity,[6] or

(b) junior in the statutory creditor hierarchy to all excluded liabilities on the balance sheet of the resolution entity, or

(c) issued by a resolution entity which does not have any excluded liabilities on its balance sheet (for example, a holding company) that are pari passu or junior to TLAC-eligible instruments on its balance sheet.

Notwithstanding the general creditor priority requirements, subordination of eligible TLAC to excluded liabilities is not required if:

• the amount of excluded liabilities on the balance sheet of the resolution entity does not exclude 5 per cent of the resolution entity's eligible external TLAC,

• the resolution authority of the G-SIB has the authority to differentiate among pari passu creditors in resolution,

• such differentiation would not give rise to a material risk of successful legal challenge or valid compensation claims, and

• this does not have a material adverse impact on resolution.

---

[6] They may, however, rank senior to capital instruments, including Tier 2 subordinated debt, in the insolvency creditor hierarchy.

4.51 The subordination requirement also does not apply in those jurisdictions in which all liabilities excluded from TLAC are statutorily excluded from the scope of the bail-in tool and therefore cannot legally be written down or converted to equity in a bail-in resolution. In this case, liabilities that rank alongside them and are included in the scope of the bail-in tool and meet the eligibility criteria for TLAC would in fact be able to absorb losses in resolution and qualify for TLAC. If this option is used, authorities must ensure that this would not give rise to a material risk of successful legal challenge or valid compensation claims, and that the terms of the TLAC eligible liabilities specify that they are subject to bail-in.

4.52 In those jurisdictions where the resolution authority may, under exceptional circumstances specified in the applicable resolution law, exclude or partially exclude from bail-in all of the liabilities excluded from TLAC, the relevant authorities may permit liabilities that would otherwise be eligible to count as external TLAC but which rank alongside those excluded liabilities in the insolvency creditor hierarchy to contribute a quantum equivalent of up to 2.5 per cent RWA of the resolution entity's common minimum TLAC requirement when the common minimum risk-weighted TLAC requirement exceeds 16 per cent and 3.5 per cent RWA when the common minimum TLAC requirement is 18 per cent. If this option is used, authorities must ensure that the capacity to exclude or partially exclude liabilities from bail-in would not give rise to material risk of successful legal challenge or valid compensation claims.

12—Redemption restrictions

4.53 G-SIBs are prohibited from redeeming eligible external TLAC without supervisory approval, except when replacing eligible TLAC with liabilities of the same or better quality and the replacement of liabilities is done at conditions which are sustainable for the income capacity of the bank.

13—Governing law

4.54 Eligible external TLAC must be subject to the law of the jurisdiction in which the relevant resolution entity is incorporated, or if issued under or otherwise subject to the law of another jurisdiction, the application of resolution tools by the relevant resolution authority is effective and enforceable under binding statutory provisions or legally enforceable contractual provisions for the recognition of resolution actions.

14—Triggers (for externally issued TLAC)

4.55 Eligible TLAC should contain a contractual trigger or be subject to a statutory mechanism which permits the relevant resolution authority to effectively write it down or convert it to equity in resolution.

15—Regulation of investors

In order to reduce the risk of contagion, G-SIBs must deduct from their own TLAC **4.56** or regulatory capital exposures to eligible external TLAC liabilities issued by other G-SIBs in a manner generally parallel to the existing provisions in Basel III that require a bank to deduct from its own regulatory capital certain investments in the regulatory capital of other banks.

16—Conformance period

Firms that were designated as G-SIBs by the FSB before the end of 2015 would **4.57** be required to comply with the TLAC standard and meet the 16 per cent of RWA and 6 per cent of total Basel III exposures requirements by 1 January 2019 (2025 if headquartered in an EME) and the 18 per cent of RWA and 6.75 per cent of total Basel III exposures requirements by 1 January 2022 (2028 if headquartered in an EME).

Firms that subsequently become G-SIBs would have thirty-six months to comply **4.58** with the FSB TLAC standard and its fully phased-in minimum TLAC ratios following the date on which they become G-SIBs.

A G-SIB that fails and enters resolution, or its successor bridge entity, would have **4.59** twenty-four months to come back into compliance with the FSB TLAC standard following the date on which it exits resolution, if it is still determined by the FSB to be a G-SIB.

A G-SIB which as a recovery measure comes to a voluntary agreement with its **4.60** creditors to convert liabilities to equity and so recapitalize the firm outside of resolution would be allowed twenty-four months to comply again with the FSB TLAC standard.

The Basel Committee is permitted to further specify this provision, including a prudential treatment for non-G-SIBs.

17—Internal TLAC

The primary purpose of internal TLAC is to facilitate cooperation between home **4.61** and host authorities and implementation of cross-border resolution strategies that are feasible and credible. The loss absorbing capacity that resolution entities have committed to material subgroups (as defined below) is referred to as internal TLAC.

Each of a G-SIB's resolution entities must maintain sufficient externally issued **4.62** TLAC-eligible instruments to cover its minimum TLAC requirement, which is to be set in relation to the consolidated balance sheet of the relevant resolution group.

Each sub-group (as defined below) of a G-SIB or of a resolution entity should meet **4.63** an internal TLAC requirement by maintaining a minimum amount of eligible internal TLAC (see below). This ensures that losses and recapitalization needs from material sub-groups that are not themselves resolution entities can be passed to a resolution entity without the need for statutory resolution tools to be applied directly to such subsidiaries.

4.64 Branches are not subject to internal TLAC requirements separate from any external or internal TLAC requirement applied to the legal entity of which they are a part.

18—Material sub-groups

4.65 A material sub-group consists of one or more direct or indirect subsidiaries of a resolution entity that is or are not resolution entities, do not form part of another material sub-group, are incorporated in the same jurisdiction outside their resolution entity's jurisdiction unless the CMG agrees otherwise, and meets certain materiality standards.

4.66 A sub-group is material if the subsidiary or subsidiaries forming the sub-group on a sub-consolidated basis at the level of the sub-group:

(a) has more than 5 per cent of the consolidated RWAs of the G-SIB group, or

(b) generates more than 5 per cent of the consolidated revenues of the G-SIB group, or

(c) has a total leverage exposure measure larger than 5 per cent of the G-SIB group's total leverage exposure measure, or

(d) has been identified by the firm's CMG as material to the exercise of the firm's critical functions.

4.67 The list of material subsidiaries should be reviewed and, if necessary, revised by the CMG on an annual basis.

19—Size of the internal TLAC requirement

4.68 TLAC generally should be distributed as necessary within resolution groups in proportion to the size and risk of exposures of its material sub-groups.

4.69 Each material sub-group must maintain internal TLAC of 75–90 per cent of the external minimum TLAC requirements applicable to resolution entities. The actual figure within that range should be determined by the host authority of the material sub-group in consultation with the home authority of the resolution group.

4.70 Unless otherwise agreed between home and relevant host authorities, this amount of internal TLAC must be pre-positioned on-balance sheet at the material sub-groups and should be sufficient at this level to facilitate effective cross-border resolution strategies for G-SIB resolution groups. TLAC that is not pre-positioned should be readily available to recapitalize subsidiaries as necessary to support the execution of the resolution strategy. Authorities should ensure that there are no legal or operational barriers to this.

To avoid 'double gearing', the resolution entity should issue and maintain at least as **4.71** much external TLAC as the sum of internal TLAC, which it has provided or committed to provide, and any TLAC needed to cover material risks on the resolution entity's own balance sheet. However, external TLAC may be lower if and to the extent this is due to consolidation effects only.

20—Core features of eligible internal TLAC

The core features of eligible internal TLAC are the same as the core features set out **4.72** above for eligible external TLAC (except with regard to the issuing entity and permitted holders), including liabilities that are excluded from eligible external TLAC are excluded from eligible internal TLAC.

Internal TLAC instruments of a subsidiary must be statutorily or contractually **4.73** subordinated to liabilities of that subsidiary that are excluded liabilities.

Internal TLAC that comprises regulatory capital instruments must comply with the **4.74** relevant provisions of Basel III, including those in relation to write-down and conversion at the point of non-viability. Internal TLAC must be subject to write-down or conversion to equity by the relevant host authority at the point of non-viability, as determined by the host authority in line with the relevant legal framework, without applying resolution tools to the subsidiary.

Any write-down or conversion to equity of internal TLAC is subject to consent **4.75** from the relevant authority in the jurisdiction of the relevant resolution entity, except where Basel III provides that such consent is not required.

This would not preclude the host authority from subjecting internal TLAC to its **4.76** own resolution bail-in or other resolution powers should the consent of the home authority not be forthcoming.

Home and relevant host authorities in CMGs may jointly agree to substitute on- **4.77** balance sheet internal TLAC with internal TLAC in the form of collateralized guarantees, subject to the following conditions:

- the guarantee is provided for at least the equivalent amount as the internal TLAC for which it substitutes;
- the collateral backing the guarantee is, following appropriately conservative haircuts, sufficient fully to cover the amount guaranteed;
- the guarantee is drafted in such a way that it does not affect the subsidiaries' other capital instruments, such as minority interests, from absorbing losses as required by Basel III;
- the collateral backing the guarantee is unencumbered and in particular is not used as collateral to back any other guarantee;
- the collateral has an effective maturity that fulfils the same maturity condition as that for external TLAC; and

- there should be no legal, regulatory or operational barriers to the transfer of the collateral from the resolution entity to the relevant material sub-group.

21—Public disclosure by G-SIBS of their eligible TLAC

4.78 G-SIBs must disclose the amount, maturity, and composition of TLAC maintained by each resolution entity and at each legal entity that forms a material sub-group and issues internal TLAC to a resolution entity.

4.79 G-SIBs must also disclose, at a minimum, the amount, nature, and maturity of any liabilities of each resolution entity which in the relevant insolvency creditor hierarchy rank pari passu or junior to liabilities which are eligible as TLAC.

4.80 Entities that are part of a material sub-group and issue internal TLAC to a resolution entity must disclose any liabilities that rank pari passu with or junior to internal TLAC issued to a resolution entity.

4.81 The Basel Committee on Banking Supervision is authorized to specify further the disclosure requirements.

PART II

THE US RESOLUTION REGIME

5

FUNDAMENTALS
OF RESOLUTION AUTHORITY

A. History

Resolution authority was first introduced in the United States in 1933 as part of the **5.01**
deposit insurance programme for banks. As originally enacted, it was little more
than the method by which the Federal Deposit Insurance Corporation (FDIC)
honoured its obligations to insured depositors. It evolved over time into a com-
plementary method of reducing contagion, preserving and restoring public confidence in the US banking system, and otherwise promoting financial stability—the
fundamental purposes of deposit insurance—as well as minimizing the cost to the
US banking system of providing deposit insurance. The most significant revision to
the FDIC's bank resolution powers was made by the Financial Institutions Reform,
Recovery and Enforcement Act of 1989 (FIRREA) during what is known in the
United States as the savings and loan crisis. The US bank resolution statute is contained within the Federal Deposit Insurance Act (FDIA).[1] It operates like a special
type of insolvency code for US insured depository institutions (IDIs) administered
by the FDIC.

When resolution authority was first introduced, US banks were generally organ- **5.02**
ized as standalone legal entities rather than as part of banking groups. Between
1933 and 1956, however, many US banks were put under holding companies in
order to find a way around restrictions on interstate branching. While a bank could
not freely branch across state lines, a single bank holding company (BHC) could
engage in interstate banking by acquiring a separate bank in each state. It could also
engage in non-banking activities by acquiring non-bank affiliates other than affiliates engaged principally in underwriting and dealing in securities, which had been
prohibited in 1933 by the Glass–Steagall Act. Although US banks were eventually

---

[1] The bank resolution statute consists of ss 11–15 of the FDIA, 12 USC ss 1821–1825, plus certain
definitions and other supplementary provisions scattered throughout the FDIA, but the most important provisions for purposes of this chapter are ss 11 and 13, 12 USC ss 1821 and 1823.

allowed to branch nationwide, virtually all of them remain structured as part of a broader group of legal entities headed by a parent BHC. Despite these structural changes, the US bank resolution regime was not expanded to apply to entire banking groups but was still limited to IDIs on the eve of the global financial panic of 2008.

5.03   The US bank resolution regime proved to be inadequate during that financial panic. It could resolve US IDIs as distinct legal entities, but not the parent BHC or other legal entities in a US banking group in a coordinated manner. Thus, Washington Mutual Bank (WaMu Bank), an insured savings association, was resolved under the bank resolution provisions of the FDIA, but its parent, Washington Mutual, Inc. (WaMu Inc.), a savings and loan holding company (SLHC), was reorganized under Chapter 11 of the US Bankruptcy Code. This resulted in a number of conflicts between the FDIC receivership and the bankruptcy proceeding, which in turn resulted in substantial litigation over the ownership of $20 billion of assets among WaMu Inc., the FDIC, and JP Morgan Chase Bank, which had purchased WaMu Bank. The FDIC ultimately settled its claim for $844 million.[2]

5.04   The US government responded to this situation in two ways. First, it enacted Title II of the Dodd–Frank Act, which created a new resolution authority for BHCs and most other non-bank financial companies when certain conditions are satisfied. The most important conditions are that the liquidation, recapitalization, or reorganization of a particular financial company under otherwise applicable insolvency law, principally the US Bankruptcy Code, 'would have serious adverse effects on financial stability in the United States' and that any action under Title II of the Dodd–Frank Act 'would avoid or mitigate such adverse effects'.[3] If a financial institution that becomes insolvent or reaches the point of non-viability can be resolved under the US Bankruptcy Code in a manner that stems contagion, preserves or restores public confidence in the US financial system, or otherwise promotes financial stability in the United States as effectively as Title II, then Title II cannot be lawfully invoked.

5.05   Second, the United States enacted section 165(d) of the Dodd–Frank Act, which requires BHCs with assets of at least $50 billion and certain other non-bank financial companies to file annual resolution plans (Title I resolution plans) showing how they and their material subsidiaries can be resolved in a rapid, orderly, and coordinated manner under the US Bankruptcy Code and any other normally applicable insolvency or resolution laws. The FDIC subsequently issued a regulation requiring IDIs with more than $50 billion in assets to file separate annual resolution plans (IDI resolution plans) showing how they can be resolved under the

---

[2] For the FDIC's description of this litigation, see FDIC, Status of Washington Mutual Bank Receivership, available at: <https://www.fdic.gov/bank/individual/failed/wamu_settlement.html> (last updated 4 August 2015).

[3] Dodd–Frank Act, s 203(b)(2) and (5), 12 USC s 5383(b)(2) and (5).

bank resolution provisions of the FDIA.[4] The institutions covered by these annual resolution planning requirements have now filed as many as four annual Title I and IDI resolution plans, starting in 2012. The applicable regulations require covered institutions to file public summaries of their resolution plans, which are posted on the FDIC's website.[5]

The FDIC has indicated that it prepares separate resolution plans for at least the **5.06** US global systemically important banking groups (US G-SIBs) under Title II of the Dodd–Frank Act. The FDIC does not disclose the contents of these plans, although it has indicated that its preferred strategy for resolving the US G-SIBs under Title II is the single-point-of-entry (SPE) recapitalization (bail-in) within the resolution model. The US G-SIBs do not have a clear window into the FDIC's Title II resolution planning process or whether the FDIC's Title II resolution plans are consistent with the Title I Resolution Plans filed annually by the US G-SIBs. The US G-SIBs are not treated as partners in the FDIC's Title II resolution planning process, although the FDIC has frequently requested the US G-SIBs to provide information that appears to be used by the FDIC in its Title II resolution planning process.

Seizing on the fact that the US Bankruptcy Code remains the principal law for **5.07** resolving failed BHCs and their non-bank subsidiaries unless the liquidation, recapitalization, or reorganization of such firms under the US Bankruptcy Code 'would have serious adverse effects on financial stability in the United States', the Bipartisan Policy Center, a private-sector think tank, published a report explaining how the existing US Bankruptcy Code could be used in a manner that would promote the financial stability goal as effectively as Title II under most circumstances, therefore reducing the need for Title II and the likelihood that it can be lawfully invoked.[6] The Hoover Institution, another private-sector think tank affiliated with Stanford University, proposed a new Chapter 14 to the US Bankruptcy Code that would include tools designed to help the US Bankruptcy Code resolve large financial companies in a manner that would promote financial stability.[7]

After the FDIC announced its development of an SPE method of resolving US **5.08** banking groups under Title II,[8] and that method was accepted around the world as

---

[4] For a comprehensive analysis of the Title I and IDI resolution planning process, see Randall D Guynn, 'Resolution Planning in the United States' in Patrick S Kenadjian (ed) *The Bank Recovery and Resolution Directive—Europe's Solution for 'Too Big to Fail'?* (Degruyter 2013).

[5] FDIC, Title I and IDI Resolution Plans, available at: <https://www.fdic.gov/regulations/reform/resplans/> (accessed 26 October 2015).

[6] John F Bovenzi, Randall D Guynn, and Thomas H Jackson, *Too Big to Fail: The Path to a Solution*, A Report of the Failure Resolution Task Force of the Financial Regulatory Reform Initiative of the Bipartisan Policy Center (May 2013).

[7] Thomas H. Jackson, 'Bankruptcy Code Chapter 14: A Proposal' in Kenneth E Scott and John B Taylor (eds) *Bankruptcy Not Bailout: A Special Chapter 14* (Hoover Institution 2012).

[8] Remarks by Martin J Gruenberg, Acting Chairman, FDIC, to the Federal Reserve Bank of Chicago Bank Structure Conference (10 May 2012).

the most promising solution to the too-big-to-fail (TBTF) problem,[9] the Hoover Institution developed a revised version of its Chapter 14 proposal that included provisions designed to facilitate an SPE strategy under the US Bankruptcy Code. The Hoover group called is revised proposal Chapter 14 2.0.[10] The US House of Representatives passed a bill in December 2014 that would have implemented the SPE portion of Chapter 14 2.0 and a nearly identical version of the bill was introduced in 2015.[11] Similar bills were introduced in the US Senate in 2013 and 2015.[12]

5.09 The FDIC's SPE strategy is a variation on a number of bail-in strategies that had been discussed most actively in Europe at least since 2010.[13] The Bank of England and the FDIC published a joint paper describing and endorsing the SPE strategy as the most promising strategy for resolving most G-SIBs, while recognizing that a multiple-point-of-entry (MPE) strategy may be more appropriate for others.[14] As noted above, the strategy was eventually described by many regulators around the world as the most promising solution to the TBTF problem.

B. Core Resolution Powers

5.10 Resolution authority, as conceived in the United States, has two principal components. The first—the *core resolution powers*—provides the FDIC or a US bankruptcy court with the authority to take control of a bank or other financial institution that has reached the point of non-viability. These powers enable the FDIC or a bankruptcy court to maximize the residual value and minimize the losses of the failed

---

[9] For a description of the process by which SPE became accepted around the world as the most promising solution to the TBTF problem, see Randall D Guynn, 'Framing the TBTF Problem: The Path to a Solution' in Martin Neil Baily and John B Taylor (eds) *Across the Divide: New Perspectives on the Financial Crisis* (Hoover Institution 2014).

[10] Thomas H Jackson, 'Building on Bankruptcy: A Revised Chapter 14 Proposal for the Recapitalization, Reorganization, or Liquidation of Large Financial Institutions' in Kenneth E Scott, Thomas H Jackson, and John B Taylor (eds) *Making Failure Feasible: How Bankruptcy Reform Can End 'Too Big to Fail'* (Hoover Institution Press 2015).

[11] Financial Institution Bankruptcy Act of 2014, HR 5421, 113th Cong, 1st Sess (2014); Financial Institution Bankruptcy Act of 2015, HR 2947, 114th Cong, 1st Sess (2015).

[12] Taxpayer Protection and Responsible Resolution Act of 2013, s 1861, 113th Cong, 1st Sess (2013): Taxpayer Protection and Responsible Resolution Act of 2015, s 1840, 114th Cong, 1st Sess (2015).

[13] See, e.g., Wilson Ervin and Paul Calello, 'From bail-out to bail-in' *The Economist* (28 January 2010); Thomas F Heurtas, 'The Road to Better Resolution: From Bail Out to Bail In' *LSE Financial Markets Group Paper Series*, Special Paper 195 (December 2010). A bail-in strategy is simply a way of recapitalizing a financial institution by converting certain types of debt to equity. Paul Tucker, Deputy Governor for Financial Stability at the Bank of England, was also an early proponent of bail-in.

[14] Bank of England and FDIC, Joint Paper, *Resolving Globally Active, Systemically Important, Financial Institutions* (10 December 2012); Martin Gruenberg and Paul Tucker, 'When global banks fail, resolve them globally' *Financial Times* (10 December 2012).

institution, preserve its critical operations, stem contagion, preserve or restore public confidence in the banking or wider financial system, and otherwise promote financial stability. There are at least two ways of accomplishing these goals:

1. **Receivership or bankruptcy.** Placing the bank or other financial institution into an FDIC receivership or a non-bank financial institution into a bankruptcy proceeding and quickly separating its capital structure liabilities from its operating liabilities and the viable parts of its business, including any critical operations, and either:
   a. quickly selling the viable parts of its business to, and requiring the assumption of its operating liabilities by, a third party for 'fair value' or transferring them to a bridge entity while leaving the equity interests and other capital structure liabilities behind in the FDIC receivership or bankruptcy proceeding and either liquidating those viable parts of its business in an orderly manner or effecting a bridge bail-in;[15] or
   b. temporarily staying the holders of the failed institution's capital structure liabilities from enforcing their rights as part of a reorganization, and effecting a direct bail-in;[16] or:
2. **Conservatorship.** Solely in the case of a failed bank under the FDIA, placing the failed bank into a conservatorship and operating it as a going concern until it can be rehabilitated for the benefit of its stakeholders or converted into a receivership to be liquidated in an orderly manner.

A critical part of the resolution process of US banks is the protection of insured **5.11** deposits. The United States, similar to most countries, protects depositors up to a stated limit. The underlying theory is that smaller depositors are not in a position to judge the financial condition of a bank, and should not be expected to bear losses when a US bank fails. The FDIC, in its role as receiver for a failed bank will, if at all possible, transfer the insured deposits to a viable third-party institution or to a bridge bank. If it is unable to do so, it will make arrangements to pay the insured depositors immediately. The immediate steps to protect insured depositors is a critical element of the US resolution process and is viewed as critical to the maintenance of financial stability and the avoidance of contagion.

---

[15] A bridge bail-in refers to the exchange of a failed legal entity's capital structure financial liabilities for the equity or other residual value of a bridge legal entity to which all or any portion of the failed legal entity's assets and liabilities have been transferred, in accordance with the priority of claims of the capital structure liabilities and in satisfaction of those claims.

[16] A direct bail-in refers to the exchange of a failed legal entity's long-term unsecured debt for equity in the same legal entity, including a write-down of the debt to reflect any shortfall in the value of the equity. The power to do a direct bail-in in the United States currently exists only under Chapter 11 of the US Bankruptcy Code and not under Title II of the Dodd–Frank Act or the bank resolution provisions in the FDIA. In contrast, the EU BRRD and the UK, German, and Swiss resolution statutes all include the power to effect either a direct bail-in or a bridge bail-in.

C. Claims Process

5.12 The second component of resolution authority, as conceived in the United States, is a *claims process* for claims either left behind or otherwise separated from the continuing parts of the business in an FDIC receivership or bankruptcy proceeding. The claims process includes the determination of the validity, amount, and holders of the claims in the FDIC receivership or bankruptcy proceeding. The entity conducting the claims process is charged with distributing the residual value of the failed institution or the bridge institution to the creditors and other stakeholders either left behind or otherwise separated from the continuing parts of the business in the FDIC receivership or bankruptcy proceeding in accordance with the priority of their claims and in satisfaction of their claims. Note that the conservatorship provisions in the FDIA do not include a claims process. The reason is simple: if a conservatorship is successful and the bank is rehabilitated, no such process is needed. If a conservatorship is unsuccessful, then the expectation is that the conservatorship would be converted into a receivership.

D. Need for Speed

5.13 In order for the core resolution powers to achieve their value maximization and financial stability goals, the essential elements of placing a failed institution into conservatorship, or placing it into a receivership or bankruptcy proceeding and separating its capital structure liabilities from its operating liabilities and the other viable parts of its business, must be completed quickly, if possible over a weekend (commonly referred to as a 'resolution weekend'). Otherwise, the residual value of the failed institution can dissipate rapidly, like a melting ice cube on a hot summer day, especially during a financial crisis. Allowing that value to dissipate will not only harm the failed institution's stakeholders, but it could also foster contagion, undermine confidence in the financial system, and otherwise destabilize the financial system.

5.14 The urgency for swift action that exists in exercising the core resolution powers does not exist for the claims process. The speed with which the pie is divided up among claimants generally does not affect confidence in the financial system or financial stability, as long as any claims against the FDIC receivership or bankruptcy estate are tradable, and the process is carried out within a reasonable period of time in an otherwise fair and equitable manner. The third party, bridge, or recapitalized firm, which succeeds to the failed institution's operations through the exercise of core resolution powers, can continue to perform the failed firm's critical operations and maximize its residual value and minimize its losses for the benefit of the claimants in the resolution or bankruptcy proceeding. Indeed, the FDIC or bankruptcy court needs enough time to identify, validate, and determine the amount of any claims and to determine the residual value of the failed institution, without having to determine that value based on fire-sale prices, especially during a financial crisis, when asset values will have dropped to excessively low levels because ordinary markets will have become dysfunctional. Requiring the claims process to be completed too quickly, such as by the Monday morning following resolution weekend, could undermine the financial stability goals that the core resolution powers are trying to achieve by undermining the public's confidence in the fairness of the claims process for the claims either left behind or otherwise separated from the continuing parts of the business in the receivership or bankruptcy proceeding.

E. Resolution vs Bankruptcy

The core resolution powers are designed to overcome what has traditionally been **5.15** viewed as the weaknesses of the traditional bankruptcy model during a financial panic.[17] The two main goals of the bankruptcy model are to maximize the value of an insolvent company for the benefit of its creditors as a group and to determine who gets what value, in what order.[18] The goals of bankruptcy have not traditionally been viewed as including the preservation or restoration of public confidence in the financial system during a financial panic or of financial stability. Nor have bankruptcy judges traditionally been viewed as having the requisite experience or tools to achieve that objective.

What is needed to achieve the financial stability goal are core resolution powers that **5.16** enable the FDIC or bankruptcy judges to move quickly to preserve the franchise value and critical operations of a failing bank or banking group in order to maximize the firm's residual value and minimize its losses for the benefit of its stakeholders and to promote financial stability. During a financial panic, credit dries up, financial assets become illiquid, and the perceived value of financial assets drops to exaggerated levels with extraordinary speed. The disorderly failure of a large bank or a large number of smaller banks can result in a contagious panic that can destabilize the financial system and result in catastrophic harm to the wider economy in terms of reduced output, increased unemployment, and social unrest. As noted above, Milton Friedman and Anna Schwartz blamed the failure and liquidation of nearly 10,000 small US banks between 1930 and 1933 for what they called The

---

[17] For a summary of the key weaknesses of the traditional bankruptcy model, see Randall D Guynn, 'Are Bailouts Inevitable?' (2012) 29 Yale J on Reg 121, 135–40.

[18] Thomas H Jackson, *The Logic and Limits of Bankruptcy Law* (Harvard University Press 2001) (Bankruptcy Law) 10–17, 20.

Great Contraction in the supply of money (and credit), resulting in or deepening the Great Depression.[19] The core resolution powers are designed to preserve value, minimize losses, and stem panics until the markets recover, credit again flows freely, and asset prices become more easily determinable.

F. Subordination of Capital Structure Liabilities

5.17 An essential element of the core resolution powers is the power to subordinate the claims of the holders of capital structure liabilities to those of the holders of operating liabilities. Both the FDIA and Title II of the Dodd–Frank Act include this power in the form of a general power to discriminate among creditors within the same class retrospectively,[20] if necessary to achieve certain value maximization, loss minimization, financial stability, or other goals.[21] This general power to discriminate among similarly situated creditors retrospectively includes, but is not limited to, the authority to subordinate the claims of the holders of capital structure liabilities to those of the holders of operating liabilities. This power is subject, however, to the condition that the disfavoured creditors receive at least as much value in satisfaction of their claims as they would have received in a hypothetical liquidation of the failed institution.[22] This condition has become widely known as the no-creditor-worse-off-than-in-liquidation (NCWOL) principle.

5.18 The purpose of the power to subordinate the claims of the holders of capital structure liabilities to those of the holders of operating liabilities is to reduce the incentive of depositors and other short-term unsecured debt holders to run, reduce the risk of contagion, and promote financial stability. The holders of demand deposits and other short-term unsecured debt have the legal right to run when they believe their bank or other financial institution is insolvent or might become insolvent. The long-term unsecured debt holders do not.

5.19 The power to discriminate between long-term and short-term unsecured claims retrospectively has been roundly criticized in the United States, however, for essentially using long-term unsecured debt to bail out short-term unsecured debt.[23] Such

---

[19] Milton Friedman and Anna Jacobson Schwartz, *A Monetary History of the United States, 1867–1960* (Princeton University Press 1963), ch 7.

[20] FDIA, s 11(i)(2) and (3), 12 USC s 1821(i)(2) and (3); Dodd–Frank Act, s 210(b)(4)(A), (h)(5)(E)(i), 12 USC s 5390(b)(4)(A), (h)(5)(E)(i).

[21] FDIA, ss 11(d)(2)(B)(iv), (D) and (E), (d)(4)(B)(i), (d)(13)(E)(i), 12 USC s 1821(d)(2)(B)(iv), (D), (E), (d)(4)(B)(i), (d)(13)(E)(i); Dodd–Frank Act, s 210(a)(9)(E), (b)(2), (b)(4)(A)(i) and (iii), (h)(5)(E)(i)(I) and (II), 12 USC s 5390(a)(9)(E), (b)(2), (b)(4)(A)(i) and (iii), (h)(5)(E)(i)(I) and (II).

[22] FDIA, s 11(i)(2) and (3), 12 USC s 1821(i)(2) and (3); Dodd–Frank Act, s 210(b)(4)(A), (h)(5)(E)(i), 12 USC s 5390(b)(4)(A), (h)(5)(E)(i).

[23] Kenneth E Scott, 'A Guide to the Resolution of Failed Financial Institutions: Dodd–Frank Title II and Proposed Chapter 14' in Kenneth E Scott and John B Taylor (eds) *Bankruptcy Not Bailout: A Special Chapter 14* (Hoover Institution 2012).

retroactive discrimination has been criticized as being unfair to long-term unsecured debt holders because they may not have been fully compensated for the risk of being subordinated to the claims of short-term unsecured debt holders. It has also been criticized for creating a moral hazard because the short-term unsecured debt holders may not have internalized the costs of being ranked senior to long-term unsecured debt holders.

The principal response to these criticisms has been to require long-term unsecured **5.20** debt and other capital structure liabilities to be legally, contractually, or structurally subordinated to short-term unsecured debt and other operating financial liabilities in advance of any FDIC receivership or bankruptcy proceeding, rather than doing so retrospectively as a matter of the FDIC's discretion. By subordinating long-term unsecured debt to short-term unsecured debt in advance, instead of retrospectively, the market should respond by causing the interest payable on long-term unsecured debt to rise in order to compensate the holders of long-term unsecured debt for the increased risk of being subordinated to short-term unsecured debt. The market should also respond by causing the interest payable on short-term unsecured debt to fall, reflecting the reduced risk the holders of such debt face because of their preferred status, thus requiring investors in short-term debt to internalize the costs of their preferred status.

The goal of subordinating long-term unsecured debt and other capital structure **5.21** liabilities to short-term unsecured debt and other operating liabilities in advance of an FDIC receivership or bankruptcy proceedings can be accomplished in the United States without amending any contracts or enacting any statutes since virtually all US banks are structured as part of a group of legal entities headed by a BHC parent. US banking groups, for example, issue virtually all of their long-term unsecured debt at the top-tier parent level. They issue virtually all of their deposits and other short-term unsecured debt at the operating subsidiary level. Unsecured debt issued at the parent level is considered to be structurally subordinated to unsecured debt at the operating subsidiary level in a bankruptcy proceeding or an FDIC receivership under Title II.

The Federal Reserve has already used its supervisory powers to ensure that US **5.22** G-SIBs maintain a sufficient amount of equity and long-term unsecured debt at the top-tier parent level to provide a meaningful buffer against losses to short-term unsecured debt holders at the operating subsidiary level. It has also used its supervisory powers to require US G-SIBs to start the process of reducing the amount of commercial paper and other short-term unsecured debt at the top-tier parent level to an immaterial amount. The Federal Reserve has also participated in developing the Financial Stability Board's proposal for total loss-absorbing capacity (TLAC),[24]

---

[24] Financial Stability Board, *Principles on Loss-absorbing and Recapitalisation Capacity of G-SIBs in Resolution: Total Loss-absorbing Capacity (TLAC) Term Sheet* (9 November 2015).

and has announced that it will issue its own version of a TLAC regulation that will ensure that US G-SIBs have sufficient TLAC at the top-tier parent level that is structurally subordinate to virtually all of the group's short-term unsecured liabilities at the operating subsidiary level.[25]

---

[25] Federal Reserve System, *Total Loss-Absorbing Capacity, Long-Term Debt, and Clean Holding Company Requirements for Systemically Important U.S. Bank Holding Companies and Intermediate Holding Companies of Systemically Important Foreign Banking Organizations*, 80 Federal Register (30 November 2015) 74926–74964. For a visual summary of the Federal Reserve's proposed rule, see Davis Polk memo *Federal Reserve's Proposed Rule on Total Loss-Absorbing Capacity and Eligible Long-Term Debt* (10 November 2015), available at: <http://www.davispolk.com/sites/default/files/2015_11_10_Federal_Reserves_Proposed_Rule_on_TLAC_and_Eligible_LTD.PDF> (accessed 6 December 2015).

6

RESOLUTION OF INSURED DEPOSITORY INSTITUTIONS

The resolution of US-insured depository institutions (including insured banks and   **6.01**
savings associations) is governed primarily by sections 11 and 13 of the Federal
Deposit Insurance Act (FDIA). The 2008 global financial panic marked the largest
wave of insured depository institution (IDI) failures in the United States since the
US savings and loan crisis ended in the early 1990s. The Federal Deposit Insurance
Corporation (FDIC) resolved 507 failed IDIs between 2008 and 2014.[1] As of the
end of the first quarter of 2015, the FDIC still had 253 IDIs on its 'problem list', with
approximately $60 billion in assets.[2] During the past hundred years, US IDIs have
typically failed in waves, with very few failures between each wave. Indeed, there have
been three principal waves of IDI failures during this period. For tabular and graphical
illustrations of these three waves, see Table 6.1 and Figures 6.1 to 6.6.

In this chapter on US IDI resolutions, we first discuss certain background issues,   **6.02**
including the chartering authorities of the institutions that are subject to resolution authority, the deposit insurance requirement, the structure of the FDIC's
resolution unit, the administrative nature of the FDIC resolution process, and the
relatively high level of legal uncertainty in this area of US law. We then describe
the supervisory and other tools designed to prevent troubled banks and thrifts
from failing. We also discuss the resolution process, including an extended discussion of FDIC-assisted purchase and assumption (P&A) transactions designed
to keep the healthy part of a failed institution alive by transferring it to a healthy
third-party or bridge bank. We also discuss the recapitalization (bail-in) within
resolution strategy, a new technique that the FDIC has developed to resolve large
IDIs. Finally, we discuss the ancillary claims process for claims left behind in the
receivership, including a detailed discussion of the FDIC's 'super powers' to avoid,
set aside, or otherwise limit the claims of creditors or other stakeholders in the
liquidation process.

---

[1] FDIC, Annual Report (2014) 126.
[2] FDIC, Quarterly Banking Profile (First Quarter 2015) 4.

Table 6.1 Waves of major US bank/IDI failures

	Number of Failed Banks	% of Total Banks that Failed (1)	Deposits of Failed Institutions (billions) (A)	Total Deposits of All Banks (billions) (2)(A)	Deposits of Failed Institutions as % of Total Deposits (2)	Estimated Losses (billions) (3)(A)	Estimated Losses as % of Total Deposits (2)(3)
Roaring 20s and Great Depression (1921–1939)	15,119	49.0%	$139.4	$612.7	22.8%	$30.1	4.9%
Savings and Loan Crisis (1982–1992)	2,799	19.4%	$981.5	$4,928.7	19.9%	$141.6	2.9%
2008 Global Financial Crisis (2008–2012)	475	6.7%	$540.2	$8,866.1	6.1%	$82.5	0.9%

(A) Stated in 2014 Dollars
(1) Number of Failed Banks / Total Number of Banks in first year of period
(2) Average of total deposits of all banks over the years of the period
(3) Data missing estimated losses for 1982–1987

Sources: FDIC Annual Report 2014, available at: <https://www.fdic.gov/about/strategic/report/2014annualreport/index.html>; FDIC, Failures and Assistance Transactions Database, available at: <https://www2.fdic.gov/hsob/SelectRpt.asp?EntryTyp=30&Header=1>; FDIC, The First Fifty Years, Chapter 3: Establishment of the FDIC at 36, available at: <https://www.fdic.gov/bank/analytical/firstfifty/chapter3.pdf>; Bureau of Labor Statistics, All Urban Consumers-Consumer Price Index Database, available at: <http://www.bls.gov/cpi/data.htm>; OCC Annual Reports 1921–1933, available at: <https://fraser.stlouisfed.org/title/?id=56#!19155>; Milton Friedman & Anna Jacobson Schwartz, *A Monetary History of the United States 1867–1960* (1963), Table 16.

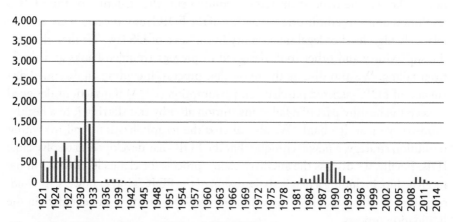

Figure 6.1 Waves of major US bank/IDI failures

© Davis Polk & Wardwell LLP.

Sources: FDIC, Failures and Assistance Transactions Database, available at: <https://www2.fdic.gov/hsob/SelectRpt.asp?EntryTyp=30&Header=1>; FDIC, The First Fifty Years, Chapter 3: Establishment of the FDIC at 36, available at: <https://www.fdic.gov/bank/analytical/firstfifty/chapter3.pdf>.

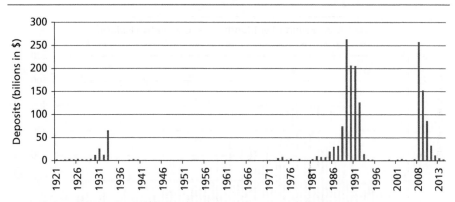

Figure 6.2 Deposits in failed US banks/IDIs (in 2014 dollars)

© Davis Polk & Wardwell LLP.

Sources: FDIC, The First Fifty Years, Chapter 3: Establishment of the FDIC at 36, available at: <https://www.fdic.gov/bank/analytical/firstfifty/chapter3.pdf>; FDIC, Failures and Assistance Transactions Database, available at: <https://www2.fdic.gov/hsob/SelectRpt.asp?EntryTyp=30&Header=1>; Bureau of Labor Statistics, All Urban Consumers-Consumer Price Index Database, available at: <http://www.bls.gov/cpi/data.htm>.

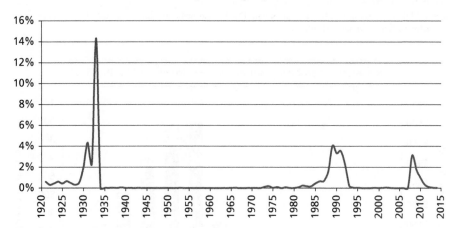

Figure 6.3 Deposits in failed US banks/IDIs as percent of total deposits

© Davis Polk & Wardwell LLP.

Sources: FDIC Annual Report 2014, available at: <https://www.fdic.gov/about/strategic/report/2014annualreport/index.html>; FDIC, Failures and Assistance Transactions Database, available at: <https://www2.fdic.gov/hsob/SelectRpt.asp?EntryTyp=30&Header=1>; FDIC, The First Fifty Years, Chapter 3: Establishment of the FDIC at 36, available at: <https://www.fdic.gov/bank/analytical/firstfifty/chapter3.pdf>; Bureau of Labor Statistics, All Urban Consumers-Consumer Price Index Database, available at: <http://www.bls.gov/cpi/data.htm>.

A. Background

Chartering authorities

IDIs may be chartered under US federal law or under the laws of any state. The **6.03** chartering authority and primary federal banking supervisor for national banks and federal savings associations, as well as the federal branches and agencies of foreign banks, is the Office of the Comptroller of the Currency (OCC). The chartering authority for state-chartered banks and savings associations, and the licensing

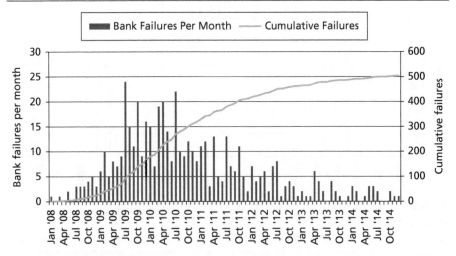

Figure 6.4 Number of US IDI failures per month (2008–2014)

© Davis Polk & Wardwell LLP.

Source: FDIC, Failures and Assistance Transactions Database, available at: <https://www2.fdic.gov/hsob/
SelectRpt.asp?EntryTyp=30&Header=1>.

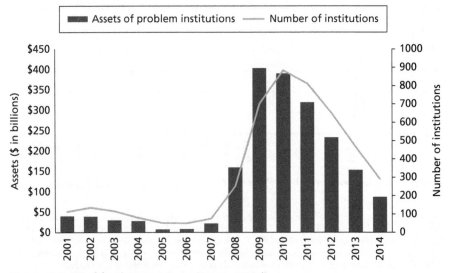

Figure 6.5 'Problem' institutions (2001–2014)

© Davis Polk & Wardwell LLP.

Source: FDIC, Quarterly Banking Profile, First Quarter 2015, available at: <https://www2.fdic.gov/qbp/
2015mar/qbp.pdf>; FDIC, Quarterly Banking Profile, First Quarter 2010, available at: <https://www2.fdic.
gov/qbp/2010mar/qbp.pdf>.

authority for state-licensed branches and agencies of foreign banks, is typically the
banking supervisor of the chartering or licensing state. State-chartered banks may
elect to be members of the Federal Reserve System or not. The primary federal
banking supervisor for state-chartered member banks is the Federal Reserve. The
FDIC is the primary federal banking supervisor for FDIC-insured state-chartered

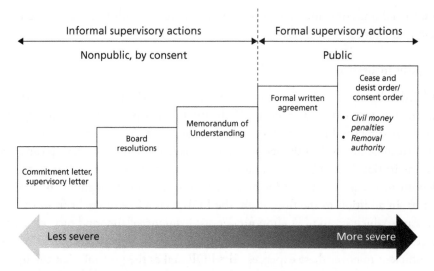

Figure 6.6 Range of supervisory actions by banking regulators

non-member banks and savings associations. All bank holding companies (BHCs) and savings and loan holding companies (SLHCs) are regulated by the Federal Reserve.

The FDIC did not traditionally have any resolution authority over BHCs, SLHCs, or the non-bank affiliates of an IDI. Instead, such holding companies were traditionally reorganized, recapitalized or liquidated under the normal bankruptcy laws. The IDI's other affiliates were also traditionally subject only to liquidation, recapitalization, or reorganization under normal bankruptcy laws, the Securities Investor Protection Act (SIPA) or some other US or non-US insolvency law that was not under the FDIC's jurisdiction. Perhaps this was because most holding companies do not engage in any significant activities other than through their IDI subsidiaries. **6.04**

The global financial crisis of 2008, however, highlighted that certain of the largest, most global BHCs and SLHCs engage in a broad range of activities either directly or indirectly through non-bank subsidiaries. As a result of the enactment of Title II of the Dodd–Frank Act, the FDIC may be appointed as the receiver of BHCs, SLHCs, and any of their non-bank financial subsidiaries, as long as certain conditions are satisfied. The most important conditions are that the holding company or the particular non-bank financial subsidiary be insolvent or in danger of becoming insolvent, its resolution under the ordinary bankruptcy laws would have serious adverse effects on financial stability in the United States and its resolution under Title II would avoid or mitigate those adverse effects. These conditions are unlikely to be satisfied except with respect to the most systemically important financial institutions during a financial crisis, but are theoretically possible with respect to most non-bank financial institutions at any time. The FDIC's power to **6.05** resolve holding companies under such circumstances are substantially similar to its resolution authority over IDIs.

Deposit insurance

6.06 All federally chartered depository institutions and virtually all state-chartered institutions are required to be FDIC-insured.[3] This means that their deposits are insured by the FDIC up to certain statutory caps. At the present time, these caps are generally $250,000 per person, per insured account ownership capacity, per institution.[4] The FDIC is an independent government agency. It maintains a deposit insurance fund paid for by assessments on IDIs throughout the United States. In addition to the fund itself, the FDIC has a line of credit from the US Treasury, which it can use to honour deposit insurance claims and provide assistance to troubled or failed depository institutions if the deposit insurance fund is insufficient to cover these expenses. The FDIC takes the position that the insurance obligations of the FDIC are backed by the full faith and credit of the United States, even though as a technical matter funds would need to be appropriated to meet the obligations if the deposit insurance fund or other resources at the disposal of the FDIC were insufficient.[5]

Structure of the FDIC's resolution unit

6.07 The FDIC is governed by a board of directors composed of five members, including the Comptroller of the Currency (the federal regulator of US national banks), the Director of the Consumer Financial Protection Bureau, and a chairman and vice chairman designated from among three appointed public members. One of the three public members must have state bank supervisory experience, and not more than three of the five members may be from the same political party.[6] It has a permanent staff that is organized into divisions and offices. The Division of Resolutions and Receiverships is the division principally responsible for the resolution of insured banks and thrifts, although the Division of Risk Management Supervision, the Division of Depositor and Consumer Protection, and the Legal Division also play important roles. The Division of Complex Financial Institutions is responsible for the FDIC's resolution authority over the largest, most complex IDIs and foreign banking organizations in the United States and their non-bank financial affiliates.

---

[3] FDIA, § 5(a), 12 USC § 1815(a).

[4] Dodd–Frank Act, § 335, 12 USC § 1821(a)(1)(E); FDIC, *Understanding Deposit Insurance* (2015).

[5] Full Faith and Credit of US Government Behind the FDIC Deposit Insurance Fund, FDIC Advisory Op, No 36 (9 November 1987); FDIC, Frequently Asked Questions: Temporary Liquidity Guarantee Program (2009).

[6] FDIA, § 2(a)(1), (b), 12 USC § 1812(a)(1), (b).

The FDIC operates primarily through regional offices. The examination and super- **6.08**
visory staff of the Division of Risk Management Supervision and the Division of
Depositor and Consumer Protection is primarily located within these regional
offices. Each of the regional offices has established local field offices to facilitate
the examination process. The Division of Resolutions and Receiverships, however,
operates primarily though the FDIC's main office in Washington DC, and a large
regional office in Dallas, Texas. Smaller offices are also located in areas where a large
concentration of failures has occurred.

Administrative nature of resolution process

In contrast to a bankruptcy proceeding under the US Bankruptcy Code, which is **6.09**
a judicial process, a proceeding under the bank resolution statute is fundamentally
an administrative proceeding conducted by the FDIC, with little input from creditors or other claimants and virtually no judicial review. As conservator or receiver,
the FDIC succeeds by operation of law to all of the rights, powers, and interests
of the failed depository institution, its officers, directors, and shareholders, and is
given plenary power to administer its affairs. Unlike a proceeding under the US
Bankruptcy Code, no creditors' committees or trustees exist, and no court oversees
the FDIC's activities. Any claims against the failed institution must first be submitted to the FDIC for its own administrative determination, and only after the FDIC
considers the claim will a claimant be permitted to assert its claim before a court
for *de novo* review.

The administrative nature of the proceedings, and the FDIC's manner of carrying **6.10**
out its authority, often creates substantial frustrations for creditors and other parties affected by the failure. In one sense, everyone other than the FDIC is a passive
observer, without direct access or input to the FDIC as it performs its functions.
Part of this frustration arises from the FDIC's inherent conflict of interest; it is
not only the sole administrator of the receivership process, but it is also typically
the largest creditor of the receivership estate. The FDIC has a statutory obligation
to insure deposits of failed institutions up to certain statutory limits. When it is
called upon to make good on those deposits, it becomes subrogated to the claims of
insured depositors and is therefore a creditor against the failed institution.[7]

Although as conservator or receiver the FDIC is supposed to function as the neutral **6.11**
arbiter of the claims process, its interest as the largest creditor is often pitted against
the interests of competing creditors. It has a strong incentive to use its extraordinary
powers to deny, avoid, or set aside conflicting creditor claims. In addition, the statutory framework gives the FDIC's subrogated deposit claims priority over the claims
of general creditors.[8]

---

[7] FDIA, § 11(g), 12 USC § 1821(g).
[8] FDIA, § 11(d)(11), 12 USC § 1821(d)(11).

Limited legal guidance

6.12 Further, unlike the extensive body of case law, legal commentary, and other guide-lines that exists with respect to reorganizations and liquidations under the US Bankruptcy Code, only a very limited body of legal guidance supplements the bank resolution statute. As described by two former general counsels to the FDIC and the Federal Home Loan Bank Board (a US government agency that has since been closed), respectively:

> This is a confusing area. The challenge arises less because of the complexity of the rules than because of their ambiguity and obscurity. The Bankruptcy Code gener-ally constitutes the starting point for rules governing the financial failure of com-panies in the United States. It contains a detailed set of rules that fill three volumes of U.S. Code Annotated, volumes of West's Bankruptcy Reporter, and over four linear feet of Collier's [on Bankruptcy]. But the statutes governing conservator-ships and receiverships of federally insured banks and thrifts fill, at most, about 111 pages of the U.S. Code Annotated. Moreover, those 111 pages were fundamentally changed less than 18 months ago in the Financial Institutions Reform, Recovery and Enforcement Act of 1989.[9]

The FDIC has only promulgated a few regulations to implement the statute,[10] and has issued only a relatively small number of advisory opinions, policy statements, and other guidelines to supplement it. The FDIC also takes the position that advis-ory opinions issued by its staff, including its general counsel, are not binding on it. In addition, the FDIC reserves the right to withdraw any of its policy statements at any time, potentially with retroactive effect. As a result, uncertainty surrounds how various issues would be resolved in the conservatorship or receivership of an insured institution.

6.13 Moreover, very little case law or legal commentary exists because IDI failures tend to occur in waves with much lower frequency than insolvencies governed by the US Bankruptcy Code. For example, nearly sixty years passed between the wave of bank failures that occurred during the Great Depression and the wave that occurred during the US savings and loan crisis of the 1980s. Approximately twenty years passed between the US savings and loan crisis and the global finan-cial panic of 2008. See Figures 6.1–6.6 for tabular and graphical illustrations of how US bank failures have occurred in three principal waves, with almost no failures between each wave, during the past hundred years. Few cases and almost no demand for legal commentaries arose in the intervening periods. As a result, the case law is sparse and little economic incentive has existed to invest time and effort into a body of legal commentary that seems irrelevant for long periods of time.

---

[9] John L Douglas, Jordan Luke, and Rex R Veal, 'Introduction', *Counselling Creditors of Banks and Thrifts: Dealing with the FDIC and RTC*, PLI Order No A4-4323 (14 January 1991).
[10] 12 CFR Part 360.

B. Supervisory and Other Tools to Ensure Resiliency

The regulation and supervision of the US banking system has historically focused **6.14** on ensuring the safety and soundness of individual banks. Since the global financial crisis of 2008, however, that sort of prudential regulation and supervision has been supplemented by macro-prudential, or systemic, regulation and supervision that focuses on promoting the stability of the overall US banking system. One of the principal goals of this new regime is to improve the resiliency of US banks against the risk of failure. The principal tools for achieving this goal for all banks include capital and liquidity regulation, source of strength obligations, prompt corrective action tools, lender-of-last-resort facilities, deposit insurance, and supervision, examinations, and enforcement actions. For banks that are considered to be systemically important, these tools are supplemented by enhanced prudential standards, early remediation tools, and recovery plans. During the 2008 global financial crisis, these tools were supplemented by a variety of extraordinary measures including the Troubled Asset Relief Program (TARP), open bank assistance, and the Temporary Liquidity Guarantee Program (TLGP).[11]

Capital and liquidity regulation

One of the most effective and flexible tools for promoting the resiliency of individual **6.15** banks and the banking system as a whole are capital and liquidity requirements. Properly calibrated capital and liquidity requirements can make banks resilient against failure under severely adverse economic scenarios, while giving them sufficient room to engage in the sort of liquidity transformation that is their core function and contribution to market efficiency.

US IDIs are subject to both risk-based and leverage capital requirements that are consistent **6.16** with Basel III.[12] Capital regulations require a bank's assets (or risk-weighted assets) be worth more than its liabilities by a specified percentage. US IDIs that are defined as systemically important are subject to higher capital requirements than other US IDIs. US banking groups are also subject to supervisory stress-testing and capital planning exercises that require them to meet certain capital requirements even after suffering the sort of losses that would be expected to occur in a severely adverse economic scenario. Banking groups that are not considered to be systemic are not subject to stress testing or are only required to conduct company-run stress tests on their capital adequacy.

---

[11] Davis Polk, 'Financial Crisis Manual' (2009).

[12] OCC, Regulatory Capital Rules: Regulatory Capital, Implementation of Basel III, Capital Adequacy, Transition Provisions, Prompt Corrective Action, Standardized Approach for Risk-weighted Assets, Market Discipline and Disclosure Requirements, Advanced Approaches Risk-Based Capital Rule, and Market Risk Capital Rule, 78 Fed Reg 62018 (11 October 2013); Davis Polk, Client Memorandum, *U.S. Basel III Final Rule: Visual Memorandum* (8 July 2013) 22.

6.17   Historically, reserve requirements were the only form of liquidity regulation applicable to all US banks. Currently applicable reserve requirements mandate that an
IDI holds cash or other forms of central bank money equal to a fraction of its
deposits and certain other liabilities.[13] US banking groups that are defined as systemically important are also subject to Basel III liquidity requirements, including
the liquidity coverage ratio, which requires that a certain percentage of their assets
consist of cash and other high quality liquid assets (HQLAs) such as US government securities.

Source of strength obligations

6.18   The Federal Reserve has long imposed a 'source of strength' obligation on bank
holding companies. The Federal Reserve has stated that it would be an unsafe or
unsound practice for a bank holding company parent to fail to serve as a source of
financial and managerial strength to a subsidiary bank, including failing to inject
additional capital into the bank to address any capital deficiency.[14] The Federal
Reserve has generally viewed this obligation as unlimited. In other words, this obligation is not subject to a cap in the same way as the guarantee of a capital restoration plan under the prompt corrective action framework discussed below. Congress
codified the Federal Reserve's source of strength doctrine in the Dodd–Frank Act
and extended it to all depository institution holding companies.[15] Notwithstanding
the Federal Reserve's position and the codification and expansion of the source of
strength doctrine by the Dodd–Frank Act, it is not clear that a US court would
uphold an order to require holding companies to inject capital into insolvent bank
subsidiaries, unless doing so would maximize the residual value or minimize the
losses of the holding company.[16] Accordingly, the source of strength obligation
is perhaps more likely to be a subject of discussion and regulatory pressure than a
strict legal obligation.

---

[13]   12 CFR § 204.5(a)(1) (requiring IDIs to hold cash reserves equal to a maximum of 10 per cent
of the amount of their deposits over a certain threshold). During the eighteenth and nineteenth centuries, US banks were subject to reserve requirements by charter, contract, or state or federal regulation.
These sources of authority originally required banks to hold gold, silver, or other commodity money
equal to a fraction of their bank notes in circulation (i.e. paper currency) and after the National Bank
Act was enacted in 1863, U.S. government securities equal to 100% of their bank notes in circula-
tion and gold, silver or other commodity money equal to a fraction of their deposit obligations. Bray
Hammond, *Banks and Politics in America: From the Revolution to the Civil War* (Princeton University
Press, 1957) 137–138, 142–143; William Graham Sumner, *A History of Banking in the United States*
(1896) 22; Joshua N Feinman, 'Reserve Requirements: History, Current Practice, and Potential
Reform' 79 *Federal Reserve Bulletin* 569, 572 (1993).

[14]   Policy Statement on the Responsibility of Bank Holding Companies to Act as Sources of
Strength to Their Subsidiary Banks, 52 Fed Reg 15707 (30 April 1987).

[15]   Dodd–Frank Act, § 616(d), adding new section 38A to the FDIA, 12 USC 1831*o*-1.

[16]   *MCorp Fin, Inc v Bd of the Governors of the Fed Reserve Sys*, 900 F 2d 852 (5th Cir 1990),
rev'd in part on procedural grounds, 502 US 32 (1991); Miller, 'Bankruptcy Code FDIC/RTC
Interplay: Holding Company vs. Subsidiary/Affiliates Interplay' in *Counselling Creditors of Banks and
Thrifts: Dealing with the FDIC and RTC*, PLI Order No A4-4323 (Practising Law Institute, 14–15
January 1991).

Since the Federal Reserve has become the supervisory agency for all SLHCs, **6.19**
the Federal Reserve issued final rules that extend the source of strength doctrine
to all SLHCs.[17] In addition, the new rule specifies that if the Federal Reserve
believes that an activity of the SLHC or a non-bank subsidiary constitutes a
serious risk to the financial safety, soundness, or stability of a subsidiary savings
association and is inconsistent with the principles of sound banking, the Federal
Reserve may require the SLHC to terminate the activity or divest control of the
non-banking subsidiary.

While neither the OCC nor the FDIC has historically imposed source of strength **6.20**
obligations on other depository institution holding companies, from time to time
both have imposed them contractually on owners of depository institutions that
are not otherwise subject to the Bank Holding Company Act. They have typically
done so as a condition to certain regulatory action in connection with acquisitions
of specialized institutions, such as trust companies, credit card banks, or industrial
banks, where the owner may not be subject to the Federal Reserve's oversight. It will
be interesting to see how they apply the new statutory source of strength doctrine to
depository institution holding companies over which they have authority now that
the Dodd–Frank Act has extended the source of strength doctrine to all depository
institution holding companies.

Prompt corrective action

If a US bank becomes undercapitalized, its appropriate federal banking agency **6.21**
and the FDIC are required by section 38 of the FDIA to take prompt corrective action designed to prevent the institution from failing. The prompt correction
action framework establishes a scale for institutions, ranging from well-capitalized
to critically undercapitalized, with the general requirement being that the agencies
must impose greater and greater restrictions on the activities of an insured institution as its condition deteriorates.

Prompt corrective action powers are triggered if an insured institution becomes **6.22**
undercapitalized, is found to be in an unsafe or unsound condition, or is found to
be engaging in an unsafe or unsound practice. Depending on the severity of the
circumstances, the institution's federal banking supervisor has the authority to take
a number of actions in response to a triggering event, including:

- requiring the insured institution to adopt a capital restoration plan that, in
  order to be acceptable, must be guaranteed by its parent (up to a maximum
  exposure of 5 per cent of the insured institution's total assets);
- imposing restrictions on dividends by the insured institution or its parent;

---

[17] 12 CFR § 238.8; see also preamble to Regulation LL, 76 Fed Reg 56508, 56514
(13 September 2011).

- restricting the insured institution's growth or requiring it to terminate certain activities or sell certain assets;
- requiring the insured institution or any affiliate to be divested;
- imposing limits on the interest rates payable on deposits; or
- imposing limits on executive compensation or requiring the insured institution's board or senior management to be replaced.[18]

6.23 The prompt corrective action provisions also create a regulatory presumption that critically undercapitalized institutions will be placed in receivership.

6.24 These prompt corrective action tools are designed to force an insured institution and its owners to take remedial action to rehabilitate a weakened institution before it becomes insolvent. Notwithstanding these provisions, however, insured institutions have typically been deeply insolvent before they have been closed since the capital measurements that trigger the prompt corrective action restrictions are largely based on historical cost rather than mark-to-market balance sheets. Historic values simply do not adequately capture the rapid deterioration of asset values. Therefore, they are often lagging indicators of the true health of an institution.

Lender-of-last-resort facilities

6.25 Despite reserve requirements and other liquidity regulation, it is possible for a solvent and even well-capitalized bank to quickly become insolvent if its short-term creditors start to run because they lose confidence in its ability to maintain its solvency or satisfy its obligations as they come due as a result of illiquidity.[19] Indeed, one of the fundamental causes of the 2008 global financial crisis was the lack of public confidence in the value of various classes of assets on the balance sheets of major financial institutions. In the absence of a lender-of-last-resort that would allow a bank to convert its illiquid assets into cash at a fair price, the bank would be forced to sell its illiquid assets at fire-sale prices in order to meet the demands of its short-term creditors to withdraw cash. In short, the lack of confidence in the bank's solvency or liquidity would become a self-fulfilling prophesy.

6.26 In order to make US banks resilient against failure as a result of such liquidity risk, Congress gave the Federal Reserve authority to provide solvent banks with a means of converting their illiquid assets into cash by selling them at a discount to the Federal Reserve or pledging them to the Federal Reserve at an appropriate haircut to secure a loan of cash through the Federal Reserve's discount window.[20] Historically, the Federal Reserve discouraged the use of the discount window by stigmatizing and imposing a penalty rate on its use. Indeed, Milton Friedman and Anna Schwartz

---

[18] FDIA, § 38(e)–(i), 12 USC § 1831o(e)–(i).
[19] Douglas W Diamond and Philip H Dybvig, 'Bank Runs, Deposit Insurance, and Liquidity', (1983) 91 J Pol Econ 401.
[20] Federal Reserve Act, § 10B, 12 USC § 347b(b); 12 CFR Part 201 (Regulation A).

argued in their classic book that the Federal Reserve's reluctance to use its discount window aggressively between 1930 and 1933 helped to trigger or deepen the Great Depression by allowing thousands of otherwise solvent banks to fail because of a lack of liquidity, which resulted in what they termed 'The Great Contraction' in the money (and credit) supply.[21] Fully aware of the Friedman and Schwartz thesis, the Federal Reserve took several steps during the period leading up to and after the global financial panic of 2008 to eliminate the stigma and encourage insured institutions to borrow from the discount window as needed during the financial crisis.

Congress also gave the Federal Reserve authority to provide emergency secured **6.27** liquidity to other financial institutions under section 13(3) of the Federal Reserve Act. Section 13(3) authorizes the Federal Reserve to provide emergency secured credit to a wide range of institutions under unusual and exigent circumstances. It was enacted in 1932, but had not been invoked until the global financial panic of 2008, during which it was used extensively. Indeed, it was the tool of choice for almost all of the Federal Reserve's emergency assistance programmes, including its rescue of AIG, its Primary Dealer Credit Facility, and its Term Asset-Backed Securities Loan Facility.[22] As a result of a perception in Congress that the Federal Reserve misused its power under section 13(3) to bail out individual firms during the 2008 financial crisis, Congress imposed restrictions on its future use in the Dodd–Frank Act. As amended by the Dodd–Frank Act, section 13(3) may only be invoked by the Federal Reserve with the consent of the Secretary of the Treasury and only to implement a program or facility with broad-based eligibility.[23]

Deposit insurance

Deposit insurance reduces the risk of runs by protecting insured depositors against **6.28** losses up to a statutory maximum, which is currently $250,000 per person per certain account capacities per bank. It is provided by the FDIC and paid for directly by the banking industry and indirectly by insured depositors based on insurance premium assessments imposed on US IDIs.

Supervision, examination, and enforcement

To make sure US IDIs comply with applicable regulation and general safety and **6.29** soundness principles, the FDIC and the other federal (and, where appropriate, state) banking regulators are granted extensive supervisory powers over depository institutions and their holding companies. This supervision is designed to address the safety and soundness of the institution and monitor compliance with laws and

---

[21] Milton Friedman and Anna Jacobson Schwartz, *A Monetary History of the United States, 1867–1960* (Princeton University Press 1963) 10, 299–305, Chapter 1 (Introduction) and Chapter 7 (The Great Contraction).

[22] Davis Polk, *Financial Crisis Manual* (2009) 144–180.

[23] Dodd–Frank Act, § 1101, 12 USC § 4511, amending section 13(3) of the Federal Reserve Act, 12 USC § 343.

regulations. The supervisory powers include both on-site and off-site examination and evaluation of the institution.

6.30 When a US bank's appropriate federal banking agency determines that the bank is operating in an unsafe or unsound manner, is violating a law, rule, or regulation, or is otherwise engaging in behaviour determined to pose a risk to the depository institution, the regulators will engage in either informal or formal enforcement actions designed to have the bank address and remedy the problems.[24] Informal tools range from simple discussions between the institution and its regulator as part of the supervisory process, to commitment letters, board resolutions, or memoranda of understanding. The FDIA also grants the regulators authority to use a variety of formal enforcement tools, such as written agreements, cease and desist orders, civil financial penalties, or removal and prohibition orders. For a graphical representation of this continuum, see Figure 6.7. Cease and desist orders are available not only to prohibit certain actions, but also to mandate corrective action on the part of the institution or those individuals or entities participating in

Enhanced Prudential Standards	Asset Size of BHC or G-SIB Status				
	<$10bn	$10–$50bn	$50–$250bn	>$250 (not G-SIBs)	U.S. G-SIBs
Recovery Plans					✓
TLAC Requirement					✓
G-SIB Capital Surcharges					✓
Supplementary Leverage Ratio (5% / 6% requirement)(1)					✓
AOCI included in Basel 3 capital				✓	✓
Full Liquidity Coverage Ratio				✓	✓
Supplementary Leverage Ratio (3% requirement)				✓	✓
Advanced Approach RWA				✓	✓
Resolution Plans			✓	✓	✓
Early Remediation Tools			✓	✓	✓
Modified Liquidity Coverage Ratio			✓	✓	✓
Annual Fed-run Capital Plan and Stress Test			✓	✓	✓
Annual Company-run Stress Test		✓	✓	✓	✓
Durbin (interchange) Amendment		✓	✓	✓	✓
Subject to Regulation by CFPB	Certain Products	✓	✓	✓	✓
Prompt Corrective Action Tools	✓	✓	✓	✓	✓
Volcker Rule	✓	✓	✓	✓	✓

(1) 5% requirement at the holding company, 6% at insured depository institutions

Figure 6.7 Enhanced prudential standards

---

[24] OCC, 'Enforcement Action Policy', *Policies and Procedures Manual* (2011); *Federal and State Enforcement of Financial Consumer and Investor Protection Laws: Hearing before the H Comm on Financial Serv*, 111th Cong 4–7 (2009) (testimony of John C Dugan, Comptroller of the Currency); Federal Reserve Bank of Kansas City, Types of Enforcement Actions (2009).

the affairs of the institution. Civil money penalties can run up to nearly $1.5 million per day per violation under certain circumstances.[25] The removal and prohibition powers can preclude an individual from participating in the affairs of any insured depository institution.

Enhanced prudential standards

As mentioned above, US banking groups that are defined as systemically important **6.31** are subject to enhanced prudential standards. These enhanced standards include more stringent capital and liquidity requirements, risk management requirements, single counterparty credit limits, and stress test requirements. They also vary depending on the size or other characteristics of a particular category of BHC. For example, all BHCs with assets of $50 billion or more are subject to enhanced prudential standards. But the most stringent enhanced standards are reserved for BHCs that have $250 billion or more in assets or have been classified as global systemically important banking groups (G-SIBs). See Figure 6.7 for a graphical illustration of some of the most important enhanced prudential standards and how they relate to certain ordinary prudential standards.

Perhaps the most controversial enhanced prudential standard is the require- **6.32** ment for supervisory stress tests and capital planning under the Federal Reserve's Comprehensive Capital Analysis and Review (CCAR). Under the CCAR stress testing, the Federal Reserve compares its own model for testing the capital adequacy of a US bank holding company against the company's own model under various economic scenarios including a severely adverse economic scenario defined by the Federal Reserve. If a US bank holding company fails the CCAR supervisory stress testing, it will not be permitted to pay dividends or take other actions without the prior permission of the Federal Reserve.

Early remediation

BHCs with $50 billion or more in assets are also subject to early remediation tools. **6.33** Early remediation tools are similar to prompt corrective action measures, except that they are triggered based on liquidity benchmarks and forward-looking indicators, rather than on backward-looking indicators such as capital levels, which are based on historical cost accounting standards that have proven to be lagging indicators of a bank's financial health.

Recovery plans

Since 2009, the Federal Reserve has required certain large, domestic US BHCs **6.34** to prepare recovery plans. Recovery plans are different from and in addition to

---

[25] FDIA, § 8(i), 12 USC § 1818(i); 12 CFR § 263.65(b)(2) (increasing maximum statutory amount for knowing or reckless violations to $1.425 million per day to adjust for inflation).

resolution plans. They establish the actions firms must take to return to a position of financial stability once it is experiencing or is likely to encounter serious financial distress short of insolvency or other failure. Recovery plans are designed to identify a range of options that must be taken to restore or enhance capital and liquidity levels to maintain the confidence of market participants during a range of stress scenarios, including the possible sale of valuable assets.[26] They require US G-SIBs to address financial weaknesses well before the point of non-viability, with the goal of substantially reducing the risk of insolvency or other failure. Recovery plans thus act as a buffer against loss of public confidence in individual firms or the broader financial system. The Federal Reserve has continued to test and require improvements in recovery plans, and expanded the range of BHCs required to develop them.

C. Resolution Process

6.35 If all these tools for preventing the failure of an IDI do not save the institution, its chartering authority will issue an order to close it (that is, revoke its charter to conduct business).[27] If the insured institution is a national bank or federally chartered savings association and a receiver is appointed, the FDIC must be appointed as its receiver. Although this requirement does not extend to state-chartered banks and savings associations, the FDIC has the power to appoint itself as the conservator or receiver of any FDIC-insured state institution, which overrides or pre-empts the appointment of any state or other federal agency.

Grounds for closing an insured institution

6.36 The grounds for closing an insured institution and appointing the FDIC as its receiver or conservator are extremely open-ended and may be satisfied well before balance-sheet insolvency. Indeed, some of the grounds overlap with the grounds for prompt corrective action. Thus, the FDIC and an institution's federal banking supervisor have considerable discretion in deciding whether and when to close an institution or to subject it to prompt corrective action. The grounds for closing an insured institution and having the FDIC appointed as its conservator or receiver include:

- the institution being unable to pay its obligations in the normal course of business;
- the institution being in an unsafe or unsound condition;

---

[26] Consolidated Recovery Planning for Certain Large Domestic Bank Holding Companies, Federal Reserve Supervision and Regulation Letter, SR 14-8 (25 September 2015).

[27] FDIC, *Resolutions Handbook: Methods for Resolving Troubled Financial Institutions in the United States* (2014), p. 6.

- the board or shareholders consenting;
- the institution being critically undercapitalized;
- the institution engaging in an unsafe or unsound practice likely to weaken its condition;
- the institution wilfully violating a cease and desist order;
- books, papers, records, or assets being concealed; or
- the institution being found guilty of a federal criminal anti-money laundering offence.[28]

Notwithstanding the wide range of the grounds for closing an institution and putting it into an FDIC receivership, the FDIC has traditionally relied either on balance-sheet insolvency or, more frequently, the inability of an institution to pay its obligations when due in the ordinary course of business because of a lack of adequate liquidity to do so.   **6.37**

The FDIC can serve as either conservator or receiver of an insured institution. A conservator takes control of an insured institution with the intent and ability to operate the institution as a going concern, until it is rehabilitated for the benefit of its stakeholders. Generally, the FDIC, as its conservator, would not engage in wholesale liquidation of the business, although it could sell assets, cease lines of business, or take other similar actions that would be consistent with restoring the institution to a sound and solvent condition, or to preserve and conserve the value of the institution, in each case for the benefit of its stakeholders. The reason is that there are no provisions in the conservatorship section of the bank resolution statute dealing with claims against an institution in conservatorship. Those provisions only apply if the conservatorship is converted to a receivership. If a conservatorship is successful in restoring the insured institution to a healthy condition, it will be terminated. If it is unsuccessful, it will be converted into a receivership and the institution's assets will be liquidated in an orderly manner.   **6.38**

Conservatorships have been extremely rare. Indeed, most historical examples of conservatorships have been limited to so-called 'pass-through' conservatorships. These conservatorships are more like receiverships with a bridge bank than a true conservatorship, because the original institution is left behind and liquidated rather than conserved. They are sometimes more accurately referred to as pass-through receiverships. Many of the savings and loan associations handled by the Resolution Trust Corporation (the specialized agency established during the savings and loan crisis of the late 1980s to handle failed thrifts) were operated as conservatorships for a period of time, until the Resolution Trust Corporation was prepared to commence liquidation of the failed institution. IndyMac, which failed in 2008, also involved a conservatorship, although in that case the original institution was placed into receivership and the FDIC as receiver transferred the assets   **6.39**

---

[28] FDIA, § 11(c)(5), 12 USC § 1821(c)(5).

and many of the liabilities to a newly chartered institution which was immediately placed into conservatorship. Before the assets of this new institution were sold to an investor group, it was placed into receivership and the FDIC effected the resolution transaction.

6.40   The conservatorships of Freddie Mac and Fannie Mae are possibly the only genuine conservatorships, and their conservatorships were effected under the Housing and Economic Recovery Act of 2008 (HERA), which was based on the bank resolution model. However, the FDIC might use a genuine conservatorship in the case of a systemically important bank.

6.41   The distinction between conservatorships and receiverships can appear fuzzy. In general, however, the FDIC uses conservatorships to operate institutions until it is prepared to effect a receivership transaction. The receivership is typically used by the FDIC to effect a sale of the assets of the failed institution to a third party, or to effect a liquidation, or both.

Effect of appointment

6.42   When the FDIC is appointed as conservator or receiver of an institution, it succeeds by operation of law to all of the rights, titles, powers, and privileges of the insured institution and its stockholders, members, directors, officers, account holders, and depositors, subject to the provisions of the FDIA. According to the US Supreme Court in *O'Melveny & Myers v FDIC*, this provision of the FDIA effectively 'places the FDIC in the shoes of the insolvent [institution], to work out its claims under state [and other applicable] law, except where some provision in [the FDIA's] extensive framework specifically provides otherwise'.[29]

Timing of appointment

6.43   An insured institution is typically closed and the FDIC is appointed receiver on a Friday after the close of business. The purpose of this timing is to minimize disruption to customers and facilitate the transfer of assets and liabilities to a new acquirer, giving the new acquirer the weekend to prepare for a Monday reopening. In the case of a systemically important institution with an international business, the deadline is typically the opening of the Asian markets on Monday morning (i.e. Sunday evening in the United States). While the FDIC will attempt to engage in a transaction that will transfer assets and liabilities to another healthy privately owned banking organization, on occasion a suitable acquirer cannot be found. In such cases, the FDIC may elect to operate the failed institution through a conservatorship or use its bridge bank authority, or it may be forced to conduct a pay-off of the depositors.

---

[29] 512 US 79, 80 (1994).

FDIC's statutory duties

The FDIC has a statutory duty to resolve all insured institutions in a manner that **6.44** is 'least costly to the deposit insurance fund of all possible methods'.[30] It also has a statutory duty to resolve all insured institutions in a manner that maximizes the residual value of the institutions and minimizes their losses for the benefit of their depositors and other stakeholders.[31] It is generally precluded from using the deposit insurance fund to benefit existing shareholders.[32] The least-cost test and no shareholder benefit duties were imposed on the FDIC in 1991 and 1993, respectively, in reaction to the perceived tendency by the FDIC and other responsible federal agencies at the time to rescue or otherwise provide open-bank assistance to troubled IDIs during the savings and loan crisis of the 1980s. The least-cost test was also added to impose some discipline on the FDIC, which had developed a tendency to do a P&A sales transaction, even if there were other less costly resolution transactions available. The FDIC also has a policy to resolve failed institutions in a manner that avoids contagion, maintains public confidence in the US financial system, and otherwise promotes financial stability.[33]

Until modified by the Dodd–Frank Act, the least-cost test contained a 'systemic **6.45** risk' exception that permitted the FDIC to provide open-bank assistance to individual IDIs if necessary to avoid 'serious adverse effects on economic conditions or financial stability' during a financial emergency.[34] The Dodd–Frank Act amended this exception, and no longer permits the FDIC to provide open-bank assistance to any individual institution.[35] It now provides an exception from the least-cost test only with respect to IDIs in receivership. If invoked, it permits the FDIC to provide financial assistance to facilitate the resolution of an IDI in receivership even if such assistance would not be consistent with the least-cost test.

Purchase and assumption sale transaction

As receiver, the FDIC has the authority to transfer the assets and liabilities of the **6.46** institution to a third party without obtaining anyone's consent or approval.[36] It uses this authority to engage in what is typically known as a P&A (purchase and assumption) transaction—that is, it identifies a third-party bank that will purchase all or some portion of the assets and assume all or some portion of the liabilities of the failed institution.[37] The purchaser must have a bank or thrift charter, although the charter may be granted at the time of the P&A transaction.

---

[30] FDIA, § 13(c)(4), 12 USC § 1823(c)(4).
[31] FDIA, § 11(d)(13)(E)(i) and (ii), 12 USC 1821(d)(13)(E)(i) and (ii).
[32] FDIA, § 11(a)(4)(C). 12 USC § 1821(a)(4)(C).
[33] FDIC, *Resolutions Handbook* (2014) 1.
[34] 12 United States Code Annotated § 1823(c)(4)(G) (West Publishing 2009).
[35] Dodd–Frank Act, § 1106(b), 12 USC § 5613(b).
[36] FDIA, § 11(d)(2)(G)(i)(II), 12 USC § 1821(d)(2)(G)(i)(II).
[37] FDIC, *Resolutions Handbook* (2014) 16–19.

6.47   The FDIC has discretion to determine which assets are sold to the acquirer. Since the FDIC remains subject to the least-cost resolution test as receiver, its determination as to which assets to sell will be based on its analysis of whether the deposit insurance fund is better off transferring the assets to the acquiring institution as part of the P&A transaction or whether it should sell the assets separately. The assets sold can include cash and securities, performing loans, non-performing loans, buildings, furniture, fixtures, and equipment, or any combination thereof. To facilitate the sale, the FDIC can offer loss-sharing or other forms of protection to the purchaser.[38]

6.48   The acquiring institution will assume the insured deposits and may elect to assume uninsured deposits as well. On occasion, the acquiring institution will assume certain secured liabilities such as Federal Home Loan Bank advances.

6.49   Any assets not purchased by the acquiring institution will be left with the FDIC as receiver, which will liquidate the assets over time. The proceeds of the asset sales, including the proceeds of the sale to the acquiring bank under the P&A transaction, will be used to satisfy the claims of creditors of the failed institution.

Bridge banks

6.50   If the FDIC is unable to sell all or any part of a failed institution before it must be closed, the FDIC may request the OCC to charter a new national bank or federal savings association to operate as a 'bridge bank'.[39] A bridge bank is an entity used by the FDIC to assume all or any portion of a failed institution's business, and thereby continue to operate the business as a going concern without interruption. The FDIC's board typically selects a CEO and board of directors for the bridge bank. In the past, they have generally consisted of senior FDIC personnel, retired FDIC executives, or experienced bankers. An acquirer can then make a bid for all or any portion of the assets and liabilities of the bridge bank, or for the bridge bank as a whole. The FDIC generally uses this option if it believes that the temporary operation and subsequent sale of the institution would be more financially attractive to the FDIC than an immediate liquidation, or if it determines that temporarily operating the business through a bridge bank will facilitate financial stability.

6.51   The FDIC has the authority to transfer any assets or liabilities from the closed bank to the bridge bank without the need for consent or approval from any party. The original bank and any of its left-behind assets and liabilities will be liquidated. The FDIC must merge, transfer, or terminate and dissolve the bridge bank within two years of its organization, with the option of three additional one-year periods at the

---

[38]   FDIA, § 13(c)(2)(A), 12 USC § 1823(c)(2)(A).
[39]   FDIA, § 11(n)(1)(A), 12 USC § 1821(n)(1)(A).

FDIC's discretion.[40] This period is designed to give the FDIC time to find one or more third-party acquirer for all or part of the bridge bank's assets and liabilities, or for the bridge bank itself. The FDIC will often enter into loss-sharing agreements or provide other financial assistance to encourage third parties to maximize the net value of the bridge bank's assets and liabilities.

Recapitalization (bail-in) within resolution

The FDIC's strategy of choice in resolving small, mid-size, and regional banks has been the P&A sale transaction, with or without loss-sharing. While the FDIC is likely to continue resolving such institutions with this strategy, it is unlikely to use this strategy to resolve the largest, most systemically important US banks, because the strategy is unlikely to be the least-cost to the deposit insurance fund or maximize the residual value of the institution or minimize its losses for the benefit of its stakeholders. Just as important, it could result in an even larger, more systemically important bank. Instead, the FDIC is likely to use some other technique for systemically important banks such as a recapitalization (bail-in) within resolution strategy or a multi-acquirer or orderly wind-down strategy. **6.52**

A recapitalization (bail-in) within resolution strategy involves the conversion of external long-term unsecured debt or intercompany unsecured debt into equity interests. Since by statute-insured deposits, uninsured deposits that are solely payable in the United States and uninsured deposits that are dually payable at a foreign branch or in the United States (collectively, domestic deposits) rank senior to the general liabilities of a US bank (including uninsured deposits that are payable solely at a foreign branch of a US bank),[41] it should be possible to convert long-term unsecured debt or intercompany liabilities into equity interests without fostering a run by the holders of domestic deposits. Assuming a large IDI has sufficient long-term unsecured debt and intercompany liabilities to result in the IDI being fully recapitalized if they are converted to equity interests, and only an immaterial amount of short-term non-deposit liabilities, it should be possible for the FDIC to use this strategy to recapitalize the failed IDI without fostering a contagious run on demand deposits or other short-term unsecured liabilities throughout the US banking system. **6.53**

---

[40] FDIA, § 11(n)(9), 12 USC § 1821(n)(9).

[41] FDIA, § 11(d)(11), 12 CFR § 1821(d)(11). Three US law firms—Cleary Gottlieb, Davis Polk, and Sullivan & Cromwell—jointly published a paper in which they argued that the term 'deposit liability' includes foreign branch deposits for purposes of section 11(d)(11). Cleary Gottlieb, Davis Polk, and Sullivan & Cromwell, *The Status of Foreign Branch Deposits under the Depositor Preference Rule* (2 January 2013). The FDIC rejected that view, however, based on an opinion by a then acting general counsel of the FDIC in 1994. FDIC, *Deposit Insurance Regulations; Definition of Insured Deposit*, 78 Fed Reg 56583 (13 September 2013); FDIC Advisory Opinion, *'Deposit Liability' for Purposes of National Depositor Preference Includes Only Deposits Payable in the US*, FDIC 94-1 (28 February 1994). According to the FDIC, a foreign branch deposit must be dually payable at both the foreign branch and in the United States to be included in the term 'deposit liability'. 78 Fed Reg (13 September 2013) 56583, 56586.

6.54 Indeed, several of the US G-SIBs have proposed recapitalization within resolution strategies in their IDI resolution plans filed with the FDIC as the method that is least-cost to the deposit insurance fund of all possible alternatives and the one that is most likely to maximize its residual value and minimize its losses for the benefit of its stakeholders.[42] Under this method, the FDIC would establish a bridge bank and transfer all of the failed IDI's assets to the bridge bank and cause the bridge bank to assume all of the IDI's insured deposits and uninsured domestic deposits. The rest of the IDI's liabilities, including external senior unsecured debt and intercompany debt, would be left behind in the IDI's receivership. By leaving these and other liabilities behind in the receivership, the FDIC will have recapitalized the business transferred to the bridge bank. After the bridge bank's operations have been stabilized and the bridge bank is able to prepare reliable financial statements, the FDIC would transfer the bridge bank to a newly created holding company ('new holdco') owned by a trust in return for the trust's promise to sell all or a portion of new holdco's equity to the public through private sales, an initial public offering (IPO), or one more follow-on public offerings and to distribute the net proceeds from such sales and any unsold equity in new holdco to the IDI's receivership to be distributed to the holders of claims against the IDI in accordance with the priority of their claims and in satisfaction of their claims.

Break-up and sell strategy

6.55 Although the IDI that emerges from a recapitalization within resolution strategy is inevitably smaller than the IDI that entered the process, and sometimes significantly so,[43] the FDIC required the US G-SIBs to include a break-up and sell strategy (which it called a 'multiple acquirer strategy') in their 2015 IDI resolution plans.[44] The FDIC described a break-up and sell strategy as a technique that 'primarily involves the separation and sale of the [IDI]'s deposit franchise, core business lines, and/or major assets to multiple acquirers'. The FDIC stated that a break-up and sell strategy 'may be accomplished through a combination of transactions, including purchase and assumption ('P&A'), initial public offering of securities ('IPO'), and liquidation'. The FDIC also stated that it expected 'at least one [break-up and sell] strategy [to] involve the recapitalization of a portion of the [IDI] through single or multiple IPO transactions'. The FDIC also provided that it expected IDI's to use a bridge bank in connection with executing a [break-up

---

[42] See FDIC, Title I and IDI Resolution Plans, available at: <https://www.fdic.gov/regulations/reform/resplans/> (accessed 26 October 2015).

[43] Statement of Randall D Guynn, Partner, Davis Polk, Hearing before the Subcommittee on Financial Institutions and Consumer Protection, Senate Committee on Banking, Finance and Urban Affairs (29 June 2015) 7–8 (discussing the reduction principle that is an inevitable by-product of the single-point-of-entry (SPE) and other recapitalization within resolution strategies).

[44] FDIC, Guidance for Covered Insured Depository Institution Resolution Plan Submissions (December 2014).

and sell] strategy because of 'the expected timeline required by the complexity of a [break-up and sell] [s]trategy'.

Orderly wind-down strategy

An orderly wind-down strategy is similar to a recapitalization within resolution **6.56** or a break-up and sell strategy in that it involves the creation of a bridge bank and the transfer of all or a portion of the failed bank's assets and liabilities to the bridge bank. The FDIC then causes the bridge bank to sell any businesses and assets transferred to it in an orderly manner over an extended period of time in order to maximize the value realized from the sale of the bridge bank's assets, with the net proceeds being turned over to the FDIC receivership to be distributed to the holders of any claims left behind in the receivership in accordance with the priority of claims and in satisfaction of such claims.

Liquidation strategy

The FDIC also required the US G-SIBs to include a liquidation strategy in their **6.57** 2015 IDI resolution plans. The FDIC did not expect a liquidation strategy to be least-cost to the deposit insurance fund of all possible alternative strategies or otherwise maximize the residual value of the bank or minimize its losses. Rather, the FDIC mandated that a liquidation strategy be included in the 2015 plans in order to establish a baseline against which a break-up and sell or other strategy could be compared for purposes of the least-cost test.

D. FDIC-assisted P&A Sale Transactions

In its resolution of failed community, mid-size, and regional banks, the FDIC **6.58** has used a P&A strategy and provided some form of financial assistance in the form of cash or other value to the acquiring institution. This is because the insured deposit liabilities assumed have usually exceeded the value of the assets transferred (even when the FDIC provided additional protection in the form of loss-sharing). Because of the importance of these assisted transactions, both to the FDIC and to potential bidders, this section provides more detail about P&A sale transactions with FDIC assistance.

Initiation of the process

The process for an FDIC-assisted transaction, like any resolution transaction, has **6.59** typically begun when the FDIC or an insured institution's chartering authority has determined that the institution is rapidly running out of sufficient liquidity to operate its business in the ordinary course (e.g. because of a 'run' on the bank) or is unlikely to have sufficient capital to continue safe and sound operations, or when the institution has received a prompt corrective action notice from its primary federal banking regulator telling it that it is critically undercapitalized. A bank is considered to be 'critically undercapitalized' when its tangible equity, which is defined as Tier 1 capital plus non-Tier 1 perpetual preferred stock, is at or below 2 per cent of total assets,[45] at which point the bank has ninety days to raise capital, complete a merger or otherwise improve its status. There is a presumption that critically undercapitalized institutions will be placed into receivership.

The decision whether to close the institution is reached by the institution's chartering authority in consultation with the FDIC.

When the chartering authority or the FDIC believes an insured institution is running out of liquidity or when the institution receives a prompt correction action notice, the FDIC has typically sent a resolution team to the failing bank or thrift to obtain the necessary data to conduct an auction process. The resolution team has prepared an information package for potential bidders, performed an asset valuation, determined the appropriate resolution structure, and conducted an on-site analysis to prepare for the closing. The time between the FDIC's determination that an institution is running out of liquidity or receipt of a prompt corrective action notice and the closing of an assisted transaction has generally been about ninety days, although it has been longer or shorter depending upon the facts and circumstances surrounding the institution.

Bidding process

6.60   As part of the bidding process, the FDIC has typically established a reserve price for the failing institution, by estimating the fair market value of the institution's assets and then deducting any estimated costs of disposition and direct marketing, arriving at a net figure that is known as the liquidation value of the assets. The estimated liquidation value of the assets has been part of the FDIC's least-cost test for the resolution of the institution. In the early 1990s, the FDIC attempted to increase the volume of assets sold at resolution by revealing its reserve price for asset pools. The FDIC has observed that revealing the reserve price has advantages and disadvantages, including, in circumstances where few bids are submitted, by biasing the bidding towards that price.[46] The FDIC does not currently reveal its reserve price, primarily to reduce the risk of receiving bids that are lower than a bidder's maximum willingness to pay.

6.61   The FDIC also does not currently disclose the names or number of bidders for a particular failing institution during the bidding process because it has an interest in maximizing the number of bidders and in fostering the belief that there are many bidders exist in every situation. After the transaction has closed, however, the FDIC

---

[45]   12 CFR § 325.103(b)(5).
[46]   FDIC, *Resolutions Handbook* (2003), pp 10–11 (superseded by 2014 edition).

has published on its website certain details about the bidders and bids received, including the winning bidder and bid and, after one year, the second-place bid. It has also revealed, at the same time as the winning bid, the names of all bidders and bids, but has not associated each bidder with a particular bid.[47]

The goal of the FDIC has been to sell as much of the bank as possible to the highest **6.62** bidder in a manner that maintains public confidence in the US financial system and results in the least disruption to insured depositors and other stakeholders of the bank, consistent with the FDIC's statutory obligation to resolve the bank in a manner that is least costly to the deposit insurance fund. The FDIC is required to reject all bids if they would result in a more costly resolution of the institution than a deposit pay-off and liquidation of the assets. If the FDIC receives at least one bid that would result in a lower amount of losses to the deposit insurance fund than a deposit pay-off and liquidation of the institution, the FDIC is required by statute (at least in theory) to accept the highest such bid it receives or use another technique such as recapitalization within resolution that will reduce the cost to the deposit insurance fund.

In deciding what structure to offer to potential bidders in a P&A transaction, the FDIC has considered a variety of factors, including the following:

- Should it offer the bank in whole or in parts? The FDIC has found that it is sometimes easier to sell certain parts of a bank separately, such as a trust business, a credit card operation, or branches. Occasionally, the FDIC has divided a bank into geographic regions if it believed doing so would facilitate the sale.
- Which types of assets should it offer to bidders?
- How should it package saleable assets? Should they be sold with or without loss-sharing?
- How should the assets be priced? Should they be sold at book value, market value, or with reserve pricing?

After the FDIC has completed its initial work on the failing institution, the **6.63** Franchise and Asset Marketing Branch of the FDIC's Division of Resolutions and Receiverships has typically sent a notice of the opportunity to bid on the failing institution to approved bidders through a secure website. Approved bidders have been required to register as such on the FDIC's secure internet channel. They have been requested to designate two contacts, and to provide the email addresses and phone numbers of the two contacts. They have also been invited to indicate their geographic preferences for future acquisitions and whether they were interested in purchasing deposit franchises or asset portfolios, or both. The FDIC has required approved bidders to keep the names of failing institutions confidential to avoid causing a 'run' on the institutions before they can be resolved in an orderly fashion.

---

[47] 5 USC § 552. The FDIC's policy on releasing bidding information in response to requests is set forth at <https://www.fdic.gov/about/freedom/biddocs.html> (accessed 26 October 2015).

6.64 In general, approved bidders have been limited to banks, thrifts, BHCs, or SLHCs that were well-capitalized and in satisfactory condition. The FDIC has generally limited access to its secure website to banks, thrifts, BHCs, or SLHCs that have registered as approved bidders. The FDIC has only given non-banking institutions access in special situations. The FDIC has tended to permit institutions to bid on institutions in their geographic areas, but has made exceptions for strong management teams. It has generally permitted an institution to bid on another institution that is smaller, not larger, in size, but has made exceptions for strongly capitalized banks with strong management teams.

6.65 It has been possible for other bidders to participate in the auction if they obtained a *de novo* bank or thrift charter. This option has occasionally been referred to as a 'shelf' charter, meaning that the FDIC and the chartering authority have received sufficient information from the proponents to be satisfied with the financial, managerial, and business plan aspects of the proponents. In that light, the regulators have indicated a willingness to activate a charter, with deposit insurance, if and when a bid from the proponents for a failed bank is accepted. The FDIC has permitted potential investors without an active charter (but with a 'shelf' charter) to participate in the bidding process when few other feasible purchasers exist. Examples include the IndyMac, BankUnited, and Silverton transactions. It has been possible to persuade the FDIC to sell these other bidders a bridge bank that will have assumed some or all of the assets and liabilities of the failed bank. The FDIC has the statutory authority to establish and sell a bridge bank in order to facilitate a transaction, but the FDIC has rarely used this transaction structure with a small, mid-size, or even regional bank.

6.66 In the past, the FDIC invited all approved bidders that indicated an interest in bidding on a particular failing institution to an information meeting where potential buyers could receive hard-copy documents from the FDIC only upon attending the meeting in person and after signing a confidentiality agreement. Since 2000, the FDIC has marketed banks using secure online data rooms and these meetings have ceased.

6.67 Under the more modern procedures, the FDIC has sent an email to banks that meet certain criteria to inform them of an FDIC transaction and to provide general information about the offering. The offering has not named the failing bank, but has generally revealed the state or region in which the bank resides and its size. Interested potential bidders have been permitted to view an executive summary with more specific information about the failing bank on the FDIC's secured website. Certain bidders have then notified the FDIC and thereby obtained full access to all available information provided through the FDIC's online data room. After signing a confidentiality agreement, each such bidder has been given access to an information package, which has included financial data on the failing institution, descriptions of the resolution methods being offered, the legal documents, including any proposed P&A or loss-sharing agreements, details on the due diligence process, and the bidding procedures. The materials available online have generally included information about the transaction structure, financial information about the target, proposed legal documentation, regulatory application information, and other relevant information. In recent situations, the FDIC has not disclosed its internal evaluation of asset values. Nevertheless, the FDIC has provided some information about valuation in connection with FDIC offerings. In particular, the FDIC has provided the intrinsic loss estimates and intrinsic shared loss estimates, which have given potential buyers information about estimated credit losses on loans and other real estate included in the offerings.

In order to participate in the bidding process, the party has been required to have **6.68** received assurance from its primary federal regulator that it would be permitted to acquire the failed institution. In order to submit a bid on the failed institution and have it considered by the FDIC, a bidder has been required to satisfy a variety of conditions, including the following:

- The bidder must have contacted all appropriate state and federal regulators and arranged to receive all necessary regulatory approvals for the transaction before the FDIC's proposed closing of the failed bank transaction.
- The institution resulting from the transaction would need to be 'well capitalized' and have a fully funded allowance for loan losses as of closing.
- If a bidder was a *de novo* institution, the resulting institution would also have been required to satisfy any additional conditions imposed by the chartering authority of the *de novo* institution, such as super capital requirements imposed on *de novo* institutions (e.g. a 10 per cent Tier 1 risk-based capital ratio for the first three years of operation), a comprehensive business plan, and qualified directors and senior executive officers.
- In the case of a bidder that is a 'private capital investor', the FDIC has imposed additional requirements.[48]

If a prospective bidder failed any of these conditions, the FDIC reserved the right **6.69** to reject the bid.

Each approved bidder has been permitted to conduct due diligence on the bank. **6.70** The FDIC has tightly controlled the due diligence process, ensuring that all bidders has had equal access to information. Approved bidders have been required to sign confidentiality agreements, have been provided access to a virtual data room, and, if sufficient time exists, may have been allowed on-site inspection of certain books and records of the institution. Potential acquirers have occasionally been given the opportunity to speak with management of the bank, but access to information may

---

[48] FDIC, *Final Statement of Policy on Qualifications for Failed Bank Acquisitions*, 74 Fed Reg 45440 (2 September 2009).

have been limited by the FDIC. For instance, the FDIC generally has taken the position that bidders should not have access to the target's examination reports or other supervisory information.

6.71   It remains an open question whether these restrictions on bidder qualifications, immediate or complete access to information, and special requirements for private equity and other types of financial bidders, depresses the prices that qualified bidders are required to bid, or discourages certain qualified bidders from bidding at all. These possibly price-depressing features of the FDIC's somewhat opaque bidding process are arguably balanced, at least in part, by loss-sharing protection and other incentives designed to encourage robust bidding when asset values are highly uncertain, such as during a financial crisis. Nevertheless, some bidders believe that the FDIC has been willing to accept below-market bids if the highest bidder is another insured institution that would be strengthened by a favourable deal. These bidders believe that the FDIC's process is subject to being exploited by the relatively small number of experienced bidders or bidders advised by the relatively small number of experienced advisors. In other words, they believe that these procedures and special requirements on private equity bidders may inhibit the FDIC's ability to receive the highest price for a failed insured institution, which raises questions about whether the FDIC is fully compliant with the least-cost test. They believe that the FDIC, the deposit insurance fund, and other creditors of a failed insured institution, might receive better value and otherwise be better off if the FDIC adopted a more open and transparent bidding process.

6.72   In contrast, the FDIC believes that its procedures are appropriately calibrated to satisfy the least-cost test. Based on a study in 2009, the FDIC concluded that immediate disclosure of losing bids, particularly the cover bid, was having an adverse effect on the FDIC's ability to minimize costs to the deposit insurance fund.[49] The study included data suggesting that immediate or full disclosure of losing bids was reducing the incentive of bidders to offer their highest bid based on analysis of previous competitions. Winning bids well above second bids might be viewed as outliers and discounted by some as anomalies. The FDIC believes that its current procedures reduce the possibility of the FDIC being exploited by experienced or well-advised bidders as described above.

Transaction structure

6.73   All FDIC-assisted transactions have revolved around the assumption of liabilities and the purchase of assets. The transaction structures have included the following options:

- On the liability side of the balance sheet:
  - insured deposits only;

---

[49]   Rosalind L Bennett and Haluk Unal, *The Effects of Resolution Methods and Industry Stress on the Loss on Assets from Bank Failures* (2009).

- insured and uninsured deposits;
- insured and uninsured deposits, with certain secured liabilities such as Federal Home Loan Bank advances and covered bonds; or
- all deposits plus secured liabilities plus certain other debt obligations.
- On the asset side of the balance sheet:
  - cash and readily marketable securities;
  - performing assets, with or without loss-sharing;
  - non-performing assets, with or without loss-sharing; and
  - premises and equipment.

In a so-called whole bank transaction, virtually all the bank's assets are purchased **6.74** and all or certain of its liabilities assumed pursuant to a P&A agreement. As described above, the parent holding company and its non-bank subsidiaries have been excluded from the FDIC's resolution process. Subsidiaries of the failed institution have not been placed into receivership when the FDIC deals with the failed institution, although the equity of a subsidiary has been treated as an asset of the receivership estate of the failed institution and has generally been sold by the FDIC.

The purchased assets have typically included the loan portfolio (including non- **6.75** performing assets and other real estate-owned), the securities portfolio, operations, intellectual property, employee relationships, equity in subsidiaries, and joint ventures. The liabilities assumed have included insured, uninsured, or brokered deposits; liabilities under liquidity funding arrangements, and borrowings from the Federal Reserve and the Federal Home Loan Board; and other secured or unsecured liabilities. The FDIC has also decided whether it needed to offer loss-sharing or other financial assistance to make the structure marketable. The FDIC has sold or liquidated assets that have not been purchased and has addressed the rights of unassumed liabilities as part of its receivership duties.

The FDIC has normally provided a cash payment to the acquirer that has approxi- **6.76** mated the difference in the value of assets and liabilities. As the other structures imply, they have involved the purchase of only part of the assets or liabilities of the failed institution.

If the FDIC has offered additional financial assistance to facilitate the transaction, **6.77** it has recently virtually always been in the form of the FDIC's standard loss-sharing arrangements. The FDIC has had two types of loss-sharing arrangements, one with two tranches, and the other with three tranches. The three-tranche loss-sharing arrangement has been reserved for banks with assets above $500 million. In those arrangements, the assuming bank has typically borne 100 per cent of the losses on an amount called the 'first loss tranche', which can be a positive number or zero. If it has been zero, loss-sharing has started immediately upon any losses. Losses incurred in excess of the first loss tranche and up to an amount called the 'stated threshold' have been shared 80 per cent by the FDIC and 20 per cent by the assuming bank.

The stated threshold has generally represented the FDIC's estimate of the maximum amount of expected losses. Any losses above the stated threshold are shared 95 per cent by the FDIC and 5 per cent by the assuming bank.

6.78 Two-tranche loss-sharing arrangements have been used for smaller banks with less than $500 million in assets. The first tranche has covered losses up to the intrinsic loss estimate, which is the FDIC's estimate of embedded credit losses in the assets offered. Loss incurred in excess of the intrinsic loss estimate has been referred to as the second tranche. The FDIC's loss share in both tranches has been capped at 80 per cent so that the assuming bank, at a minimum, has shared 20 per cent of the losses. If potential bidders are willing to share a greater portion of the loss, bidders have been able to change this loss share percentage by submitting a bid to lower the FDIC's loss-share percentage. Potential bidders have also bid on each tranche separately.

6.79 Not all assets passing to the assuming bank in the context of an FDIC loss-share transaction have been covered by loss share. For example, consumer loans and government guaranteed loans have not been covered, and often neither have single-family residential mortgage loans. In addition, the FDIC has maintained the right to claw back some upside from the assuming bank when the actual losses have been significantly less than estimated.

6.80 The FDIC used a variety of different assisted transaction structures during the savings and loan crisis of the 1980s and early 1990s. But a major study of these structures after the savings and loan crisis persuaded the FDIC that whole bank or asset pool transactions, with loss-sharing, were the most effective structure in producing the least-cost result for the FDIC in most closed-bank transactions.[50] As a result, the FDIC has been exceedingly resistant to any asset structure other than whole bank or asset pool transactions, with its standard loss-sharing provisions.[51]

6.81 Several important reasons explain why FDIC-assisted transactions have been attractive to bidders. First, the FDIC process has given purchasers the option to avoid assuming certain types of liabilities. Thus, any unsecured senior or subordinated debt has typically not been assumed, nor has any obligation to shareholders. For example, in the JP Morgan Chase Bank (JPMCB) acquisition of Washington Mutual Bank (WaMu Bank), JPMCB was able to avoid approximately $30 billion in unsecured debt of WaMu Bank.

6.82 Second, as a general proposition, contingent claims, including litigation exposure, can be avoided. Accordingly, the assuming bank generally has not had to worry about past actions of the institution and its management.

---

[50] FDIC, *Managing the Crisis: The FDIC and RTC Experience 1980–1994*, Vol 1 (1998).
[51] For a discussion of some of the other structures, which the FDIC now strongly resists, see FDIC, *Resolutions Handbook* (2003) 19–40 (superseded by 2014 edition).

Third, the acquirer has been able to piggyback off the FDIC's repudiation power. As **6.83** explained more fully in paragraphs 6.113 to 6.119 below, the FDIC has the power to repudiate any contract that it finds burdensome within a reasonable period of time after the institution is closed. This repudiation power applies to both executory and non-executory contracts. As a practical matter, the FDIC has not repudiated contracts that have been fully executed. It is only where some performance obligation remains on the part of the failed bank that the FDIC has exercised the repudiation power. The FDIC also has the power to cherry-pick the contracts it will repudiate, unless the contract is a special type of contract called a qualified financial contract (QFC). QFCs include securities contracts, commodities contracts, forward contracts, repurchase agreements, swap agreements, and master agreements for any of the foregoing. In the case of QFCs, the FDIC must repudiate all or none of the QFCs with a particular counterparty and its affiliates.[52]

When the FDIC repudiates a contract, it must pay the counterparty damages. But **6.84** rather than measure damages as the lost benefit of the counterparty's bargain, the FDIA provides that damages are generally limited to 'actual direct compensatory damages', determined as of the date the FDIC was appointed as conservator or receiver.[53] This damages formula excludes punitive or exemplary damages, damages for lost profits, or opportunity or damages for pain and suffering.[54] Special rules exist for leases, which require the FDIC to pay accrued and unpaid rent through the date of repudiation of the lease.[55]

An exception is made for QFCs, where damages are measured as of the date of **6.85** repudiation and damages may include the cost of cover and are calculated in light of industry practices.[56] However, damage claims arising from repudiation are generally unsecured claims against the receivership estate. They are treated as general creditor claims, subordinate in priority to the claims of depositors. General creditor claims have rarely been paid in full following a receivership, and in many instances receive no recovery at all.

The FDIC has effectively passed this repudiation power on to the winning bidder, **6.86** by giving it the option for up to ninety days or more to assume certain contracts, including leases for bank premises or data processing facilities and most other contracts providing for services to or by the failed bank. Because the FDIC has typically repudiated any contract or lease for which the option to assume has not been exercised by the winning bidder, the counterparty on any such contract or lease has had a powerful financial incentive to renegotiate the terms of any contract or lease that has terms that are above market at the time of the closed-bank transaction in

---

[52] FDIA, § 11(e)(11), 12 USC § 1821(e)(11).
[53] FDIA, § 11(e)(3)(A), 12 USC § 1821(e)(3)(A).
[54] FDIA, § 11(e)(3)(B), 12 USC § 1821(e)(3)(B).
[55] FDIA, § 11(e)(4)–(5), 12 USC § 1821(e)(4)–(5).
[56] FDIA, § 11(e)(3)(C), 12 USC § 1821(e)(3)(C).

order to induce the bidder to exercise the option. If a bidder exercises the option to assume any leases for bank premises, the bidder has been required to purchase the related furniture, fixtures, and equipment at fair market value. The FDIC has also typically given the winning bidder the option for up to ninety days or more to purchase any owned bank premises, and the related furniture, fixtures, and equipment, at fair market value.

6.87 Closely related to the repudiation power is the ability of the FDIC to avoid termination of any contract solely as a result of the institution's insolvency. See paragraphs 6.110 to 6.112 below. Thus, the acquirer has generally had the ability to keep in effect those contracts it needs for the operation of the institution, even if it later determines to use the option to have the FDIC repudiate them when they are no longer necessary.

Marketing the structure

6.88 The FDIC has generally been quite rigid in the way it has marketed failed banks. The FDIC has decided—without any input from potential bidders—which transaction structures to offer bidders, based on what it has believed to be the options most likely to produce the least-cost result for the deposit insurance fund. It alone has decided the structure of any assistance, such as loss-sharing. It has marked up its standard form P&A agreement to reflect the selected structure, and then instructed bidders to bid on that structure on a take it or leave it basis. In other words, the FDIC generally has not permitted any negotiation of the legal documentation it has proposed. Instead, it has purported to require bidders simply to increase or decrease their bids to reflect any perceived flaws in the non-financial terms of the proposed legal documentation, rather than to negotiate the non-financial terms.

6.89 While the FDIC's standard forms are not publicly available, examples of executed P&A agreements have been available on the FDIC's website, including those with loss-sharing (e.g. Downey Savings) and those without loss-sharing (e.g. Washington Mutual). Most posted forms have followed a common pattern, but a few appear to have been highly negotiated (e.g. IndyMac and BankUnited) probably because bidding was less competitive.

6.90 The FDIC has been more successful in enforcing this marketing strategy in a competitive bidding situation. Instances have arisen where strategic buyers (i.e. other financial institutions) have been unable or unwilling to bid on a particular institution. The FDIC has shown a willingness to consider modifications proposed by potential bidders, but at the end of the process, the FDIC has nonetheless determined the legal form of documentation and the required bidding format. It has reserved the right to reject, and has generally rejected, any bid that it has considered to be 'non-conforming'—that is, a bid that has reflected a modification of the legal documentation—because that modification would introduce a variable that the FDIC has found hard to compare with those that bid in accordance with the predetermined format. Moreover, accepting a non-conforming bid may conflict with the statutory requirement that the FDIC conduct its operations in a manner that 'ensures adequate competition and fair and consistent treatment of offerors' and prohibits discrimination.[57]

In situations where the FDIC has been faced with a single serious bidder or **6.91** liquidation, it has shown far more flexibility in negotiating both financial and non-financial terms. Even in such extreme situations, a bidder would find the FDIC to be far less willing to negotiate terms than a typical private counterparty in a merger or acquisition transaction. Bidder have therefore needed to be sparing in the changes it has proposed to the FDIC's standard documentation in order to avoid having its bid rejected by the FDIC staff. While the FDIC's rigidity can be extremely frustrating to many bidders, it can work to a well-advised bidder's advantage by providing it with opportunities to make lower bids and therefore real opportunities for enhanced value.

Bank failures have tended to come in waves, and a backlog of insolvent or near insolv- **6.92** ent banks has often developed. See Figures 6.1–6.6 for tabular and graphical illustrations of the three principal waves that occurred during the past century. Several reasons can account for this condition. First, the FDIC typically has become over-worked and understaffed, placing limits on its ability to process failures through its pipeline.[58] Second, some strategic buyers have had their own problems or otherwise have had limited capacity to absorb all the failed banks. The FDIC has also created disincentives for private capital investors to bid on failed banks.[59] These factors, in turn, have discouraged early intervention, resulting in greater deterioration in asset values before a failed bank has been closed and lower bids from approved bidders. This, in turn, may have resulted in increased cost to the deposit insurance fund of resolving failed banks. These conditions have created two potential opportunities for bidders—greater leeway on legal documentation and the ability to make a least-cost bid closer to the FDIC's actual cost of liquidation.

As noted above, the FDIC is required to accept any least-cost bid.[60] If a particular **6.93** bidder is the only bidder for a particular institution, the FDIC's only other options are to liquidate the bank or transfer its assets and liabilities to a bridge bank to wait for better market conditions. The FDIC's net liquidation cost therefore becomes its only alternative to the bidder's bid. The FDIC calculates its net liquidation cost based upon its experience as liquidator with the type of assets it will be required to dispose of. Bids are evaluated against this net liquidation cost. The best bid will be

---

[57] FDIA, § 11(d)(13)(E), 12 USC § 1821(d)(13)(E).

[58] Testimony of Mitchell L Glassman, Director, Division of Resolutions and Receiverships, Federal Deposit Insurance Corporation, at 9, in *Hearing before the Subcomm. on Financial Institutions and Consumer Credit, H. Comm. on Financial Servs* (21 January 2010).

[59] FDIC, *Final Statement of Policy on Qualifications for Failed Bank Acquisitions*, 74 Fed Reg 45440 (2 September 2009).

[60] FDIA, § 13(c)(4), 12 USC § 1823(c)(4).

the one that ultimately costs the FDIC the least amount of money. If no bid results in a cost to the FDIC that is less than its net liquidation cost, the FDIC will refuse to sell the institution and proceed with liquidation.

6.94 If a bidder can accurately estimate the FDIC's net liquidation cost and there are no other bidders, it can bid $1 above that amount and qualify as the least-cost bid. For example, assume that the FDIC is selling an institution with $100 of insured deposit liabilities and assets with a net liquidation value of $75. In this example, the FDIC's loss as a result of liquidation would be $25. Assuming the FDIC is not confident that its costs would fall if it transferred the institution's assets and liabilities to a bridge bank, a single bidder would be able to be the least-cost bid by submitting a negative bid of $24, meaning that the FDIC will, upon the bidder's assumption of the deposit liabilities and purchase of the assets, pay the bidder $24 in cash to entice the bidder to purchase the institution.

6.95 After the FDIC has accepted one or more bids in a closed-bank auction, it has determined which bid satisfies the least-cost test, cleared the bid with the other relevant regulators, notified the winning bidder, and signed the appropriate legal documentation. The chartering authority has then closed the bank, typically on Friday after the close of business, and the FDIC has simultaneously announced the agreement with the winning bidder. The failed institution has reopened for business as a subsidiary or part of the new owner on Saturday or Monday. This is an important aspect of the FDIC process. The winning bidder must be prepared to operate the bank immediately. No extended period will be provided to prepare for the process of assuming operational control of the failed institution.

6.96 The FDIC's resolution handbook contains further details on assisted transactions.[61] Most of the material in the current edition reflects the FDIC's policies, but the current edition is woefully incomplete compared to the prior edition. The prior edition, which the FDIC no longer makes available online, included a lot more details about assisted transactions, but only some of it reflected current FDIC policies.[62] Much of the still valid information was interwoven with historical information and discussions that did not reflect current FDIC policies and practices. Similarly, the FDIC's review of the savings and loan crisis—*Managing the Crisis*[63]—includes some material that generally reflects current FDIC policies and practices (e.g. Chapter 2), but other parts are historical and do not reflect its current practices. The FDIC staff has made certain PowerPoint presentations available that reflect the FDIC's current closed-bank bidding process.[64] In

---

[61] FDIC, *Resolutions Handbook* (2014).

[62] FDIC, *Resolutions Handbook* (2003)(superseded by 2014 edition) (current policies largely reflected only in overview, chapter 2, section 3–6, chapter 8, and glossary).

[63] FDIC, *Managing the Crisis: The FDIC and RTC Experience 1980–1994* (1998).

[64] FDIC, Staff Presentation, *The Failing Bank Marketing Process: Whole Bank Transactions and Loss Share Transactions* (American Bankers Association, 2 September 2009); FDIC Staff Presentation, *Resolutions: The Process of Bidding on Distressed Banks in the New Millennium* (18 July 2008).

addition, the FDIC recently launched a Failing Bank Acquisitions webpage on the FDIC website, which contains information that allow institutions to better understand FDIC-assisted transactions and how the FDIC markets failing financial institutions.[65]

E. Claims Process and the FDIC Super Powers

As an ancillary proceeding to the resolution transaction, the FDIC conducts a **6.97** claims process and distributes the residual value of the failed bank, including the net proceeds from any sale or liquidation of the failed bank's assets, to the deposit, general creditor, and other claims left behind in the receivership in accordance with the priority of their claims and in satisfaction of their claims. The FDIC administers the claims process, sorting out valid from invalid claims, determining priorities, and administering distributions from the receivership estate, which it refers to as dividends. When the various claims and priorities are sorted out, the FDIC uses the institution's assets to satisfy accepted claims to the extent of such assets in accordance with the statutory priorities. Section 11 authorizes the FDIC to conduct the claims process without any court supervision. Indeed, it makes the FDIC's decision to disallow a claim unreviewable by any court, although the validity of a claim is subject to *de novo* judicial consideration following completion of the administrative claims process.

In general, the FDIC notifies potential claimants of the failure after the institu- **6.98** tion is closed. Claimants have ninety days in which to submit a claim and the FDIC has 180 days to consider the claim. If the FDIC denies the claim, or if the 180-day consideration period lapses without a determination, only then can the claimant obtain judicial consideration of the claim, but the litigation must be filed within sixty days of the earlier to occur of the denial or the lapse of the period. Failure to abide by these time limits will result in a bar of further prosecution of the claim.

The FDIC has a variety of 'super powers' that allow it to avoid, set aside or other- **6.99** wise limit the claims of creditors and other stakeholders. The last ten super powers have been referred to as the 'ten most significant rules'.[66] But their impact has been largely overshadowed by the depositor preference rule, which was enacted last. With only a few important differences, the FDIC's super powers are the same whether it acts as a receiver or conservator.

---

[65] See FDIC, Failing Bank Acquisitions (last updated 27 April 2015), available at: <https://www.fdic.gov/buying/FranchiseMarketing/> (accessed 26 October 2015).
[66] John L Douglas, Jordan Luke, and Rex R Veal, 'Introduction', *Counselling Creditors of Banks and Thrifts: Dealing with the FDIC and RTC*, PLI Order No A4-4323 (14 January 1991).

Depositor preference rule

6.100 The FDIC's most important super power is simply the statutory priority that was given to domestic deposit claims in 1993 by the National Depositor Preference Law.[67] Section 11(d)(11) of the FDIA now gives deposits payable in the United States (domestic deposits) priority over all other unsecured claims, including those of depositors whose claims are payable solely outside the United States (foreign branch deposits) and general unsecured creditors. In summary, section 11(d)(11) contains the following priority of claims:

- administrative expenses of the receiver;
- any deposit liability (other than foreign branch deposits);[68]
- any other general or senior liability (including foreign branch deposits);
- any obligation subordinated to depositors or general creditors; and
- any obligation to shareholders or members.[69]

6.101 The reason why this super power has been so important and has even diminished the importance of the other super powers is that most insured institutions have very few unsecured liabilities other than domestic deposit liabilities and the assets of a failed institution have typically been insufficient to satisfy the claims of both the holders of domestic deposits and the holders of any claims junior to domestic deposits. For example, based on our review of ten of the largest institutions to fail in 2008 and 2009, domestic deposits generally accounted for at least 97 per cent of the failed institution's liabilities[70] and the value of each institution's assets averaged just 65 per cent of total liabilities.[71] Under these conditions, the assets will

---

[67] Omnibus Budget Reconciliation Act of 1993, § 3001, 107 Stat 312, 336, which added §11(d)(11) to the FDIA, 12 USC § 1821(d)(11).

[68] Three US law firms—Cleary Gottlieb, Davis Polk, and Sullivan & Cromwell—jointly published a paper in which they argued that the term 'deposit liability' includes foreign branch deposits for purposes of section 11(d)(11). Cleary Gottlieb, Davis Polk, and Sullivan & Cromwell, *The Status of Foreign Branch Deposits under the Depositor Preference Rule* (2 January 2013. The FDIC rejected that view, however, based on an opinion by a then acting general counsel of the FDIC in 1994. FDIC, *Deposit Insurance Regulations; Definition of Insured Deposit*, 78 Fed Reg 56583 (13 September 2013); FDIC Advisory Opinion, *'Deposit Liability' for Purposes of National Depositor Preference Includes Only Deposits Payable in the US*, FDIC 94-1 (28 February 1994). According to the FDIC, a foreign branch deposit must be dually payable at both the foreign branch and in the United States to be included in the term 'deposit liability'. 78 Fed Reg (13 September 2013) 56583, 56586.

[69] FDIA, § 11(d)(11), 12 USC § 1821(d)(11).

[70] Our review was based on data contained in the closed institution's call report as of the quarter ended immediately before it was closed. See ANB Financial, NA (closed 9 May 2008) (98 per cent); BankUnited (closed 21 May 2009) (95.5 per cent); Colonial Bank (closed 14 August 2009) (98 per cent); Corus Bank, NA (closed 11 September 2009) (99 per cent); Downey Savings and Loan, FA (closed 21 November 2008) (99.5 per cent); First National Bank of Nevada (closed 25 July 2008) (95 per cent); Georgian Bank (closed 25 September 2009) (99 per cent); Guaranty Bank (closed 21 August 2009) (98 per cent); Indymac, FSB (closed 11 July 2008) (98 per cent); Silver State Bank (closed 5 September 2008) (95 per cent); Washington Mutual Bank (closed 25 September 2008) (89 per cent).

[71] See ANB Financial, NA (closed 9 May 2008) (79 per cent); BankUnited (closed 21 May 2009) (56 per cent); Colonial Bank (closed 14 August 2009) (76 per cent); Corus Bank, NA (closed

be insufficient to satisfy the claims on all domestic deposit liabilities; as a result, nothing will be left for general unsecured claims or any other claims junior to domestic deposits.

The other super powers are likely to be far more important if an IDI subsidiary **6.102** of a US G-SIB were to fail and be resolved in an FDIC receivership. There are at least two reasons for this prediction. First, the FDIC is likely to put such IDIs into receivership when they run out of liquidity long before they are balance sheet insolvent. Second, the domestic deposit liabilities of such IDIs (except for Morgan Stanley Bank) account for a substantially smaller percentage of their total liabilities compared to most US IDIs.[72] All of the IDI subsidiaries of US G-SIBs (except Morgan Stanley Bank) have significant amounts of liabilities that are subordinate to domestic deposit liabilities, including foreign branch deposits, federal funds liabilities, trading liabilities, other borrowed money, subordinated debt, and other liabilities.[73] As a result, the value of the assets of such an IDI in receivership is far more likely to be sufficient to satisfy all the claims on domestic deposits, thus resulting in no loss to the deposit insurance fund.[74] This means that an IDI subsidiary of a US G-SIB is likely to have excess assets for the junior creditors to fight over. Thus, the FDIC's other super powers will be relevant because the domestic depositor preference rule will not have decided the whole game.

Contingent claims not provable

Although it has no statutory basis for doing so, the FDIC has long taken the pos **6.103** ition that claims against an insured institution for contingent obligations are not provable in a conservatorship or a receivership. Thus, the beneficiary of an undrawn line of credit, letter of credit, or guarantee has no provable claim to draw down additional amounts or to exercise its indemnification or guarantee rights once the

---

11 September 2009) (65 per cent); Downey Savings and Loan, FA (closed 21 November 2008) (81 per cent); First National Bank of Nevada (closed 25 July 2008) (60 per cent); Georgian Bank (closed 25 September 2009)(49 per cent); Guaranty Bank (closed 21 August 2009) (63 per cent); Indymac, FSB (closed 11 July 2008) (57 per cent); Silver State Bank (closed 5 September 2008) (63 per cent).

[72] Our data are based on the figures provided by the US G-SIBs in their call reports dated 30 June 2015: Bank of America, NA, 83 per cent; The Bank of New York Mellon, NA, 52 per cent; Citibank, NA, 37 per cent; Goldman Sachs Bank USA, 78 per cent; JP Morgan Chase Bank, NA, 60 per cent; Morgan Stanley Bank, NA: 97 per cent; State Street Bank & Trust, 44 per cent; Wells Fargo Bank, NA, 77 per cent.

[73] This data are based on the figures provided by the US G-SIBs in their call reports dated 30 June 2015: Bank of America, NA, 17 per cent; Bank of New York Mellon, NA, 48 per cent; Citibank, NA, 63 per cent; Goldman Sachs Bank USA, 22 per cent; JPMorgan Chase Bank, NA, 40 per cent; Morgan Stanley Bank, NA: 3 per cent; State Street Bank & Trust, 56 per cent; Wells Fargo Bank, NA, 23 per cent.

[74] This conclusion is consistent with the public summaries of the 2015 Title I and IDI resolution plans filed by the US G-SIBs, which generally concluded they could be resolved under a severely adverse economic scenario without any loss to the deposit insurance fund. See FDIC, Title I and IDI Resolution Plans, available at: <https://www.fdic.gov/regulations/reform/resplans/> (accessed 26 October 2015).

FDIC has been appointed receiver or conservator. Alternatively, the FDIC has taken the position that contracts for contingent obligations can be repudiated as 'burdensome', and that damages for such repudiation will be zero.

6.104 On rare occasions, the FDIC may include contingent obligations in any assets or liabilities transferred to a third-party bank in a P&A agreement. If they are transferred, the beneficiaries may enforce their rights against the third-party bank. For example, the FDIC transferred certain contingent obligations in both the JP Morgan/WaMu and the US Bank/Downey Savings transactions. Whether the FDIC would do so in other bank failures is uncertain, although we could envision the FDIC doing so in connection with resolving a US G-SIB if it believed that doing so would promote financial stability and be consistent with the least-cost test.

High bar to enforceability of contracts

6.105 Section 13(e) of the FDIA provides that any agreement with an insured institution that tends to 'diminish or defeat the interest of the [FDIC] in any asset acquired by it [as receiver or conservator under the FDIA], either as security for a loan or by purchase or as receiver' is not enforceable against the institution or the FDIC, and may not form the basis of a claim against the institution, unless the agreement:

- is in writing;
- was executed by the insured institution and any person claiming an interest under it contemporaneously with the acquisition of the asset by the institution;
- was approved by the board of directors of the insured institution or its loan committee and the approval is reflected in the minutes of the board; and
- has continuously been an official record of the insured institution.[75]

6.106 Section 13(e) has been one of the most litigated provisions, because it goes so far beyond the normal enforceability requirements under otherwise applicable non-insolvency law and is so difficult to satisfy as a practical matter.

6.107 These requirements were added in 1950 to codify and expand the Supreme Court's decision in *D'Oench Duhme & Co v FDIC*.[76] They defeat the enforceability against an insured institution in receivership or conservatorship of any otherwise enforceable oral contracts. They also create a substantial risk that many otherwise enforceable written contracts will not be enforceable against an insured institution in receivership or conservatorship.

6.108 For example, if a creditor had an otherwise enforceable and perfected security interest in certain assets, but the security agreement failed to satisfy one of the requirements in section 13(e), the security interest could be unenforceable against the FDIC and could not form the basis of a claim against the institution. While these

---

[75] FDIA, § 13(e), 12 USC § 1823(e).
[76] 315 US 447 (1942).

provisions were designed to protect the FDIC against 'secret' or 'side' agreements not reflected on the records of the institution (e.g. a guarantor that a loan officer supposedly promised would never be called upon), in practice the breadth of the provisions can be traps for the unwary.

The contemporaneous execution requirement is particularly difficult to satisfy in **6.109** the context of contractual arrangements that purport to govern a series of transactions over a long period of time before or after the contract is executed, such as a revolving line of credit or a security agreement that grants a security interest in previously or subsequently acquired collateral. The statute contains an exception for agreements for revolving lines of credit from the Federal Reserve or any Federal Home Loan Bank. Such lines of credit agreement are deemed to have been executed contemporaneously with any drawdown. The FDIC has also issued a policy statement on security interests to the effect that the FDIC 'will not seek to avoid otherwise legally enforceable and perfected security interests solely because the security agreement granting or creating such security interest does not meet the "contemporaneous" requirement of [the Federal Deposit Insurance Act]'.[77] Of course, the FDIC has the right to withdraw its policy statements at any time,[78] potentially with retroactive effect.

Power to enforce contracts despite ipso facto clauses

The FDIC has the power to 'enforce any contract... entered into by the depository **6.110** institution notwithstanding any provision of the contract providing for termination, default, acceleration, or exercise of rights upon, or solely by reason of, insolvency or the appointment of or the exercise of rights or powers by a conservator or receiver'.[79]

This means that contractual counterparties are prohibited from accelerating, ter- **6.111** minating, or otherwise exercising any rights under any contract against the insured institution solely as a result of the appointment of a receiver or conservator for the institution.

Two exceptions to this rule exist. First, the rule does not apply to QFCs in receiver- **6.112** ship (as distinguished from conservatorship) after a one business day cooling-off period.[80] Second, the rule does not apply to directors' or officers' liability insurance contracts or depository institution bonds in either conservatorship or receivership.[81] Counterparties to such contracts may accelerate, terminate, or otherwise exercise

---

[77] Statement of Policy Regarding Treatment of Security Interests After Appointment of the FDIC as Conservator or Receiver, 58 Fed Reg 16833, 16834 (31 March 1993).

[78] Statement of Policy on the Development and Review of Regulations, 63 Fed Reg 25157 (7 May 1998).

[79] FDIA, § 11(e)(12)(A), 12 USC § 1821(e)(12)(A).

[80] FDIA, § 11(e)(8)(G)(ii), 12 USC § 1821(e)(8)(G)(ii).

[81] FDIA, § 11(e)(13)(A), 12 USC § 1821(e)(13)(A).

the rights solely because of the insolvency or the appointment of a conservator or receiver.

Repudiation of contracts

6.113 The FDIC also has the power to disaffirm or repudiate any contract or lease, including QFCs, to which the insured institution is a party if the FDIC determines within a reasonable period of time that:

- the contract would be burdensome, and
- the repudiation or disaffirmance of the contract would promote the orderly administration of the institution's affairs.[82]

6.114 This repudiation power was added to the FDIC's toolkit by section 212(e) of the Financial Institutions Reform, Recovery and Enforcement Act of 1989 (FIRREA). Prior to FIRREA, the FDIC relied on the common law right of an equity receiver to disaffirm executory contracts.

6.115 Under the US Bankruptcy Code, executory contracts and unexpired leases must either be assumed and performed, or rejected and not performed with the approval of the bankruptcy court.[83] In contrast, the FDIC's repudiation power applies to both executory and non-executory contracts, although repudiation of a contact that has been fully executed presents substantial difficulties and to our knowledge has not been attempted by the FDIC. The FDIC may cherry-pick in exercising this power, even among similar contracts involving the same parties, except in the case of QFCs, where it must repudiate all or none of the contracts with a particular counterparty and its affiliates.[84]

6.116 The statute itself does not define what constitutes a reasonable period of time. The FDIC has indicated, however, in the context of security interests, that a reasonable period of time would generally be no more than 180 days after the FDIC's appointment as receiver or conservator,[85] and in its standard P&A agreement, appears to operate under the six-month guideline. At least one court has indicated that approximately six months to one year should generally qualify as a reasonable period of time.[86] But a more recent decision states that the amount of time that is 'reasonable' must be determined according to the circumstances of each case.[87] The statute contains no definition of the term 'burdensome', so the FDIC has wide latitude to interpret that standard, provided that its interpretation is reasonable.

---

[82] FDIA, § 11(e)(1)(C), 12 USC § 1821(e)(1)(C).

[83] 11 USC § 365(a).

[84] FDIA, § 11(e)(11), 12 USC § 1821(e)(11).

[85] Statement of Policy Regarding Treatment of Security Interests After Appointment of the FDIC as Conservator or Receiver, 58 Fed Reg 16833 (31 March 1993).

[86] See *Texas Co v Chicago & AR Co*, 36 F Supp 62, 65 (D Ill 1940), revised on other grounds, 126 F 2d 83, 89–90 (7th Cir 1942).

[87] *Resolution Trust Corp v CedarMinn Bldg Ltd P'ship*, 956 F 2d 1446, 1455 (8th Cir 1992).

Indeed, one court has held that the FDIC is not required to make a formal finding as to why a contract is burdensome.[88]

If the FDIC disaffirms or repudiates a contract, it must pay the counterparty **6.117** damages.[89] But rather than measure damages as the lost benefit of the counterparty's bargain, the FDIA provides that the damages are generally limited to 'actual direct compensatory damages; and determined as of the date of the appointment of the conservator or receiver'.[90] This very narrow definition of damages was added by section 212(a) of the FIRREA. In contrast, under the US Bankruptcy Code, breach of contract damages are generally allowed for rejected contracts, and administrative expense claims are often allowed to the extent that the debtor accepted benefits under the contract after the petition date. The damages formula in the FDIA excludes punitive or exemplary damages, damages for lost profits or opportunity, or damages for pain and suffering. The FDIA contains a special rule for QFCs, under which damages include the cost of cover and are determined based on industry standards.[91]

As noted, the damages are generally measured as of the date the FDIC was **6.118** appointed as conservator or receiver.[92] The FDIA does not require the FDIC to pay interest for the period between appointment and repudiation. Thus, for instance, if the FDIC repudiated a debt obligation, the institution would be required to pay the counterparty damages in the form of principal plus accrued interest until the date of appointment, but not until the date of repudiation or the original maturity date of the debt obligation. The FDIC is not required to pay post-appointment interest. In the case of QFCs, damages are measured as of the date of disaffirmance or repudiation, which eliminates the post-appointment interest issue through the later date but does not necessarily preserve the benefit of the original bargain.

The statute contains special rules for leases, governing both cases where the failed **6.119** institution is the lessor and cases where it is the lessee.[93] In general, when the institution is the lessee the FDIC will pay rent until the effective date of repudiation.[94] This is particularly important for leased bank premises, where the FDIC or third-party acquirer will take a period of time to determine whether it wishes to continue use of the property. Generally, if repudiated, the FDIC will not be obligated to pay future rent or be subject to acceleration or other penalties associated with unpaid future rent.

---

[88] *1185 Ave of Americas Assoc v Resolution Trust Corp*, 22 F 3d 494, 498 (2nd Cir 1994).
[89] FDIA, § 11(e)(3), 12 USC § 1821(e)(3).
[90] FDIA, § 11(e)(3)(A), 12 USC § 1821(e)(3)(A).
[91] FDIA, § 11(e)(3)(C), 12 USC § 1821(e)(3)(C).
[92] FDIA, § 11(e)(3)(A)(ii)(I), 12 USC § 1821(e)(3)(A)(ii)(I).
[93] FDIA, §§ 11(e)(4)–(5), 12 USC §§ 1821(e)(4)–(5).
[94] FDIA, § 11(e)(4)(B), 12 USC § 1821(e)(4)(B).

Special treatment for QFCs

6.120 QFCs are a special class of contract that receives preferential treatment in receivership and, to a far lesser extent, in conservatorship. QFCs include securities contracts, commodities contracts, forward contracts, repurchase agreements, swap agreements, and master agreements for any of the foregoing.[95] They are basically the same as the list of protected contracts under the US Bankruptcy Code.[96]

6.121 The enforceability of *ipso facto* clauses in QFCs is different depending on whether the institution is in receivership or conservatorship. If in receivership, counterparties have the right to exercise any contractual rights to terminate, liquidate, close out, net, or resort to security arrangements upon the appointment of the FDIC as receiver, subject to a one business day cooling-off period.[97] This right overrides the general prohibition against the enforceability of *ipso facto* clauses by counterparties. During the one business day cooling-off period, the FDIC has the option to transfer all, but not less than all, of the QFCs with a particular counterparty to a single third-party financial institution.[98] If the FDIC exercises this option, the counterparty is not permitted to terminate, accelerate, or otherwise exercise its rights with respect to the transferred QFCs.

6.122 In a conservatorship, the general rule against the enforceability of *ipso facto* clauses applies. Counterparties may not terminate, close out, or net QFCs solely on account of the insolvency, financial condition, or appointment of the conservator.[99] This, in effect, continues all relationships under their existing contractual provisions.

6.123 If the FDIC repudiates any QFCs, it is not permitted to cherry-pick with respect to a particular counterparty and its affiliates. It must repudiate all or none of the QFCs with a particular counterparty and its affiliates.[100] Damages for repudiated QFCs are determined as of the date of repudiation, and may include the cost of cover, and are calculated in light of industry practices.[101]

6.124 The FDIA prohibits the enforceability of walkaway clauses, even in QFCs, in both conservatorship and receivership.[102]

6.125 The FDIA does not, however, include a provision like section 210(c)(16) of the Dodd–Frank Act,[103] which gives the FDIC the power to override cross-defaults in QFCs that are tied to the insolvency or financial distress of the insured institution's parent or other affiliate if certain conditions are satisfied. Instead, if they are

---

[95] FDIA, § 11(e)(8)(D)(i), 12 USC § 1821(e)(8)(D)(i).
[96] 11 USC § 362(b)(6).
[97] FDIA, § 11(e)(10)(B)(i), 12 USC § 1821(e)(10)(B)(i).
[98] FDIA, § 11(e)(9)(A)(i), 12 USC § 1821(e)(9)(A)(i).
[99] FDIA, § 11(e)(10)(B)(ii), 12 USC § 1821(e)(10)(B)(ii).
[100] FDIA, § 11(e)(11), 12 USC § 1821(e)(11).
[101] FDIA, § 11(e)(3)(C), 12 USC § 1821(e)(3)(C).
[102] FDIA, § 11(e)(8)(G)(i), 12 USC § 1821(e)(8)(G)(i).
[103] Dodd–Frank Act, § 210(c)(16), 12 USC § 5390(c)(16).

overridden at all, such cross-defaults would be overridden pursuant to section 2 of the 2014 International Swaps and Derivatives Association (ISDA) Resolution Stay Protocol ('ISDA Protocol') if contained in ISDA Master Agreements between counterparties that have agreed to be bound by the ISDA Protocol.[104]

Security interests

Notwithstanding the FDIC's general repudiation power, the FDIA protects **6.126** legally enforceable and perfected security interests from being avoided for any reason, unless:

- the underlying security agreement does not satisfy the requirements of section 13(e);
- the security interest was taken in contemplation of the institution's insolvency;[105] or
- the security interest was taken with the intent to hinder, delay, or defraud the institution or its creditors.[106]

An exception to the avoidance powers exists for any extension of credit from any **6.127** Federal Home Loan Bank or any Federal Reserve Bank, and for any security interest in assets securing such an extension of credit.[107]

In the case of national banks and possibly federally chartered savings associations, **6.128** the FDIC is also permitted to rely on the preference avoidance powers contained in 12 USC §91 to set aside security interests that amount to preferential transfers. By contrast, under the US Bankruptcy Code, preferential transfers made on account of antecedent debt, within ninety days of bankruptcy while the debtor was insolvent, and which allow the creditor to receive more than the creditor would receive in liquidation, may be avoided, subject to defences if the transfer was for 'new value' or outside the ninety-day preference period.[108]

Because all security interests are in some sense taken 'in contemplation of an insti- **6.129** tution's insolvency', depending on how it is interpreted the second exception could swallow the rule. The FDIC has provided no guidance on how the second exception would be interpreted generally, but has not attempted to avoid security interests taken in the normal course of business. In 2005, however, the FDIA was amended to delete the second exception for collateral securing QFCs.[109] Such security interests are avoidable only if taken with the actual intent to defraud, and not merely because they were taken in contemplation of an institution's insolvency.[110]

---

[104] International Swaps and Derivatives Association, Inc. (ISDA), ISDA 2014 Resolution Stay Protocol.

[105] FDIA, § 11(e)(12), 12 USC § 1821(e)(12).

[106] FDIA, § 11(e)(12), 12 USC § 1821(e)(12).

[107] FDIA, § 11(e)(14), 12 USC § 1821(e)(14).

[108] 11 USC § 547.

[109] Bankruptcy Abuse Prevention and Consumer Protection Act of 2005, Pub L No 109-8 § 903, 119 Stat 23, 160–65. See also FDIA, § 11(e)(8)(C)(ii), 12 USC § 1821(e)(8)(C)(ii).

[110] Krimminger, *Adjusting the Rules: What Bankruptcy Will Mean for Financial Markets Contracts* (2005) 4 and note 9.

Discretion to discriminate among similarly situationed creditors

6.130 Section 11(i)(2) of the FDIA provides that the maximum liability of the FDIC to a person having a claim against an insured institution is the amount the claimant would have received if the FDIC had liquidated the assets and liabilities of the institution without using its bridge bank power.[111] It was added by section 212(a) of FIRREA in reaction to *First Empire Bank v FDIC*,[112] which had held that the FDIC was required to comply with the pro rata distribution rules in the National Bank Act in resolving a national bank,[113] which required the FDIC to treat similarly situated creditors equally.[114] Read solely as a maximum liability provision, section 11(i)(2) would seem to permit the FDIC to keep the difference between the value it would have realized on a hypothetical liquidation of the institution's assets and liabilities and any greater amount the FDIC actually realizes by resolving the institution in manner that maximizes its residual value—such as by a P&A sale to a third party, the use of a bridge bank to liquidate the assets and liabilities in an orderly fashion, or a recapitalization within resolution.

6.131 But that is not how the provision has generally been understood. Instead, it has generally been understood by both the FDIC and most commentators to permit the FDIC to treat similarly situated creditors unequally—to award some creditors more than their pro rata share of the residual value of the institution, and some less than their pro rata share—provided that all creditors receive at least as much value as they would have received in a hypothetical liquidation of the assets and liabilities of the failed institution.[115] In other words, it has been construed to impose a ceiling on the FDIC's liability if it exercises its discretion to favour some creditors over others and a floor on the recovery by any disfavoured creditors. In contrast, Chapter 11 of the US Bankruptcy Code requires equal treatment within classes of creditors, unless it can be shown that favouring certain creditors, such as critical vendors, over others will maximize the residual value of the estate for the benefit of all creditors.[116]

6.132 In the absence of a priority rule that subordinates long-term unsecured debt to demand deposits and other short-term unsecured debt, the FDIC probably needs this discretionary authority in order to favour short-term unsecured creditors over long-term unsecured creditors in order to stem runs and otherwise promote financial stability in the course of resolving a failed bank.

6.133 Section 11(i)(3) of the FDIA also permits the FDIC to use its own resources (or theoretically other resources of the receivership) to make additional payments to

---

[111] FDIA, § 11(i)(2), 12 USC § 1821(i)(2).

[112] 572 F.2d 1361 (9th Cir 1978).

[113] 12 USC §§ 91, 194.

[114] *First Empire Bank v FDIC*, 572 F.2d 1361, 1371 (9th Cir 1978).

[115] See, e.g., FDIC, Treatment of Uninsured Depositors and Other Receivership Creditors, in *Managing the Crisis: The FDIC and RTC Experience 1980–1994*, vol 1, part 1 (August 1998).

[116] Douglas Baird, *The Elements of Bankruptcy* (6th edn, 2014), 229–30, 261.

certain claimants if it believes that it would help minimize its losses. If it elects to do so, it is not obligated to make such payments to any other claimant or category of claimant, even if of the same type. As an example, the FDIC may determine that unpaid utility bills should be paid in full in order to assure uninterrupted service. The payment of a utility bill, which is a general unsecured claim, does not require the FDIC to pay an unpaid bill for legal services.

Super priority over fraudulent transfers by insider or debtor

As conservator or receiver of an insured institution, the FDIC has the right to avoid **6.134** and recover any fraudulent transfer by an insider or debtor of the insured institution to a third party that occurs within five years of appointment.[117] The FDIC's claim is senior to any claim by a trustee in bankruptcy or other person (except another federal agency) in a proceeding under the US Bankruptcy Code.[118] But the transfer must have been made with the intent to hinder, delay, or defraud the insured institution or the receiver or conservator.[119] The FDIC may recover from any immediate or intermediate transferee, except for a transferee who took as a good-faith purchaser for value.[120]

Cross guarantees

The FDIC has the right to recover any losses incurred in assisting or resolving any **6.135** insured institution from any other insured institution under common control with the first institution.[121] The FDIC's claim may be estimated and assessed in advance of any expenditure of funds and is subordinated to general creditors and depositors, but senior to the claims of shareholders and affiliates.[122]

Statute of limitations, tolling, and removal powers

The FDIC enjoys special powers with respect to litigation and claims involving **6.136** failed institutions.

First, any ongoing litigation against the failed institution will be stayed. The FDIC **6.137** would like to drive all potential claimants through the administrative claims process; however, the stay will only last forty-five days in the case of a conservatorship and ninety days in the case of a receivership.[123] Courts are required to grant the stay upon the request of the FDIC.[124] Note that the filing of a claim with the receiver

---

[117] FDIA, § 11(d)(17)(A), 12 USC § 1821(d)(17)(A).
[118] FDIA, § 11(d)(17)(D), 12 USC § 1821(d)(17)(D).
[119] FDIA, § 11(d)(17)(A), 12 USC § 1821(d)(17)(A).
[120] FDIA, § 11(d)(17)(B)–(C), 12 USC § 1821(d)(17)(B)–(C).
[121] FDIA, § 5(e)(1), 12 USC § 1815(e)(1).
[122] FDIA, § 5(e)(2)(A)–(C), 12 USC § 1815(e)(2)(A)–(C).
[123] FDIA, § 11(d)(12)(A), 12 USC § 1821(d)(12)(A).
[124] FDIA, § 11(d)(12)(B), 12 USC § 1821(d)(12)(B).

(which many claimants often do in order to preserve all remedies) does not affect the ability of the claimant to continue any action that was filed before the appointment of the FDIC as receiver.[125]

6.138 Second, claimants (unless they had previously commenced litigation) will be required to file an administrative claim that will be handled by the FDIC.[126] When a claimant files an administrative claim under the claims procedure, it will be deemed to have commenced an action for applicable statute of limitations purposes, even though the plaintiff may be precluded from actually commencing litigation in court until the administrative process concludes.[127]

6.139 Third, the FDIC will have the power to remove most actions filed in state court to federal court.[128]

6.140 Fourth, with respect to claims that the FDIC might wish to assert as receiver, the FDIC enjoys a special statute of limitations of six years for contract claims and three years for tort claims or, if longer, the statute provided by state law.[129] The statute of limitations does not begin to run until the date of the FDIC's appointment as conservator or receiver or, if later, the date the cause of action accrues.[130] Accordingly, unless a cause of action has expired as of the date of conservatorship or receivership, the FDIC has the benefit of an entirely new statutory period within which to bring claims. Indeed, for claims of fraud or intentional misconduct resulting in unjust enrichment or substantial loss to the institution, unless the cause of action accrued more than five years from the date of appointment, the FDIC is entitled to take advantage of the special statute of limitations.

6.141 These litigation powers are extremely important. In addition to having to address litigation to which the failed institution was a party, as receiver the FDIC will both initiate and be subject to multiple claims. For instance, following a failure it routinely investigates director and officer liability claims and professional malpractice claims. The extended statute of limitations provides ample opportunity for the FDIC to conduct investigations and bring claims without having to worry about rapidly expiring state statutes of limitation.

---

[125] FDIA, § 11(d)(6)(A), 12 USC §1821(d)(6)(A).

[126] FDIA, § 11(d)(12), 12 USC § 1821(d)(12). See also Self-Help Liquidation of Collateral by Second Claimants in Insured Depository Receiverships, FDIC Advisory Op, No 49 (15 December 1989).

[127] FDIA, § 11(d)(5)(F)(i), 12 USC § 1821(d)(5)(F)(i).

[128] FDIA, § 11(d)(13)(B), 12 USC § 1821(d)(13)(B).

[129] FDIA, § 11(d)(14)(A), 12 USC § 1821(d)(14)(A).

[130] FDIA, § 11(d)(14)(B), 12 USC § 1821(d)(14)(B).

7

RESOLUTION OF NON-BANK FINANCIAL COMPANIES

With some notable dissenters,[1] a consensus developed in the United States after the **7.01** financial panic of 2008 that some form of resolution authority based on the bank resolution model should be extended to most non-bank financial institutions under certain circumstances. Proponents argued that resolution authority is essential to ending bail-outs. They argued that because ordinary bankruptcy proceedings have the potential to trigger a chain reaction of failures throughout the financial system during a financial panic, such proceedings produce an irresistible temptation to bail out financial institutions that are considered to be too big or interconnected to fail during such a panic.[2] Opponents countered that far from being a solution to bail-outs, resolution authority actually institutionalizes bail-outs.[3]

The Obama Administration released its original proposal on 25 March 2009 and **7.02** a revised version on 23 July 2009.[4] The US House of Representatives passed an amended version of the Administration's proposal as part of the Wall Street Reform and Consumer Protection Act of 2009 ('House Bill').[5] The Senate passed a different version as part of the Restoring American Financial Stability Act of 2010 ('Senate Bill'), and previous versions of the Senate Bill included other versions of the resolution authority proposal.[6] The House and Senate Conference Committee used the

---

[1] See, e.g., Paul Mahoney and Steven Walt, 'Viewpoint: Treasury Resolution Plan Solves Nothing', *Am Banker*, 20 November 2009; Peter J Wallison and David Skeel, Op-Ed: 'The Dodd Bill: Bailouts Forever', *Wall St J*, 7 April 2010; John B Taylor, Op-Ed: 'How to Avoid a "Bailout Bill"', *Wall St J*, 3 May 2010.

[2] See *Too Big to Fail: The Role of Bankruptcy and Antitrust Law in Financial Regulation Reform: Hearing Before the Subcomm. on Commercial and Administrative law*, H. Comm. on the Judiciary, 111th Cong (2009) (testimony of Michael S Barr, Assistant Secretary of the Treasury).

[3] See, e.g., Hearings Before the House Financial Services Committee (29 October 2009) (remarks of Rep Hensarling).

[4] See Davis Polk, 'Client Memorandum', *Treasury's Proposed Resolution Authority for Systemically Significant Financial Companies* (30 March 2009); Davis Polk, 'Client Memorandum', *The Regulatory Reform Marathon* (28 July 2009).

[5] Wall Street Reform and Consumer Protection Act of 2009, HR 4173, 111th Cong, 1st Sess, §§ 1601 et seq (2009).

[6] Restoring American Financial Stability Act of 2010, Senate Substitute Amendment for HR 4173, 111th Cong, 2nd Sess, §§ 201–214 (20 May 2010).

version contained in the Senate Bill, after reflecting certain technical amendments, as its base text ('Conference Base Text').[7] On 21 July 2010, the United States passed the final version as Title II of the Dodd–Frank Act.[8] The purpose of this chapter is to summarize the key elements of the new resolution authority in Title II, identify the main policy issues raised in the debate over the various proposals, and summarize certain alternative proposals that were made based on the bankruptcy model.

A. Orderly Liquidation Authority Framework

7.03 The orderly liquidation authority in Title II of the Dodd–Frank Act is modelled largely on sections 11 and 13 of the Federal Deposit Insurance Act (FDIA), but with several significant differences. These differences were designed to harmonize the rules defining creditors' rights with those contained in the US Bankruptcy Code, discourage bail-outs, and reduce the moral hazard that could result if shareholders or unsecured creditors are insulated from the losses they would have suffered in a liquidation or reorganization under the US Bankruptcy Code. Thus, Chapter 6 of this book provides a good summary of the basic framework of Title II, except for the following key differences:

- **Orderly liquidation authority.** The resolution authority provided for in Title II has been named the 'orderly liquidation authority' to emphasize that it does not include a conservatorship option or permit bail-outs of failed institutions. This does not mean that the statute requires or even authorizes the Federal Deposit Insurance Corporation (FDIC) to do a fire-sale liquidation of a failed institution. Instead, the statute includes a duty to maximize the value of the failed institution and minimize losses for the benefit of its stakeholders[9] and includes the ability to transfer all or any part of the assets and liabilities of the failed institution to a bridge financial company. While the FDIC is required to liquidate any bridge within two years, with possible extensions of up to a total of five years, the bridge option provides the FDIC with the power to preserve the firm's franchise value and critical operations so that it can be liquidated in an orderly manner or recapitalized pursuant to a bridge bail-in.
- **Covered companies.** Unlike almost any other statute, the orderly liquidation authority is not limited to a fixed category of persons, determinable in advance, such as all systemically important financial companies. Instead, it could apply to any 'financial company'[10] if certain determinations are made. The required determinations depend as much on general market conditions as they do on

---

[7] Restoring American Financial Stability Act of 2010, Conference Base Text for HR 4173, 111th Cong, 2nd Sess, Title II (10 June 2010).
[8] Dodd–Frank Act, Title II (21 July 2010).
[9] Dodd–Frank Act, § 210(b)(9)(E)(i) and (ii), 12 USC § 5390(b)(9)(E)(i) and (ii).
[10] Dodd–Frank Act, § 201(a)(11), 12 USC §5381(a)(11).

the systemic importance of a particular firm in a vacuum. The conditions for coverage are more likely to be satisfied during a financial panic. They are less likely to be satisfied during periods of relative calm.

• Subject to the exceptions described below for broker-dealers or insurance companies, a financial company will be designated as a covered financial company, and the FDIC will be appointed as its receiver, if at any time (including on the eve of bankruptcy) the Treasury Secretary makes certain financial distress[11] and systemic risk determinations,[12] upon the recommendation of two-thirds of the Federal Reserve and two-thirds of the FDIC Board (or in the case of a broker-dealer, the Securities and Exchange Commission (SEC)), and in consultation with the President.[13] Title II applies to all financial subsidiaries of a covered financial company other than insured depository institutions (IDIs) (which continue to be covered by the FDIA's resolution provisions). Systemically important insurance companies could be covered financial companies, but they would be resolved by state insurance authorities under otherwise applicable state insurance insolvency laws, rather than by the FDIC under the substantive provisions of the new resolution authority.[14] Insurance company subsidiaries, however, would not be covered financial companies merely because they are subsidiaries of a covered financial company.[15]

• **Harmonized with the US Bankruptcy Code.** The final law reflects a substantial harmonization of the rules defining creditors' rights with those contained in the US Bankruptcy Code, thus narrowing the gap between these two laws on this important issue. The rules are therefore very different from the FDIC's super powers discussed in section E of Chapter 6 of this book, which remain in place without substantial modification only for the resolution of IDIs under the FDIA. Important differences include:

  • *No depositor preference rule.* Since the covered financial companies are not authorized to take deposits, the statute does not include a depositor preference rule.

  • *Key contingent claims are provable.* Contingent claims in the form of guarantees, letters of credit, lines of credit, and other similar claims are recognized as provable claims equal to their estimated value as of the date of the FDIC's appointment as receiver, which is essentially the same as under the US Bankruptcy Code.[16]

  • *Special enforceability requirements.* Although agreements against the interest of the receiver or a bridge financial company must be in writing and meet

---

[11] Dodd–Frank Act, § 203(b)(4), 12 USC § 5383(b)(4).
[12] Dodd–Frank Act, § 203(b), 12 USC § 5383(b).
[13] Dodd–Frank Act, § 203(a), 12 USC § 5383(a).
[14] Dodd–Frank Act, § 203(e), 12 USC § 5383(e).
[15] Insurance company subsidiaries are carved out of the definition of 'covered subsidiaries'. Dodd–Frank Act, § 201(a)(9), 12 USC § 5381(a)(9).
[16] Dodd–Frank Act, § 210(c)(3)(E), 12 USC § 5390(c)(3)(E).

certain other special enforceability requirements as required by the bank resolution statute (but not the US Bankruptcy Code), any written agreement that is duly executed or confirmed in the ordinary course of business that the counterparty can prove to the satisfaction of the receiver is enforceable (closer to the US Bankruptcy Code).[17]

- *Damages for a repudiated debt obligation.* Damages for the repudiation of such obligations are calculated as the face amount of the obligation plus accrued interest and accreted original issue discount, determined as of the date of the receiver's appointment.[18]
- *Limited right to 'post-appointment' interest.* Similar to the 'post-petition' interest provisions of the US Bankruptcy Code for a secured claim, any accrued interest is calculated through the date of repudiation, to the extent that such allowed secured claim is secured by property worth more than the amount of such claim.
- *Security interests and security entitlements.* Legally enforceable or perfected security interests and legally enforceable security entitlements in respect of assets held by the covered financial company must be respected as property rights.[19]
- *Preferential or fraudulent transfers.* Legally enforceable or perfected security interests and other transfers of property are not avoidable if 'taken in contemplation of the company's insolvency', as the FDIC has consistently asserted under the FDIA. Instead, they are avoidable only if they amount to preferential or fraudulent transfers under language that was lifted directly from sections 546, 547, and 548 of the US Bankruptcy Code.[20]
- *Set-off rights.* Set-off rights must be respected as under the US Bankruptcy Code, with some qualifications to permit the receiver to transfer liabilities to a third party or a bridge financial company even if the transfer destroys the mutuality of offsetting claims.[21]
- *Choice-of-law rules.* Non-insolvency choice-of-law rules determine the applicable non-insolvency law governing the perfection of security interests and the creation and enforcement of security entitlements.[22]
- *Additional due process.* This narrows the gap between the due process protections of the US Bankruptcy Code and those provided under the bank resolution statute, including a gatekeeping role of the US Federal District Court for the District of Columbia, additional opportunity for judicial review of the claims process, and certain notice and hearing rights.[23]

---

[17] Dodd–Frank Act, § 210(a)(6), 12 USC § 5390(a)(6).
[18] Dodd–Frank Act, § 210(c)(3)(D), 12 USC § 5390(c)(3)(D).
[19] Dodd–Frank Act, § 210(c)(12), 12 USC § 5390(c)(12).
[20] Dodd–Frank Act, § 210(a)(11), 12 USC § 5390(a)(11).
[21] Dodd–Frank Act, § 210(a)(12), 12 USC § 5390(a)(12).
[22] Dodd–Frank Act, § 210(a)(1)(I), 12 USC § 5390(a)(1)(I).
[23] Dodd–Frank Act, § 202, 12 USC § 5382.

- *Minimum recovery right.* To ensure minimum due process, all creditors are entitled to receive at least what they would have received in a liquidation of the covered financial company under Chapter 7 of the US Bankruptcy Code, at least if the FDIC exercises its power to favour some creditors over others within the same class.[24] A creditor's maximum entitlement is both its maximum and minimum entitlements.[25] This minimum recovery right is analogous to the no-creditor-worse-off-than-in-liquidation (NCWOL) principle described in the Financial Stability Board's Key Attributes document.[26]
- *Mandatory rule-making.* The FDIC is required to promulgate rules to implement the orderly liquidation authority in a manner that further reduces the gap between how creditors are treated in a liquidation under the US Bankruptcy Code and how they are treated under the orderly liquidation authority.[27]

Despite these important differences, Title II is still modelled on the bank resolu- **7.04** tion authority and therefore shares most of its features, including some of the super powers given to the FDIC. The FDIC is the resolving authority. It has the power to take control of certain troubled or failing financial institutions, if certain financial distress and systemic risk determinations are made. It may transfer any part of a covered institution's business to a third party at fair value. If a third-party buyer cannot be found at fair value, the FDIC may establish a bridge financial company to hold the part of the business worth preserving until it can be sold to a third party at fair value, liquidated in an orderly fashion or recapitalized pursuant to a bridge bail-in.

The FDIC has the power to provide a wide range of financial assistance, including **7.05** loss-sharing arrangements, to facilitate the transfer of assets and liabilities to a third party in connection with the liquidation of a covered institution.[28] But certain limitations are imposed on the FDIC's discretion that do not apply when it resolves IDIs under the FDIA, including that:[29]

- unsecured creditors must bear losses (up to the amount they would have suffered in a liquidation under Chapter 7 of the US Bankruptcy Code); and
- the management and board members responsible for the failed condition must be removed.

The FDIC is generally responsible for liquidating the covered institution left behind **7.06** in receivership (after transferring all or any portion of its assets and liabilities to a

---

[24] Dodd–Frank Act, § 210(a)(7)(B); (b)(4), (d)(4), and (h)(5)(E), 12 USC § 5390(a)(7)(B); (b)(4), (d)(4), and (h)(5)(E).

[25] Dodd–Frank Act, § 210(b)(4), (d)(4), and (h)(5)(E), 12 USC § 5390(b)(4), (d)(4), and (h)(5)(E).

[26] Financial Stability Board, *Key Attributes of Effective Resolution Regimes for Financial Institutions* (Updated Version, 15 October 2014) 11.

[27] Dodd–Frank Act, § 209, 12 USC § 5389.

[28] Dodd–Frank Act, § 204(d), 12 USC § 5384(d).

[29] Dodd–Frank Act, § 206, 12 USC § 5386.

bridge financial company) and conducting an administrative claims process for claims left behind in the receivership with very limited judicial oversight.[30] In both its exercise of core resolution powers and its administration of the claims process, the FDIC has some of the 'super powers' that it has under the bank resolution provisions of the FDIA. For example, it has the power to treat similarly situated creditors differently by cherry-picking which assets and liabilities to transfer to a third party or a bridge financial company, provided that each creditor left behind in the receivership receives no less for its claims than the value it would have received in a hypothetical liquidation under Chapter 7 of the US Bankruptcy Code as if no such transfer had taken place.[31] The FDIC has the power to treat all oral and some written contracts as unenforceable, even if they would be enforceable under applicable state or other non-insolvency law. It has the power to enforce contracts despite any so-called *ipso facto* clauses that purport to accelerate the contracts upon the commencement of a resolution or insolvency proceeding, subject to the same exceptions for qualified financial contracts as in the bank resolution statute.[32] The FDIC also has the discretion to repudiate any burdensome contract within a reasonable period of time, and limit the amount of any claim for damages as a result of repudiation to 'actual direct compensatory damages', subject to the same exceptions for qualified financial contracts (QFCs) and to certain new exceptions for contingent claims and debt obligations.[33] And it enjoys the same special powers with respect to litigation.[34]

7.07 Because Title II could apply to securities broker-dealers that are members of the Securities Investor Protection Corporation (SIPC), the statute includes provisions that are intended to provide customers with the same level of protection for customer property as would be provided in a normal SIPC proceeding under the Securities Investor Protection Act (SIPA).[35] If the FDIC were appointed receiver of a systemically important or other covered broker-dealer that is a member of SIPC, the FDIC would be required to appoint SIPC as trustee for the liquidation of the broker-dealer. Effectively, the FDIC would exercise the core resolution powers and SIPC would conduct the claims process for left-behind claims and assets, including left-behind customer claims and customer property. The FDIC would have the power to transfer any assets and liabilities of a covered broker-dealer (including any customer claims and corresponding customer property held by the covered broker-dealer) to a bridge financial company, and SIPC would be required to satisfy any left-behind customer claims 'in the same manner and amount' as if the FDIC

---

[30] Dodd–Frank Act, § 210(a), 12 USC § 5390(a).
[31] Dodd–Frank Act, § 210(b)(4), (d)(4), and (h)(5)(E), 12 USC § 5390(b)(4), (d)(4), and (h)(5)(E).
[32] Dodd–Frank Act, § 210(c)(13), 12 USC § 5390(c)(13).
[33] Dodd–Frank Act, § 210(c)(1)–(3), (c)(8)–(12), 12 USC § 5390(c)(1)–(3), (c)(8)–(12).
[34] Dodd–Frank Act, § 210(a)(8)–(10), 12 USC § 5390(a)(8)–(10).
[35] Dodd–Frank Act, § 205, 12 USC § 5385.

had not been involved in the receivership and no transfer of assets or liabilities to a bridge financial company had taken place.

Title II also contains certain provisions designed to reduce the moral hazard poten- **7.08** tially caused by allowing the FDIC to transfer certain 'cherry-picked' liabilities to a third party or a bridge financial company, while preserving the FDIC's authority to use its 'cherry-picking' power to preserve, promote, or restore financial stability during a financial panic. The new resolution authority attempts to strike an appropriate balance between these anti-moral hazard, anti-bail-out, and pro-financial stability goals by requiring the FDIC to recover any costs incurred in resolving a covered financial company from any of the company's creditors who received 'excess benefits' in the resolution proceeding, but only to the extent of such excess benefits and over an extended period of time.[36]

The FDIC may incur costs in a resolution proceeding in a variety of ways, including **7.09** by being required to top up any left-behind creditors for any *shortfall* between what the creditors would have received in a hypothetical liquidation under Chapter 7 of the US Bankruptcy Code and any lesser amount they actually received in the resolution proceeding. Transferred creditors could receive an 'excess benefit' to the extent they received more on their claims as a result of the transfer than they would have received in a hypothetical liquidation under Chapter 7 of the US Bankruptcy Code. The FDIC would have the power to finance any costs it incurs by borrowing from the Treasury, but would be required to repay such borrowed funds within five years, first, by recovering any 'excess benefits' from any creditors, and second, by imposing assessments on financial companies with assets of $50 billion or more.[37] Because the FDIC could take up to five years to complete the resolution of a covered company, it could conceivably allow transferred creditors to use their 'excess benefits' for up to ten years from the time the institution is first put into receivership (if the cost and the borrowing were incurred at the end of the receivership).

Unlike the proposed resolution authority in the House Bill, the final resolution **7.10** authority in the Dodd–Frank Act does not include a pre-funded orderly liquidation fund or a provision allowing the FDIC to impose haircuts on secured creditors. The House Bill would have required the creation of a pre-paid systemic dissolution fund of at least $150 billion, which would have been funded through assessments on all financial companies with assets of $50 billion or more and all financial companies that manage a hedge fund with assets under management of $10 billion or more.[38] The House Bill also would have allowed the FDIC to recover some of its losses by imposing a 10 per cent haircut on the claims of certain secured creditors.[39]

---

[36] Dodd–Frank Act, § 210(o)(1), 12 USC § 5390(o)(1).
[37] Dodd–Frank Act, § 210(o)(1), 12 USC § 5390(o)(1).
[38] Wall Street Reform and Consumer Protection Act of 2009, HR 4173, 111th Cong, § 1609(n)(6) (2009).
[39] Wall Street Reform and Consumer Protection Act of 2009, HR 4173, 111th Cong, § 1609(a)(4) (D)(iv) (2009).

This provision would essentially have allowed the FDIC to convert up to 10 per cent of a secured claim into an unsecured claim. It was aimed primarily at short-term financing in the form of repurchase agreements based on non-US government security collateral.

7.11 Title II gives the FDIC one business day to decide whether to transfer or repudiate QFCs.[40] This is the same as the bank resolution statute. The original Senate proposals would have given the FDIC a longer period of time, such as three or five business days, to make this decision. The FDIC argued that it needed this extra time to make the required determination with systemically important financial companies because they generally have more complex QFC portfolios than the type of IDIs that the FDIC has experience resolving. Critics argued that three or five days was too long during a financial crisis when asset and collateral values can be extremely volatile.

B. Key Policy Issues

7.12 The debate over the treatment of systemically important non-bank financial companies following their insolvency is extremely important, for the debate frames the key policy issues that must be addressed before any new insolvency framework is introduced. The insolvencies of AIG and Lehman Brothers convinced the Obama administration and Congress that new powers were needed, but there was vigorous debate over the proper approach. This section outlines the key policy issues that were debated.

What's wrong with bankruptcy?

7.13 In the absence of the required financial distress and systemic risk determinations under the new resolution authority, the US Bankruptcy Code would govern the liquidation, recapitalization, or reorganization of a financial company other than an IDI or insurance company. Even broker-dealers that are members of the SIPC are resolved under the US Bankruptcy Code, with SIPA supplementing its provisions with respect to customer property. The US Bankruptcy Code prevents moral hazard—that is, the incentive to take excessive risks if investors are entitled to the upside from their investments but are protected from the downside—by ensuring that shareholders, creditors, and counterparties of covered financial companies suffer appropriate losses if such companies are insolvent. The US bankruptcy process is generally considered to be transparent and consistent with due process. It has rules governing creditors' rights that are widely understood and considered to be neutral among similarly situated classes of creditors.

---

[40] Dodd–Frank Act, § 210(c)(10), 12 USC § 5390(c)(10).

Unless harmonized with the US Bankruptcy Code or other applicable insolvency **7.14** laws, any new resolution authority would change the 'rules of the game' for creditors and counterparties on the eve of bankruptcy, and thereby disrupt their reasonable expectations with little or no prior notice. Creditors, counterparties, customers, and other stakeholders have very different rights depending on whether their claims are governed by the US Bankruptcy Code or the FDIA, and changing the rules of the game on the eve of bankruptcy could itself create systemic risk. This problem was addressed in the Dodd–Frank Act by largely harmonizing the rules that define creditors' rights in Title II with their counterparts under the US Bankruptcy Code. This approach leaves a federal agency in charge of the process, with the bridge financial company option, but otherwise requires it to apply the substantive rules defining creditors' rights as they currently exist in the US Bankruptcy Code, with only a few exceptions.

While there remain substantial procedural differences in the way failures are han- **7.15** dled under the US Bankruptcy Code and the new orderly liquidation authority under Title II of the Dodd–Frank Act (primarily in the judicial oversight and relative transparency of US bankruptcy proceedings), Congress attempted to strike a reasonable balance between the desired need for government control over how these systemically important institutions should be addressed and the expectations of creditors.

The 'too big to fail'/moral hazard debate

The US Treasury and other proponents of the new resolution authority argued **7.16** that some form of resolution authority was necessary to eliminate taxpayer-funded bail-outs of financial companies that are perceived to be too big to fail, and the moral hazard that such bail-outs produce, in a way that does not destabilize the financial system. These proponents noted that a resolution authority would combat the notion that certain firms are 'too big to fail' by providing a mechanism to allow them to be liquidated in an orderly fashion. For example, Federal Reserve Chairman Bernanke stated that establishing a credible process for imposing such losses is essential to restoring a meaningful degree of market discipline and addressing the too-big-to-fail problem. According to resolution authority proponents, the only alternatives to resolution authority were to allow these companies to fail in a disorderly fashion the way Lehman Brothers was or to rescue them in an ad hoc fashion the way AIG was.

No one understood at the time that it was possible to do a single-point-of-entry **7.17** (SPE) recapitalization of a failed bank holding company under Chapter 11 of the US Bankruptcy Code, using the authority for quick sales under section 363 of the US Bankruptcy Code. When Professor Thomas Jackson, one of the leading bankruptcy scholars in the country and the principal author of the original Chapter 14 proposal, first heard about SPE under Chapter 11, he called it a genuine breakthrough and immediately suggested how the proposed new Chapter 14 might be revised to facilitate the successful use of SPE under the US Bankruptcy Code.

7.18 Critics asserted that the new resolution authority in Title II would not end 'too big to fail' or reduce moral hazard, but would rather institutionalize them. These commentators expressed a concern that having a resolution authority under which certain creditors could be protected against losses by having their claims assumed by third parties or a bridge financial company would create moral hazard by insulating the claims against losses they would have suffered in a bankruptcy proceeding.

7.19 These critics pointed to the financial assistance provided to Freddie Mac and Fannie Mae in connection with their conservatorships as examples, and argued that the new resolution authority would create twenty new Fannie Maes and Freddie Macs. They asserted that the institutionalization of such bail-outs would increase moral hazard and give potentially covered companies a funding advantage over their competitors. Such critics would leave the US Bankruptcy Code in place to insure that shareholders, creditors, and counterparties of non-depository institution financial companies suffer appropriate losses if such companies fail.

7.20 The Dodd–Frank Act attempted to strike an appropriate balance between the anti-moral hazard, anti-bail-out, and pro-financial stability goals by:

- prohibiting the Federal Reserve or the FDIC from providing any financial assistance to a financial company unless the assistance is part of a market-wide programme, or unless, in the case of the FDIC, the company is being liquidated in an FDIC receivership;[41] and
- requiring the FDIC to recoup any costs incurred in the receivership of a systemically important financial company by clawing back any 'excess benefits' received by any of its creditors whose claims are transferred to a third party or a bridge financial company in the receivership proceeding, while giving the FDIC an extended period of time (up to five to ten years) to recoup such excess benefits.[42]

Claims process

7.21 Some proponents of the general concept of resolution authority strongly supported giving a federal agency core resolution powers modelled on the FDIA. But they believed that the FDIA was the wrong model for the claims process for left-behind claims, as applied to non-depository institution financial companies. They argued that an administrative claims process modelled on the FDIA is too opaque and does not provide the same level of due process and judicial review as

---

[41] Dodd–Frank Act, §§ 1101–1106.
[42] Dodd–Frank Act, § 210(o), 12 USC § 5390(o).

the US Bankruptcy Code. They also argued that the rules defining creditors' rights in the FDIA should not be used for the resolution of non-depository financial companies. They asserted that using such rules would be inconsistent with provisions in the resolution authority statute which guarantee all creditors that they will receive the same recovery as they would have received in a liquidation under the US Bankruptcy Code.

In addition, critics asserted that the FDIA rules are deliberately designed to **7.22** reinforce the priority of deposit creditors—a class of creditors that does not exist for non-depository institutions—over unsecured non-deposit creditors—a class of creditors that account for only a tiny portion of the balance sheets of most depository institutions. The rule allowing the FDIC to set aside security interests if they were taken 'in contemplation of insolvency' would also create a serious risk that otherwise perfected security interests may be set aside when applied to non-bank financial companies, thus causing secured credit to dry up during times of financial stress.

Instead, they argued that the resolution authority needed to be adapted so that it **7.23** provides a more transparent claims process, additional judicial review, neutral rules governing creditors' rights, and protection of secured creditors' rights modelled on the US Bankruptcy Code.

Finally, they argued that unless the proposed resolution authority reflected a **7.24** compromise between the FDIA and bankruptcy or other applicable insolvency models, it would have the unintended consequence of making our credit markets inefficient—creating uncertainty as to creditor treatment; increasing the cost and reducing the availability of credit to these financial companies, consumers, small businesses, and others in the system; slowing jobs growth; increasing unemployment; and causing liquidity to dry up during times of financial stress.

Defenders of the bank resolution model for both the core resolution powers and **7.25** the ancillary claims process countered that the right of *de novo* judicial review after the administrative claims process has been completed would provide adequate due process for creditor claims. They argued that no significant difference in outcomes would arise between the FDIC's application of the rules defining creditors' rights in the FDIA and a typical bankruptcy court's application of the rules in the US Bankruptcy Code. As a result, they asserted that the unintended consequences are more feared than real.

Proponents of the bankruptcy model for the ancillary claims process had responses **7.26** to each of these defences. First, they asserted that the administrative claims process under the FDIA was in fact more opaque and would provide far less due process and judicial review than a bankruptcy process. Second, significant differences in outcomes would arise between the two sets of rules. Moreover, if no significant differences in outcomes really would arise, the FDIC should be required to apply the rules under the US Bankruptcy Code to avoid creating any legal uncertainty about the matter and to avoid any inconsistencies between the applicable rules and the minimum recovery guarantees in both the House and Senate versions.

7.27 Other defenders of the bank resolution model for both the core resolution powers and the ancillary claims process argued that if the rules governing creditors' rights in the proposed resolution authority would impose greater losses on creditors or subject them to greater legal uncertainty of recovery than the Bankruptcy Code, the rules would serve the important public policy purpose of further enhancing market discipline and reducing moral hazard.

7.28 Proponents of the bankruptcy model argued that this argument seemed over-wrought and ill-conceived, and was inconsistent with numerous provisions in the Title II that were designed to ensure that creditors and other stakeholders would never fare worse in a Title II proceeding than they would in a bankruptcy proceeding.[43] For example, Title II cannot even be lawfully invoked unless resolution of the company under the US Bankruptcy Code would result in serious adverse effects on financial stability in the United States *and* Title II would mitigate or avoid such adverse effects.[44] There is perhaps no better way to foster contagion and cause serious adverse effects on financial stability in the United States than to use Title II in a manner that treats creditors and other stakeholders worse than they would have been treated in a bankruptcy proceeding. Thus, if Title II were used in this manner, the FDIC would have violated a fundamental condition for invoking it in the first place.

7.29 They also argued that imposing greater losses on creditors than they would have suffered in a liquidation under the Bankruptcy Code is inconsistent with the minimum recovery provisions Title II.[45] Moreover, the public policy goals in favour of market discipline and reducing moral hazard must be balanced against the important public policy goals of due process and fundamental fairness, and encouraging a healthy level of credit during normal times. Otherwise, Congress could deny all recovery to creditors even if some assets were available to satisfy all or part of their claims.

Funding

7.30 A significant policy discussion arose over who should bear the costs of failure of a systemically important financial company and whether an *ex ante* resolution fund should be established to address future failures of systemically important institutions, or whether *ex post* funding would be more appropriate. While under the Dodd–Frank Act, Congress adopted an *ex post* funding model that attempts to

---

[43] Dodd–Frank Act, § 201(a)(7)(B), (b)(4)(B), (d)(2)–(3), (h)(5)(E), 12 USC § 5381(a)(7)(B), (b)(4)(B), (d)(2)–(3), (h)(5)(E).
[44] Dodd–Frank Act, § 203(b)(2), (5), 12 USC § 5383(b)(2), (5).
[45] Dodd–Frank Act, § 201(a)(7)(B), (b)(4)(B), (d)(2)–(3), (h)(5)(E), 12 USC § 5381(a)(7)(B), (b)(4)(B), (d)(2)–(3), (h)(5)(E).

impose the costs first on creditors of the failed institution and, to the extent of any shortfall, other large financial institutions, the debate over the proper approach for funding these liquidations is likely to continue.

As adopted, the Dodd–Frank Act gives the FDIC the power to recover liquidation **7.31** costs, first, by clawing back any 'excess benefits' received by any claimants that received more in the resolution of a covered company than they would have received in a liquidation of the company under Chapter 7 of the Bankruptcy Code.[46] To prevent this power from being destabilizing, the FDIC has the discretion to recoup any excess benefits over an extended period of time, instead of imposing immediate haircuts on creditors. If the FDIC is not able to recover all of its costs in this manner, it may recover any shortfall by imposing assessments on certain large US financial companies. To meet short-term funding needs in connection with a resolution, the FDIC is empowered to borrow from the US Treasury.[47]

The first aspect of this debate is who should bear the costs of failure. Many argued **7.32** that the costs should be imposed on the large, complex financial institutions that ultimately might have to be resolved under the new authority. Critics questioned whether it was appropriate to impose the cost of the new resolution authority on the targeted pool of large companies. The direct beneficiaries of the financial assistance would not be these companies, except to the extent that they were among the creditors or counterparties whose claims are assumed by a third party or a bridge financial company pursuant to the FDIC's exercise of its core resolution powers. Instead, the direct beneficiaries would be the creditors and counterparties whose claims are assumed. To the extent the transfer of these claims helps to stabilize the financial system, the indirect beneficiaries would be everyone who benefits from financial stability.

Critics also argued that unless the creditors and counterparties whose claims would **7.33** be assumed bear the cost of the financial assistance, they would in fact be insulated from losses, undermining market discipline and creating a degree of moral hazard that would not exist if all US financial companies were resolved under the Bankruptcy Code or other applicable insolvency law. On the other hand, if there were to be some form of claw-back from these creditors and counterparties equal to the difference between what they would have received in a bankruptcy liquidation and what they actually received because of the third-party assumption of liabilities, it might undo the stabilization benefits of giving the FDIC the power to transfer the claims.

As noted, the Dodd–Frank Act attempted to resolve this policy issue by giving the **7.34** FDIC power to recover its costs, first, by recouping any 'excess benefits' from any claimants who received more in the resolution than they would have received in

---

[46] Dodd–Frank Act, § 210(o), 12 USC § 5390(o).
[47] Dodd–Frank Act, § 210(n), 12 USC § 5390(n).

a liquidation under Chapter 7 of the Bankruptcy Code, and second, from large financial companies.[48] Only time will tell whether such a claw-back power can be exercised in a way that is consistent with promoting financial stability or whether it will have a destabilizing effect by creating an incentive for short-term creditors to 'run' at the slightest hint of financial trouble.

7.35 A vigorous debate has also arisen over whether the tax to recover these costs should be imposed before or after the resolution authority is exercised. The principal argument advanced in favour of an *ex ante* tax is that an *ex post* tax would allow the companies that are resolved to escape bearing any of the cost of their own resolution. The principal arguments advanced against an *ex ante* tax and in favour of an *ex post* tax are (i) it is impossible to know whether the resolution authority will ever be used or how much it will cost if used, and (ii) the creation of a fund makes it more likely the fund will be put to use by placing an entity into resolution under this authority, and creating an incentive on the part of the government to bail out creditors and counterparties rather than using the claw-back procedure to impose the costs of failure on those creditors and counterparties.

Is the FDIC qualified?

7.36 Under the Dodd–Frank Act, the FDIC must be appointed as the receiver for all covered financial companies, except for insurance companies. The FDIC would be required to consult with the state or federal regulators of a covered financial company in carrying out its functions as receiver.[49] The FDIC is required to prepare an orderly liquidation plan acceptable to the Treasury Secretary before it could borrow any funds to cover its resolution costs.[50] It would not be permitted to take any action inconsistent with this plan without the Treasury Secretary's consent. But otherwise, nothing would require the FDIC to follow the direction of any other regulator.

7.37 Until recently, the FDIC had little to no experience with the type of large, complex, and global financial institutions that would be the subject of the new resolution authority. Its supervisory experience was limited to community banks and other relatively small IDIs. Although the FDIC had resolved at least one relatively large savings association (Washington Mutual),[51] that savings association had relatively simple and purely US domestic activities compared to the more complex, cross-border operations of the core targets of the new resolution authority, and that institution was resolved in such a way as to minimize FDIC involvement as essentially all assets were transferred to a single institution buyer.

---

[48] Dodd–Frank Act, § 210(o), 12 USC § 5390(o).
[49] Dodd–Frank Act, § 204(c), 12 USC § 5384(c).
[50] Dodd–Frank Act, § 210(n)(9), 12 USC § 5390(n)(9).
[51] Washington Mutual had total assets of $309 billion as of 30 June 2008. See Washington Mutual, Inc., Quarterly Report on Form 10-K for quarterly period ended 30 June 2008.

Given the FDIC's lack of experience, a debate ensued over the degree of auton- **7.38**
omy the FDIC should be granted as it handled the resolution of a large, complex financial institution. Many argued that some form of oversight board
should be formed, consisting of the Treasury Secretary, the Chairman of the
Federal Reserve, the Chairperson of the FDIC, and the primary federal regulator of the company being resolved. The FDIC would carry out the resolution
powers under the new authority, subject to the direction of this oversight
board. They proposed that the oversight board would also be the rule-making
authority under the proposed resolution authority and be responsible for
international coordination.

In the end, none of these proposals was enacted. After the passage of Title II, the **7.39**
FDIC made substantial efforts to increase its experience with global systemically
important banking groups (G-SIBs). It established a new Office of Complex
Financial Institutions. It reviewed comment letters from the private sector,[52]
and participated in a series of public/private workshops about how to use its new
authority to resolve G-SIBs. As a product of these comment letters and workshops,
it developed its SPE recapitalization within resolution strategy for resolving US
G-SIBs under Title II. The SPE strategy has since been widely praised or endorsed
as the most promising strategy for resolving G-SIBs in a manner that will promote
financial stability without the need for taxpayer-funded bail-outs. The FDIC has
now had several years to review dozens of resolution plans submitted by some of
the largest and most complex G-SIBs under section 165(d) of the Dodd–Frank Act
and the FDIC's rules for IDIs.[53]

Mandatory rule-making

The FDIC does not have a history of transparency in providing *ex ante* legal cer- **7.40**
tainty on how ambiguities in the FDIA are to be resolved. Although it has permissive rule-making authority under the FDIA, it has rarely exercised that authority.
It has also been very sparing in providing other forms of legal guidance, including
policy statements, general counsel opinions, and other interpretations. In addition,
all of these sources of legal guidance may be withdrawn by the FDIC at any time
with, or in some cases without, notice.

---

[52] Joint Comment Letter from the Securities Industry and Financial Markets Association and
The Clearing House Association in Response to FDIC's Second Notice of Proposed Rulemaking
under Title II of the Dodd–Frank Act (23 May 2011) (advocating recapitalization within resolution
under Title II); *Certain Orderly Liquidation Authority Provisions under Title II of the Dodd–Frank Wall
Street Reform and Consumer Protection Act (Final Rule)*, 76 Federal Register 41626 (15 July 2011),
41634–41635 (FDIC praising the joint comment letter from the Securities Industry and Financial
Markets Association (SIFMA) and The Clearing House Association (TCH) 'as an example of the
value generated by constructive dialogue between the private financial markets and the federal government on topics such as this one').

[53] See Title I and IDI Resolution Plans, available at: <https://www.fdic.gov/regulations/reform/
resplans/> (accessed 26 October 2015).

7.41   Further, FDIC receiverships are handled primarily within the FDIC, with little judicial oversight or review. This is to be contrasted with the US Bankruptcy Code, where there are extensive statutes, rules, and procedures, and a well-developed body of case law. Further, in a bankruptcy proceeding, the judge is directly involved, providing significant and substantial oversight.

7.42   To counter this culture and tradition, the Dodd–Frank Act includes mandatory rule-making authority, with the requirement that the FDIC use its authority to further harmonize the rules governing creditors' rights with those in the Bankruptcy Code.[54]

Valuation issues

7.43   Neither the new resolution authority nor any of its earlier versions has included any specific procedures for ensuring that the FDIC obtains the highest possible price for any assets and liabilities sold or transferred pursuant to its exercise of core resolution powers, or assigns a fair value to what the assets would have been worth in a liquidation under Chapter 7 of the US Bankruptcy Code. Because the amount received for such assets and liabilities, and the value placed on those assets as if they had been liquidated under the US Bankruptcy Code, has a direct relationship to the size of the minimum recovery rights of left-behind claimants, the law may eventually need to be amended to include some incentives and procedures, as well as judicial review, to ensure that the FDIC does not sell any assets or liabilities at below the maximum value possible over some reasonable time period or assigns an artificially low value to what the assets would have been worth in a hypothetical liquidation under the US Bankruptcy Code.

Remedies

7.44   The Dodd–Frank Act also lacks a clear and practical remedy for left-behind claimants who believe they did not receive their minimum recovery entitlement in a resolution proceeding (i.e. the amount they would have received in a liquidation under Chapter 7 of the US Bankruptcy Code, at least if they were treated differently from similarly situated creditors). Each such claimant has the implied right to bring a separate proceeding in federal court to recover the shortfall from the FDIC. But the cost of such individual proceedings could be prohibitive and exceed the shortfall amount. The policy issue is whether to provide aggrieved parties with an express right to a collective proceeding in a single federal district court after the termination of the receivership. Proponents argued that such a collective proceeding, or just the threat of such a proceeding, would 'keep the FDIC honest' in carrying out its duty to make sure all left-behind claimants receive what they would have received in a liquidation under Chapter 7 of the Bankruptcy Code. It would also give them

---

[54] Dodd–Frank Act, § 209, 12 USC § 5389.

a practical remedy if the FDIC violated its trust. Critics argued that the FDIC is a federal agency that can be trusted to carry out its statutory duties responsibly, and that a collective proceeding could subject the FDIC to unnecessary litigation costs.

Haircuts on secured claims?

Early in the process of considering the new resolution authority, the FDIC argued **7.45** for a provision that would have given the FDIC the discretionary authority to impose a 10 per cent haircut on certain secured claims (other than those of certain favoured creditors like the Federal Reserve), effectively turning 10 per cent of an otherwise secured claim into an unsecured claim. While incorporated into the House Bill, neither the Senate Bill nor the final legislation included such a provision. Proponents argued that such a haircutting power would be an appropriate way to help the FDIC recoup its resolution costs. Perhaps more importantly, they argued that exposing a portion of a secured claim to unsecured risk would increase the incentive of the secured creditor to monitor its debtor and create greater market discipline. In the absence of such risk, proponents argued, secured creditors would not adequately monitor their debtors. Critics of the proposal vigorously argued that this power would reduce the supply of secured credit and increase its cost. Secured creditors would respond by exiting the market or reducing the term of their credit to overnight or intraday periods in order to be able to 'run' at the slightest sign of trouble. It would also make secured creditors unwilling to provide credit during a financial crisis, at the very time when any liquidity—even secured liquidity—is most needed from the private sector. It could transform central banks from lenders of last resort during a financial crisis to the only willing lenders during a financial crisis.

As noted, the final legislation did not incorporate the haircut provision. However, it **7.46** required the Financial Stability Oversight Council to prepare a report for Congress on whether haircuts 'could improve market discipline and protect taxpayers'.[55] The Financial Stability Oversight Council submitted its report to Congress in July of 2011.[56] The report concluded that haircuts on secured credit were unnecessary.

Extend automatic stay to QFCs?

A final policy issue is whether to impose a stay on the ability of counterparties on **7.47** QFCs to exercise their close-out rights (liquidate collateral, etc) upon the insolvency of a covered financial company. Such counterparties are exempt from the automatic stay under the US Bankruptcy Code. They are subject to a one-business-day stay under the FDIA and the new resolution authority.[57] This one-business-day stay is designed to give the FDIC time to decide whether to repudiate or transfer

---

[55] Dodd–Frank Act, § 216.
[56] Report to the Congress on Secured Creditor Haircuts (July 2011).
[57] Dodd–Frank Act, § 210(c)(10), 12 USC § 5390(c)(10).

a failed institution's QFCs to a third party or a bridge bank, or simply to allow the counterparties to exercise their close-out rights. The Conference Base Text would have imposed a three-business-day stay, and earlier versions of the Senate Bill would have imposed a five-business-day stay. The House Bill would have imposed only a one-business-day stay.

7.48 Some commentators argued for an indefinite stay. They contended that the exemption of QFCs from an automatic stay is a major source of instability when a financial institution fails. During the debate of the Senate Bill, Senator Nelson proposed an amendment that would have eliminated the exemption for QFCs from the automatic stay under the Bankruptcy Code and subject them to a ninety-day stay under the new resolution authority.

7.49 Critics countered that such a rule would be far from stabilizing when looked at from an *ex ante*, rather than *ex post*, point of view. They argued that the prospect of an automatic stay would destabilize the derivatives markets, reduce the supply of credit including repurchase agreement credit, and increase its cost. QFC counterparties would seek to protect themselves from such a rule by reducing the term of their QFCs to the shortest term possible (including overnight or even intraday) in order to facilitate a 'run' at the slightest hint of financial trouble.[58]

C. Single-Point-of-Entry Strategy

7.50 The most significant development since the enactment of Title II has been the FDIC's development of its SPE recapitalization within resolution strategy for resolving US G-SIBs under Title II. The SPE strategy has been widely recognized as the most promising solution to the 'too-big-to-fail' problem since it was first publicly announced by then-acting FDIC Chairman Martin Gruenberg in May 2012.

7.51 Under the SPE strategy, the FDIC would put the top-tier parent of a failing US G-SIB into a receivership under Title II. It would immediately set up a bridge financial company and transfer all of the parent's assets, including its operating subsidiaries,

---

[58] Professors Mark Roe and Stephen Adams recently argued that both the current safe harbours in the US Bankruptcy Code and their outright repeal would result in value destruction and thus be suboptimal from a public policy perspective. In contrast, they argued that a temporary stay of ten days (with a possible extension of another ten days) on the right to close out QFCs, together with the express authority to break up a derivatives book and sell it along product lines (e.g. interest rate swaps, foreign currency swaps, etc), would maximize the value of a failed institution's derivatives book. Mark J Roe and Stephen D Adams, 'Restructuring Failed Financial Firms in Bankruptcy: Selling Lehman's Derivatives Portfolio', 32 Yale J Reg 363 (2015). The authors do not provide a persuasive reason, however, why a derivatives book could not be broken up and sold along product lines pursuant to an SPE recapitalization within resolution strategy under the US Bankruptcy Code or Title II of the Dodd–Frank Act where the operating subsidiaries (which are the counterparties on virtually all QFCs) remain open and operating.

to the bridge. It would leave behind in the parent's receivership all of the equity interests in and long-term unsecured debt and other unsecured liabilities of the parent, except for an immaterial amount of essential operating liabilities. Essential operating liabilities assumed by the bridge would include obligations to pay rent and utilities, guarantees of operating subsidiary liabilities, and derivatives used to hedge the bridge's ongoing treasury operations. The FDIC would keep the parent's operating subsidiaries open and operating, and out of insolvency or other resolution proceedings. A step-by-step graphical illustration of how the SPE strategy works is contained in a report by the Failure Resolution Taskforce of the Bipartisan Policy Center.[59]

The FDIC would recapitalize the business transferred to the bridge by leaving **7.52** behind in the parent's receivership enough long-term unsecured debt and other unsecured liabilities to ensure that the bridge is well capitalized. It would recapitalize any undercapitalized operating subsidiaries by forgiving any of their intercompany debt liabilities to the parent, including deposit liabilities, or contributing parent assets to the operating subsidiaries where needed. It would borrow whatever it needed from the US Treasury to provide the bridge and its operating subsidiaries with sufficient liquidity to convert their illiquid assets into cash. It would provide liquidity in accordance with the classic principles established by Walter Bagehot, namely only to solvent entities on a fully secured basis at above-market interest rates. The bridge and its operating subsidiaries would be more than solvent—they would all be well-capitalized as a result of implementing the recapitalization within resolution strategy.

Because US G-SIBs issue virtually all of their long-term unsecured debt out of **7.53** their parent holding companies and virtually all of their demand deposits and other short-term unsecured debt out of their operating subsidiaries, their long-term unsecured debt will be structurally subordinate to their demand deposits and other short-term unsecured debt. In addition, because most US G-SIBs already have enough regulatory capital and long-term unsecured debt to be recapitalized at fully phased in Basel III levels if they ran out of all their required regulatory capital,[60] there is very little risk that demand deposits or other short-term unsecured debt would suffer any losses. As a result, the FDIC should be able to use the SPE strategy to resolve US G-SIBs in a manner that will maximize the residual value of the US G-SIB for the benefit of its stakeholders yet should stem runs and contagion and otherwise preserve financial stability without the need for a taxpayer-funded bail-out.

---

[59] John F Bovenzi, Randall D Guynn, and Thomas H Jackson, *Too Big to Fail: The Path to a Solution*, A Report of the Failure Resolution Task Force of the Financial Regulatory Reform Initiative of the Bipartisan Policy Center (May 2013) 23–31.
[60] Statement of Randall D Guynn, Hearing Before the Subcomm on Fin Inst and Consumer Protection, S Comm on Banking, Fin and Urban Affairs (29 June 2015) Exhibit F.

7.54 The FDIC would then conduct a claims process for the equity interests, long-term unsecured debt, and other liabilities left behind in the parent's receivership. After it had identified, validated, and determined the amount of all allowed claims after a six-to-nine-month process, and the value of the bridge and its operating subsidiaries will have stabilized and they could satisfy all of their liquidity needs from the private sector, the FDIC would distribute the residual value of the bridge to the claims left behind in the parent's receivership in accordance with the priority of their claims and in satisfaction of their claims. The FDIC has various options as far as the form of value it could distribute. It could do a public offering of the bridge's equity and distribute the net proceeds to the receivership. It could distribute shares in the bridge to the receivership. Or it could distribute a combination of shares and the net proceeds from a partial public offering of the bridge's shares. Once a majority of the bridge's shares are sold to a trust in return for a promise to sell the shares to the public and distribute the net proceeds of the shares to the parent's receivership, the bridge should cease to be a bridge and its charter should be converted to that of an ordinary private-sector entity.[61]

7.55 The overarching benefit of the SPE method is that only the parent holding company is put into a receivership; the operating subsidiaries remain open and operating. This is important for several reasons. If the financial institution in question has cross-border operations, including foreign branches, the transfer of any assets of the branches is generally unenforceable or prohibited without the consent of foreign counterparties, foreign regulators or foreign courts. SPE avoids the need for those consents. It reduces or eliminates the incentive for foreign regulators to ringfence the foreign branches of operating subsidiaries, which are kept open and operating, and reduces the need for the FDIC to rely on cooperation from foreign authorities.

7.56 Another benefit is that by taking advantage of the structural subordination of long-term unsecured debt to short-term unsecured debt, the SPE strategy reduces or eliminates the incentive of demand depositors or other short-term creditors to run and the right of derivatives counterparties to terminate. This reduces or eliminates the likelihood of contagious panic throughout the financial system. Meanwhile, the orderly liquidation fund ensures that the bridge financial company will have access to sufficient secured liquidity to preserve going-concern value and prevent value destruction of valuable but illiquid assets.

D. Resolution under the US Bankruptcy Code

7.57 Despite the enactment of Title II of the Dodd–Frank Act, the US Bankruptcy Code remains the principal law under which non-bank financial companies are to be liquidated, recapitalized, or reorganized when they fail. Title II is only lawfully

---

[61] Dodd–Frank Act, § 210(h)(13) and (14), 12 USC § 5390(h)(13) and (14).

permitted to be invoked if resolution of a covered company would result in serious adverse effects to financial stability in the United States and Title II would avoid or mitigate those adverse effects.[62]

Existing US Bankruptcy Code

The US G-SIBs recently submitted their Title I resolution plans for 2015. Most of **7.58** them indicated in the public summaries of their plans that they believed they could be resolved under Chapter 11 of the existing US Bankruptcy Code pursuant to an SPE recapitalization strategy.[63] They identified the strategy as the one most likely to enable them to be resolved in a rapid and orderly manner without extraordinary government support and without imposing serious adverse effects on financial stability in the United States. Under this strategy, only the top-tier parent would be put into a bankruptcy proceeding. Most of the assets of the parent, including its ownership interests in all of its operating subsidiaries, would be transferred to a newly formed bridge company pursuant to section 363 of the US Bankruptcy Code. The failed parent's long-term unsecured debt would be left behind in the bankruptcy estate. The largely debt-free bridge holding company would be held by a trust for the benefit of the bankruptcy estate. Its shares would be sold in public or private sales or transferred to the parent's bankruptcy estate for distribution under a plan of reorganization in accordance with the priority of claims and interests in the bankruptcy case. Some or all of the operating subsidiaries would be recapitalized and remain open and operating, though they would shrink by 30–80 per cent as a by-product of the SPE strategy. Others would be sold or wound down in an orderly fashion outside of insolvency proceedings (i.e. a solvent wind-down).

The Failure Resolution Taskforce of the Bipartisan Policy Center issued a report **7.59** showing how an SPE recapitalization strategy could be carried out under Chapter 11 of the existing US Bankruptcy Code. But it also argued in favour of a proposed new Chapter 14 in order to make that outcome more legally certain and to minimize the need to use Title II of the Dodd–Frank Act in order to avoid or mitigate serious adverse effects on financial stability in the United States.[64]

Proposed new Chapter 14

In 2012, a working group at Stanford University's Hoover Institute proposed a new **7.60** Chapter 14 of the US Bankruptcy Code.[65] The purpose of new Chapter 14 was

---

[62] Dodd–Frank Act, § 203(b)(2) and (5), 12 USC § 5383(b)(2).

[63] Federal Reserve, Pubic Summaries of Title I Resolution Plans, available at: <http://www.federalreserve.gov/bankinforeg/resolution-plans.htm> (accessed 26 October 2015) (see Bank of America, Citigroup, Goldman Sachs, JP Morgan Chase, Morgan Stanley, and State Street).

[64] John F Bovenzi, Randall D Guynn, and Thomas H Jackson, *Too Big to Fail: The Path to a Solution*, A Report of the Failure Resolution Task Force of the Financial Regulatory Reform Initiative of the Bipartisan Policy Center (May 2013) 33–5, 80, 87.

[65] Thomas H Jackson, 'Bankruptcy Code Chapter 14: A Proposal' in Kenneth E Scott and John B Taylor (eds) *Bankruptcy Not Bailout: A Special Chapter 14* (Hoover Institution 2012).

either to replace Title II of the Dodd–Frank Act or minimize the circumstances under which Title II could be lawfully invoked.[66] As noted above, Title II may only be lawfully invoked if the resolution of a particular non-bank financial company under the US Bankruptcy Code would result in serious adverse effects to financial stability in the United States and the use of Title II would avoid or mitigate those effects.[67] The proponents of the new Chapter 14 believed that it would be more consistent with the rule of law than the Orderly Liquidation Authority in Title II of the Dodd–Frank Act and more likely to result in losses being imposed on the private sector instead of taxpayers.

7.61   The original version of proposed Chapter 14 defined 'financial institution' as any institution, including any subsidiaries, with $100 billion or more in assets 'that is substantially engaged in providing financial services or financial products.' However, while the original version of Chapter 14 would apply to insurance companies, stock brokers, and commodity brokers, it would not extend to IDIs.

7.62   The proposal greatly expanded the role of the failed institution's primary regulator. It granted the primary regulator standing to be heard as a party or to raise motions relevant to its regulations in any Chapter 14 proceeding. Moreover, to address potential systemic consequences from the failure, the primary regulator would be empowered to commence an involuntary case against the institution, including on the grounds of mark-to-market balance sheet insolvency or 'unreasonably small capital'. The primary regulator would also have standing to file motions for a quick sale of the failed company or any of its assets under section 363 of the Bankruptcy Code subject to court review. Finally, the primary regulator would be empowered to file a plan of reorganization for the institution at any time after the order for relief.

7.63   Another major element of the original proposal would be to permit the debtor-in-possession (DIP), through DIP financing provided by the government or the private sector, to 'advance' a partial or complete payout to certain liquidity-sensitive creditors before final distribution. These payouts would be subject to court approval and several burden of proof requirements including showings that the payout is necessary either for liquidity or systemic reasons, that the payout is less than a conservative estimate of the creditors' likely eventual payout, and that such prepayment is not likely to favour particular creditors. If the government provides the funding, the petitioners for such funding must show that no private funding on reasonably comparable terms is available.

---

[66]   Kenneth E Scott, 'A Guide to the Resolution of Failed Financial Institutions: Dodd–Frank Title II and Proposed Chapter 14' in Kenneth E Scott and John B Taylor (eds) *Bankruptcy Not Bailout: A Special Chapter 14* (Hoover Institution 2012) 23.

[67]   Dodd–Frank Act, § 203(b)(2) and (5), 12 USC § 5383(b)(2) and (5).

The proposal also directly addressed longstanding concerns over a lack of judi- **7.64**
cial experience and political pressure in bankruptcy proceedings, specifically those
involving large financial institutions. Here, the proposal required Chapter 14 cases
to be heard by a panel of Article III district court judges in the Second and DC
Circuits who have been selected by the Chief Justice of the United States.[68] The
idea is that the quality of US Article III judges would, on average, be higher than
that of US bankruptcy judges, and that Article III judges would be more resistant
to political pressure because unlike bankruptcy judges they have life tenure.[69] These
Article III judges would have exclusive jurisdiction along with the power to appoint
a special master from a pre-designated panel to hear the case and all proceedings
under it that could normally have been heard by a bankruptcy judge.

Proposed new Chapter 14 2.0

Largely in response to the development of the SPE recapitalization within resolu- **7.65**
tion strategy under Title II of the Dodd–Frank Act, the Hoover group updated and
expanded its original Chapter 14 proposal to include provisions that would facilitate an SPE strategy under the US Bankruptcy Code, calling this updated version
Chapter 14 2.0.[70]

The most significant change in Chapter 14 2.0 is the 'section 1405 transfer' provi- **7.66**
sion that would expressly authorize the 'quick sale' of a covered company's assets
to a newly created bridge financial company, while leaving behind in the bankruptcy estate all or any portion of the covered company's liabilities. By leaving
enough liabilities behind in the bankruptcy estate, such a quick sale to a bridge
financial company would result in the recapitalization of the business transferred
to the bridge financial company. Professor Jackson, the author of Chapter 14 2.0,
calls this technique the 'two-entity' recapitalization strategy, but he notes that it is
substantially identical to the FDIC's SPE strategy. At the core of this two-entity
recapitalization technique lie two principles: (i) that sufficient long-term unsecured debt must exist to be 'left behind' in the bankruptcy estate, and (ii) that
the bridge company otherwise owns the assets, rights, and liabilities of the former
holding company.

The section 1405 transfer allows either the institution or the Federal Reserve to **7.67**
make a motion to transfer the estate's property, contracts, and liabilities other than
capital structure debt to the newly created bridge company. The section 1405 transfer motion must be heard no sooner than twenty-four hours after its filing, and the

---

[68] Article III judges are those who have been appointed under Article III of the US Constitution.
District court judges are appointed under Article III. Bankruptcy judges are not.

[69] Bankruptcy judges are appointed for fourteen-year terms. 28 USC § 152.

[70] Thomas H Jackson, 'Building on Bankruptcy: A Revised Chapter 14 for Recapitalisation,
Reorganisation, or Liquidation of Large Financial Institutions' in Kenneth E Scott, Thomas H
Jackson, and John B Taylor (eds) *Making Failure Feasible: How Bankruptcy Reform Can End 'Too Big
to Fail'* (Hoover Institution 2015) 30–1.

court must rule within forty-eight hours after its filing. The court may approve the section 1405 transfer only upon finding (or the Federal Reserve certifying that it found) that 'the bridge company adequately provides assurance of future performance of any executory contract, unexpired lease, or debt agreement being transferred.' Although the bridge company is not generally subject to the jurisdiction of the Chapter 14 judge subsequent to the transfer, upon application by the bridge company the judge does retain jurisdiction for up to six months to award financing on terms applicable to DIP financing in section 1413.

7.68 The SPE provisions of Chapter 14 2.0 contain rules applicable to debts, executory contracts, and unexpired leases—including QFCs. Thus, these assets and liabilities may successfully be transferred to or assumed by the bridge company within the forty-eight-hour window and remain there, so 'business as usual' is taken over by the bridge company upon assumption. Specifically, this requires overriding certain contractual provisions regarding change of control, as well as '*ipso facto*' clauses allowing the termination or modification of contracts based on the commencement of a bankruptcy proceeding or a deterioration in the financial condition of the covered company, including ratings downgrades. Chapter 14 2.0 would also modify the 'safe harbours' for QFCs that would otherwise allow the immediate termination of QFCs of the covered company. These modifications and overrides would allow a bridge company to assume debt, executory contracts (including QFCs), and unexpired leases 'as if nothing happened' as opposed to it having been breached and accelerated. Importantly, they would apply equally with respect to contracts held by subsidiaries that are transferred to the bridge company. As the newly created bridge company will by definition have no long-term unsecured debt, Chapter 14 2.0 provides the bridge company a window during which it need not be in compliance with certain long-term unsecured debt requirements, such as those included in the Financial Stability Board's international standard for total loss absorbing capacity (TLAC).[71] This window terminates at the earlier of either (i) confirmation of the debtor's plan of reorganization that involves the distribution of securities (or proceeds from sales) of the bridge company, or (ii) one year from the section 1405 transfer.

7.69 In addition to the section 1405 transfer provision, Chapter 14 2.0 would make other significant changes to the initial Chapter 14 proposal. The definition of 'covered financial corporation' is revised to include institutions with consolidated assets of more than $50 billion, other than bank (subject to FDIC resolution), stockbroker, or commodity broker subsidiaries. The definition expressly excludes 'financial market infrastructure corporations' such as central counterparty clearinghouses. Also, the new version of Chapter 14 would require at least one district court judge in each circuit to be selected by the Chief Justice of the United States for Chapter 14

---

[71] Financial Stability Board, Principles on Loss-absorbing and Recapitalisation Capacity of G-SIBs in Resolution: Total Loss-absorbing Capacity (TLAC) Term Sheet 9 November 2015.

cases. Those cases that involve a section 1405 transfer need only be handled by the designated judge up to the point of transfer, and the designated judge may appoint a bankruptcy judge to assist as special master.

The role of the regulators would differ significantly in Chapter 14 2.0. If the Federal **7.70** Reserve determines, after consultation with the Secretary of the Treasury and the FDIC, that commencement of a Chapter 14 case is 'necessary to avoid serious adverse effects on the financial stability of the United States', it may file a petition on behalf of the company that is equivalent to a voluntary petition. The Federal Reserve and the primary regulator would retain their standing from the initial proposal to be heard on any issue relevant to the regulation of the institution and the Federal Reserve also has standing to be heard on any issue affecting 'the financial stability of the United States'. The FDIC is granted more limited standing, relating solely to the opportunity to be heard in a section 1405 transfer.

Financial Institutions Bankruptcy Act

On 1 December 2014, the US House of Representatives passed the Financial **7.71** Institutions Bankruptcy Act (FIBA), which would add a new subchapter V to existing Chapter 11 of the US Bankruptcy Code.[72] FIBA resembles in many ways the SPE provisions of Chapter 14 2.0. The House introduced a new bill in 2015 that is substantially identical to the 2014 bill.[73] Like the SPE portion of Chapter 14 2.0, this bill was designed primarily to facilitate an SPE resolution strategy under the US Bankruptcy Code. In particular, it would expressly authorize the transfer of all or substantially all of the assets of a covered company to a new bridge company, while leaving all capital structure liabilities behind in the bankruptcy case. In exchange, the debtor institution would retain a beneficial interest in the new bridge company through a private trust that holds the bridge company's equity, or sale proceeds thereof, for the benefit of the bankruptcy estate.

FIBA applies to 'covered financial corporations', which mirror the 'covered **7.72** financial companies' definition in Title II of the Dodd–Frank Act, and would include (i) BHCs and (ii) corporations that have total consolidated assets greater than $50 billion and are primarily engaged in financial activities, other than stockbrokers, commodity brokers, or institutions such as banks, insurance companies, and similar institutions that are not eligible to be debtors under the Bankruptcy Code.

---

[72] Financial Institutions Bankruptcy Act of 2014, HR 5421, 113th Cong (2014) (as passed by the House on 8 December 2014). Statement of Donald S Bernstein, Partner, Davis Polk, *Hearing Before The Subcomm on Regulatory Reform, Commercial and Antitrust Law, H Comm on Judiciary* (15 July 2014).
[73] Financial Institutions Bankruptcy Act of 2015, HR 2947, 114th Cong (2015) (as introduced in the House on 7 July 2015). Statements of Donald S Bernstein and Richard Levin, *Hearing Before The Subcomm on Regulatory Reform, Commercial and Antitrust Law, H Comm on Judiciary* (9 July 2015).

7.73 Taken together, FIBA's provisions would accomplish four things: (i) expressly permit a quick transfer of a covered company's assets to a new bridge company; (ii) facilitate the recapitalization of the business transferred to the bridge by permitting the covered company to leave behind in the bankruptcy estate all capital structure debt; (iii) impose certain restrictions on creditors' rights; and (iv) amend the safe harbours for QFCs to impose a temporary forty-eight-hour stay on the exercise of close-out rights and a permanent override of any cross-defaults based on the parent's or another affiliate's failure or financial condition, if certain conditions are satisfied.

7.74 As proposed, FIBA authorizes the Federal Reserve to file an involuntarily case against a covered company if it shows that the commencement of the case and the transfer to a bridge company is necessary to prevent imminent substantial harm to financial stability in the United States. Any dispute over an involuntary filing must be resolved within twenty-four hours after the petition is filed. Regulators, including the Federal Reserve, the SEC, the Office of the Comptroller of the Currency, and the FDIC each have standing to appear and be heard on any issue in the case. Finally, FIBA mandates that the Chief Justice of the Supreme Court designate at least ten bankruptcy and at least twelve appellate court judges, three in each of four districts, to be available to hear cases under subchapter V.

Taxpayer Protection and Responsible Resolution Act

7.75 The Taxpayer Protection and Responsible Resolution Act (TPRRA) was introduced in the Senate in December 2013.[74] A substantially revised version of TPRRA was reintroduced in 2015.[75] The new version is substantially similar to FIBA, except that it would add a new Chapter 14 to the US Bankruptcy Code instead of a new subchapter V of Chapter 11, repeal Title II of the Dodd–Frank Act, and impose restrictions on the Federal Reserve's authority to provide DIP financing to the covered company or the bankruptcy estate. It also would not give the Federal Reserve a right to initiate an involuntary petition and would not impose a minimum dollar threshold on the definition of covered financial corporation.

National Bankruptcy Conference

7.76 The National Bankruptcy Conference (NBC), a voluntary, non-partisan, not-for-profit organization composed of about sixty of the leading bankruptcy judges, professors, and practitioners in the United States, wrote a letter

---

[74] Taxpayer Protection and Responsible Resolution Act, S. 1861, 113th Cong (2013).
[75] Taxpayer Protection and Responsible Resolution Act, S. 1840, 114th Cong, 1st Sess (2015). Statements of Thomas H Jackson, Randall D Guynn, and John B Taylor, *Hearing before the Subcomm on Fin Inst and Consumer Protection, S Comm on Banking, Fin and Urban Affairs* (29 June 2015).

commenting on FIBA and TPRRA.[76] While commending both bills for facilitating the SPE resolution strategy under the Bankruptcy Code, the NBC provided five comments:

- Title II of the Dodd–Frank Act should not be repealed;
- regulators should have the power to continue supervising the operations of a systemically important financial institution (SIFI) being resolved in a bankruptcy case;
- regulators should not be given the power to commence a bankruptcy case against a covered company;
- the legislation should not impose any limitations on the power of the Federal Reserve to provide lender-of-last-resort liquidity to a recapitalized firm; and
- bankruptcy judges should not be replaced by Article III district judges in bankruptcy cases for resolving SIFIs.

---

[76] Letter dated 18 June 2015 from the NBC to the Honourable Tom Marino, Chairman, House Subcommittee on Regulatory Reform, Commercial and Antitrust Law; the Honourable Hank Johnson, Ranking Member, House Subcommittee on Regulatory Reform, Commercial and Antitrust Law; the Honourable Chuck Grassley, Chairman, Senate Committee on the Judiciary; and the Honourable Patrick J. Leahy, Ranking Member, Senate Committee on the Judiciary.

8

RESOLUTION PLANNING

A. Title I Plans

8.01 Section 165(d) under Title I of the Dodd–Frank Act requires all bank holding companies (BHCs) and foreign banking organizations with assets of $50 billion or more, as well as any non-bank financial institution that has been designated as systemically important, to prepare and regularly update a resolution plan (Title I Resolution Plan).[1] A resolution plan is a plan for liquidating, reorganizing, or otherwise resolving a systemically important financial institution (SIFI) that has reached the point of insolvency, non-viability, or failure. It is the last stage along the full continuum of contingency planning from risk management to early remediation to recovery planning to resolution planning that is sometimes referred to as a 'living will'.[2] Activating the resolution plan would be a last resort, when various ex ante solutions designed to reduce the likelihood of failure have been unsuccessful.

8.02 The Title I Resolution Plans are required to be divided into a public section and a confidential section. The confidential section is more extensive than the public section and must include an executive summary, detailed information about organizational structure, resolution strategies, corporate governance, management information systems, interconnections and interdependencies, supervisory and regulatory issues, and contact information.[3] The public section is similar, but the description is meant to be significantly less detailed so that financial institutions can protect confidential proprietary and supervisory information.

8.03 Most importantly, the Title I Resolution Plan must include specific information about the financial institution's resolution strategies, which is its plan for 'rapid and orderly resolution'.[4] This is defined as 'a reorganisation or liquidation of the covered company...under the Bankruptcy Code that can be accomplished within a

---

[1] Dodd–Frank Act, § 165(d), 12 USC § 5365(d).
[2] The Federal Reserve and the FDIC have used the term 'living will' interchangeably with 'resolution plan'. See 76 US Federal Register 67323, 67323 (1 November 2011).
[3] 12 CFR § 243.4.
[4] 12 CFR § 243.4(c).

reasonable period of time and in a manner that substantially mitigates the risk that the failure of the covered company would have serious adverse effects on financial stability in the United States'.[5] Under the implementing regulations, these resolution plans must assume that the covered company is resolved under the US Bankruptcy Code or other applicable insolvency law, and that no 'extraordinary support' from the United States or any other government would be available. Each Title I Resolution Plan is also required to explain how it would work under the most recent 'baseline', 'adverse', and 'severely adverse' macroeconomic scenarios provided to the financial institution by the Federal Reserve in connection with the Comprehensive Capital Analysis and Review (CCAR) stress-testing and capital planning process.[6]

Domestic financial institutions must include information for their worldwide **8.04** operations, including material entities, critical operations, and core business lines.[7] 'Material entity' refers to a subsidiary or foreign office of the financial institution that is significant to the activities of a critical operation or core business line.[8] 'Critical operations' are the operations of the financial institution and its material entities, including associated services, functions, and support, the failure or discontinuation of which, in the view of the financial institution or as jointly directed by the Federal Reserve and the Federal Deposit Insurance Corporation (FDIC), would pose a threat to the financial stability of the United States.[9] 'Core business lines' means the business lines of the financial institution and its material entities, including associated operations, services, functions, and support that, in the view of the financial institution, upon failure would result in a material loss of revenue, profit, or franchise value.[10] For foreign banking organizations, the information is only required with respect to their operations that are domiciled or conducted in whole or in part in the United States, along with information about any interconnections or interdependencies between the United States and foreign operations, and how the US resolution plan is integrated into the organization's overall resolution or contingency planning process.

B. IDI Plans

The FDIC separately requires all US insured depository institutions (IDIs) with **8.05** assets of $50 billion or more to submit and regularly update a separate resolution plan (IDI Resolution Plan).[11] Although the two processes were designed to be complementary of each other and the requirements for both have been substantially

---

[5] 12 CFR § 243.2(o).
[6] 12 CFR § 243.4(a)(4)(i).
[7] 12 CFR § 243.4(a)(1).
[8] 12 CFR § 243.2(l).
[9] 12 CFR § 243.2(g).
[10] 12 CFR § 243.2(d).
[11] 12 CFR § 360.10.

similar, there is a growing divergence between the sets of assumptions each firm is supposed to use for the two types of resolution plans. For example, the FDIC issued new guidance in December 2014 that requires financial institutions to provide a fully developed discussion and analysis of a range of realistic resolution strategies, including a break-up and sell strategy, which the FDIC calls a multi-acquirer strategy. It also requires IDI Resolution Plans to include a second strategy that involves the liquidation of the company, including a payout of insured deposits.[12] These changes may create greater divergence between the two types of resolution plans.

8.06 The IDI Resolution Plans have substantially similar requirements as Title I Plans, including a requirement to file public and confidential portions of the plans. There are, however, important differences between the two types of plans, the most important of which relates to their objectives. The FDIC has indicated that the Title I Plans focus principally on financial stability, whereas the IDI Plans may focus on other objectives.

C. Grading the Plans

8.07 In order to facilitate review of a financial institution's Title I Resolution Plan, the institution must provide the Federal Reserve and the FDIC with such information and access to personnel as the Federal Reserve and the FDIC jointly determine is necessary to assess the credibility of the plan and the ability of the financial institution to implement it. The Federal Reserve and the FDIC must jointly determine within sixty days of receiving an initial or annual resolution plan under Title I whether the plan satisfies the minimum informational requirements. If the regulators decide that the plan is deficient, the financial institution must submit the additional requested information no later than thirty days after receiving notice.

8.08 If the regulators both decide that a Title I Resolution Plan is not credible, they must jointly notify the financial institution in writing of such a determination. Neither agency may unilaterally give such notice of deficiencies without the consent of another.[13] After such an issue is issued, the financial institution must submit a revised resolution plan within ninety days of receiving such a notice, unless the Federal Reserve and the FDIC jointly determine otherwise.

8.09 If the financial institution fails to cure the deficiency in its Title I Resolution Plan, the Federal Reserve and the FDIC may jointly impose on the institution, or any of its subsidiaries, more stringent capital, leverage, or liquidity requirements or restrictions on growth, activities, or operations.[14] Any requirements

---

[12] FDIC, *Guidance for Covered Insured Depository Institution Resolution Plan Submissions* (17 December 2014).

[13] 12 CFR § 243.5(a)(2).

[14] 12 CFR § 243.6(a).

or restrictions imposed in response to a failure to cure resolution plan deficiencies would apply until the date when the Federal Reserve and the FDIC jointly determine that the financial institution has submitted a revised resolution plan that adequately remedies the deficiencies.[15] If the financial institution fails to do so within the first two years following the imposition of such requirements, the financial institution would face the further threat of mandated divestitures (ie, breakup).[16] There are conditions and procedures that the Federal Reserve and the FDIC must follow prior to making such determinations and neither agency may unilaterally act without the consent of the other. The regulations for the IDI Resolution Plan are not so specific in detailing the possible list of consequences for non-compliance.

In 2014, the Federal Reserve and the FDIC issued letters to each of the eleven larg-   **8.10** est US and non-US global SIFIs, known colloquially as the 'first-wave' or July filers, listing the shortcomings of the filers' 2013 Title I Resolution Plans.[17] The FDIC determined that the plans submitted by these first-wave filers were not credible and did not facilitate an orderly resolution. The Federal Reserve did not make a credibility determination. Instead, the Federal Reserve simply joined with the FDIC in writing letters to each of the eleven first-wave filers outlining the shortcomings in their 2013 plans and requiring them to address these shortcomings in their 2015 plans. As only one of the two agencies have determined that the 2013 plans are not credible, the draconian remedies under section 165(d) of the Dodd–Frank Act were not activated. However, both agencies agreed that, if the July filers do not submit plans responsive to the identified shortcomings in their 2015 plans, the agencies would expect to use their authority under section 165(d) of the Dodd–Frank Act to jointly determine that the resolution plans are not credible.

The US regulators have continued to issue new guidelines and expectations, which   **8.11** will probably continue to evolve over time. The increasing burden of new regulations will also continue to put downward pressure on the market value of the US G-SIBs. This escalating burden could eventually result in shareholder pressure to downsize or restructure, if that would actually reduce the regulatory burden, which is far from clear.

D. Cross-border Cooperation and Coordination

Many large US financial companies have international operations outside the   **8.12** US through a network of branches, offices, and subsidiaries. These branches,

---

[15]   12 CFR § 243.6(b).
[16]   12 CFR § 243.6(c).
[17]   Joint Press Release, Federal Reserve and the FDIC, *Agencies Provide Feedback on Second Round Resolution Plans of 'First-Wave' Filers* (5 August 2014).

offices, and subsidiaries are generally subject to different insolvency laws or special resolution regimes in different national jurisdictions. For a long time, there was no set of international agreements or arrangements that existed to provide any overarching coordination if a major cross-border financial firm failed. Following the global financial panic of 2008, regulatory agencies in different national jurisdictions have turned their attention to making arrangements for a potential cross-border failure. If such arrangements are not put into place or turn out to be unsatisfactory, there is a fear that each jurisdiction will attempt to grab assets and control as much of the process as possible in order to protect its own citizens—perhaps beneficial for the residents of the country fortunate enough to have substantial assets within its boundaries, but perhaps not helpful in promoting global financial stability.

8.13 Under the Dodd–Frank Act, the FDIC is required to consult with the state and federal regulators of each covered financial company in exercising its powers as receiver.[18] The FDIC is also required to consult with the primary regulators for non-US subsidiaries and coordinate regarding the resolution of those entities.[19]

8.14 As part of its efforts to improve cross-board coordination of resolutions, the FDIC has contacted regulators in a number of foreign jurisdictions on an individual basis. In 2012, the FDIC released a joint paper with the Bank of England, *Resolving Globally Active, Systemically Important, Financial Institutions.*[20] In the paper, the FDIC and the Bank of England expressed a commitment to developing an SPE resolution strategy in both jurisdictions. As the paper notes, one advantage of the SPE resolution strategy for cross-border coordination is that it does not require the commencement of separate territorial or entity-focused insolvency proceedings. The home jurisdiction would oversee a resolution of the top entity while the foreign subsidiaries and branches largely continue to operate as they did before, albeit with substantially smaller balance sheets reflecting the losses at subsidiaries that gave rise to the parent's failure and the sale of subsidiary assets during the resolution process to ensure sufficient funding for their continuing operations.[21] The paper was an outgrowth of a Memorandum of Understanding (MOU) entered into in 2010 by the FDIC and the Bank of England.[22] The FDIC has pursued MOUs with a

---

[18] Dodd–Frank Act, § 204(c), 12 USC § 5384(c).

[19] Dodd–Frank Act, § 210(a)(1)(N), 12 USC § 5390(a)(1)(N).

[20] FDIC and Bank of England, Joint Paper, *Resolving Globally Active, Systemically Important, Financial Institutions* (10 December 2012).

[21] For examples of this balance sheet reduction under an SPE resolution strategy, see the public summaries of the 2015 Title I resolution plans of Bank of America, Citigroup, Goldman Sachs, J.P. Morgan Chase, Morgan Stanley, and State Street which are available at <https://www.fdic.gov/regulations/reform/resplans/> (accessed 12 January 2016).

[22] FDIC and Bank of England, Memorandum of Understanding Concerning Consultation, Cooperation and the Exchange of Information Related to the Resolution of Insured Depository Institutions with Cross-Border Operations in the United States and the United Kingdom (22 January 2010).

number of regulators around the world in an effort to secure similar commitments to cross-border cooperation.[23]

In 2011 at the Cannes summit, the G20 endorsed the *Key Attributes of Effective* **8.15**
Resolution Regimes for Financial Institutions ('Key Attributes') which had been published by the Financial Stability Board.[24] The Key Attributes identified the core elements a resolution framework should include in order to bring about an orderly resolution of financial firms. A revised draft of the Key Attributes was adopted by the G20 in 2014 that retained the original twelve Key Attributes and added appendices to deal with financial market infrastructures, insurers, and the treatment of client assets.[25]

The Key Attributes have become a common starting point for discussions of **8.16**
cross-border cooperation in resolution. Several of the Key Attributes promote the establishment of specialized resolution regimes that are designed to facilitate cross-border cooperation. At the most basic level, this takes the form of promoting resolution regimes that are predisposed to a cross-border perspective. For example, the Key Attributes call for specialized resolution regimes to be enacted with one of their statutory objectives being that the resolution authorities duly consider the potential impact of their resolution actions on the financial stability of other jurisdictions. Another of the Key Attributes is that part of the statutory mandate of a resolution authority should be to strongly encourage a cooperative solution with foreign resolution authorities whenever possible.

In addition to promoting a general disposition towards cross-border cooper- **8.17**
ation, the Key Attributes recommend the creation of Crisis Management Groups (CMGs) as an important element of an effective resolution regime. A CMG is focused on the orderly resolution of a specific financial institution and can include the supervisory authorities, central banks, resolution authorities, and finance ministries from that financial institution's home jurisdiction and from any jurisdiction that is host to subsidiaries or branches of that institution that are material to its resolution. CMGs are charged with reviewing the coordination and information-sharing between the entities in the CMG and with other authorities where the

---

[23] FDIC and China Banking Regulatory Commission, Appendix to Memorandum of Understanding between the China Banking Regulatory Commission and the Federal Deposit Insurance Corporation to Address Cross-Border Resolutions (26 May 2010); FDIC and Canadian Deposit Insurance Corporation, Memorandum of Understanding Concerning the Resolution of Insured Depository Institutions and Certain Other Financial Companies with Cross-Border Operations in the United States and Canada (12 June 2013); FDIC and People's Bank of China, Memorandum of Understanding between Federal Deposit Insurance Corporation and People's Bank of China Regarding Cooperation, Technical Assistance and Cross Border Resolutions (24 October 2013).

[24] Financial Stability Board, *Key Attributes of Effective Resolution Regimes for Financial Institutions* (October 2011).

[25] Financial Stability Board, *Key Attributes of Effective Resolution Regimes for Financial Institutions* (Updated Version, 15 October 2014).

financial institution has a systemic presence, as well as reviewing the recovery and resolution planning process for that financial institution. The CMG provides periodic updates to the Financial Stability Board of the progress that has been made in these areas. By the autumn of 2014, CMGs were put in place for all banking groups designated as global systemically important banks (G-SIBs) by the Financial Stability Board. The FDIC has been an active participant in the CMGs for the US G-SIBs.

8.18 The 2014 International Swaps and Derivatives Association Resolution Stay Protocol (ISDA Protocol)[26] and the Financial Stability Board's international standard on total loss-absorbing capacity (TLAC),[27] which was finalized in 2015 represent two of the most important accomplishments in cross-border cooperation.[28] Among other things, the ISDA Protocol requires adhering parties to give extraterritorial effect to provisions in special resolution regimes that would impose temporary stays on the exercise of remedies in ISDA Master Agreements or would override cross-defaults in those agreements based on a parent or other affiliate's failure or financial distress, as well as agree to contractual limitations on the exercise of cross-defaults to a parent or other affiliate becoming subject to proceedings under the US Bankruptcy Code or certain other US insolvency regimes. Eighteen G-SIBs have agreed to adhere to the ISDA Protocol.[29] US, European, and other regulators are exploring ways to expand the range of financial contracts and counterparties that are subject to the provisions of the ISDA Protocol.

8.19 In response to the global financial panic of 2008, a strong interest in expanding resolution authority took root in the United States. This chapter has described the fundamental characteristics of resolution authority as conceived and implemented in the United States. The United States has long had a workable model for resolving community banks, mid-size banks, and even some regional banks. It has recently adapted that model to larger and more complex financial institutions, including the US G-SIBs. The FDIC has developed an SPE recapitalization within resolution framework that is widely viewed as the most promising model for resolving the US G-SIBs in a manner that maximizes the value of the enterprise for the benefit of its stakeholders, preserves critical operations, and promotes financial stability without the need for any taxpayer-funded bail-outs. Various bankruptcy lawyers have also

---

[26] International Swaps and Derivatives Association, Inc. (ISDA), ISDA 2014 Resolution Stay Protocol.

[27] Financial Stability Board, *Adequacy of Loss-Absorbing Capacity of Global Systemically Important Banks in resolution* (10 November 2014).

[28] Financial Stability Board, Principles on Loss-absorbing and Recapitalisation Capacity of G-SIBs in Resolution: Total Loss-absorbing Capacity (TLAC) Term Sheet (9 November 2015). For summary of the FSB's final international TLAC standard, see chapter 4 of this book. ; Federal Reserve Board and FDIC Joint Press Release, *Federal Reserve Board and FDIC Welcome ISDA Announcement* (October 2014).

[29] News Release, ISDA, *Major Banks Agree to Sign ISDA Resolution Stay Protocol* (11 October 2014).

developed ways to implement that strategy under either Title II of the Dodd–Frank Act or Chapter 11 of the US Bankruptcy Code. The United States is also examining various proposals to add a new Chapter 14 to the US Bankruptcy Code in order to facilitate the successful implementation of an SPE strategy under the US Bankruptcy Code. The FDIC has also engaged in substantial efforts to coordinate the cross-border resolution of a US G-SIB with other resolution authorities around the world.

PART III

THE EU RESOLUTION REGIME

9

RESOLUTION IN
THE EUROPEAN UNION

A. Introduction

The threat of bank failures forced many individual EU member states to intro- **9.01**
duce domestic legislation before the European Union as a whole could respond.
However, these regimes tended to follow a common pattern, in that their draftsmen
all, to one degree or another, looked to the bank resolution provisions of the US
Federal Deposit Insurance Act (FDIA) as an intellectual template.[1] Whereas bank
failure in the European Union has been relatively uncommon, the structure of the
US banking market means that the FDIC has, since its formation in 1933, resolved
an average of forty-three insured banks and other insured depository institutions a
year since 1933[2] when the FDIA was first enacted, and as a result the FDIC is the
undisputed leader in the field of bank resolution mechanisms. This means that the
bank resolution regimes introduced by many states after the global financial crisis
of 2008 tended to share a common intellectual DNA.

Scope

In general, regulators tend to make a clear distinction between banks and other **9.02**
forms of financial business, and a bank resolution regime was initially envisaged
as being applicable—as the name implies—only to banks. The logic of this—that
banks are special because they accept retail deposits and provide access to the
payment system—is clear. However, in the aftermath of a crisis in which the
first victims—Bear Stearns and Lehman Brothers—were not banks, it rapidly

---

[1] The bank resolution statute consists of §§ 11–15 of the FDIA, 12 USC §§ 1821–1825, plus
certain definitions and other supplementary provisions scattered throughout the FDIA, but the most
important provisions for purposes of this chapter are §§ 11 and 13, 12 USC §§ 1821 and 1823.

[2] FDIC website, 'Historical statistics on banking'. This figure includes the year 1989, when at
the peak of the savings and loan crisis FDIC resolved 534 banks. In a 'normal' year (such as the years
between 1940 and 1980, and 1994 and 2008) there might be around ten resolutions. There have
only been two years in the whole of FDICs history when there were no bank resolutions at all (2005
and 2006).

became abundantly clear that the failure of an investment firm could do just as much damage to the financial system as the failure of a deposit taking bank. As a result, the EU resolution regime is explicitly applied to banks and investment firms alike.

9.03 Mention at this point should also be made of the EU financial group legislation. The European Union does not have the equivalent of the US Bank Holding Company legislation—there is no process set out in the European Union by which an EU bank or investment firm holding company is registerable as such, or which imposes formal legal restrictions and obligations on bank holding companies.[3] However, the EU does impose regulatory reporting obligations on bank holding companies indirectly through the bank concerned (for this purpose a 'bank holding company' is an unregulated entity a majority of the activities of whose subsidiaries consist of either banking or investment business). As a result, the EU resolution regime also provides powers to resolve these entities.

9.04 Another EU difficulty arises in the context of central counterparties (CCPs). CCPs perform a number of bank-like functions, and in particular they hold collateral balances like banks for their members. More importantly for our purposes, they also take the (generally cash) margin deposited with them and invest it in assets, generating their profits from this spread. They are therefore vulnerable to runs in the same way that banks are, and as a result a number of EU jurisdictions require that CCPs be authorized banks; partly (prior to the European Markets and Infrastructure Regulation[4]) in order to subject them to capital requirements and partly to ensure that they have access to the liquidity window of the local central bank in case of need. The application of bank resolution tools to CCPs remains, at the time of writing, one of the biggest policy challenges facing government, and as a result when the scope of the BRRD is set out it is made clear (in recital 8) that they are excluded from the current directive.

Commencement of resolution

9.05 As regards the commencement of resolution, recital 41 of the Bank Recovery and Resolution Directive (BRRD) sets out the default position that the determination as to when resolution should be commenced should be made by the supervisory authority, and only exceptionally and by concession by the resolution authority. It also summarizes the basic principles for a resolution determination as follows:

> The fact that an institution does not meet the requirements for authorization should not justify per se the entry into resolution, especially if the institution is

---

[3] Although equally there is nothing that prevents it, and some member states do regulate bank holding companies as such.

[4] However, European Market Infrastructure Regulation (EMIR) recognizes the continuation of dual-status, with some EU clearing houses being both banks and EMIR-authorized CCPs.

still or likely to still be viable. An institution should be considered as failing or likely to fail when it is or is likely in the near future to be in breach of the requirements for continuing authorization, when the assets of the institution are or are likely in the near future to be less than its liabilities, when the institution is or is likely in the near future to be unable to pay its debts as they fall due, or when the institution requires extraordinary public financial support except in the particular circumstances set out in this Directive. The need for emergency liquidity assistance from a central bank should not in itself be a condition that sufficiently demonstrates that an institution is or will be, in the near future, unable to pay its liabilities as they fall due.

The recital also provides that resolution should not be triggered where, as a precau-   **9.06**
tionary measure, a member state takes an equity stake in an institution, including an institution which is publicly owned, which complies with its capital requirements. It gives as an example of this situation the position where an institution is required to raise new capital by scenario-based stress test, but is unable to raise capital privately in markets.

In the context of holding companies, the trigger for resolution must of course be the   **9.07**
insolvency of the bank subsidiary, not the holding company itself.

The BRRD sets out two sets of conditions for the commencement of   **9.08**
resolution—one for institutions[5] (Article 32) and one for holding companies and financial institutions (Article 33). The core conditions for both are set out in Article 32(1):

> Member states shall ensure that resolution authorities shall take a resolution action in relation to an institution referred to in point (a) of Article 1(1) only if the resolution authority considers that all of the following conditions are met:
> (a) the determination that the institution is failing or is likely to fail has been made by the competent authority, after consulting the resolution authority, or subject to the conditions laid down in paragraph 2, by the resolution authority after consulting the competent authority;
> (b) having regard to timing and other relevant circumstances, there is no reasonable prospect that any alternative private sector measures, including measures by an Institutional Protection Scheme, or supervisory action, including early intervention measures or the write down or conversion of relevant capital instruments in accordance with Article 59(2) taken in respect of the institution, would prevent the failure of the institution within a reasonable timeframe;
> (c) a resolution action is necessary in the public interest pursuant to paragraph 5.

Article 32(4) sets out the detailed meaning of the first condition—'failing or likely   **9.09**
to fail'—as follows:

(a) the institution infringes or there are objective elements to support a determination that the institution will, in the near future, infringe the requirements for continuing authorization in a way that would justify the withdrawal of

---

[5] Referred to in the vernacular of the BRRD as 'an institution referred to in point (a) of Article 1(1)'.

the authorization by the competent authority including but not limited to because the institution has incurred or is likely to incur losses that will deplete all or a significant amount of its own funds;

(b) the assets of the institution are or there are objective elements to support a determination that the assets of the institution will, in the near future, be less than its liabilities;

(c) the institution is or there are objective elements to support a determination that the institution will, in the near future, be unable to pay its debts or other liabilities as they fall due;

(d) extraordinary public financial support is required except when, in order to remedy a serious disturbance in the economy of a member state and preserve financial stability, the extraordinary public financial support takes any of the following forms:

    (i) a state guarantee to back liquidity facilities provided by central banks according to the central banks' conditions;

    (ii) a state guarantee of newly issued liabilities; or

    (iii) an injection of own funds or purchase of capital instruments at prices and on terms that do not confer an advantage upon the institution, where neither the circumstances referred to in point (a), (b), or (c) of this paragraph nor the circumstances referred to in Article 59(3) are present at the time the public support is granted.

9.10 It should be noted that (a) indicates that any breach of the threshold conditions, and not merely one which is financial, may be sufficient to trigger resolution. Threshold conditions set out the minimum requirements that regulated firms must meet in order to be permitted to carry on regulated activities (such as taking deposits) and include requirements to maintain liquidity, to have appropriate resources to measure, monitor and manage risk, to be fit and proper and to conduct their business prudently, as well as requirements to maintain sufficient capital.

9.11 The second condition is that it must not be reasonably likely that action will be taken—outside the resolution regime—that will result in the firm no longer failing or likely to fail. In effect, this means that the recovery plan must have been exhausted, and that no further proposals made by the management of the firm concerned have any reasonable likelihood of being successful. When making this determination, the resolution authority must take into account the requirement that any remaining regulatory capital must be written down or converted once the firm is no longer viable (that is, once it is failing or likely to fail) before stabilization tools can be used.

9.12 Part of the reason that this is likely to be an increasingly difficult determination for the authorities to make is the fact that bank creditors, faced with the threat of resolution action by the authorities, are increasingly likely to want to renegotiate financing themselves. It is notable in this respect that in the United

Kingdom, the proposed bail-in of the Co-op Bank in 2013[6] resulted not in an actual bail-in, but in a negotiated restructuring with the bank's bondholders. Bondholders faced with the threat of bail-in will prefer to negotiate their positions, but will wish to maintain a hard line with bank management whist negotiations continue. Thus those responsible for triggering resolution in the future will face a difficult determination as to when negotiated restructuring is no longer possible. In this regard it is important to remember that the determination which the authorities are required to make is based on judgement; for example, the standard is 'reasonably likely' to rather than 'certain' to, and forward-looking, for example, action could be taken if the firm is 'likely to fail', rather than 'will fail'.

It is very unlikely that any institution will in fact be found to be balance-sheet insolv- **9.13**
ent. Institutions in general fail because of lack of access to liquidity well before they reach balance-sheet insolvency. Thus the judgement to be made by the authorities will never be a simple valuation exercise.

Financial institutions

Where the power to impose resolution is to be deployed as regards other group **9.14**
members, Article 33 specifies how the triggers are to be applied as regards group members other than the bank itself. By Article 33(1), this extends to 'financial institutions'.[7]

The concept of 'financial institution' is an essential but imponderable element **9.15**
of the EU regulatory framework. In essence, a 'financial institution' for this purpose is an entity which engages in one of a number of particular types of activity,[8] whether regulated or not. The list of activities giving rise to this status includes lending, leasing, payment services, custody, giving guarantees, and (importantly) acting as a holding company. Because not all of these activities require regulation, the class of 'financial institutions' includes a number of entities which are not authorized. The key issue as regards 'financial institution' status for this purpose is that only financial institutions may be included in the consolidated return produced by a bank group—entities within the group which are not financial institutions are not consolidated into the regulatory return, and equity investments in them are required to be deducted from the capital of the consolidated group.

Where a financial institution has as its parent a regulated bank, Article 33(1) pro- **9.16**
vides that the financial institution itself may be placed in resolution provided that

---

[6] 'The Co-operative Group announces outcome of review of The Co-operative Bank's capital position', The Co-operative Banking Group, 17 June 2013.
[7] Again, referred to in the BRRD vernacular as 'an institution referred to in point (b) of Article 1(1)'.
[8] Specifically, those listed in Annexe 1 to the Capital Requirements Directive (CRD).

the ordinary resolution conditions apply both to the financial institution itself and to a bank which is its parent. Article 33(2). Thus, a financial institution may not be placed in resolution where it does not itself satisfy the conditions for resolution, even if its parent does satisfy them. The same principle is—in theory—applied to holding companies[9] and parent companies in EU member states.[10,11] However, Article 33(4) provides an override to this principle, in that parent and holding companies may be placed in resolution even if they do not themselves satisfy the criteria for resolution provided that 'their assets and liabilities are such that their failure threatens an institution or the group as a whole...and [their] resolution is necessary for the resolution of such subsidiaries as are banking institutions'. It is hard to think of many bank parent or holding companies which would not satisfy this condition.

9.17 This process does, however, create an interesting problem where a bank in one EU jurisdiction has a holding company in a different jurisdiction. Although the bank may be failing, the holding company may not be, and it is necessary in such a situation for the authorities in the jurisdiction where the holding company is located to be able to intervene. In such a case, responsibility for commencement cannot be left with the competent authority of the holding company, since the holding company may not be regulated by that competent authority, or at all. Thus the determination as to whether to commence resolution at the holding company level must be made by the resolution authority (in the United Kingdom, the resolution authority is given this power by ss 81A and 81B of the Banking Act (BA), which enable it to be exercised directly where an institution in the group is likely to fail. Where the institution is in a different jurisdiction, however, that determination is properly made by the competent authority in the jurisdiction concerned. Thus the Bank of England, as resolution authority, is given a power to intervene to resolve a holding company which has a bank subsidiary in a member state other than the United Kingdom, where the competent authority in the jurisdiction where the subsidiary institution is located determines that that institution is failing.

9.18 In May 2015 the European Banking Authority (EBA) published guidance on what is meant by 'failing or likely to fail' in the context of the BRRD. This was an attempt by the EBA to promote the convergence of supervisory and resolution practices regarding the interpretation of the different circumstances when an institution should be considered as failing or likely to fail,[12] and is required by Article 32(4) of the BRRD. The Guidelines provide guidance on the objective

---

[9] Including financial holding companies, mixed financial holding companies, and mixed-activity holding companies, collectively 'Institutions referred to in point (c) of Article (1)'.

[10] Institutions referred to in point (d) of Art 1(1).

[11] Art 33 2(2).

[12] EBA/GL/2015/07 of 26 May 2015.

elements that should guide competent authorities and resolution authorities in determining that:

– an institution infringes, or is likely to infringe in the near future, the requirements for continuing authorization in a way that would justify the withdrawal of its authorization by the competent authority, including but not limited to because it has incurred or is likely to incur losses that will deplete all or a significant amount of its own funds;
– an institution's assets are, or there are objective elements to support a determination that its assets will be, in the near future, less than its liabilities;
– an institution is, or is likely to be in the near future, unable to pay its debts or other liabilities as they fall due.

The guidance notes that although the BRRD prescribes that the determination that **9.19** an institution is failing or likely to fail should be made by the competent authority (i.e. the prudential regulator) after consulting with the resolution authority, member states may also permit this determination to be made by the resolution authority after consulting the prudential regulator, provided that the resolution authority has the necessary tools and, in particular, adequate access to the information required. Ordinarily it would be expected that prudential regulator and resolution authorities would take very different approaches to such determinations, and one of the primary aims of the guidance is to harmonize methodologies and encourage exchange of information.

The EBA takes the view that this determination should be based on the outcomes **9.20** of a supervisory review and evaluation process (SREP) as described in Article 97 of CRD IV. The EBA has provided guidelines as to how such SREPs should be conducted,[13] in particular setting out common procedures and methodologies. Authorities must also take into account the results of the application of supervisory and early intervention measures, recovery options applied by institutions, and the results of the valuation of an institution's assets and liabilities.

Principles of resolution

An important part of the protection of creditors within the resolution process is the **9.21** application of the resolution principles (Article 34), and in particular the objective that resolution authorities should apply the bail-in tool in a way that respects the pari passu treatment of creditors and the statutory ranking of claims under the applicable insolvency law.[14] Losses should first be absorbed by regulatory capital instruments and should be allocated to shareholders either through the cancellation or transfer of shares or through severe dilution. Where those instruments are

---

[13] EBA/GL/2014/13 of 19 December 2014.
[14] Art 34(1)(f) and (g).

not sufficient, subordinated debt should be converted or written down. Senior liabilities should be converted or written down if the subordinate classes have been converted or written down entirely.

Types of resolution

9.22 The main difference between the approaches taken by the United States and the European Union to resolution are that the US approach is effected through the transfer of some or all of the assets and liabilities of the failed institution to a healthy third party or new legal entity (the 'separation approach').[15] The EU approach can be effected either through such a separation approach, or by leaving assets and liabilities in place and exercising a power to write down senior creditors until the existing entity is sufficiently recapitalized (the direct 'bail-in' approach).

The 'separation' approach

9.23 The basis of the separation approach in the European Union, as in the United States, is to divide the bank concerned into a 'good'—that is, solvent—bank and a 'bad' bank. Such separation is effected by transferring all or a portion of the failed bank's assets and liabilities, together with any payments from the deposit guarantee scheme (DGS) to make up any shortfall in the value of any such assets over any such liabilities that are guaranteed by the DGS, to a healthy third party or 'bridge' bank, and leaving behind enough liabilities in the failed bank's receivership to ensure that the transferred assets, liabilities and DGS payments result in a 'good' bank.[16] The aim of all such separations is ultimately that the good bank should be able to continue in business, providing continuing services to its customers, whilst the 'bad' bank is wound down, crystallizing losses. All activities relating to essential services should be transferred as part of the good bank. The separation approach can effect a bridge bail-in by leaving enough liabilities behind in the failed bank's receivership to recapitalize the business transferred to the bridge bank. The liabilities left behind in the receivership than receive the equity interests in the bridge bank or the net proceeds from the sale of such equity interests in satisfaction of their claims in accordance with the priority of their claims. Any shortfall in value received amounts to a write-down of the liabilities left behind in the receivership.

---

[15] Although the bank resolution provisions of the FDIA contain a conservatorship option that authorize the FDIC to conserve and rehabilitate US-insured institutions that fail instead of separating them into a good bank and bad bank, the FDIC has virtually never exercised its conservatorship option. Instead, it has virtually always exercised its receivership option, which is limited to a quick sale, bridge bail-in or other separation strategy. Moreover, the conservatorship provisions in the FDIA do not contain the legal tools necessary to perform a direct bail-in.

[16] John L Douglas, 'Too Big to Fail: Do we Need Special Rules for Bank Resolution? The Treatment of Creditors in Bank Insolvencies' in Patrick S Kenadjian (ed) *Too Big to Fail: Brauchen wir in Sonderinsolvenzrecht für Banken?* (DeGruyter 2011).

The 'bail-in' approach

A bail-in, whether direct or indirect, operates by writing down some of the creditors **9.24**
of the bank, thereby recapitalizing it. The EU variety of direct bail-in may be used
to write down not only the claims of subordinated creditors but also some senior
creditors, converting their claims to equity.

The write-down power

It is important to distinguish between the power to bail in creditors and the power **9.25**
to write down Additional Tier 1 and Tier 2 capital instruments. The BRRD prescribes both powers. However, it is important to emphasize that whereas resolution authorities may choose to apply bail-in powers or not as they see fit, they
are required (BRRD Article 59(3)) to apply the write-down power as soon as
they determine that the issuing institution has reached the point of non-viability.
Another important aspect of the write-down power is that, where this power is
exercised, relevant creditors will not have the benefit of the 'no-creditor-worse-off-
than-in-liquidation' (NCWOL) protection—indeed, Additional Tier 1 and Tier 2
holders may end off worse off than equity holders, in that their claims may be written down without compensation.

The BRRD therefore contains both powers to write down obligations of a bank **9.26**
in resolution and also powers to write down capital instruments—Alternative
Tier 1 and Tier 2 instruments—outside resolution.[17] The write-down power dif-
fers from the resolution power in a number of important respects; most notably
in that it is not covered by the NCWOL safeguard.[18] Somewhat confusingly,
the trigger for the use of the write-down power is not notably different from
the trigger for the use of the resolution power. The write-down power must be
automatically triggered where the conditions for resolution are satisfied,[19] but
must also be capable of being used once the issuer has reached the 'point of
non-viability' (generally referred to as PONV). The BRRD definition of PONV
is as follows:

    (a) the institution or the entity referred to in point (b), (c), or (d) of Article 1(1) or
        the group is failing or likely to fail; and
    (b) having regard to timing and other relevant circumstances, there is no reason-
        able prospect that any action, including alternative private sector measures or
        supervisory action (including early intervention measures), other than the write
        down or conversion of capital instruments, independently or in combination
        with a resolution action, would prevent the failure of the institution... within a
        reasonable timeframe.[20]

---

[17] Art 59(1)(b).
[18] See para 13.33 for the UK's solution to the problem posed by the coexistence of these powers.
[19] Art 56(3)(a).
[20] Art 59(4).

9.27   This is of course pretty much identical to the threshold condition for resolution set out in Article 32—the primary difference being that Article 32 condition is only satisfied if write-down of capital instruments itself would not solve the problem. Article 59(5) makes clear that a group shall be deemed failing or likely to fail for this purpose where it has infringed, or is likely to infringe, its consolidated prudential requirements. This compares with the threshold conditions for resolution, which specify breach of any authorization requirement, not just as regards capital. The write-down power must also be exercised where extraordinary public support is required by the entity concerned.[21]

9.28   One of the primary differences between the commencement of resolution action and the exercise of the write-down power is that BRRD mandates member states to require that their resolution authorities exercise the write-down power, 'without delay', where the conditions for its exercise are satisfied.[22] There is thus intended to be a degree of automaticity about the exercise of the write-down power.

9.29   However, before the exercise of the power to write down instruments, the resolution authority must carry out the same independent valuation as is required for a resolution.[23]

9.30   Finally, Article 59(3)(a) purports to make the exercise of the write-down power a precondition to resolution, since it provides that the write-down power must be recognized where the determination has been made that conditions for resolution specified in Articles 32 and 33 have been met, before any resolution action is taken.

9.31   The write-down power is a wholly new type of power for the United Kingdom— under the pre-BRRD Banking Act, powers could only be used once the entity concerned has been placed in resolution. It is also a breach of the general convention that pre-resolution powers are exercised by the supervisory rather than the resolution authority.

9.32   This power does raise cross-border issues. Where a group has capital instruments issued by both a parent and a subsidiary, it is entirely possible that one or other of these entities may theoretically be viable even without the write-down. Article 59(3) of the BRRD therefore provides a mechanism whereby the relevant authorities as regards the parent and the subsidiary may collectively make a determination that without a write-down the group as a whole will not be viable. This permits both authorities to write down the relevant instruments, subject to the constraint in Article 59(7) that '[a] relevant capital instrument issued by a subsidiary shall not be written down to a greater extent or converted on worse terms...than equally ranked capital instruments at the level of the parent undertaking which have been written down or converted'. However, it should be noted that the UK view is that

---

[21] Art 59(4)(d).
[22] Art 59(3).
[23] Art 59(10), and see para 9.33 below.

this only applies where the subsidiary is not otherwise failing—if the subsidiary itself is failing, then the requirement for equivalence of treatment between holders of subsidiary capital and parent capital no longer applies.

Valuation

One of the unique features of the BRRD is its focus on valuation. Its basic require- **9.33** ment is that '[b]efore any resolution action is taken, a fair and realistic valuation of the assets and liabilities of the institution should be carried out'. Also, a comparison between the treatment that shareholders and creditors have actually been afforded and the treatment they would have received under normal insolvency proceedings should be carried out after resolution tools have been applied. If these shareholders and creditors have received less that they would have received in insolvency, they should be compensated.

BRRD envisages a rapid provisional valuation of the assets or the liabilities of a fail- **9.34** ing institution, and the authority should be able to rely on this until an independent valuation is carried out.

B. Resolution Funding under the BRRD

The BRRD requires each member state to establish a national resolution financing **9.35** arrangement, which may use the same administrative structure as national bank deposit guarantee schemes—that is, an organized and dedicated fund. Within the eurozone these arrangements are to be pooled into a common SRM resolution fund, but outside the eurozone each member state is required to create its own domestic fund financed by its national banking industry.

Such resolution financing arrangements are to be empowered to levy *ex ante* indus- **9.36** try contributions from institutions authorized in the member state and from local branches of third-country firms. However, member states[24] need not set up such a fund provided that they have a 'resolution financing arrangement' which is funded through general industry contributions.[25] This provision is relied on by the United Kingdom, which takes the view that the bank levy, whose proceeds are paid into the general exchequer, satisfies these requirements (the UK Bank levy[26] is a tax levied specifically on banks[27]).

---

[24] Art 100(6).
[25] Subject to certain requirements, including that the amount raised be equal to the amount that a dedicated fund would raise, and that the resolution authority be entitled to access the contributions for resolution purposes.
[26] Sch 19 Finance Act 2011.
[27] There are some problems with this analysis—notably that the bank levy itself excludes banks with equity and liabilities below £20bn. It is therefore imposed on a subset (albeit a large subset by value) of the banks which might require to have recourse to resolution funding.

9.37 The BRRD sets a number of purposes for which resolution financing may be used, including (but not limited to):

(a) funding NCWOL compensation payments to shareholders and creditors;

(b) making loans to or purchase assets from, an institution in resolution;

(c) to guarantee the assets or liabilities of an institution in resolution, its subsidiaries, a bridge institution or an asset management vehicle;

(d) to contribute in lieu of write down or conversion where the carve out from bail-in has been extended to exclude the bail-in of certain creditors otherwise susceptible to bail-in.

9.38 Critically, the BRRD expressly prohibits the use of the resolution financing arrangement directly to absorb losses or recapitalize a failing institution. This express prohibition may be problematic when weighed against the idea that NCWOL acts as an *ex ante* limitation in the Directive.

9.39 The BRRD sets a resolution fund 'target level' of at least 1 per cent of the value of insured deposits of all authorized institutions in a member state. The Directive aims to reach this minimum level, through industry contributions, by 31 December 2024 (with scope to extend that deadline where payouts have been made in the meantime and with a mechanism to maintain that target level beyond the deadline date on an ongoing basis). The Directive also requires the EBA to report to the Commission by 31 October 2016 with an analysis as to whether total liabilities would be a more appropriate reference point for setting resolution financing arrangements than insured deposits.

9.40 In addition to annual *ex ante* industry contributions, the Directive also establishes a framework for extraordinary *ex post* industry contributions to be levied in cases where existing resources are inadequate. Such *ex post* contributions are capped at three times the normal annual contributions.

Depositor preference

9.41 The BRRD establishes a preference in the ordinary insolvency hierarchy for both insured depositors (or a DGS subrogating to the depositors' rights having made a payout to depositors or otherwise contributed to the costs of resolution) and for all other deposits of individuals and micro, small, and medium-sized enterprises held in both European Economic Area (EEA) and non-EEA branches of an EEA bank.

9.42 This requirement needs to be considered alongside the recast EU Directive on deposit guarantees (DGD), which will increase the volume of deposits that are insured (and thus preferred) to include all deposits, including all corporate deposits (unless the depositor is a public sector body or financial institution) plus some temporary high value deposits.

Under the Directive, a deposit guarantee scheme can be used to contribute to reso-   **9.43**
lution to the extent that it would have suffered loss on paying out bank depositors if the bank had gone into ordinary insolvency proceedings.[28] However, the
preference for insured depositors in winding up means that it is very unlikely
that there will be an absolute loss to depositors, except in exceptional cases.
This in turn means that Article 109 of the BRRD—which provides that a DGS
should not be liable to contribute to a bank resolution to a greater extent than
'the amount of losses that it would have had to bear had the institution been
wound up under normal insolvency proceedings' has the effect in practice of
barring any recourse to DGSs to fund resolution. Thus the only real usefulness
of the DGS in resolution is likely to be to act as a source of liquidity to help
meet the target of seven days for paying out insured deposits under the DGD in
the event that a bank is not placed into resolution but instead enters ordinary
insolvency proceedings.

Recapitalization

Banks, like certain other companies, are capable of entering into a state where   **9.44**
they are, in the view of a classically trained lawyer, neither solvent nor insolvent.
Not insolvent, because they have a positive equity value and do not satisfy any of
the ordinary balance-sheet tests for insolvency. Viewed from the perspective of the
Insolvency Act 1986, they are solvent.[29] However, from the perspective of a bank
regulator they are insolvent, since in order to be permitted to continue to engage in
their business they need to be not just solvent but to maintain a level of capital in
excess of a specified level. Merely filling in the holes in a bank balance sheet leaves
the bank in an 'undead' state, where it is technically solvent but does not have sufficient capital to be permitted to continue operating.

The key point here is that in order to restore a bank to a fully 'alive' state, there are   **9.45**
in fact two separate processes which have to be undertaken:

- allocation of the historic losses, which—in the new world—will and should
  be made to fall on the existing creditors of the bank. This is the process which
  approaches such as bail-in are designed to accomplish.
- bank recapitalization.

---

[28] Art 109. The United Kingdom has implemented this by inserting protected deposits within the
list of preferred creditors on insolvency set out in Schedule 6 to the Insolvency Act 1986—see the
Banks and Building Societies (Depositor Preference and Priorities) Order 2014 2014/3486.

[29] There was some discussion in the *Eurosail* case (*BNY Corporate Trustee Services Limited v Eurosail-
UK* 2007-3BL PLC appeal [2013] UKSC 28) as to whether it should be possible to declare an entity
insolvent where, although viable today, it would certainly become unviable tomorrow. However, the
UK Supreme Court made clear the fact that insolvency is a balance-sheet test triggered of the ability
to meet liabilities today, and is unconnected with issues such as the ability of the firm to conduct its
business at some time in the future.

9.46   There is a necessary tension between the second of these elements and the NCWOL safeguard. Once a firm has been restored to balance-sheet solvency, the expectation of a creditor is that he will be paid 100 per cent, of the value of his claim, and (under the BRRD approach at least) it will then become impossible to write him down any further. The question then becomes one as to whether a creditor is 'worse off' if his claim of 100 is exchanged for eighty of new debt and an equity stake in the resulting business. In principle, of course, he is worse off, since the balance-sheet value of the equity is the same as that of the debt it replaces, so he has in effect exchanged a senior claim of twenty for a subordinated claim of twenty. However, the equity carries an entitlement to future profits, and it is entirely possible that the current market value of the equity could be more than the twenty of debt cancelled in order to create it.

C. The EU Resolution Fund

9.47   Given the amount of political capital which has been expended on the European Resolution Fund, it would be tempting for the casual observer to conclude that this fund will be the major resource to be drawn upon in resolving EU banks. The size of the fund—€55 billion—means that the resources which it will have at its disposal in respect of bank resolution will be broadly similar to those of the European Stability Mechanism (ESM)[30] (although the ESM has a greater total capacity, the direct recapitalization instrument (DRI), which governs the use of its resources to recapitalise banks directly, indicates that its capacity for assuming direct exposures to resolved institutions will be limited to €60bn).

9.48   However, the circumstances in which this fund can be used are set out in the BRRD, and the constraints imposed on it are considerable. Article 101(1) of the BRRD provides that:

> The financing arrangements established in accordance with Article 100 may be used by the resolution authority only to the extent necessary to ensure the effective application of the resolution tools, for the following purposes:
> - to guarantee the assets or the liabilities of the institution under resolution, its subsidiaries, a bridge institution or an asset management vehicle;
> - to make loans to the institution under resolution, its subsidiaries, a bridge institution or an asset management vehicle;
> - to purchase assets of the institution under resolution;
> - to make contributions to a bridge institution and an asset management vehicle;
> - to pay compensation to shareholders or creditors in accordance with Article 75;
> - to make a contribution to the institution under resolution in lieu of the write down or conversion of liabilities of certain creditors, when the bail-in tool is applied and the resolution authority decides to exclude certain creditors from the scope of bail-in in accordance with Article 44(3) to (8);

---

[30] See paras 6.56 et seq below.

- to lend to other financing arrangements on a voluntary basis in accordance with Article 106;
- to take any combination of these actions.

Critically, none of these permits the resolution fund to contribute new equity to the recapitalize the institution concerned, unless it can be shown that the contribution is made in substitution for the write-down of certain excluded creditors. The resolution fund can, however, capitalize a bridge institution or asset management vehicle without limit.[31]   **9.49**

Once these criteria have been satisfied, the amount of funding provided by the fund may not amount to more than 5 per cent of the total liabilities of the fund (assuming that the fund has sufficient assets—a resolution fund may never be required to contribute more than it has or can raise within three years). When the fund is fully constituted, this will amount to a total of €3bn.   **9.50**

If recourse to the fund is insufficient, the resolution authority is permitted to seek funding from 'alternative financing arrangements'—euro-code for direct financing by the ESM.   **9.51**

D. The European Stability Mechanism

The ESM is the successor to the European Financial Stability Facility (EFSF). It is not an EU institution, but was created by a separate intergovernmental treaty signed in February 2012 and was inaugurated on 8 October 2012.[32] Although it is not an EU body, it is perceived as a key element of the EU legislative programme known as 'banking union' as agreed by the European Council in 2012. This project had three planks—the Single Supervisory Mechanism (SSM), the Single Resolution Mechanism (SRM), and direct recapitalization of banks by the ESM.[33] These elements are intended to be interoperative—thus the ESM should not recapitalize banks directly until the SSM is in place.   **9.52**

The main distinction between the EFSF and the ESM is that the EFSF was restricted to advancing funds only to member states. A number of member states deployed the funds thus received in order to prop up their banking systems—Ireland being a prime example. However, the difficulty that this created was that the borrowings inflated the debt to gross domestic product (GDP) ratio of the government concerned, thereby weakening its credit. Since banks generally hold large amounts of the domestic debt of the government in whose territory they   **9.53**

---

[31] Art 101.

[32] The ESM had been intended to be an EU institution, but this proposal was vetoed by the UK as part of an (unsuccessful) attempt to create negotiating leverage.

[33] It envisaged a fourth plank, a common deposit guarantee mechanism, but this has been postponed *sine die*.

are established, this weakening generally caused the debt concerned to reduce in value, and created further losses for the banks concerned. The idea behind the establishment of the ESM was that this phenomenon could be eliminated if the funds concerned were advanced directly to the bank rather than indirectly through the government concerned.

9.54 The ESM operates in this regard under the direct recapitalization instrument, or 'DRI',[34] which sets out the terms on which the ESM will contribute to a bank recapitalization. The conditions for ESM participation in any resolution are tightened as from 1 January 2016.[35] As from that date, the ESM will only make any contribution to any resolution provided that:

(a) there has been a write-down or conversion of capital and other instruments equal to 8 per cent of shares, capital instruments, and other minimum requirement for eligible liabilities (MREL) liabilities at the time of resolution;

(b) a contribution of the resolution financing arrangement of 5 per cent of total liabilities has been made;

(c) all unsecured non-preferred liabilities, other than eligible deposits, have been written down or converted in full.

9.55 A further condition of ESM participation in a recapitalization is that the institution concerned must have at least the legal minimum Common Equity Tier 1 of 4.5 per cent of risk-weighted assets (RWAs) (if the institution has less than this, the member state concerned is required to make good the shortfall itself out of its own resources). The member state must then contribute alongside the ESM up to 20 per cent of the total amount of the public contribution.[36]

9.56 The ESM Board of Governors may, however, agree that the member state's contribution may be partially or fully suspended. This is clearly intended to address situations such as that encountered in the Cyprus case where the member state faces such severe fiscal pressures that it is in practice unable to fund any contribution.

9.57 The broad criterion which the ESM must satisfy before granting any sort of assistance is that the financial assistance is indispensable to safeguard the financial stability of the eurozone as a whole or of its member states.

9.58 A member may only request contributions from ESM where it is or would be unable to provide financial assistance to the beneficiary bank without very serious effects on its own fiscal sustainability, or if the alternatives available would endanger the continuous access to markets of the requesting ESM

---

[34] Guideline on Financial Assistance for the Direct Recapitalisation of Institutions, 8 December 2014.
[35] DRI Art 8 para 3.
[36] DRI Art 9.

member, thereby forcing the country concerned to seek financial assistance from the ESM.

The bank would have to currently be (or likely to be in the near future) unable to **9.59** meet the capital requirements established by the European Central Bank in its capacity as supervisor under the SSM. It would also have to be unable to obtain sufficient capital from private sources. The bank in question must also be of systemic relevance or pose a serious threat to the financial stability of the eurozone as a whole or of its member states.

E. Bail-in and the Resolution Fund

BRRD begins with the proposition that all liabilities of an institution are poten- **9.60** tially subject to bail-in. This is then subject to a list of claims which are automatically excluded and another list which may, at the discretion of the relevant resolution authority, be excluded.

Where a resolution authority decides to exclude or partially exclude an eligible **9.61** liability or class of eligible liabilities under this paragraph, the level of write-down or conversion applied to other eligible liabilities may be increased to take account of such exclusions, provided that the level of write-down and conversion applied to other eligible liabilities complies with the NCWOL principle.

Where any of these obligations are in fact excluded, it is envisaged that the resolu- **9.62** tion fund may be called upon to make good the amount which would have been generated had these obligations been bailed in. However, it may only be called upon provided that a contribution equal to the lesser of (a) 8 per cent of total liabilities or (b) 20 per cent of RWAs[37] has been made by (i) shareholders, (ii) holders of relevant capital instruments, and (iii) other eligible liabilities.

The final characteristic of this odd arrangement is that if a resolution authority **9.63** wishes to exclude a liability from bail-in, it is required to notify the European Commission, which has power to veto the exclusion where the fact of the exclusion results in recourse to the resolution fund or the ESM.

F. BRRD Resolution in Practice

Bank capital levels are very substantially larger than they were. Modern banks **9.64** have Tier 1 capital levels in excess of 5 per cent of their total assets, generally

---

[37] The latter is only permitted if the institution has below €900bn of assets—thus for large institutions the binding constraint will be the 8 per cent figure.

translatable into a figure well in excess of 12 per cent of RWAs, compared with the low single-digit figures seen before the crisis. This in turn means that the problems we should anticipate in the future are different from those encountered in the past. In particular, historic models of bank default tended to envisage a loss sufficient to wipe out the capital of the bank concerned completely, and to envisage how such a loss might be rectified. A modern bank crisis, by contrast, is likely to leave an institution with a shortfall as against its capital requirements but a net positive value.

Let us begin by assuming a bank whose balance sheet is roughly as follows:

ASSETS				
Loan Assets	250	Off-balance-sheet commitments		50
		Risk-weighted assets		100
LIABILITIES				
Deposits	100			
Senior debt	130			
	230			
Capital	20			
Composed of		Tier 2		7.5
		Common equity		12.5
				20.0
CAPITAL REQUIREMENTS				
Capital requirement	15% of RWAs			15.0
Tier 1 capital requirement	12.5% of RWAs			12.5
Leverage ratio capital requirement	3% of assets plus commitments			9.0

9.65 We will say for example that this bank is required by its regulator to maintain a capital requirement of 15 per cent of RWAs (that is, 20) and a 3 per cent leverage ratio (i.e. Tier 1 equal to 3 per cent of assets plus commitments—that is, 3 per cent of 300, or 9). Our bank therefore (barely) meets its current capital requirements.

9.66 We now assume that the bank realizes that it has been grossly over-optimistic in valuing its loan book. This results in a sudden one-off charge of fifteen. This is less than 4 per cent of the loan book, but is sufficient to place the bank in crisis mode. Accounting principles state that this is applied in reduction of the common equity balance, which is wiped out, leaving a 2.5 per cent deficit.

9.67 At this point, it is necessary to consider the question of what victory looks like. A good starting point for this is to ask what is the minimum amount of

capital which the institution would have to have before it could regard itself
as recapitalized.

In broad terms, an EU bank is subject to three cumulative Tier 1 requirements. **9.68**
One is a requirement to maintain capital according to the calculations set out in the
Capital Requirements Regulation (CRR) (Pillar 1). The second is the requirement
applied by its national competent authority in respect of the non-quantitative
measures set out in Articles 97–110 of the CRD. Article 104(2) does provide that
a competent authority 'shall' impose these requirements unless it is satisfied that
they are already addressed in other ways, and it is very hard to see how a competent
authority which had taken the view up to the time that a particular buffer was
required could suddenly conclude that it was now not required. A third requirement is the array of further discretionary buffers set out in Articles 128–140 of the
directive—the capital conservation buffer, the institution-specific countercyclical
capital buffer, the global systemically important institution (G-SII) buffer, and the
systemic risk buffer.

The second and third of these are—broadly—waivable by the competent authority **9.69**
concerned; the CRR requirements are not. However, the CRR requirement itself
is divided in two:

ii) 4.5 per cent is the minimum Tier 1 requirement set out in the CRR (Article 92).
    Competent authorities have no power to dispense with this—it is a hard minimum.
iii) A 2.5 per cent capital conservation buffer is required by Article 129 of the
    CRD. If capital falls below this level, the bank is subject to 'capital conserva-
    tion measures' in accordance with Articles 141 et seq of the CRD.

It is therefore broadly true that a competent authority may allow the Tier 1 **9.70**
capital requirement for a bank to fall to the CRR minimum of 4.5 per cent provided that the bank is able to present a plausible recapitalization strategy aimed
at restoring it to full compliance with the headline requirements. However,
it would, in practice, be extremely difficult to present a bank as having been
'resolved' if it was still subject to capital conservation measures and a capital
replenishment plan.

Article 46(2) of the BRRD sets out a different (and much more realistic) standard. **9.71**
This provides that an institution in resolution should be recapitalized to a level
'to sustain sufficient market confidence in the institution under resolution or the
bridge institution and enable it to continue to meet, for at least one year the conditions for authorization and to carry on the activities for which it is authorized'.[38]
This probably translates into the pre-crisis capital requirement of 15 per cent.

---

[38] BRRD 46(2).

9.72 If we assume that the conversion of the Tier 2 holders is done either under the terms of those notes or through regulatory powers equivalent to those contained in BRRD, we now have Tier 1 equity of 5 per cent. Thus the bank will meet the bare minimum Tier 1 capital requirement of 4.5 per cent. However, there is more to life than Tier 1. Article 92 of the CRR specifies that an institution must maintain total capital of 8 per cent.[39] Thus by converting its Tier 2, the institution has placed itself in a position where it is (a) solvent but (b) non-compliant with the CRR minimum capital requirements.

9.73 In a perfect world, it would now be possible for the bank to access the market to raise new equity and Tier 2 capital or to seek a capital injection from a buyer. This is unlikely to happen for an institution which will be perceived as in trouble. Thus in practice it is at this point that the bank will require recourse to other sources.

9.74 Classical resolution theory would suggest that at this point a bail-in of senior creditors could be undertaken. However, as discussed above, this will depend on the value of the equity in the bank thus recapitalized compared with the 'cost' to creditors of creating it. A simple example will illustrate. Imagine that the bank above is resolved through conversion of Tier 2 holders plus a bail-in. Tier 2 holders will be converted into 7.5 of equity, of which 2.5 will be applied immediately to meet the residual loss after common equity has been wiped out, leaving five of new equity. Senior debt holders will be written down by ten, to create a further ten of new equity—thus the new bank will have fifteen of equity. The question of what the shares in this equity are worth will be a function of the profitability of the asset book concerned. If the spread on the remaining assets is 0.5 per cent, the return on this 15 of equity will be 1.25 before tax, suggesting that the equity is worth 7.5.[40] However, if the spread on the remaining assets is 2 per cent, the return on equity will be 5, suggesting that the equity is worth 30. In the former case, bail-in will be impossible, since the noteholders, having given up 10 of senior claim, will have received 5 worth of junior claim. They are therefore worse off than they would have been on insolvency. In the latter case, however, they will be better off, having given up 10 of senior claim in order to receive 20 of equity value. In this case it is the Tier 2 holders who are likely to complain that the bank has been over-bailed-in, with the effect that value has been transferred from them to the senior noteholders.

9.75 A possible solution to the first case—where the asset book is low-yielding and the equity consequently lowly valued—is the approach applied in some of the UK resolutions. This involves arguing that the correct baseline for the NCWOL safeguard is not the balance-sheet position as at the date of resolution, but the

---

[39] And Tier 1 of 6 per cent.
[40] On the basis of a share price multiple of six times pre-tax profit, a number plucked out of a hat for ease of calculation which is broadly in line with the bank market at the time of writing.

balance sheet as it would exist at the end of the most disorderly possible wind-down of the institution. A picture of an analysis of this kind can be gleaned from the report of the independent valuer into the Dunfermline Building Society,[41] under which (on an asset book of £3.2bn) an £88m surplus on the onset of resolution was reckoned to be likely to have become a deficit of £80m on the completion of insolvency. It is of course true that a disorderly wind-down would destroy significant value in the institution concerned, and the larger the hypothetical value destruction the greater the scope for bail-in of creditors. However, the question of whether a sufficiently large value destruction can be hypothesized is a difficult one, depending as it does on a variety of issues such as the nature of the financial crisis concerned, the composition of the asset book and the funding structure of the institution in resolution. In general, an asset book which is largely composed of market traded assets can be hypothesized as vulnerable to disorderly wind-down with significant loss of value. The recent announcement by its liquidators that Lehman's unsecured senior creditors will in fact be paid in full[42] will, if nothing else, make it hard for the official sector to argue that creditors will inevitably suffer significant losses if a firm is placed in liquidation rather than resolution.

G. State Intervention under the BRRD

State bail-out

Perhaps surprisingly for a measure aimed at 'eliminating "too big to fail"', state aid is explicitly provided for in the BRRD, and Articles 56–58 set out a regulatory schema for government support of banks. **9.76**

In principle, any state aid granted a member state government to a bank should trigger resolution, since Article 32 of the BRRD deems the grant of any state aid to be ipso facto proof that the institution is failing or likely to fail. However, Article 32(4)(d)(iii) provides an escape from this, in that resolution is not automatically triggered where the state injects capital into an institution on arms-length terms and in circumstances where none of the other criteria of failure have been met.[43] The Article does, however, mandate the commission to consider whether to dispense with Article 32(4)(d)(iii), so it is not clear for how long this useful provision will continue to exist. If it is dispensed with, it is likely that all state investment in the capital of firms will automatically trigger resolution of those firms. **9.77**

---

[41] <http://www.fscs.org.uk/uploaded_files/final_report.pdf> (accessed 26 October 2015).

[42] <http://www.pwc.co.uk/business-recovery/administrations/lehman/creditor-update-forth-interim-distribution-to-unsecured-creditors-28-february-2014.jhtml> (accessed 26 October 2015).

[43] Recourse to this provision proved essential in the 2015 Greek bank recapitalizations, where otherwise solvent and profitable banks were required to raise further capital in response to stress tests.

9.78 Article 56 provides that member states may provide extraordinary public financial support for the purpose of participating in the resolution of an institution or group member, including by intervening directly in order to avoid its winding up. Such intervention must be conducted by the relevant ministry in close cooperation with the resolution authority, is only permitted provided that:

(a) it is conducted for the purposes of meeting one or more of the objectives of resolution[44] in relation to the member state or the Union as a whole;

(b) it is in accordance with the EU state aid framework;

(c) it is used as a last resort after having assessed and exploited the other resolution tools to the maximum extent practicable whilst maintaining financial stability, as determined by the competent ministry or the government after consulting the resolution authority;

(d) the competent ministry or government and the resolution authority determine that the application of the resolution tools would not suffice to avoid a significant adverse effect on the financial system, or would not suffice to protect the public interest, where extraordinary liquidity assistance from the central bank has previously been given to the institution.

9.79 If these conditions are satisfied, member states may apply either the 'public equity support tool' or the 'temporary public ownership tool'. The public equity support tool is simply a participation by the government in an offering of common equity or alternative Tier 1 (but not Tier 2) instruments by the institution or a parent. It must be a condition of the purchase of the instruments that the institution be managed on a commercial and professional basis, and that the holding of capital instruments be transferred back to the private sector as soon as commercial and financial circumstances allow.[45] The temporary public ownership tool is given effect by transferring ownership of the institution or parent concerned to a company wholly owned by the member state or its nominee. Again, it must be a condition of the transfer that the institution be managed on a commercial and professional basis, and that the holding of capital instruments be transferred back to the private sector as soon as commercial and financial circumstances allow.[46]

EU restrictions on state aid in bank resolution

9.80 The BRRD provides that in order to be permissible in resolution, state intervention must satisfy the EU state aid guidelines. This means that it is necessary here to summarize these guidelines as they apply to bank recapitalization.

9.81 During the crisis, the only tool that the European Union had to regulate the recapitalization of banks by member states was the EU competition regime, and in

---

[44] Art 31(2).
[45] Art 57.
[46] Art 58.

particular the treaty limitation on state aid. Thus, EU control of state aid to banks has developed through these guidelines.

It is interesting in this regard to remind ourselves of the fact that although the finan- **9.82**
cial stability objective may be best served by preserving institutions, this may not be the optimum outcome for the markets as a whole. As the Commission say in their 2009 communication:[47]

> Where banks compete on the merits of their products and services, those which accumulate excessive risk and/or rely on unsustainable business models will ulti-mately lose market share and, possibly, exit the market while more efficient competi-tors expand on or enter the markets concerned. State aid prolongs past distortions of competition created by excessive risk-taking and unsustainable business models by artificially supporting the market power of beneficiaries. In this way it may cre-ate a moral hazard for the beneficiaries, while weakening the incentives for non-beneficiaries to compete, invest and innovate...Financial stability remains the overriding objective of aid to the financial sector in a systemic crisis, but safeguard-ing systemic stability in the short-term should not result in longer-term damage to the level playing field and competitive markets. In this context, measures to limit distortions of competition due to State aid play an important role . . .

The latest iteration of the Commission's state aid rules is set out in the *Communica-* **9.83**
tion from the Commission on the application, from 1 August 2013, of State aid rules to support measures in favour of banks in the context of the financial crisis ('Banking Communication').[48]

When the commission considers state aid, it is inclined to begin by considering **9.84**
whether such aid is reversible or irreversible. Reversible aid may be rapidly approved subject to after-the-event consideration and the possibility for a finding that the aid should be returned along with the cost of funding advantage obtained by the recipi-ent during the period when he held it. Much industrial subsidy can be dealt with in this way. Bank recapitalizations, however, are in general irreversible, and as a result the Commission can in principle only authorize them once the member state con-cerned demonstrates that all measures to limit such aid to the minimum necessary have been exploited to the maximum extent. Any application to give state aid made by a member state is therefore required to contain a capital raising plan setting out proposed measures to be taken by the bank to raise new capital and to inflict existing losses on shareholders and holders of capital instruments. It is notable that the commission does not require either shareholders or capital instruments to be completely written down before state aid will be permitted.

The commission will proceed by assessing the gap between the actual capital pos- **9.85**
ition of the bank and the required capital position of the bank. This assessment will require a thorough asset quality review of the bank, as well as a forward-looking

---

[47] *Communication on the return to viability and the assessment of restructuring measures in the finan-cial sector in the current crisis under the State Aid rules* (2009/C 195/04).
[48] 2013/C 216/01.

capital adequacy assessment. In theory, only once these have been completed will the commission be able to determine precisely the (residual) capital shortfall of a bank that should be permitted to be covered with state aid.

9.86 If the commission accepts that state aid is justified, it will require a restructuring plan, and this restructuring plan is likely to require asset disposals, exit from markets, or other measures designed to reduce the degree of competition offered by the institution in the market. The Commission will authorize any recapitalization or impaired asset measure as restructuring aid only after agreement on the restructuring plan has been reached.

9.87 It is likely that for an institution facing resolution, the raising of new capital from external sources may be deemed to be impossible within any practical timescale.

9.88 Interestingly, if the commission take the view that recourse to state aid could have reasonably been averted through appropriate and timely management action, any entity relying on state aid for its restructuring or orderly winding down should normally replace the Chief Executive Officer of the bank, as well as other board members if appropriate. Even if executives are not dismissed, it is a condition of approval of state aid that any bank in receipt of it should restrict the total remuneration to staff, including board members and senior management, to an appropriate level. There is a particularly mad provision in the criteria that '[t]he total remuneration of any such individual may therefore not exceed fifteen times the national average salary in the Member State where the beneficiary is incorporated or ten times the average salary of employees in the beneficiary bank' which, if strictly implemented, would constitute an insuperable bar to the use of state aid in respect of any bank with investment banking operations. However, this is mitigated slightly by a provision that these restrictions must apply only 'until the end of the restructuring period or until the bank has repaid the state aid, whichever occurs earlier'. Thus, it is just possible that an investment banking business within a bank subject to these measures might be capable of being retained provided that there was a clear path towards rapid repayment of the aid concerned.

9.89 The key point within the commission guidelines relates to what will be regarded as 'adequate' burden-sharing by existing investors. The commission provides that:

> Adequate burden-sharing will normally entail, after losses are first absorbed by equity, contributions by hybrid capital holders and subordinated debt holders. Hybrid capital and subordinated debt holders must contribute to reducing the capital shortfall to the maximum extent. Such contributions can take the form of either a conversion into Common Equity Tier 1 or a write-down of the principal of the instruments.

9.90 The commission states the position that where the bank has failed a stress test or similar but retains a capital position above the required regulatory minimum, it should be possible to raise new equity but, if it is not, subordinated debt must be converted into equity before state aid will be approved. Where the bank has fallen below its regulatory minimum, equity, hybrid capital, and subordinated debt must have fully contributed to offset any losses before state aid will be approved. This is all, however, backstopped by the observation that 'the "no creditor worse off principle" should be adhered to. Thus, subordinated creditors should not receive less in economic terms than what their instrument would have been worth if no State aid were to be granted'.

Given that the communication was written in 2013—and therefore before the **9.91** finalization of the bail-in provisions of the BRRD—its provisions on the treatment of senior creditors may have been overtaken by events. However, it is notable that it provides that:

> The Commission will not require contribution from senior debt holders (in particular from insured deposits, uninsured deposits, bonds and all other senior debt) as a mandatory component of burden-sharing under State aid rules whether by conversion into capital or by write-down of the Instruments.

These provisions, taken together, constitute a robust statement that no state aid will be permitted whilst equity or subordinated debt holders remain unaffected.[49] However, this gives rise to a further problem.

In general, placing an institution in resolution has various undesirable side-effects, **9.92** and if state aid is to be provided to an institution, it is likely to be considerably more effective if the aid is provided whilst the institution is still solvent in order to keep it out of resolution. This, however, will only be permissible under the Guideline if it is possible to ensure that the holders of subordinated debt are all capable of being written down or converted outside the scope of resolution. If all of the subordinated debt issued by the bank contains contractual conversion provisions which have been triggered, then this criterion could be satisfied without putting the bank into formal resolution. However, most bank Tier 2 does not contain such clauses, and for some such bonds (notably 'low-trigger' contingent convertibles (CoCos)), it is possible that the relevant triggers might not have been reached. In this situation, it would be a necessary precondition to ESM intervention for the Tier 2 holders either to agree to a voluntary exchange of their notes for equity, or to place Bank B

---

[49] Paras 43 and 44 of the Guideline make this explicit:

  – 43. Where the capital ratio of the bank that has the identified capital shortfall remains above the EU regulatory minimum, the bank should normally be able to restore the capital position on its own, in particular through capital raising measures as set out in point 35. If there are no other possibilities, including any other supervisory action such as early intervention measures or other remedial actions to overcome the shortfall as confirmed by the competent supervisory or resolution authority, then subordinated debt must be converted into equity, in principle before state aid is granted.
  – 44. In cases where the bank no longer meets the minimum regulatory capital requirements, subordinated debt must be converted or written down, in principle before state aid is granted. State aid must not be granted before equity, hybrid capital and subordinated debt have fully contributed to offset any losses.

into formal resolution in order to enable the relevant resolution authority to use its powers to write down subordinated debt. Thus, in some cases, the commencement of resolution by the member state may be a necessary precondition for it or the ESM to be able to provide direct support.

9.93 The BRRD does of course contain provision for writing down capital instruments without placing the institution concerned into resolution—thus it may be possible to ensure that he criteria set out in the Guidelines have been satisfied without placing the institution concerned into formal resolution.

9.94 However, there is a substantial qualification to this provision in the form of a statement that:

> An exception to [these] requirements can be made where implementing such measures would endanger financial stability or lead to disproportionate results. This exception could cover cases where the aid amount to be received is small in comparison to the bank's RWAs and the capital shortfall has been reduced significantly in particular through capital raising measures.

10

DIRECT BAIL-IN IN
THE EUROPEAN UNION

One of the key differences between the EU regime and the US resolution structure is **10.01** the fact that the EU regime permits bail-in to be implemented both directly—by varying the terms of the obligations of the institution in resolution—and indirectly—by transferring assets within the group so as to reduce the size of the pools of assets available to certain creditors. The second of these approaches—indirect bail-in—is common to the United States and the European Union. The first—direct bail-in—is an EU phenomenon. It is important to note that both direct and indirect bail-ins produce the same result (write-down of certain specific creditors), as set out below. However, the legal powers necessary to facilitate direct bail-in mean that the EU's resolution legislation is in this regard structurally very different from that of the United States.

We begin with a bank whose equity has been wiped out by losses, so that its assets **10.02** are equal to its liabilities, as shown in Figure 10.1.

In an indirect bail-in, assets and protected liabilities are moved to a new bridge **10.03** bank, the residual value of which is held for the benefit of the shareholders and unprotected liabilities left behind in the failed (bad) bank. This results in a position shown in Figure 10.2.

The effect of this transfer is that the protected liabilities—primarily depositors and any **10.04** secured creditors—are preserved intact with a significant buffer of capital to fall back on. The value and risks of the portfolio are thus held for the benefit, first, of the protected creditors. These will be repaid in full if the bridge bank can be sold to a third party for an amount above the claims of the protected liabilities, but will suffer losses if the value of the asset portfolio falls below the claims of the protected liabilities. Another way of looking at this is that the protected creditors are now senior creditors of an entity whose only competing claimants are equity interests and subordinated debt, and the protected creditors have therefore become, in practice, senior to such competing claimants.[1]

---

[1] The position of the competing claimants left behind in the failed (bad) bank is known as 'structural subordination'.

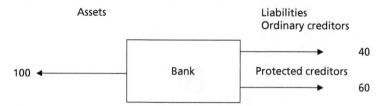

Figure 10.1 Stage 1

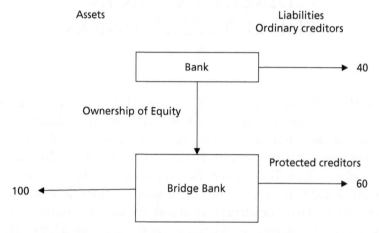

Figure 10.2 Stage 2

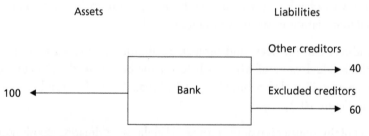

Figure 10.3 Stage 1

10.05 If we compare this outcome with a direct bail-in, the comparison works as shown in Figure 10.3. The key difference is at the starting point.

Here, liabilities are divided into those which are formally excluded from the scope of the bail-in power and those which are not. This is a clearer and more definite distinction than that which arises in a resolution by transfer, since in a resolution by transfer the question of which liabilities are transferred to the bridge bank is largely in the discretion of the relevant EU authorities.

The effect of this—shown in Figure 10.4—is that the other creditors effectively have their claims cancelled and are given equity in the bank in exchange.

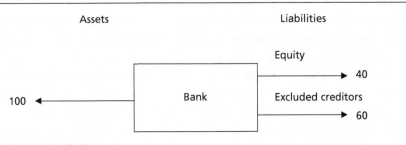

Figure 10.4 Stage 2

The primary appeal of the direct bail-in structure is the fact that there is no necessity **10.06** to establish a new entity and transfer assets to it. As the Federal Deposit Insurance Corporation's history of resolving small, domestic US-insured depository institutions demonstrates, this is a relatively straightforward process where the assets are all in one country and governed by the laws of that country. However, for European (and global) entities whose business is multi-jurisdictional or significantly governed by the laws of other countries, the legal risk inherent in such transfers is substantial when the resolution entity has branches in other countries.[2] It is also argued that the increase in certainty for creditors which arises from a predetermined list of which creditors will be bailed in and which will not should decrease uncertainty and reduce funding costs.

The challenge, therefore, in dealing with banks, is to create a mechanism that deliv- **10.07** ers the same broad outcomes as the insolvency process but which can be executed quickly, outside insolvency legislation, and without triggering a formal insolvency process. Bank resolution regimes are in this regard best regarded as specialized insolvency regimes for banks.

The idea of bail-in, although initially greeted by regulators and market participants **10.08** with some scepticism, has now been widely accepted around the world as the most promising solution to the 'too big to fail' problem, at least in its single-point-of-entry (SPE) form.[3] Regulators are familiar with the concept of banks issuing debt which is described as being capable of supporting the bank through its difficulties, and Tiers 3, 2, and alternative Tier 1 capital have all been recognized as providing this utility to some extent. It is therefore not too difficult for them to accept the proposition that making some senior debt (and subordinated debt) capable of being written down in some contexts would have a beneficial effect on the stability of banks.

---

[2] These cross-border issues are largely avoided in an SPE resolution in which the only entity to enter resolution is a top-tier holding company, with any bank subsidiaries with an international branch network and foreign subsidiaries being transferred to the bridge entity, recapitalized and kept out of their own insolvency or other resolution proceedings.

[3] See Randall Guynn, 'Framing the TBTF Problem: The Path to a Solution' in Martin Neil Baily and John B. Taylor (eds) *Across the Great Divide: New Perspectives on the Financial Crisis, Chapter 13* (Hoover Press 2014).

10.09 The optimal environment for a bail-in would be in circumstances where a systemically important institution failed for reasons idiosyncratic to itself or its
business model, and where the remainder of the financial system remained
stable. When dealing with an entire financial system subjected to a substantial
exogenous shock affecting many different business models, the likely usefulness
of a bail-in approach would be a direct function of the amount of cross-holding
of debt within that system—if bail-in debt was substantially owned by other
banks, then bail-in could increase systemic risk, whereas if bail-in debt were
predominantly held by end investors, then bail-in could substantially reduce
systemic risk. The trend amongst regulators (particularly through the Basel III
proposals) is to penalize inter-bank holdings of debt and, in particular, holdings of other banks' capital instruments, and the market appears to be moving towards an environment where the majority of long-term bank debt issued
by global systemically important banking groups (G-SIBs) is held outside the
banking system—this should increase the appeal to regulators of bail-in as a tool
for dealing with bank failure.

A. How does a Direct Bail-in Work?

10.10 Bail-in, by definition, is a process which applies to some but not all of the creditors of an institution—not all, since the object of the process is to protect some
of these creditors. Chief amongst those to be protected are depositors, although
banks have for some time had depositor protection schemes in place to address
such issues.[4] However, for the reasons given above, if the bank is to be preserved
as a going concern its 'trade creditors'—payment services customers, short-term
creditors, securities, trading exposures, etc—must be preserved intact, and for the
purposes of illustration it can be assumed that the bail-in process will be applied to
the long-term investment creditors of the bank—loosely, bondholders and holders
of subordinated debt.

10.11 The essence of a direct bail-in is the idea that some creditors of an entity should,
in certain circumstances, have part of their claim against the entity written down
(in whole or in part) whilst other creditors of the same entity remain intact. Bail-in
should only occur after the write-down of lower ranking subordinated claims and
equity. Bailed-in creditors may receive new shares in the bank, and existing equity
holders may have their claims simply extinguished.

---

[4] However, 'depositor protection' is in some respects a misnomer, since what is also sought to
be protected is payment accounts and other facilities. Individual depositors did not queue outside
branches of Northern Rock only because they believed they were exposed to credit risk (because of
the self-insured portion of their claim under the United Kingdom's then deposit protection scheme),
many of them queued because an insured deposit balance which cannot be withdrawn is useless for
most of the ordinary purposes for which we keep money in a bank.

There are really two aspects to direct bail-in. First, shareholders of the institution will **10.12** have their claims reduced in order to *absorb losses* on the institution's assets. Thus, the institution's Common Equity Tier 1 and Additional Tier 1 capital (i.e. its going concern) capital is reduced in order to restore the institution to solvency. This loss absorption is hardwired into Basel III requirements (reflected in the European Union via the Capital Requirements Regulation). Absorbing losses restores solvency but this process consumes the capital that prudential rules require the institution to hold in order to do business as a viable financial institution. So, in the second stage of a bail-in, holders of the institution's 'gone concern' capital instruments (additional Tier 2 and potentially some debt instruments and other liabilities that do not count towards regulatory capital) will be 'bailed in' to the extent necessary to *recapitalize* the institution, that is, their claims will be converted (into equity or other highly loss-absorbent capital) so that the revived institution is not merely balance sheet-solvent but also in compliance with regulatory capital rules. Both processes are illustrated in Table 10.1 below.

In theory, the effect of any special bank resolution measure (including bail-in) **10.13** should be to leave all creditors in no worse a position than would have prevailed in a case where the institution was liquidated under general insolvency law.

Table 10.1 Bail-in example

Bank Balance Sheet Pre-Bail-in			
Assets		Liabilities	
Loans	50	Deposits	50
Cash	5	Repo	20
Securities	45	Long-term unsecured debt	20
		Equity	10
Total Assets	100	*Total Liabilities + Equity*	100

Bank Balance Sheet—after equity absorbs a loss of 10 in the loan book (Bank is solvent but in breach of prudential rules)			
Loans	~~50~~ 40	Deposits	50
Cash	5	Repo	20
Securities	45	Long-term unsecured debt	20
		Equity	~~10~~ 0
Total Assets	90	*Total Liabilities + Equity*	90

Bank Balance Sheet—after bail-in recapitalization (Bank is solvent and complies with prudential rules)			
Loans	40	Deposits	50
Cash	5	Repo	20
Securities	45	Long-term unsecured debt	~~20~~ 10
		Equity	~~0~~ 10
Total Assets	90	*Total Liabilities + Equity*	90

Compensation is supposed to restore a creditor's position where it is determined that they would made a better recovery in liquidation than they did in the resolution. While the *concept* of leaving no creditor worse off than in liquidation (NCWOL) is easily enough understood, its application in practice is an altogether different matter. First, as a compensation standard, it relies on the calculation of counterfactual, so the rules governing the valuations which are input into that calculation are critically important. Second (and particularly for senior creditors), cash compensation in two or three years' time may fail to take account of the immediate detrimental consequences suffered when claims are bailed in or transferred. Third (and of particular relevance to bail-in), if NCWOL is not only a benchmark for *ex post* compensation but also (as for example the BRRD appears to suggest) an *ex ante* constraint that limits the way in which resolution tools can be applied, how will resolution authorities ever know which liabilities they can bail in unless a sufficient amount of liabilities to be bailed in are made contractually, statutorily or structurally subordinate to protected liabilities in advance of bail in. The extent to which set-off rights affect the quantum of 'bail-in-able' liabilities is potentially a significant issue, particularly in the United Kingdom and other 'insolvency set-off-friendly' jurisdictions.

10.14 One of the most interesting of the issues which arise out of this example is the assumption that equity is extinguished in a bail-in if the residual value of the failed bank or bridge bank is not sufficient to provide full recovery to all creditors and still have excess value left over. In principle, this is clearly right—a bail-in conducted under these circumstances without a cram-down of existing equity holders would result in those equity holders receiving a windfall profit. The conversion of contingent capital, by contrast, involves the creation of new equity which ranks pari passu with the existing equity (although it may heavily dilute it). The implicit sequencing is therefore:

1. subordinated or contingent capital is written off and converted in full to equity;
2. bail-in is triggered, and existing share capital (old and new) is written off; and
3. new equity is issued to the holders of the bailed-in senior bonds.

10.15 It probably goes without saying that in order to have any confidence in this system, regulators require a power to require that a bank maintain at least a specified minimum proportion of its financing in the form of either contingent capital or bail-in eligible debt or some combination of the two (although the requirement could also be met by equity or bail-in eligible subordinated debt). This is the gone concern loss absorbing capacity (GLAC), discussed in Chapter 8, or minimum requirement for eligible liabilities (MREL) requirement discussed below at paras 10.47–10.48.

10.16 In principle, the larger the volume of bail-in eligible debt, the lower the potential losses for bailed-in creditors. However, the primary aim of a bail-in is to recapitalize the relevant institution, and it is argued in some quarters that ensuring that creditors do suffer significant losses is an appropriate and necessary part of the process, whose development will enhance market discipline.

B. Impact of Bail-in on Debt Pricing

An objection which is sometimes raised to bail-in capital is that because the pulling of the bail-in trigger and the quantum of the resulting write-down or conversion are in the discretion of the regulator, it is not possible for holders of bail-in eligible debt to make any meaningful pre-estimate of their risk of loss. This, it is argued, will make such debt difficult or impossible to price on the market. Although there is something in this, it is possible by analysing the likely structure of a bail-in regime to draw some useful conclusions which may assist the pricing process.

10.17

Contingent capital instruments generally have defined trigger and conversion/ write-down mechanisms specified in the terms of the instrument, whereas the triggering of a bail-in and the resulting conversion/write-down are at the regulator's discretion under a special resolution (in contrast to the US Bankruptcy Code where a failing institution controls the timing of bail-in). However, as noted above, an economically identical outcome to direct bail-in can be achieved by the authorities through a resolution by transfer to a bridge bank, which permits the transfer of a variable quantity of valuable assets out of the failing bank in such a way as to reduce the assets available to meet the claims of residual senior creditors of that bank (indirect bail-in). It is notable that the introduction of the power to effect indirect bail-in in the United Kingdom by statute (through the Banking (Special Provisions) Act 2008, the precursor of the Banking Act 2009) had almost no impact on the prices of the bonds subject to it. This may be because dealers and investors made the simplifying assumptions that the making of a resolution order under the Act was functionally equivalent to the default whose probability was already used to price bonds—that is, that such an order would be made only where the institution would otherwise have defaulted—and that the NCWOL and compensation safeguards provided by the Act should have the effect that their losses in a resolution would be no worse than those to which they would expect to be subject in a disorderly liquidation. Thus, the new powers created under the Act may not have affected their fundamental calculation as to the probability of the issuer defaulting or their loss given default.

10.18

The same is broadly true for direct bail-in—the fact of a bond being bail-in-eligible should only be material to pricing if the probability of a bail-in and the losses given bail-in are significantly different from the probability of a default and losses given default absent bail-in. If an institution were permitted to operate using only the minimum Tier 1 regulatory capital, and relied on a bail-in to cover all of its other risks, the chance of bail-in occurring would clearly be significant, and this phenomenon might well be observed. However, any bail-in regime would also

10.19

need to ensure that institutions maintain sufficient regulatory capital to satisfy regulators, plus a balance of contingent capital sufficient to cover the residual risk of unexpected losses. The risk covered by the bail-in debt would therefore be the risk that the losses suffered by the institution would exceed both expected and unexpected loss. In principle, this is a 'tail' risk, of a kind which is not generally reflected in pricing.

10.20 A bail-in regime does concentrate any loss (not absorbed by equity or subordinated debt) on a sub-set of senior creditors, whereas insolvency regimes spread losses across a wider group. Realistically, however, the increased losses resulting from a liquidation or the dismembering of an institution in a resolution are likely to outweigh these risks—in most cases investors in bail-in eligible debt are likely to be better off than under the alternatives of insolvency or the use of other resolution tools—and investors should in any event analyse their likely loss in resolution on a worst case outcome. In addition, the NCWOL safeguard applies equally to the use of the debt write-down tool, which should mean that the likely loss given default (LGD) on bail-in is at least no worse than the LGD on other resolution outcomes.

10.21 One further concern is that since the power to require a bail-in will necessarily involve an element of discretion on the part of the relevant authority, the price of bail-in eligible debt would rise if it were perceived that the regulator were minded to exercise that power in circumstances in which the institution would not have defaulted. This is a behavioural matter, and as such very difficult to model—although the impact could be mitigated if regulators were prepared to give broad guidance as to in what circumstances they would ordinarily expect to use their bail-in power.

10.22 However, a more fundamental issue is the possibility that the market does not price the potential adverse impact of existing resolution regimes into outstanding subordinated or, more importantly, senior bank debt, on the basis that the existing regimes are not perceived to present a credible threat of imposing losses on bondholders, precisely because of the difficulties of using resolution tools that require the dismembering of a large, international, systemically important institution. This seems less and less likely with every passing month—rating agencies have now formally varied credit ratings of different classes of bank exposures to take account of bail-in risk,[5] and market discussion of the valuation of putative MREL issuance is widespread.

10.23 Finally, there are concerns that a significant number of current investors in bank senior or subordinated debt would be unable to buy bail-in eligible debt because their investment mandates restrict their ability to purchase debt which is convertible into equity and that the resulting restricted market for bail-in eligible debt will

---

[5] See, e.g., Thomas Hale, 'Rating Agencies Warn on Bank Bail-in Rules', *Financial Times*, 14 January 2016 at <http://www.ft.com/cms/s/0/55c6fa9c-baaa-11e5-b151-8e15c9a029fb.html#axzz3yuvlc3Ek>.

drive up funding costs. This could be a particular issue if a bail-in regime is structured based on the use of contractual conversion clauses in debt issues. However, the risk of ultimate conversion into equity is a risk which is taken by every senior creditor of any corporate issuer which can be subjected to a Chapter 11 or similar restructuring regime under which creditors can be required to exchange their claims for equity without their consent. These regimes do not seem to restrict investor appetite for senior debt. This suggests that a statutory bail-in regime which is clearly seen as a form of compulsory debt restructuring would be less likely to restrict investor demand. It may also be possible to reduce the impact of investor mandate concerns by building in a trust or similar mechanism under which debtholders can elect not to receive shares but to have them sold for their benefit. Nevertheless, in one respect, there is likely to be a more restricted investor base in the future for bail-in eligible senior debt than current senior bank debt, as bank regulators are raising the capital charges for exposures to other banks and could decide to treat a bank's holding of bail-in eligible senior debt of another bank as the holding of another bank's capital instruments which may be required to be deducted from core Tier 1 capital under the new Basel III regime.

C. Bail-in, Public, and Private Recapitalization

The primary aim of any public authority as regards resolution is to do the minimum **10.24** necessary to facilitate the continuation of the services provided by the entity in resolution. The existence of a power to bail-in can facilitate this in a non-intuitive way, since the possibility of suffering a bail-in may provide a powerful incentive to private creditors to agree a voluntary restructuring.

Privately funded recapitalization is a technique which has a surprisingly long his- **10.25** tory. Central banks have had considerable experience over the years with a technique which involves identifying the largest creditors of the troubled institution concerned, locking them in a room together, and explaining that their mutual self-interest clearly indicates their assembling a resolution fund out of their own resources. For example, in the 1970s, the Bank of England dealt with the secondary banking crisis by organizing a 'lifeboat' amongst the major clearing banks which at its peak amounted to 40 per cent of their capital, and in 1998 the Federal Reserve facilitated the rescue of LTCM by a group of the largest US commercial and investment banks.

The primary problem with this model of privately funded recapitalization is that it **10.26** is more or less impossible to identify every significant creditor of a SIFI in any reasonable timescale, and even harder to persuade them to agree amongst themselves in the short period available to those charged with resolving a bank. These issues are more acute where a bank is significantly dependent on capital markets funding with a dispersed bondholder group. Even within a small 'lifeboat' group under great time pressure the prisoners' dilemma will arise and, as the Lehman Brothers experience shows, orchestrating all the parties towards a consensual solution in a weekend timetable may just prove too challenging.

10.27 This could be accomplished by providing in the terms of the agreement by which the creditor becomes a creditor that, in the event of a recapitalization being required, the amount due to him will be reduced by the amount of his contribution to the recapitalization in exchange for shares in the bank or by giving the authorities statutory powers to achieve this result (or a hybrid combination of the two methods).

10.28 There is, however, one final point which should be made as regards the use of this technique. For any firm in any business, a financial crisis can be defined as the moment when it runs out of cash. Extinguishing liabilities, whilst restoring balance-sheet solvency, does not produce a penny of new cash. A balance-sheet restructuring, therefore, is only useful if it is sufficient to restore credibility—and therefore access to liquidity—to the institution concerned. A private recapitalization done using bail-in techniques will therefore involve a significantly greater write-down of creditor assets than the amount which would be required if those creditors were to agree to advance new money to the troubled institution. It may, therefore, be the case that the principal effect of the possibility of a bail-in might be to resolve the prisoner's dilemma[6] and make it easier for central banks to provide secured liquidity where necessary. This would not be a bad or an undesirable outcome.

D. Bail-in, Subordinated Capital, and Contingent Capital

10.29 The idea that banks should be able to subordinate some of their debt in order to enhance their solvency ratios has been around for many decades. The results have included innovative hybrid subordinated capital (qualifying as Tier 1 capital), perpetual subordinated debt (upper Tier 2), or term subordinated (lower Tier 2). However, regulators objected—and events proved—that although this subordination would have had the effect of protecting depositors in an insolvency, it provided no benefit where a bank was in difficulty but liquidation was not a real option. In particular, where it is not clear whether short-term debt is senior to subordinated debt, taxpayers could end up bailing out subordinated debtholders along with senior creditors and subordinated debt might also impede resolution options such as the sale of the whole entity to a purchaser.

10.30 As a result of this, Basel III introduced a rule that neither subordinated debt instruments nor preference shares should count as capital unless either (i) the terms and conditions of the instruments contain a provision that required them, at the option

---

[6] Or, alternatively expressed, to restore Pareto optimality to the class of outcomes of individual choices.

of the relevant regulator, to be written off or converted into common equity at the trigger point of non-viability, or (ii) the bank's home state had laws which required that debt to be written off at that trigger point or otherwise required those instruments to fully absorb loss before taxpayers are exposed to loss.[7] The trigger point under special resolution regimes is when the regulator determines either that the firm cannot continue in business without an injection of public capital or that the firm will be required to take a write-off in order to be recapitalized.[8] Thus, these proposals, in common with more general bail-in proposals, envisage that subordinated debt at least must be exposed to loss at a gone concern (or near-gone concern) trigger point, in order to facilitate a going concern outcome.

The increased focus on the loss absorbency of banks has also led to the development **10.31** of new instruments capable of absorbing losses on a going concern basis, by being written down or converting into equity at a trigger point intended to occur some time before the point of non-viability. These contingent convertible or contingent capital bonds aim to restore the health of a bank by either converting the debt into equity or writing down the outstanding amount of the debt—thus creating additional core Tier 1 capital—at a trigger point generally set by reference to the issuer's capital ratio falling below a level set at a point well above the point at which the bank will be in real crisis.[9] The intention is that these instruments should count towards increased regulatory measures of loss-absorbency.

It is therefore clear that there is some similarity between contingent capital and bail- **10.32** in eligible debt. Both are, in effect, debt instruments that have the capacity to create or restore a bank's core equity capital at a defined trigger point, to secure a going concern outcome for the institution as a whole. Both can take the form of either senior or subordinated debt and both could be required to be converted or written down in whole or in part as needed to achieve their ends.

There are, however, three principal differences between the two. First, contin- **10.33** gent capital is based on a going concern trigger, in contrast to the gone concern (or near-gone concern) trigger envisaged by bail-in proposals. Second, for that reason, contingent capital can be structured with an objectively defined trigger point and a pre-defined conversion or write-down mechanism, which requires no regulatory intervention to achieve its outcome and no (or minimal) exercise of discretion by the bank's board. In contrast, a bail-in is triggered at a point of non-viability which inevitably requires an exercise of regulatory discretion. At least for bail-ins of senior debt, there will also need to be discretion exercised by

---

[7] The EU regime follows the second of these routes—see Art 59 BRRD.

[8] See the Basel press release of 13 January 2011 at <http://www.bis.org/press/p110113.pdf> (accessed 26 October 2015). This articulates the policy which was consulted on in its 'Proposal to ensure the loss absorbency of regulatory capital at the point of non-viability'—BCBS 174 of August 2010 at <http://www.bis.org/publ/bcbs174.pdf> (accessed 26 October 2015).

[9] At the time of writing there have only been a small number of such issues, notably by Lloyds in 2009, Rabobank and Credit Suisse in 2011.

regulators as to the quantum of the debt that is subject to conversion or write-down and, in the case of conversion, the quantum of shares issued in exchange. Third, as a result of the two previous features, contingent capital can more readily be structured on a wholly contractual basis, where, as discussed below, bail-in proposals (at least for senior debt) are likely to require the backing of a statutory regime empowering regulators to take the necessary actions and to deal with consequential issues, such as the cancellation or dilution of existing equity and the overriding of events of default.

E. Direct Bail-in

10.34 The classical bank resolution mechanism involves transferring assets (usually good loans) and liabilities (usually retail and corporate deposits) to a 'good bank' (a 'bridge bank') in such a fashion that the bridge bank remains solvent (and can be wound down or sold at a later stage) or to a rival purchaser. The remainder (including ownership of the good bank) will be left in the initial institution—now the 'bad bank'—which is likely to be very bad indeed. The residual creditors of the bad bank will generally be entitled to what enterprise value may be secured from the sale of the ownership of the good bank (or the sale to the purchaser) and the realization proceeds of any (usually illiquid and often toxic) assets left in the bad bank, but are likely to be left short.

10.35 This approach has been tried and tested around the world, and in particular is the usual modus operandi of the US Federal Deposit Insurance Corporation, which may have more experience of managing bank failures than any other organization. However, it is a tried-and-tested technique in the context of smaller or primarily domestic retail-financed banks, whose structures are generally straightforward and whose funding is non-complex. The difficulty in using this technique in other circumstances is that the more complex the business of the institution, the harder it is to perform the division of assets into 'good' and 'bad'. This difficulty is then magnified many times over if the institution has significant assets or liabilities governed by foreign law or held through foreign branches or subsidiaries, which are subject to their own investor protection or regulatory regime and in the case of overseas subsidiaries with creditors of their own.

10.36 Banks exist in an industry in which viability is measured minute to minute. In many businesses it is possible for a business to suspend its activities for days or even weeks without doing irreparable damage to its commercial success. However, if a bank ceases to function even for a period measured in minutes, its viability as a business may be gone. A successful bank resolution is therefore one which can be completely effected in a period in which the bank is closed for business—classically between the close of business in the United States on Friday evening and opening of business in Tokyo on Monday morning, or around fifty hours.

There can therefore be a point at which an institution can become too large or too **10.37** complex to divide into a 'good' and a 'bad' bank in the fifty available hours. This point is well below the size of any institution which could reasonably be considered systemically significant. Resolution planning ('living wills') can increase the confidence of regulators that these techniques can be used, but the usefulness of the bail-in option is that it can provide a more credible, readily understood alternative.

Alternatively, the simplest way to effect a bank resolution is to arrange for those **10.38** parts of the bank's undertaking which it is sought to preserve to be transferred to a solvent purchaser with sufficient resources to sustain them (although such transactions may be subsequently criticized as leading to over-concentration in the market). However, even if potential purchasers exist for the insolvent business, the problem which may well have to be faced is that there is a tremendous difference between knowing that an undertaking is in trouble and knowing exactly the extent of the trouble that the undertaking is in. Resolution purchases may simply have the effect of imperilling the stability of the purchaser, and in such cases the usefulness of the existence of a bail-in option may be considerable.

F. Which Creditors should be Bailed In?

The question of legal effectiveness is frequently confused with the question of **10.39** the scope of the bail-in itself. The reason for this is that when considering bail-in regimes, an apposition is sometimes posed between a 'targeted' regime, under which the bail-in is only possible for certain pre-designated exposures, and a 'comprehensive' regime, in which the bail-in is extended to all creditors subject to a closed list of exceptions.[10] It should be clear from the foregoing that a 'comprehensive' regime may be legally ineffective, depending on the existence of cross-border insolvency recognition statutes such as those based on the 1997 United Nations Commission on International Trade Law (UNCITRAL) Model Law on Cross-Border Insolvency[11] or judicial recognition of bail-in based on the longstanding judicial doctrine of international comity, for any institution whose debt was not entirely subject to the laws of the country of its home state regulator. Since it would in practice be impossible to require a global institution to enter into all of its financial contracts under the law of its place of incorporation, the next best operative solution would be to require the bank as a matter of regulation to identify the cross-border recognition statutes or judicial cross-border

---

[10] These are the labels adopted in the European Commission discussion document referenced in n 1 above.

[11] The UNCITRAL model law is clear that it is not expected to apply to (and is not in practice applied to) banks and insurance companies (see para 56 of the Guide to Enactment). However, it does apply to non-bank-holding companies, and is therefore likely to be applicable in respect of resolution effected on an SPE basis at the level of an unregulated holding company.

recognition doctrines in the jurisdictions of its material foreign branches and subsidiaries or include in all of its relevant contracts language which would give effect to the bail-in. At this point, the distinction between the 'targeted' regime and the 'comprehensive' regime disappears—in both cases, the mechanism by which the bail-in is effected is the inclusion of language in the documentation creating the relevant exposure, and the principal remaining distinction is the means by which the scope is defined.

10.40 Consideration of this exposes another issue regarding a 'comprehensive' bail-in regime. It is accepted that not all creditors should be bailed-in—in addition to the 'trade' creditors who would have to be preserved, there would clearly be other classes of contracts—purchase of goods, occupation of real estate, unpaid salaries, outsourcing fees, and many others—which would also have to be outside the scope of the regime. The legal difficulties which would be caused for banks by the existence of a continuing obligation to consider every material contract entered into across the bank against this issue would be considerable, and the legal uncertainties raised by the question of whether the bank had correctly categorized the material exposures which it had entered into would result in legal uncertainty affecting the bail-in as a whole—an outcome which would be toxic for the success of the bail-in when required.

10.41 Consideration of the 'targeted' approach, however, immediately flushes another legal chimera—the idea that creditors could 'contract out of bail-in'. This is clearly possible (it is true of all creditors in all possible structures)—the question is whether it is a problem, and the answer to the question of whether it is a problem, depends on the way in which bail-in is approached by regulators.

10.42 In the context of any bail-in arrangement, it is clear that certain creditors must be capable of being excluded from the possibility of bail-in (secured creditors are an obvious example). It is therefore essential for the institution concerned to be able to say clearly to any creditor whether or not it will be caught by a bail-in possibility. Since the factors which drive that determination must be mechanical and predictable, it will always be possible for any claim to be taken outside the scope of bail-in. The issue is not the fact that this is possible—it is inevitable—but the question of whether the fact of the possibility weakens the reliance which the regulator would seek to place on the bail-in mechanism under a special resolution regime.

10.43 In order to answer this, we need to think about the bail-in mechanism under a special resolution regime from the perspective of the regulator. In general, we expect regulators to determine their approach to bail-in capital levels in the context of a 'living will' analysis. Regulators should assess the question of whether:

(a) there is sufficient existing equity capital to meet anticipated losses,

(b) there is sufficient contingent capital available to meet unanticipated or crisis losses, and

(c) in the event of a catastrophic unexpected losses, there is sufficient bail-in eligible debt available to avoid the necessity for a government bail-out.

This process should yield a quantifiable requirement for the institution concerned **10.44** to maintain a specified amount of bail-in debt—defined as debt that can be written down or partially converted to equity on the determination of the relevant authority under its resolution powers. If the institution does not maintain sufficient bail-in eligible debt (i.e. permits too many counterparties to contract out of bail-in) the required amount of contingent capital or equity would simply be increased proportionately. However, if the institution does have sufficient bail-in eligible debt to satisfy the regulator, there is no reason to assume that the regulator should care whether new creditors fall inside or outside this scope. Since it should be assumed that it will be clear to all creditors how much of the institution's total debt is bail-in eligible and how much is not, an institution which sought to reduce the amount of its debt which was bail-in eligible would be expected to suffer a significant increase in its cost of funding from its remaining bail-in-able debt, and, of course, vice versa. Thus provided that the institution maintained sufficient bail-in debt to satisfy its regulator, there is no reason for concern about 'contracting out'. Indeed, the flexibility to issue additional non-bail-in eligible debt—which is the remaining distinction between the comprehensive and the targeted approach—may be a source of strength. It allows additional funding, presumably at lower cost, in normal times and, in times of stress when it may not be possible to issue further bail-in eligible debt because of the increased risk of loss, would allow the institution to continue to access the capital markets without the need to create a further category of super-senior creditors or debtor in possession financing.

G. The Limits of Bail-ins

Bail-ins are not necessarily a panacea, and will not produce a zero-failure environ- **10.45** ment for all banks. Recapitalization only works for good businesses with bad balance sheets—businesses which are fundamentally bad will not be and should not be bailed in, but will be left to a resolution regime in the ordinary way. It is also perfectly possible for a bail-in to fail—if the initial assessment of the extent of the losses of an institution is sufficiently adrift, the amount of new capital created by the bail-in may be insufficient to support the business. Possibly more importantly, a bailed-in bank will only survive if counterparties, creditors, and customers believe that the institution is now robust. Leaving aside uncertainties as to the legal robustness of the bail-in (which should be largely eliminated by the use of the SPE method and appropriate safeguards), it will be important that the market be satisfied that the recapitalized institution has enough capital for its needs, and in response to the regulators assurance that this is now the case the market might not unreasonably respond 'yes, but that is what you said last time'. It has been suggested that this problem could be addressed by creating an equivalent of 'debtor-in-possession' financing which could be used in such cases, whereby a bailed-in institution could contract on terms that new creditors were senior to existing creditors. However, this proposal is outside the scope of this chapter.

10.46 The most significant obstacle to the use of bail-ins, however, is that at the end of the day a bail-in is simply a mechanism for allocating an existing loss. It will only be possible to use it to allocate such losses to the bank's creditors if the bank's creditors are sufficiently robust to absorb that loss. In a systemic crisis, where all systemic institutions are simultaneously at risk due to external circumstances, a bail-in could be counter-productive if the institutions own significant amounts of each other's bail-in-able debt, sending cascades of default across the system. However, even in this case bail-in is preferable to 'sudden-stop' liquidation, since such liquidation would result in greater losses throughout the system and therefore increase the damage to the system—thus no matter how bad the overall systemic problem, it will always be the case that a bail-in response will be preferable to a liquidation response.

H. Loss Absorbency and MREL

10.47 As noted above, it is clear that in order to recapitalize a bank, it is first necessary to have some identifiable debt that can be written down without fostering runs, contagion or otherwise destabilizing the financial system. This is the basis of the proposed Financial Stability Board (FSB) requirement that banks raise a minimum amount of their funding in the form of long-term unsecured debt, referred to as total loss absorbing capacity (TLAC). The EU implementation of the TLAC requirement is through Article 45 of BRRD. This requires EU banks to maintain a minimum proportion of their liabilities in the form of 'eligible liabilities', which in turn produces a 'minimum requirement for eligible liabilities', or MREL. Although the definition of MREL is set out in Article 45 of BRRD, the most important part of that Article is 45(17) and (18), which provides that the commission shall submit a legislative proposal to revise these provisions by the 31 December 2016. This rare manifestation of a law which provides that it should be changed before it comes into force is a result of a sincere desire on the part of the European Union to adopt the FSB structure now that it is finalized, and the sequence of events that is currently anticipated is that now that the FSB has finalized its international TLAC standards the European Union will incorporate them into its definition of MREL.

10.48 The primary difference between the FSB TLAC approach and the EU MREL approach, however, lies in the fact that whereas the FSB is explicitly designing a standard for the largest G-SIBs, the EU MREL requirement applies—in theory— to every bank in the European Union. The European Banking Authority (EBA), in its final draft of the regulatory requirements to apply to MREL,[12] provides the following three examples of how the MREL requirement might work in practice for banks of different sizes:

Bank A is a small bank, assumed to have a minimum total capital requirement of 8 per cent of risk-weighted assets (RWAs) and a combined buffer requirement of 2.5 per cent (i.e. no pillar 2 or discretionary buffer requirements) and total RWAs equal to 35 per cent of total liabilities and own funds.

The resolvability assessment process concludes that it is both feasible and credible to liquidate the bank. The resolution authority therefore determines a loss absorption amount by translating the overall capital requirement of 10.5 per cent of RWAs into the equivalent percentage of total liabilities and own funds—in this case, 3.7 per cent. The recapitalisation amount is zero, as the bank could be liquidated without affecting financial stability.

Bank B is a medium-sized bank, again with an overall capital requirement of 10.5 per cent and RWAs equal to 35 per cent of total liabilities and own funds. The loss absorption amount determined by the resolution authority is therefore also 3.7 per cent of total liabilities and own funds. However, the resolution authority assesses that liquidation is not credible because the bank carries out some critical functions that need to be preserved. The resolution plan adopted is to transfer assets and liabilities associated with the critical functions to a bridge bank and liquidate the remaining assets and liabilities. The planned bridge bank accounts for half of the RWAs of Bank B, so the resolution authority sets a recapitalisation amount of 1.8 per cent of total liabilities and own funds. This gives a total MREL of 5.5 per cent. If a leverage ratio requirement had been applied, this would also need to be considered and could lead to a higher level of MREL.

Bank C is a large, systemically important bank with a capital conservation buffer requirement of 2.5 per cent, a G-SIB surcharge requirement of 2.5 per cent, and a pillar 2 capital requirement of 2 per cent of RWAs, giving an overall capital requirement of 15 per cent of RWAs. Again RWAs are 35 per cent of total liabilities and own funds. If the pillar 2 and G-SIB surcharges are included in the resolution authority's assessment of the required loss absorption amount, it would be 5.4% of total liabilities and own funds. The resolution authority determines that the only feasible and credible resolution strategy is SPE bail-in, and so resolution will not result in any immediate reduction in RWAs. The resolution authority therefore sets a recapitalisation amount also equal to 5.4 per cent of total liabilities, and a total MREL of 10.8 per cent. If a leverage ratio requirement had been applied, this would also need to be considered and could lead to a higher level of MREL.[13]

---

[12] EBA/RTS/2015/05 3 July 2015.
[13] Ibid at p. 8.

11

INSTITUTIONAL
AND CROSS-BORDER ISSUES

A. BRRD and the Single Resolution Mechanism

11.01 The Bank Recovery and Resolution Directive (BRRD) provides a basis for resolution across the European Union. However, it also provides the framework for the EU Single Resolution Mechanism (SRM), implemented within the eurozone[1] by the Single Resolution Mechanism Regulation (SRMR)[2] and overseen by the Single Resolution Board (SRB). This regulation repeats some parts of the BRRD, but is designed to operate alongside it. Thus, an EU bank group with three bank subsidiaries, two within the eurozone area and one in the United Kingdom, would find the SRB charged with resolution of two of the subsidiaries, operating under the SRM, and the Bank of England acting as resolution authority of the third. In this situation the SRB is simply another resolution authority, and the two authorities follow the procedures set out within the BRRD as regards their interaction. However, as regards the two subsidiaries within the SRM, the SRB can disregard those parts of the BRRD which would apply across borders and act under the relevant provisions of the SRMR.

11.02 Although the SRM is in some respects a complement to the Single Supervisory Mechanism (SSM), the SRM was implemented some time after the SSM, The Single Supervisory Mechanism Regulation[3] (SSMR) came into force some time ago, and the European Central Bank (ECB) assumed the powers as the single supervisor for the eurozone on 4 November 2014. However, BRRD required member states to adopt implementing legislation and to apply that legislation from 1 January 2016. The SRMR also applies (in operative part) from 1 January 2016,

---

[1] The SRM does make provision for non-eurozone member states to apply to join the SRM, and at least one non-eurozone state (Denmark) has indicated that it may join. The SRM is envisaged as operating in parallel with the Single Supervision Mechanism, so it would be necessary for a joining country to join both.

[2] 2015/81.

[3] 1022/2013.

and the SRB assumed its responsibilities as the resolution authority for the euro-zone on that date.

B. Scope

The BRRD and the changes it requires to national laws apply across all EU member **11.03**
states. In contrast, the SSM Regulation and the SRM Regulation create a supervision and resolution framework only for participating member states, that is, euro-zone member states and other member states that agree to join the SSM (none have yet done so).[4]

BRRD—allocation of functions

The BRRD requires member states to confer on their resolution authorities the full **11.04**
set of resolution tools and powers set out therein. However, there are certain roles under the BRRD for the home state national competent authority (NCA), that is, the banking supervisor.[5] In particular:

- The NCA assesses recovery plans and requires remedial action, but the resolution authority reviews and comments as well.[6]
- The resolution authority consults with the NCA on the resolution plan, the resolvability assessment, and remedial action, and the NCA plays a role in information-gathering for resolution planning and in implementing requirements for remedial action.[7]
- The NCA reviews and approves intragroup financial support agreements and action under it, subject to notice to the resolution authority.[8]
- The NCA has powers to take early intervention measures with respect to an institution (including removal of management and temporary administration), which are notified to the resolution authority.[9]
- Generally it is the NCA that determines whether an institution is failing or is likely to fail and it is the resolution authority that determines whether the other conditions for resolution are met (i.e. whether other actions could prevent

---

[4] The BRRD is marked as a 'text with EEA [European Economic Area] relevance'. This means that it should be implemented in Norway as well. However, there is currently a dispute between the European Union and the members of the EEA about how EU single market legislation should apply in EEA states where it provides powers for the European Supervisory Authorities (ESAs), such as the European Banking Authority and the European Securities Markets Authority. The EEA states do not participate in the ESAs on an equal footing. It is currently expected that Norway and others will implement equivalent regimes which replicate the provisions of BRRD but do not confer powers on ESAs.

[5] Note, not the national resolution authority (NRA).

[6] Art 6.

[7] Arts 10, 11, 15, and 16.

[8] Art 20 and 25.

[9] Arts 27–29.

failure within a reasonable time and whether resolution action is in the public interest), and takes the overall decision on whether to take resolution action. However, in appropriate cases, the member state can confer the function of deciding whether the institution is failing or is likely to fail on the resolution authority.[10]

- The NCA would be responsible for authorization of any purchaser of the business and any change of control authorizations[11] or a bridge bank, including potential waiving of some of the normal conditions for authorization.[12]
- The NCA also retains the role in approving any changes of control resulting from bail-in[13] and agrees the business reorganization plan in conjunction with bail-in.[14]
- The resolution authority consults the NCA on the minimum requirement for eligible liabilities (MREL).[15]
- The NCA plays a role in the use of national government stabilization tools.[16]
- The member state can decide whether it is the NCA or the resolution authority that makes the determinations necessary for the use of the write-down tool.[17]
- There are procedures for notices between the NCA and the resolution authority (Articles 81ff and 90).
- The NCAs also participate in cooperation agreements with relevant non-EU states (Article 97(4)).

11.05 If the entity has 'significant branches' in another member state (broadly, branches which are of local systemic importance), then there is a role for the NCA and resolution authority from that member state (primarily rights to be consulted).

Impact of SSM Regulation

11.06 The SSM Regulation only has limited effect on the allocation of functions under the BRRD, even for those institutions for which the European Central Bank (ECB) becomes the direct supervisor. The structure of the SSM Regulation is that the ECB is given specific tasks with respect to institutions in participating member states. It will directly carry out those tasks with respect to some, more significant institutions (directly supervised institutions), acting with the assistance of the NCA. With respect to other institutions (indirectly supervised institutions), the NCAs retain the frontline responsibility for carrying out those tasks, acting within the framework and guidelines set by the ECB, which allow the ECB to control the decisions

---

[10] Art 32.
[11] Art 38.
[12] Art 41(1).
[13] Art 47(4).
[14] Art 52.
[15] Art 45(6) and (15).
[16] Arts 56 ff.
[17] Art 61(2).

of the NCA, although the ECB always retains responsibility for authorizations and change of control approval for institutions in the participating member states.

For the most part, the tasks described above in relation to the role of the NCA **11.07** under the BRRD will remain with the NCA in relation to a bank, even if that bank is directly supervised by the ECB under the SSM. However:

- supervisory tasks relating to recovery plans and early intervention measures are ECB tasks and thus would be directly exercised by the ECB if the ECB directly supervises a bank, or by the relevant NCA, if the ECB indirectly supervises the bank, but within the framework and guidelines set by the ECB;
- the ECB would have the function of authorizing any purchaser or bridge bank and approving change of control in relation to the bank in the context of a resolution;
- only the ECB could withdraw the authorization of the bank, which means that the ECB could close the bank even if the NCA and member state concerned choose not to trigger resolution action;
- in practice, the NCA, the ECB, and the resolution authority would need to cooperate in relation to resolution action even if this remains, in effect a national issue.

Impact of the SRMR

The SRMR creates an EU Single Resolution Board with resolution responsibilities **11.08** and creates a (gradually) mutualized resolution fund. It also moves some tasks to the ECB that were exercised by the NCAs.

In summary, if a bank is directly supervised by the ECB, the effect of the SRMR **11.09** is to move most of the resolution responsibilities under the BRRD from the national level, although the member state's national resolution authority (NRA) remains responsible for implementing the resolution decisions of the SRB. The SRB's decisions on resolution actions are subject to a measure of control by the Commission and the Council of the European Union (which represents the member states).

If a bank is not directly supervised by the ECB, the effect of the SRMR is largely **11.10** to leave things unchanged as described above, except if the SRB intervenes to take over resolution and to displace the national authority (and in any event the national authorities will need to coordinate their actions with the SRB).

The SRMR divides the tasks as follows: **11.11**

- For entities and groups directly supervised by the ECB and cross-border groups (i.e. groups which have supervised entities in two or more participating member states), the SRB is responsible for resolution planning, setting MREL, adopting resolution decisions, and writing down capital instruments. In addition, a member state may decide that the SRB shall exercise the tasks in the SRMR for all entities and groups established in its territory.

- For other institutions and groups, NRAs are responsible for resolution planning, setting MREL, adopting resolution actions, and writing down capital instruments, except that if the resolution action involves the use of the Fund, the SRB must adopt the resolution scheme. In addition, the SRB can at any time displace the national resolution authority and take over all the tasks under the SRMR (e.g. at the request of the national resolution authority or if the SRB is not satisfied with national actions taken).

Where the SRB is taking resolution decisions, the ECB (not the NRA) is responsible for deciding whether the entity is failing or likely to fail. In addition, there is a defined process for the SRB to initiate resolution which starts with the SRB adopting a resolution scheme if the conditions to resolution are met and sending it to the Commission.

- The Commission may either endorse or object to the scheme except in the areas reserved to the Council.
- The Commission may propose to the Council to object on the grounds that the public interest test is not satisfied or to approve or object to a material modification of the amount of the Fund provided for the SRB's scheme. The Council votes by simple majority on this.

11.12 The scheme only enters into force if no objection has been expressed by the Commission or the Council within twenty-four hours of the scheme being sent to the Commission. If the Commission objects or the Council approves a modification as to the use of the Fund, the SRB has to amend its scheme to reflect the reasons given. The Commission can direct changes to the scheme where the exclusion of liabilities from bail-in results in a contribution by the Fund. If the Council objects on the grounds that the public interest test is not met, the institution must be wound up.

11.13 The Commission may be required to give state aid approval in relation to the resolution and the use of the Fund.

11.14 Where the SRB is exercising tasks or powers under the BRRD, it is considered to be the NRA or relevant group level resolution authority (Article 5(1)). However, implementation of the SRB's scheme is carried out by the NRA using its national powers implementing the BRRD (Article 16(8) and Article 26).

11.15 Where the national resolution authority is acting under the SRMR it must notify the SRB in advance and coordinate its measures with the SRB.

11.16 The SRM regulation operates as an overlay to the provisions of the BRRD so that it is necessary to read the two together to determine how particular functions will be exercised by the authorities, including by national resolution authorities, where they are responsible for resolution.

C. Cross-border Branching

The BRRD requires each member state to recognize in their law the effect of reso- **11.17**
lution actions taken by other member states. This means that as regards foreign
resolution action which purports to transfer assets located in their jurisdiction, or
rights or liabilities governed by their law, or write-down or convert liabilities governed by their law or owed to creditors in their jurisdictions, their law must make
provision for such transfers or conversions to take effect automatically[18] and cannot
be prevented, challenged, or set aside under their law.

In principle this means that where a bank in a member state has a branch in another, **11.18**
the resolution activities undertaken in the home member state will have automatic
effect in respect of assets and liabilities of the branch.

The mechanism by which this is achieved is—broadly—through the amendment **11.19**
of the existing Credit Institutions Winding Up Directive (CIWUD) (2001/24/
EC) so that:

- exercise of resolution measures and powers under the BRRD are treated as
  'reorganisation measures'
- only the home member state is entitled to take reorganization measures (or
  winding up proceedings) with respect to an institution. This means that there
  can be no proceedings in the branch states
- other member states are required to give effect to the home member state measures.

The CIWUD provides:[19] **11.20**

> The reorganisation measures shall be applied in accordance with the laws, regula-
> tions and procedures applicable in the home member state, unless otherwise pro-
> vided in this Directive.
>
> They shall be fully effective in accordance with the legislation of that member state
> throughout the Community without any further formalities, including as against
> third parties in other member states, even where the rules of the host member state
> applicable to them do not provide for such measures or make their implementation
> subject to conditions which are not fulfilled.
>
> The reorganisation measures shall be effective throughout the Community once
> they become effective in the member state where they have been taken.
> - The provisions of the BRRD allowing the home state authority powers to suspend
>   termination rights and impose temporary stays override netting and repurchase
>   agreements governed by other member states' laws.
> - However, there are some exceptions to the general rule of universality, including
>   that set off provisions remain governed by national law.

---

[18] Art 66.
[19] Art 2(2).

11.21 The SRMR does not completely supplant the national law implementing the BRRD. When it comes to resolution involving the Board, the relationship between the Board and national resolution authorities (NRA) is that the NRAs implement decisions of the Board using their powers under their national law implementing the BRRD.

11.22 The SRMR also affects third-country resolutions. Under Article 31 of the SRMR, the SRB must assess and issue a recommendation addressed to the national resolution authorities in the participating member states (i.e. eurozone states, plus those member states participating in the single supervisory mechanism) on the recognition and enforcement of third-country resolution proceedings in relation to a third-country institution within the scope of Article 94 BRRD. The national resolution authorities must comply (by implementing the recommendation using their powers under national law implementing Article 94) or provide a reasoned explanation why they cannot implement the recommendation of the SRB.

D. Cross-border Issues

11.23 A resolution regime will be useless unless it is immediately accepted by the bank's customers and counterparties as legally effective. A resolution, by itself, is purely an accounting adjustment. Its usefulness lies in the fact that by writing off debt, it improves the creditworthiness of the bank concerned to a stage where it can access the money markets and raise liquidity. In order to achieve this objective, providers of liquidity must be left with no grounds to doubt that the write-off is immediately effective and cannot be credibly challenged.

11.24 Achieving this level of legal certainty requires solid legal analysis. In a situation where the bank and all the relevant creditors were located in a single jurisdiction, simple legislation in that jurisdiction would suffice. However, this is not—and will never be—the case for any global systemically important banking group (G-SIB). The challenge is therefore to construct a legal solution which employs a variety of legal techniques to achieve a robust outcome without falling into impossible demands for global harmonization of bank resolution legislation.

11.25 It might be possible in some jurisdictions—including possibly the United Kingdom—to create a bail-in regime entirely by private contract by including the relevant provisions in debt instruments issued by the entity and in the constitution of that entity. However, this would give rise to some interesting legal conundrums, since the issuer would be seeking to create debts on terms allowing the debtor, at its discretion, to eliminate all or part of the debt and to replace that debt with new shares. Even if this were possible, it seems unlikely that it would be acceptable to those creditors or the entity's shareholders that such a regime could be operated by the board of the relevant company entirely in its discretion, and even more unlikely that, in the context of the modern law on directors' liability, any board of directors would in practice be prepared to exercise such a discretion. Thus even if the regime were based entirely on private law, it seems likely that the contractual provisions would need to be structured so that the initiation of the bail-in is triggered by an external act of an appropriate regulator or other public body and to ensure that any discretion about the extent of any necessary write-down or any compensatory issue of equity is also exercised by or jointly with the authorities rather than solely by the bank's board. This might create procedural and technical difficulties for public authorities, who in many cases might perceive unacceptable risks to acting pursuant to private rights rather than public obligations.

An alternative approach is to provide for bail-in by legislation. Bail-in backed by legislation has a number of appealing aspects—in many jurisdictions legislation will be necessary to deal with company law issues, and legislative backing would clearly underpin market confidence in the robustness of a bail-in. However, legislation is an imperfect solution for all but the smallest banks, since for the majority of banks a significant portion of their debt is likely to be governed by laws other than that of their place of incorporation—for example, most large continental European banks are likely to have bonds and other long-term unsecured debt governed by English or New York law.   **11.26**

The problem which arises in this case is known to English lawyers as the 'Metliss' problem. In *National Bank of Greece v Metliss*,[20] the English courts decided that where a Greek bank owed money under bonds governed by English law, a Greek statute passed for the purpose of varying liability on the bonds had no effect under English law, since—at its simplest—you cannot vary English legal rights by Greek statute. This principle might be applied by courts of at least some other jurisdictions—thus, if the contractual obligations of a UK bank were varied by UK law, there might be a risk that the variation would not be effective as against holders of New York law-governed bonds, unless Chapter 15 of the US Bankruptcy Code applied or the New York courts gave effect to the action in the UK resolution law as a matter of international comity. The litigation commenced in New York by Fir Tree Capital against Anglo Irish Bank Corporation is an example of a creditor seeking to rely on rights under New York-law-governed documentation alleged to conflict with the exercise of resolution powers, in this case those conferred on the Irish authorities by the Irish Credit Institutions (Stabilisation) Act 2010.[21]   **11.27**

---

[20] *National Bank of Greece and Athens SA v Metliss* [1958] AC 509.

[21] *Fir Tree Capital Opportunity Master Fund LP et al v Anglo Irish Bank Corp. Ltd*, case number 1:11-cv-00955, in the US District Court for the Southern District of New York. The conflicts issues raised were never decided, since the court at first instance found that Anglo Irish, having been nationalized, was a government entity and therefore shielded from lawsuits by the US Foreign Sovereign Immunities Act of 1976.

11.28 It is important not to overstate *Metliss*. In particular, the EU proposals would, if enacted, produce a regime in which a bail-in or write-down effected by the law of one member state would be recognized by the laws of other member states. In addition, a number of jurisdictions including the United States have adopted cross-border recognition statutes based on the United Nations Commission on International Trade Law (UNCITRAL) Model Law on Cross-Border Insolvency and have longstanding judicial doctrines that reflect a strong public policy in favour of deferring to foreign insolvency and similar proceedings, such as resolution proceedings, based on principles of international comity. Thus, courts in most cases may well be prepared to recognize compromises of creditors' rights arising under the insolvency or resolution laws of other jurisdictions. However, such recognition in practice has in the past been applied to insolvency proceedings, and predicated on the assumption that a similar process would be possible under the domestic law of the court concerned. It has not yet been tested in the context of proceedings under special resolution regimes, although such regimes are strikingly similar to traditional insolvency laws in purpose and effect. In short, there is a certain amount of legal uncertainty as to whether courts will give effect to foreign resolution proceedings as readily as they currently give effect to foreign insolvency proceedings. As between common law systems (and particularly as between the United States and the United Kingdom), this residual amount of legal uncertainty could probably be addressed adequately by including consent to insolvency and other resolution proceedings under the issuer's home country laws in debt instruments issued under foreign law. However, given the much greater variety of types of legal system within the European Union, the BRRD addresses the issue of legal certainty of cross-border recognition directly.

11.29 The BRRD has two provisions dealing with the recognition in EU member states of resolution measures taken in other EU member states. First, the BRRD amends the CIWUD[22] to require EU member states to recognize resolution measures taken in other member states in the same way that reorganization and winding up measures are recognized in accordance with the CIWUD.[23] Second, Article 66 of the BRRD has specific recognition provisions regarding transfers and write-downs.

E. Changes to the Credit Institutions (Winding-Up) Directive

11.30 The CIWUD provides for 'reorganisation measures' in respect of an EU credit institution implemented in one member state to be effective throughout the European Union (Article 3). The definition of 'reorganisation measures' in

---

[22] 2001/24/EC.
[23] Recital (119) and Art 117 of the BRRD.

Article 2 of CIWUD has been amended by Article 117(2) of the BRRD so that it now covers:

> measures which are intended to preserve or restore the financial situation of a credit institution or an investment firm as defined in Article 4(1), point (2) of Regulation (EU) No 575/2013 [ie, the Capital Requirements Regulation (CRR)] and which could affect third parties' pre-existing rights, including measures involving the possibility of a suspension of payments, suspension of enforcement measures or reduction of claims; those measures include the application of the resolution tools and the exercise of resolution powers provided for in Directive 2014/59/EU [ie, the BRRD].[24]

For these purposes: **11.31**

(a) 'resolution tools' are the sale of business tool, the bridge institution tool, the asset separation tool, and the bail-in tool (Articles 2(19) and 37(3) of the BRRD); ie, all the resolution tools prescribed by the BRRD, and

(b) 'resolution powers' are the powers in Articles 63–72 of the BRRD (eg, the power to transfer shares, to transfer rights, assets, and liabilities, to alter the maturity of debt instruments, to close out and terminate financial contracts and derivatives for the purpose of writing down the liability, to make transfers free of liabilities and encumbrances, to impose a short-term suspension of delivery and payment obligations, and to cancel or modify the terms of any contract) (Article 2(20) of the BRRD).

Accordingly, the starting point is that, under the CIWUD, each EU member   **11.32**
state is required to recognize and give effect to resolution measures taken in other member states. The law of another EU member state should, therefore, be able to transfer or reduce the liabilities on a contract governed by English law, a situation contrary to the general EU conflict of laws rule (Article 12 of the Rome I Regulation).[25]

However, there are exceptions in the CIWUD, as amended by the BRRD, to the   **11.33**
ability of foreign reorganization measures to modify English law obligations. In particular:

(a) reorganization measures do not affect the rights *in re* of creditors or third parties in respect of tangible or intangible, movable or immovable assets—both specific assets and collections of indefinite assets as a whole which change

---

[24] The original definition of 'reorganisation measures' in the CIWUD was as follows: '[M]easures which are intended to preserve or restore the financial situation of a credit institution and which could affect third parties' pre-existing rights, including measures involving the possibility of a suspension of payments, suspension of enforcement measures or reduction of claims.'
[25] The Rome I Regulation provides that it shall not prejudice the application of provisions of EU law which, in relation to particular matters, lays down conflict of laws rules relating to contractual obligations (Art 23). The provisions of the CIWUD and the BRRD therefore override the Rome I Regulation.

from time to time—belonging to the credit institution, which is situated in the territory of another member state at the time of the adoption of the measures;[26]

(b) reorganization measures do not affect seller's rights based on reservation of title where the asset in question is situated in a member state other than that in which the measures were adopted;[27]

(c) reorganization measures do not affect the rights of creditors to demand set-off of their claims against the claims of the credit institution where set-off is permitted by the law applicable to the credit institution's claim;[28]

(d) the enforcement of proprietary rights in instruments the existence or transfer of which presupposes their recording in a register, an account, or a centralized deposit system held in a member state shall be governed by the law of the member state where the register, account, or centralized deposit system in which those rights are recorded or held is located;[29]

(e) without prejudice to Articles 68 and 71 of the BRRD, netting arrangements are governed solely by the law of the contract which governs such arrangements;[30]

(f) without prejudice to Articles 68 and 71 of the BRRD and Article 24 of CIWUD, repurchase agreements are governed solely by the law of the contract which governs the agreement;[31] and

(g) without prejudice to Article 24 of CIWUD (above), transactions carried out in the context of a regulated market are governed solely by the law of the contract that governs the transactions.[32]

F. Cross-border Provisions of BRRD

11.34 In addition to amending the CIWUD regarding recognition, Article 66 of the BRRD sets out further new obligations on member states to recognize other member state's resolution activities. Article 66 has two elements:

(a) Article 66(1)–(3) deals with 'transfers of shares, other instruments of ownership, or assets, rights or liabilities' which are in a state other than that of the resolution authority or are governed by the law of another state. EU member states are obliged to ensure that transfers have effect under their laws, that they assist the relevant resolution authority and that their laws and courts

---

[26] Art 21 CIWUD.
[27] Art 22 CIWUD.
[28] Art 23 CIWUD.
[29] Art 24 CIWUD.
[30] Art 25 CIWUD.
[31] Art 26 CIWUD.
[32] Art 27 CIWUD.

cannot be used to obstruct the transfers. Since these provisions deal with transfers, they are presumably catering for the sale of business tool, the bridge institution tool, and the asset separation tool in Articles 37–42 of the BRRD, together with the powers in, for example, Article 63(1)(d) (power to transfer shares, or other instruments of ownership) and Article 63(1)(e) (power to transfer rights, assets, and liabilities).

(b) Article 66(4)–(6) deals with 'write-down or conversion powers,[33] including in relation to capital instruments in accordance with article 59 (ie, Additional Tier 1 and Tier 2 capital (Article 2(1)(74)) issued by a parent or subsidiary and eligible liabilities or relevant capital instruments of the institution under resolution), including liabilities governed by the law of, or owed to creditors in, another member state. That other member state is obliged to ensure that the principal amount of the liability or instrument is reduced, or liabilities converted, in accordance with the exercise of the write-down or conversion powers by the resolution authority of a member state. 'Eligible liabilities' are 'liabilities and capital instruments that do not qualify as Common Equity Tier 1, Additional Tier 1 or Tier 2 instruments of an institution or entity referred to in point (b), (c), or (d) of Article 1(1) (ie, parents or subsidiaries of a credit institution) that are not excluded from the scope of the bail-in tool by virtue of Article 44(2)'. Sums due under an International Swaps and Derivatives Association Master Agreement are eligible liabilities for these purposes. Since Article 66(4)–(6) is concerned with writing down and conversion, it is presumably directed to, for example, the power in Article 63(1)(e) (power to reduce, including to zero, eligible liabilities) and Article 63(1)(f) (power to convert eligible liabilities into shares).

In addition, the BRRD provides that: **11.35**

(c) a resolution authority can only exercise write-down and conversion powers for derivatives on or after closing out and netting the derivatives (Article 49(1) and (3))

(d) a resolution authority can close out derivatives for the purpose of applying Article 49 (Article 63(1)(k))

(e) member states must ensure that there is 'appropriate protection' for title transfer collateral arrangements and netting and set-off arrangements so as to

---

[33] '[W]rite-down and conversion powers' are defined in Art 2(1)(66) as the powers in Art 59(2) and in points (e)–(i) of Art 63(1). Art 59(2) provides that resolution authorities must have the power to write down or convert into shares 'capital instruments' (i.e. Additional Tier 1 and Tier 2 regulatory capital) 'of institutions or entities referred to in points (b), (c) and (d) of Article 1(1)', i.e., of parents and subsidiaries of banks. Art 63(1)(e)–(i) gives powers to reduce and convert various liabilities of the institution in resolution (NB, the power to close out derivatives is in Art 63(1)(k), and is not therefore a write-down or conversion power).

prevent the transfer of some, but not all, of the rights and liabilities protected under a netting or set-off arrangement or a title transfer financial collateral arrangement (Article 77). If some transactions could be transferred, netting would cease to be possible, depriving the counterparty of the capital benefits that the ability to net offers.

11.36 The effect of these Directives is, therefore, that the United Kingdom must ensure that English law gives effect to reorganization measures, including resolution measures, properly implemented in other EU member states even if those measures affect English law contracts. As mentioned above, this is contrary to the normal conflict of laws principle that foreign law cannot change the terms of an English law contract, still less terminate it.

G. Third-country Banks

11.37 This refers to United States and other banks who operate in the European Union.

11.38 Article 93 of the BRRD makes somewhat optimistic provision for the recognition at EU level of international agreements on cross-border bank resolution. The relevant parts of the BRRD as regards non-EU cross-border business therefore begin with Article 94. The basic approach is that the relevant EU authorities (or the EU resolution college, if there is one) shall take a decision as to whether to recognize the proceedings in the third country. If such recognition is granted, the national authorities should 'seek the enforcement of the recognized third-country resolution proceedings in accordance with national law. In general, the BRRD provisions are only triggered where the third country entity has either subsidiaries or branches in the European Union, or assets or liabilities located in member states or governed by the laws of member states.[34] To this end, they are required to have at least the following powers:

(a) exercise the resolution powers in relation to the following:
   (i) assets of a third-country institution or parent undertaking that are located in their member state or governed by the law of their member state;
   (ii) rights or liabilities of a third-country institution that are booked by the Union branch in their member state or governed by the law of their member state, or where claims in relation to such rights and liabilities are enforceable in their member state;
(b) perfect, including to require another person to take action to perfect, a transfer of shares or other instruments of ownership in a Union subsidiary established in the designating member state;

---

[34] Art 94(2). It is hard to see how these provisions could be relevant to an entity which did not have any of those characteristics.

(c) exercise the powers in Article 69 (suspension of payment or delivery obligations), 70 (restriction of the enforcement of security interests), or 71 (temporary suspension of termination rights) in relation to the rights of any party to
a contract with (a third-country entity in resolution) where such powers are
necessary in order to enforce third-country resolution proceedings; and

(d) render unenforceable any right to terminate, liquidate, or accelerate contracts,
or affect the contractual rights, of (a third-country entity in resolution) and
other group entities, where such a right arises from resolution action taken in
respect of the third-country institution, parent undertaking of such entities
or other group entities, whether by the third-country resolution authority
itself or otherwise pursuant to legal or regulatory requirements as to resolution arrangements in that country, provided that the substantive obligations
under the contract, including payment and delivery obligations, and provision of collateral, continue to be performed.

This in effect mandates member state authorities to recognize and enforce non-EU **11.39**
resolution under EU law.

There is, of course, a qualification to this. Article 95 sets out a range of grounds
on which recognition of third-country resolution proceedings can be rejected.
These are:

(a) that the third-country resolution proceedings would have adverse effects on
financial stability in the Member State in which the resolution authority is
based or that the proceedings would have adverse effects on financial stability in
another Member State;

(b) that independent resolution action...in relation to a Union branch is necessary
to achieve one or more of the resolution objectives;

(c) that creditors, including in particular depositors located or payable in a Member
State, would not receive the same treatment as third-country creditors and
depositors with similar legal rights under the third-country home resolution
proceedings;

(d) that recognition or enforcement of the third-country resolution proceedings
would have material fiscal implications for the Member State; or

(e) that the effects of such recognition or enforcement would be contrary to the
national law.

It is generally believed (although nowhere stated) that the concern behind a num- **11.40**
ber of these reservations is that national resolution authorities in other countries
may seek to prefer domestic over foreign creditors in resolutions. It would of course
be unconscionable for any EU authority to cooperate in a resolution effected on
this basis.

Finally, the BRRD requires[35] that member states have a fall-back power to **11.41**
resolve branches of third-country entities established in their jurisdictions.

---

[35] Art 96.

These powers are to be used in one of two cases: either where the bank concerned is in trouble but its home state authorities have not commenced resolution, or where resolution has been commenced but for one of the reasons set out in Article 95 cannot be given effect in the European Union. In this case, the BRRD is strangely silent on the specifics of the measures that ought to be taken to resolve the branch.

PART IV

THE UK RESOLUTION REGIME

12

UNITED KINGDOM— GENERAL APPROACH

The United Kingdom is unusual amongst EU countries in a number of ways as **12.01** regards resolution. Most importantly, the United Kingdom's first emergency legislation (the Banking (Special Provisions) Act 2008), created under enormous time pressure in response to a crisis which threatened to swallow up the country's banking system, has proved surprisingly enduring. Its outline is clearly visible in current UK legislation (the Banking Act 2009 (BA)), and there are substantial parts of its intellectual architecture which are clearly visible in the Bank Recovery and Resolution Directive (BRRD). Another aspect, however, is that both the Treasury and the Bank of England, as resolution authority, have produced relatively detailed statements of policy setting out their likely approach to future bank resolutions. It is therefore possible to give some detail as to how a UK bank resolution would be managed.

The Bank of England is the UK Resolution Authority (i.e. the UK NRA). In its **12.02** document 'The Bank of England's Approach to Resolution',[1] it divides all bank resolutions into three phases:

- stabilization phase, in which the provision of critical economic functions is assured, either through transfer to a solvent third party or through bail-in to recapitalize the failed firm;
- restructuring phase, during which any necessary changes are made to the structure and business model of the whole firm or its constituent parts to address the causes of failure; and
- exit from resolution, where the involvement of the resolution authority in the failed firm and any successor firms comes to a close.

In many respects the second and third of these phases are common to all restructurings, financial and otherwise. What distinguishes resolution of financial firms from resolution of other entities is therefore the first: the stabilization phase.

---

[1] Bank of England, October 2014.

12.03 The essence of the stabilization phase is that it is intended to avoid panic. It must therefore be immediate, and as a result the resolution authority is empowered to— and will—act without seeking the consent of shareholders, creditors, or the existing management of the firm.

12.04 In broad terms, restructuring takes time, and—except in the case of emergency nationalization—the most important element of a stabilization intervention is likely to be an announcement of what will be done, as opposed to an announcement of what has been done. The Bank will therefore seek to act as rapidly as possible.

12.05 It is reasonably well-known that in practice banks do not fail because of loss of capital, but because of loss of access to liquidity—the point at which a bank must close its doors is the point at which it can no longer access cash to pay its obligations, regardless of the state of its balance sheet. This means that any firm facing resolution is almost certainly in a liquidity crisis, and part of the immediate stabilization measures required is the creation of access to new liquidity. It is unlikely that the institution will have sufficient available high-quality liquid assets available to be able to access conventional central bank liquidity, so it is highly likely that the central bank concerned will, in effect, be required to provide bilateral, individually tailored facilities to ensure that the financial stability objectives of the resolution are achieved. The structuring of such facilities presents the further problem that it must be on arms-length terms in order to avoid falling foul of the EU state aid regime.[2]

12.06 It is also likely to be essential for the continuation of client services that the institution remains a member of relevant payment, clearing, and settlement systems, and of any relevant central counterparties. This is likely to be problematic, since the rules of such systems generally permit (and sometimes require) the system operator to immediately terminate the membership of any member who is or is likely to become unable to meet its obligations within the system. There provisions are, of course, put in place for the purpose of preserving the system as a whole, and the systems (and their regulators) generally argue that the preservation of these systems is a more important policy goal than the preservation of any individual member of the system. The resolution authority will seek to preserve such access and such memberships. To complicate matters further, the resolution authority is very likely to find that at least some of the systems which are essential to the continuation of client services of the firm concerned are outside its jurisdiction—thus, the UK authorities can require UK systems operators to continue to deal with a UK bank in resolution, but can only ask politely where the system concerned is outside the European Union.

12.07 The necessity for stabilization to take place immediately explains why resolution is almost invariably viewed as being executed over a weekend, since this gives

---

[2] See BRRD Art 32(4)(d)(iii).

the authorities forty-eight hours outside normal market hours to conduct the initial transactions.

In contrast to the United States, where all resolutions are envisaged to be effected by transfer, the BRRD sets out two approaches to resolution: resolution by transfer, and resolution by write-down (known as 'bail-in').

A. Resolution by Transfer

Resolution by transfer can be effected in a number of different ways: **12.08**

- transfer of a whole firm to a private sector purchaser;
- transfer of part of the firm—its critical economic functions such as deposit-taking—to a purchaser, backed by good-quality assets;
- temporary transfer of all or part of the firm to a bridge bank, backed by good-quality assets in preparation for an onward sale (via transfer to a purchaser or an initial public offering)—any part of the firm not transferred to a purchaser or bridge bank, such as poor-quality assets and remaining liabilities, would be placed into administration or into an asset management vehicle.[3]

The transfer to a purchaser would generally be effected through an auction process **12.09** over a 'resolution weekend', with resolution powers used to effect the purchase. Transfer to a purchaser is almost always likely to be the preferred solution of the resolution authorities.

If a purchaser for the whole entity cannot be found, the focus is likely to shift **12.10** to depositors. The likely approach here is to transfer the failed firm's depositors to a purchaser along with sufficient assets to meet the liabilities thus assumed. In such a case there is no necessary link between the assets transferred and the liabilities assumed—the idea is simply to ensure that the entity which assumes the deposits is appropriately compensated. Authorities do, however, have to recall that it is important that the transaction does not end up destabilizing the transferee, especially since the transferee is itself a deposit-taking institution. The residual assets will then be dealt with through either insolvency or an asset management vehicle.

---

[3] It is, of course, possible for the bridge institution tool to be used to create a 'bad bank', with the remaining entity being restored to stability. However, a conventional 'bad bank' approach is now barred by Art 40(3) of BRRD, which provides that the total value of liabilities transferred to a bridge institution may not exceed the value of assets transferred to it, and by Art 41(1), which provides that a bridge institution must comply with (inter alia) the Capital Adequacy Directive (2013/36/EU) and the Capital Requirements Regulation (648/2012). Such a transfer therefore cannot increase the position of the transferor entity, and in practice it is unlikely that a traditional bad bank could now be created.

12.11 In the absence of any purchaser, the next step will be the creation of a 'bridge bank'. A bridge bank is a newly created entity, authorized to act as a bank. The bridge bank acts as a purchaser, in that the critical economic functions of the failed firm are transferred to it, along with sufficient assets to ensure its economic viability. A bridge bank is not intended to be a long-term vehicle,[4] and its primary envisaged purpose is to facilitate the sale of the business to one or more purchasers or to the public in an initial public offering and one or more follow-on offerings. A further difficulty in this regard derives from the BRRD requirement.[5]

Executing a transfer

12.12 A transfer will be given effect through one or more statutory transfer instruments. Transfer instruments set out which parts of the business have been transferred and to whom—for example to one or more purchasers and/or a bridge bank. A court order would also be prepared to place the remainder of the business into administration.

12.13 The transferred assets and liabilities would have a net asset value sufficient to meet capital requirements. This would either support the sale to a private sector purchaser, or provide capital if the business was transferred to a bridge bank. Thus the failed entity would have a significant capital shortfall after the transaction with the bridge bank, although it would have a claim to the residual value of the bridge bank.

12.14 Following resolution, the Treasury would appoint a valuer to provide an independent assessment of the 'no creditor worse off than in liquidation' (NCWOL) value of the firm at the point it entered resolution.[6] If any unprotected creditor is worse off than their position would have been in liquidation, they would be entitled to compensation.

12.15 An essential precondition for the authorities to agree to any transfer is that the transferee should remain solvent post-transfer. The United Kingdom has learned through bitter experience that this is not simply a matter of evaluating the balance sheet on the transfer date, and appropriate consideration must be given to likely losses emerging post-transfer. In a transfer of shares, the acquirer would need to seek approval for any change in control from the Prudential Regulation Authority (PRA) or Financial Conduct Authority (FCA).[7]

---

[4] Indeed the BRRD specifies, at Art 41(5) and (6), that it should not exist for a period of longer than three years after the last transfer of property to it under a resolution power.

[5] Art 40(3).

[6] The reason that the valuer is appointed by Treasury rather than the resolution authority is that it is the Treasury which is ultimately responsible for paying any compensation which the valuation may reveal. It therefore wishes to maintain control of the valuation process.

[7] The PRA regulates all deposit-takers and most large financial entities, but it is possible that an FCA-regulated firm could be the subject of resolution proceedings.

The Financial Services Compensation Scheme (FSCS) also has a role in a trans-   **12.16**
fer that uses stabilization tools. It can be required to provide a contribution to
the cost of resolving the failed firm, including by contributing to recapitalization costs or making payments which provide capital to the bridge bank or
purchaser, up to the amount that it would otherwise have incurred on a payout,
after recoveries.

As an example, the FSCS contributed to the costs of the resolution of Dunfermline   **12.17**
Building Society in March 2009. This firm was resolved using a combination of the
transfer of some of the business to a willing buyer, the temporary transfer of other
parts of the business to a bridge bank, with the remainder being placed into a building society administration procedure.

B. Resolutions Involving a Bail-in

The size and complexity of most global banks and investment firms greatly increases   **12.18**
the difficulty of rapidly separating critical economic functions from the rest without causing systemic disruption. For such large firms, a transfer of part or all of the
business is likely to be difficult to achieve during a short period, such as a resolution
weekend. This has led to the development of the concept of bail-in, although as a
stabilization tool, it is available for any firm where use of an insolvency procedure
would not meet the resolution objectives.

Bail-in stabilizes a failing firm by ensuring that, after the interests of existing   **12.19**
shareholders are cancelled, diluted, or transferred, and the claims of unsecured
creditors are written down sufficient to absorb the losses incurred, creditor
claims are converted into equity to recapitalize the firm. This ensures that the
essential functions of the firm can continue, without any need to split up the
firm immediately.

Where possible, the bail-in will be an SPE bail-in carried out in a holding com-   **12.20**
pany of the failing firm. This should result in a situation where only the holding company is required to be placed in resolution, and the bank subsidiary or
subsidiaries of that holding company continue to trade without being placed in
resolution. This would help to maintain the critical functions located in those
operating companies.

Following a bail-in, the firm in resolution (or a successor firm) will continue to be   **12.21**
authorized and regulated by the PRA and by the FCA (as market conduct regulator,
and in the case of many investment firms, prudential regulator). Each will assess
whether the firm complies with their threshold conditions and other regulatory
requirements in the usual way.

The recapitalization produced by bail-in satisfies the NCWOL requirement by   **12.22**
transferring to bailed-in creditors equity shares with a value corresponding to all

or a substantial part of the net asset value of the firm following the write-down of liabilities—to cover any losses—during the bail-in.

Executing a bail-in

12.23 The Bank of England's plan for a bail-in is as follows, and falls into the four stages set out below:

- the run-up to a resolution, where preparations are put in place for the resolution weekend;
- the bail-in period, including the resolution weekend;
- the announcement of final bail-in terms and compensation arrangements; and
- restructuring of the firm after bail-in.

12.24 In the run-up to a resolution, the Bank of England will create a draft resolution instrument setting out the terms of the bail-in. As part of its preparation, it will identify those liabilities which are within scope for the bail-in and capable of being relatively easily evaluated, and, more importantly, those creditors such as derivatives counterparties whose claims may be more problematic.

12.25 During the resolution weekend, the Bank of England will confirm which liabilities are within scope of the bail-in, for example shares plus subordinated debt, or shares plus subordinated debt plus senior unsecured debt. The FCA may suspend trading in those instruments. The Bank of England has the power to transfer the legal title of the shares to a third-party commercial bank appointed by the Bank of England to act as a depositary bank for the duration of the resolution, but there is no requirement for it to do so. It will also appoint a resolution administrator, acting under the Bank's direction.

12.26 At the end of the weekend, the Bank of England will announce:

- that the firm has entered resolution, probably on the Sunday evening (prior to the re-opening of Asian financial markets);
- the nature of the resolution strategy being carried out—in this case a bail-in without any immediate changes to the structure and functioning of the firm— and the liabilities that will be affected;
- that the firm's core functions will continue without disruption and that those depositors and investors protected by the FSCS continue to be protected (as always); and
- that the firm will open for business on Monday morning, providing information on the expected financial strength of the firm.

12.27 If shares are transferred to a depositary bank, it will hold the shares on trust until they can be distributed to former bondholders or other creditors identified as being entitled to compensation, once the final terms of the bail-in are announced. The Bank of England believes this period would need to be as short as possible, while allowing sufficient time to ensure that the valuation, on which write-downs are based, is robust.

During this period, further valuation work will be undertaken by the authorities so **12.28** that the resolution administrator can announce the final terms of the write-down of liabilities within the scope of the bail-in as soon as possible.[8]

There is no necessary argument for 'freezing' the claims of creditors during this valu- **12.29** ation period—especially since it may, for a large bank, take a considerable period of time for this valuation to be completed. One idea floated by the Bank of England is for the depositary bank to issue instruments known as 'certificates of entitlement'. This mechanism would enable former creditors to be provided with shares or other instruments in due course, with the relevant depositary bank maintaining legal title until the final valuation is complete.

Once valuation is complete, the terms of bail-in will be announced, including the **12.30** terms on which the certificates of entitlement will be exchanged for shares in the firm. The resolution administrator will continue to exercise voting rights on behalf of the former creditors until a sufficient number have come forward to claim their shares (at least a majority) or a set time period has passed. Depending on the number of shares issued, formal approval of a change in control may be needed.

The NCWOL safeguard applies to bail-in as well as to partial property transfers, **12.31** so that any shareholders and creditors directly affected by the resolution must not be left worse off than if the whole firm had been placed into insolvency. However, this may be achieved by writing down the debt owed to the unprotected creditor to a level below that which the creditor would have been entitled to receive in a hypothetical liquidation, and making good the creditors claim by the issue to him of shares or other securities in the resolved firm. This gives rise to a necessity for a second valuation, since where a creditor is compensated in this way it is necessary to establish that the shares or other securities are sufficiently valuable to make good the shortfall. Thus a first valuation is necessary to establish the amount by which the creditors claim must be written down, and a second valuation is necessary to establish the value of the creditor's position post-write-down.

Role of asset management vehicles

The asset separation tool gives the Bank of England the power to transfer assets, **12.32** rights, and liabilities of a firm to an asset management vehicle (AMV). In UK Banking Act (BA) terms, the asset separation tool is classed as a stabilization tool, but unlike the other stabilization tools, it can only be used in conjunction with another stabilization tool.[9]

---

[8] There is a potential discontinuity between the UK provisions on valuation and those required by EU law–see paras 13.37 et seq.

[9] BA, s 8ZA(2).

12.33 The key point about an AMV is that it is not a bank. It is therefore not required to have any particular level of capitalization. Equally, it is not permitted to conduct banking activities. Thus, when assets are transferred to an AMV, they are not transferred as part of a going concern, but are transferred for the purpose of sale or orderly wind-down to maturity. It can only be used if liquidating the assets using normal insolvency proceedings would have adverse effects on financial markets.[10] What this means in practice is that an AMV exists for the purpose of allowing a portfolio to be liquidated slowly and over time where that strategy will result in better recoveries.

12.34 An AMV may be used both in connection with an asset transfer and in connection with a bail-in. In both cases, a transfer of high-risk assets to the AMV could be used to reduce the risk profile of the remaining firm, thus facilitating either disposal or recovery.

C. Restructuring Phase

12.35 Once the firm has been stabilized, either through bail-in or transfer, the next stage will be to consider what further restructuring will be required in order to address the causes of failure and restore confidence in it. The logic of this is inexorable—any restructuring plan will need to ensure that critical economic functions are maintained, this will only be possible if the entity continues to operate, and this in turn can only happen if counterparties are prepared to continue dealing with the firm.

12.36 The nature of the restructuring will be determined by reference to the cause of the failure. Where the cause of the failure was a single idiosyncratic event—a large loss arising from a rogue trader or excessive risk concentration—restructuring is likely to involve internal systems and controls, but may not require asset restructuring. Conversely, where the cause of the failure was a bad business model, significant restructuring of the entire undertaking, including significant asset and liability restructuring, may have to be undertaken. In both cases, it is unlikely that pre-failure management can be left in place.

12.37 In the case of a bail-in, the Bank will require a resolution administrator or one or more directors of the firm under resolution to submit a business reorganization plan in respect of the group as a whole.[11] This plan would provide, among other things, a diagnosis of the factors and problems that caused the failure of the firm, a description of the measures aimed at restoring the long-term viability of the firm, and a timetable for carrying out those measures. The measures may include:

- the reorganization of the activities of the group;
- a withdrawal from loss-making activities;

---

[10] BA, s 8ZA(3)(a).
[11] BA, s 48H.

- sale or transfer of assets or business lines; and
- a restructuring of existing activities to restore competitiveness.

There is, of course, a circularity between the resolution plan and the necessary valu- **12.38**
ations inherent in a bail-in. Where bailed-in creditors are to be compensated by a
delivery of shares or other securities issued by the relevant institution, the value of
those securities will depend on the future shape, revenue, and profitability of the
business, which will in turn be affected by the terms of the resolution plan adopted
by the resolution administrator.

Bridge bank

With a bridge bank, the restructuring effectively takes place over the resolution **12.39**
weekend, as critical functions (such as retail deposit liabilities) are transferred to
the bridge bank backed with supporting assets. Shares, debt, and other unsecured
liabilities are likely to remain in the residual bank, which will be placed in a bank
administration procedure,[12] along with any assets which are not transferred to the
bridge bank.

D. Exit from Resolution

In some cases, the path to exit from resolution is clear. A sale of all or part of a busi- **12.40**
ness to a private sector purchaser is a complete exit. Where a bridge bank is used,
there should have been a clear route to an onward sale to a private sector purchaser
or to a floatation or public offering,[13] and if this is not achieved within two years of
the property transfer to the bridge bank, it must be wound up.[14] Similarly, where
all or part of a business is put into administration or insolvency, the administration
or insolvency procedure will run its course. And, where the asset separation tool is
used, the objective of this is to ensure that certain assets of the firm are disposed of
in an orderly fashion.

The most important aspect of the exit from resolution is the fact that the firm must **12.41**
be recapitalized to a level that is sufficient to restore market confidence and allow
the firm to access private funding markets. This level is likely to be much higher
than the minimum capital requirement prescribed by the bank regulator. In practice, it is likely that the structure of the entire resolution process will be determined
by this very last factor—what level of capital would be required for the successor
institution to be able to operate as a normal private company.

---

[12] BA, s 12(3A).
[13] BA, s 12(1A)(c)(c).
[14] BA, s 12(3A). If this appears a possibility, it is permissible to transfer part of the activity of a
bridge bank to another entity (an 'onward bridge bank') so that the process can be repeated—BA,
s 12(4) and (5)—subject to the same constraint.

E. Bank Resolution and Insolvency

12.42 The story of the separate UK insolvency regimes begins with the Lehman's administration. Within a relatively short time after the placing of Lehman's into ordinary UK administration it was felt that there were aspects of the existing regime which fitted very badly indeed into the process necessary for a bank. Thus, separate regimes were created. We now have four of these: bank administration, bank insolvency, building society special administration, and investment bank special administration.

12.43 Bank resolution is optional—no major bank resolution regime provides that all banks must be placed in formal resolution. Resolution is an alternative to insolvency, and in general the approach is that resolution tools may be applied only if some form of public interest test in their use is met. If that test is not met, resolution tools are not used, and the bank is placed in ordinary insolvency.

12.44 The design philosophy of the UK regime was—and is—intended to make the barrier to the commencement of resolution a high one. The idea is to make insolvency the norm and resolution the exception. The Code of Practice which accompanies the Banking Act notes that 'the Bank of England may only exercise [resolution] powers if satisfied that the exercise of the power is necessary having regard to the public interest in the stability of the financial system of the UK, the maintenance of public confidence in the stability of that system, or the protection of depositors... The test of "necessity" is a high one'.[15]

12.45 However, when considering whether or not to place an institution in resolution, the determination which falls to be made—that is, whether public welfare will be improved by resolution action—is in fact a comparison of the outcome of resolution with the outcome of the application of insolvency law. One of the consequences of this is that the worse the outcome of the application of insolvency law, the stronger the incentive to apply resolution measures, and the lower the bar to their application. Thus, one of the key features of the BA is that it both creates the resolution regime and amends the applicable UK insolvency regime to create a special 'Bank Insolvency Regime'. The BRRD, by contrast, establishes a resolution regime but does not address the underlying insolvency issues.[16] Thus in applying the tests for the commencement of resolution set out in the BRRD, individual member states will be applying a common EU test in respect of common EU remedies against distinctly different national insolvency outcomes.

---

[15] Banking Act 2009 Special Resolution Regime: Code of Practice, November 2010, paras 5.12–5.15
[16] The European Union has traditionally struggled to justify interference in the domestic insolvency regimes of individual member states under the doctrines of subsidiarity and proportionality, although it can and does intervene in cross-border insolvency issues.

Conversely, however, the BRRD addresses a wide variety of issues which in the **12.46** United Kingdom are regarded as matters of supervision rather than resolution. The mechanisms set out in the BRRD as regards recovery planning, early intervention, the imposition of special measures on firms in recovery, and the assessment of resolvability are all matters which in the United Kingdom are addressed by giving powers to supervisors under the Financial Services and Markets Act 2000 (FSMA) rather than in resolution legislation.

Role of insolvency

Where the public interest test outlined above is not met, firms may be put into a **12.47** modified form of insolvency procedure, providing they hold protected deposits or client assets (or both). The alternative procedures, which vary according to the type of firm concerned, are discussed below. Where the firm holds neither protected deposits nor client assets, it would be placed into ordinary insolvency.

Banks and building societies

The bank insolvency procedure involves putting the whole bank into an insolvency **12.48** process designed to allow for rapid payment of deposits protected by the FSCS (up to the limit of £85,000) or the transfer of the accounts of protected depositors to a viable bank. In the case of a building society, the building society insolvency procedure would be used. The bank insolvency procedure was used in June 2011, when the Southsea Mortgage and Investment Company failed.[17]

These modified procedures require the insolvency practitioner appointed to manage **12.49** the wind-down of the firm to prioritize either the transfer of protected depositors' accounts to another deposit-taker or to facilitate a payout to protected depositors by the FSCS. In both cases, the FSCS provides funding and becomes a creditor in the insolvency, 'standing in the shoes' of protected depositors. The FSCS will levy the industry to meet the costs of a payout or transfer.

If necessary, the FSCS may borrow from the government where its own funds are **12.50** insufficient at the point when the payout or transfer takes place. These funds would be repaid subsequently. The FSCS will make a claim in the insolvency to recover these costs, which helps to reduce the impact on its levy-payers.

The BRRD makes deposits protected by EU guarantee schemes and deposit guar- **12.51** antee schemes themselves (including the FSCS) 'super-preferred'. This means that in insolvency the FSCS has the first unsecured claim in the estate, along with other preferred creditors, and is likely to recover more of its costs than under the previous creditor hierarchy. Deposits from individuals and micro, small, and medium-sized enterprises that are higher than the protected amount of £85,000 are preferred to

---

[17] Bank of England Press Release 2011/0060.

other senior unsecured liabilities but not super-preferred. This makes insolvency a viable option for entities which have largely insured deposits.

F. Bank Administration

12.52   The original UK resolution legislation used the term 'special administration' to refer to administration proceedings other than bank administration. Thus, it is usual to refer to the 'bank administration regime' as applying to banks, in contra-distinction to 'special administration regimes', or SARs, which are the building society and investment firm administration procedures.

12.53   Bank administration can only be ordered by a court on the application of the Bank of England as resolution authority (s 142 BA). Section 143 provides that such an application may only be made if the Bank of England intends to make a property transfer order, and that the residual bank is unable to pay its debts, or is likely to become unable to pay its debts as a result of the property transfer that it intends to make. Bank administration may not be sued as an alternative to ordinary administration—if the Bank of England does not intend to use a transfer power, the bank must be placed in ordinary administration. A bank administration is not conducted under the ordinary insolvency rules, but under special Rules.[18]

12.54   The primary envisaged use of the bank administration regime is to administer the insolvent rump of a firm whose continuing business has been transferred to a bridge bank or private sector purchaser through resolution action.[19] Its aim is to ensure that essential services, systems, contracts, and other facilities that cannot be imme-diately transferred from a failing bank to a bridge bank or private purchaser con-tinue to be provided by the insolvent residual bank for a period of time to enable the bridge bank or private purchaser to operate effectively. However, once this aim has been achieved, the administrator then falls back to the position of a normal administrator, charged with either resolving the rump as a going concern or—in reality—achieving a better outcome for the residual bank's creditors as a whole than would be the case if it were wound up.[20]

12.55   Section 145 of the BA sets out tables that show how the relevant provisions of the Insolvency Act (IA) 1986 are modified in bank administration. The main effect of these modifications is to remove certain procedural steps with the aim of making the process faster.

Also—importantly—bank administrators are given powers to disclaim onerous property (s 178 of the IA 1986) and to bring actions for wrongful trading (s 214 of

---

[18]   The Bank Administration (England and Wales) Rules 2009 (SI 2009/357).
[19]   BA, s 136(2).
[20]   BA, s 140.

the IA 1986). These are powers which are ordinarily reserved for liquidators, and administrators of normal companies do not have them.

Part 3 of the BA also applies to building societies in a modified way.[21]   **12.56**

G. Investment Bank Special Administration Regime

The investment bank special administration regime (SAR) was introduced under   **12.57**
Part 7 of the BA.[22]

The primary aim of the investment bank special regime is the safeguarding of client   **12.58**
assets. Unlike bank administration, the directors or creditors of an investment bank
may apply for an investment bank to have an administrator appointed under the
special regime[23] as well as the authorities. An application for an investment bank
special administration order can be made on the following grounds:

(a) Ground A. The investment bank is, or is likely to become, unable to pay its debts.
(b) Ground B. It would be fair to put the investment bank into investment bank
    special administration.
(c) Ground C. It is expedient in the public interest to put the investment bank
    into investment bank special administration.[24]

An investment bank special administrator has three, equal-ranking, statutory   **12.59**
objectives:[25]

(a) Objective 1. To ensure the return of client assets (including money) as soon
    as is reasonably practicable (Investment Bank (Amendment of Definition)
    Order 2011 (SI 2011/239)).
(b) Objective 2. To engage with market infrastructure bodies and regulators in a
    timely fashion.
(c) Objective 3. To resolve the investment bank as a going concern or to wind it
    up in the best interests of the creditors.

Unlike bank administration, these objectives rank equally.

The SAR for investment firms is available for the whole firm to be placed into an   **12.60**
insolvency proceeding.[26] In the SAR, the administrator of a failed investment firm

---

[21] The Building Societies (Insolvency and Special Administration) Order 2009 (SI 2009/805), made under BA, s 158.
[22] Investment Bank Special Administration Regulations 2011 (SI 2011/245).
[23] Reg 5(1).
[24] This ground can only be advanced where the applicant is the Treasury (reg 6(2)). The grounds on which such a petition may be advanced probably correspond closely to these set out in s 124A of the Insolvency Act 1986 for petitions to wind up a company on the grounds of public interest.
[25] Reg 10.
[26] Although the investment firm SAR was devised in the light of the Lehman administration, it was created after that administration was commenced and did not apply to it. To date, there have

has certain objectives, including the return of client money or assets as soon as is reasonably practicable and ensuring timely engagement with market infrastructure bodies and the authorities. The administrator also has the normal insolvency objective to resolve the firm as a going concern or wind it up in the best interests of creditors.

12.61 The PRA or FCA can direct the administrator to prioritize one or more of the SAR objectives. This might be considered necessary if this would be in the interests of the stability of the financial systems, or the maintenance of public confidence in the stability of the financial markets, of the United Kingdom.

Firms with deposits and client assets

12.62 Some firms that fail may have both deposits protected by the FSCS and client assets (including client money). In these circumstances, although the administrator must immediately begin to work on the objectives relating to client assets, the special objectives for depositors take precedence. This means that the administrator must work with the FSCS to ensure that protected deposits are either paid out or transferred to another financial institution.

12.63 The Investment Bank Special Administration Rules 2011 apply to UK investment banks, which broadly speaking means those that hold client assets (as agent or principal) and are permitted to carry out regulated investment activity. In addition, and as if the process was not already complicated enough, where the investment bank is also a deposit-taking bank, there are a further two variations on the special administration process: special administration (bank administration) and special administration (bank insolvency).

12.64 The most interesting aspects of the Rules are the provisions designed to protect the interests of the clients with assets held by the failed investment bank. It introduced a mechanism to modify insolvency principles in the administration of a failed firm holding or controlling assets belonging to its clients. In particular, it:

1. gives the administrator jurisdiction over the distribution or transfer of those assets;
2. requires the administrator to prioritize dealing with those assets;
3. imposes on the administrator and certain third parties duties designed to facilitate the identification, collection, and transfer or return of client assets;
4. establishes certain continuity of supply rights for the benefit of the administrator in relation to key services;

---

been five sets of proceedings under these Rules—MF Global UK Limited, Pritchard Stockbrokers Limited, WorldSpreads Limited, Fyshe Horton Finney Limited, and, most recently, City Equities Limited. As yet, this regime may be regarded as unfinished—the comprehensive 'Final review of the Investment Bank Special Administration Regulations 2011' by Peter Bloxham, which appeared in January 2014, contained a number of proposals for reform of this legislation which currently remain unimplemented.

5. allows for the use of a bar date mechanism in connection with distributions (currently limited to non-cash client assets); and

6. includes some provisions concerning the rights of clients to submit claims as creditors in the distribution of the general estate of the failed firm:

   • Where there is a shortfall in particular, client assets that shortfall is to be shared pro rata between the clients claiming those assets.

   • The special administrator has the power to set a bar date for claims to client assets.

   • The rules impose certain safeguards to avoid late claims by providing sufficient notice and time for the formulation of claims, including the fact that no distribution of client assets is to be made before the period of three months has expired after the bar date. The special administrator is also obliged proactively to notify those clients who appear from the investment bank's records to be entitled to such assets.

   • The distribution plan for client assets must also be approved by the creditors' committee and the court. There does not appear to be any bespoke mechanism for individual clients seeking to challenge the proposed distribution. The only opportunity appears to be to by formally objecting to the distribution plan at the court hearing which considers whether the plan should be approved.

   • The Rules provide that the special administrator's costs, insofar as they are incurred in dealing with the return of client assets, are to be recouped out of the client assets.

   • Clients with assets invested with the failing investment bank may also vote at creditors' meetings (as a separate class of creditors) and may be represented on any creditors' committee (whereas in an ordinary administration process only creditors have a say regarding the administrator's proposals).

12.65 These Rules were created as the Lehman insolvency was taking place; indeed, it is clear that many of them are there specifically to address difficulties encountered in that process. The reason that they were required was that the Lehman administrators had sought to incorporate many of these features into their initial settlement, but were told by the Court of Appeal[27] that client asset claims—unlike ordinary creditor claims—were not susceptible to being regulated in this way.

H. Bank Insolvency

12.66 In addition to the Bank Administration procedure, the BA also provides for a special bank insolvency regime. This provides for the orderly winding up

---

[27] See *Re Lehman Brothers International (Europe) (in administration)* [2009] EWCA Civ 1161.

of a failed bank. A bank insolvency can only be applied for by the Bank of England, the PRA, or the government, and only in respect of a bank which holds FSCS-insured deposits. The FSCS has the right to be heard in the application (s 123(4), BA).

12.67 There are three grounds on which an application for a bank insolvency order may be made:

(a) Ground A. The bank is unable, or likely to become unable, to pay its debts.
(b) Ground B. The winding up of the bank would be in the public interest (ie, where the bank may not be technically insolvent, but its winding up would protect its customers and the public generally).
(c) Ground C. The winding up of the bank would be 'fair' (as defined in s 93(8) of the BA).

12.68 The aim of a bank insolvency is to enable depositor creditors to be paid out rapidly. It should be noted that the bank insolvency procedure was created before the implementation of depositor preference in the United Kingdom, and it is sometimes argued that the introduction of this preference should of itself enable a liquidator in an ordinary liquidation to pay such claims out rapidly. The usefulness of the separate insolvency regime is therefore questionable.

12.69 Bank insolvency can only be used where a bank has depositors who are eligible for compensation under the FSCS.

12.70 Again, bank insolvency is based on the insolvency procedure under the IA, but conducted under special Rules.[28] Section 103(6) of the BA sets out the way in which the relevant provisions of the IA are modified in bank insolvency. However, the most important modification is effected by s 119 of the BA, which provides that a moratorium on creditors rights (normally only available in an administration) also applies in a bank insolvency. Also, the Rules are modified[29] to disapply ordinary insolvency set-off where:

> the relevant creditor is an eligible depositor in respect of the amount protected. Thus, where the bank has a counterclaim against a depositor, it may only set off that counterclaim to the extent that the deposit exceeds the £85,000 FSCS compensation limit.

12.71 A bank liquidator has two statutory objectives:

1. Objective 1. To work with the FSCS to ensure that, as soon as reasonably practicable, each eligible depositor has either their account (or accounts) transferred to another financial institution, or receives compensation from (or on behalf of) the FSCS.

---

[28] Bank Insolvency (England and Wales) Rules 2009 (SI 2009/356).
[29] Rules 72 and 73.

2. Objective 2. To wind up the affairs of the bank to achieve the best result for the bank's creditors as a whole.

The first of these objectives takes precedence.

Finally, it should be noted that Part 6 and schedules 6 and 7 of the Financial Services **12.72** (Banking Reform) Act 2013 set out a special resolution regime for Financial Market Infrastructure providers (inter-bank payment systems and UK securities settlement systems, but not derivative central clearing counterparties (CCPs)). However, this regime has not yet been brought into force.

13

POWERS OF
THE UK RESOLUTION AUTHORITY

A. Scope—Banks, Groups, and Branches

13.01 One of the most important issues with bank resolution legislation is as to the precise identity of the entities which can be subject to resolution. All bank resolution regimes must, by definition, apply to banks. However, there are issues both as to application as to regulated non-banks ('Can we resolve Lehmans?') and as to non-bank group entities ('Can we intervene at the holding company, as opposed to the bank, level?').

Group companies

13.02 The UK Banking Act 2009 (BA), as initially drafted, applied only to banks—that is, to the legal entities which held a UK deposit-taking authorization.[1] However, since in general, banks conduct their activities through banking groups rather than as single entities, it rapidly became clear that for a group of any size it was necessary for the resolution authority to act in respect of group companies other than the authorized bank. Thus, as from 1 August 2014, the resolution powers and tools set out in the Act can be applied to any UK-incorporated member of a bank group.[2]

13.03 Article 1(1) of the Bank Recovery and Resolution Directive (BRRD) provides that member states must have resolution powers which apply to 'financial holding companies, mixed financial holding companies and mixed-activity holding companies that are established in the EU'. This, in principle, creates a problem for banks owned by non-banks. In very broad terms, EU bank law distinguishes between a financial holding company—a holding company the majority of whose subsidiaries are financial institutions—and a mixed-activity holding company (MAHC), a majority

---

[1] Although even then there were some carve-outs—for example, many UK insurance companies have deposit-taking authorizations, and it was necessary to exclude them from the scope of the act—see now the Banking Act 2009 (Exclusion of Insurers) Order 2010 S.I. 2010/35.

[2] For this purpose, a 'group company' has the meaning given in the Companies Act 2006.

non-financial entity which holds some financial institutions (a typical MAHC would be a supermarket or manufacturer with a captive bank subsidiary). Article 33(3) of BRRD provides that member states are not required to take action against MAHCs 'where the subsidiary institutions of a mixed-activity holding company are held directly or indirectly by an intermediate financial holding company'. This is reflected in the United Kingdom by the Banking Group Companies Order 2014,[3] which provides that a resolution power can only be exercised in respect of a bank group company which is within the bank group. Where the bank is a sub-group under a holding company whose activities are not mainly financial (i.e. an MAHC), the MAHC does not count as a parent for this purpose. This means that only members of the sub-group containing the bank can be resolved. The UK approach to implementing this has been to give powers to the Bank of England to require any MAHC to hold its regulated subsidiaries through an intermediate financial holding company.

Investment firms

The BRRD applies to 'institutions', that is, to banks and to those investment firms **13.04** which are subject to the Capital Requirements Directive.[4] The BA, as initially drafted, applied only to banks, but has been extended by the Financial Services Act 2012[5] to apply to investment firms.

Within the United Kingdom this creates an interesting tension as regards the inter- **13.05** face between supervision and resolution. In general, UK banks are supervised as to prudential issues by the Prudential Regulation Authority (PRA) and as to conduct by the Financial Conduct Authority (FCA), whereas investment firms are supervised exclusively by the FCA. However, it is possible for the PRA to be a supervisor of an investment firm,[6] and, conversely, for a deposit-taker to be prudentially supervised by the FCA rather than the PRA.[7] Thus, in practice, the resolution authority will have to work with multiple supervisors. It is interesting to note in this context that the Bank of England's resolution powers are in this regard wider than those of the European Single Resolution Board (SRB) acting as the single resolution authority for the eurozone. For reasons of consistency with the Single Supervisory Mechanism, the resolution powers of the SRB are confined to those institutions which are supervised by the ECB as single supervisor.[8] Thus, within the eurozone banks subject to ECB supervision (either directly or indirectly) will be subject to SRB resolution, but investment firms outside the scope of that supervision will be

---

[3] 2014/1831.
[4] 2013/36/EC. This means all investment firms other than those identified in Art 29 of the CRD—that is, investment firms which deal for their own account and hold client money or assets.
[5] Section 101(1), inserting a new s 89A into the UK BA.
[6] PRA may designate investment firms for prudential supervision by it—para 3(4) of the Financial Services and Markets Act 2000 (PRA Regulated Activities) Order 2013, 2013/556.
[7] See BA, s 83A.
[8] See Art 2 of the Single Resolution Mechanism Regulation 806/2014, which cross-refers to Art 4(1) the Single Supervisory Mechanism Regulation (1024/2013).

subject to resolution by national resolution authorities working with national securities authorities. The United Kingdom, by contrast, has a single resolution authority charged with resolving all banks and investment firms, which faces multiple national supervisors. It should also be noted that the bank's resolution directorate is currently structurally separate from the PRA supervisory function which is also discharged by the Bank.

Branch resolution

13.06 The powers which are available in order to resolve a UK branch of a non-UK bank vary depending on whether the branch is a branch of an EU or a non-EU institution. The position of an EU branch has already been considered.[9] In respect of branches of non-European Economic Area (non-EEA) institutions, the PRA, along with the Treasury and the Bank of England, are given powers under the BA to take measures under the UK's 'Special Resolution Regime' to assist in the stabilization or resolution of credit institutions which are in financial difficulties. As part of the implementation of the BRRD,[10] the scope of the BA is extended to permit the Bank of England to employ its stabilization options and Stabilization Powers (see paras 14.02 and 14.03) in respect of assisting non-EEA regulators resolve a non-EEA bank, including any branches or subsidiaries of such bank in the United Kingdom. Where the Bank of England is notified of a resolution action undertaken by a non-EEA regulator, the Bank of England may either recognize the action, refuse to recognize the action, or recognize only part of the action. However, the Bank of England is limited in when and how it can use such powers. It may only use its powers under the BA to recognize actions of a non-EEA regulator where such actions correspond to the Bank of England's stabilization objectives as set out in the BA, and may be refused if any of the following conditions exist:

(a) recognition of the resolution action would have an adverse effect on financial stability in the United Kingdom or another EEA state;

(b) recognition of the resolution action would involve the taking of action in relation to a branch of a non-EEA entity located in the United Kingdom;

(c) under the resolution action of the non-EEA regulator, creditors (including in particular depositors) located or payable in an EEA state would not, by reason of their location, receive the same treatment as creditors (including depositors) who are located or payable in the non-EEA state concerned;

(d) steps taken pursuant to the recognition of the non-EEA resolution action would have material fiscal implications for the United Kingdom; or

(e) recognition of the resolution action would be unlawful under the Human Rights Act 1998 or contrary to a provision of EU law.[11]

---

[9] See paras 11.35–11.42 in this volume.
[10] Arts 93–98 BRRD.
[11] BA, ss 89H–89J.

This means that the Bank of England retains wide discretion to not recognize a **13.07** resolution action of a non-EEA regulator (in particular where it involves taking action in relation to a branch in the United Kingdom). Consequently, there is no obligation on the Bank of England to recognize any resolution actions undertaken by the Regulator which relate to a London branch of a non-EEA bank. The Bank of England has indicated that it would only want to employ its own powers under the BA to support an existing resolution plan by a non-EEA regulator in the event that co-operation with that non-EEA regulator alone proves ineffective and where recognizing the resolution action was required to protect the public interest. In its consultation on the implementation of these powers in the United Kingdom, the UK Government said:

> Powers to act in relation to the UK branch of a third country institution are therefore 'back-stop' powers to be used in the event that this co-operation proves ineffective, and where action is required to protect the public interest.[12]

B. Powers of Pre-Resolution Intervention

In general, the power to intervene in the affairs of a firm which has not failed are **13.08** reserved to its regulator. Thus, the PRA and FCA have powers to instruct authorized firms to take specific action under ss 55L and 55M of the Financial Services and Markets Act 2000 (FSMA). In practice, the existing approved person regime is sufficient to give the competent authorities power over individual staff—however, it will be necessary to give them a further power to require an institution to remove members of its board and/or senior managers who are directly accountable to the board.

The BA, however, gives the Bank of England, as resolution authority, wide pow- **13.09** ers under s 3A to give directions to a 'relevant person' at any time. For this purpose, a 'relevant person' is an institution, its parent or holding company, or a financial institution subsidiary thereof.[13] The Bank can in effect give any direction it feels appropriate in order to achieve the aim of reducing or elimination 'impediments to' the effective exercise of Stabilization Powers or the winding up of that person.[14]

Section 3A sets out a dizzying array of circumstances and fact-patterns in which **13.10** these powers might be used. These include:

- amending a group financial support agreement, or requiring the group to enter into one;

---

[12] Transposition of the Bank Recovery and Resolution Directive, July 2014, para 15.7.
[13] BA, s 3A(1).
[14] BA, s 3A(2).

- requiring a person to enter into an agreement for the provision of services relating to the provision of critical functions;
- limiting a person's maximum individual and aggregate exposures to any counterparty;
- providing any information to the Bank of England;
- disposal of specified assets;
- cessation of any specified activities, or restricting such activities;
- cessation of new or existing business operations, or imposing restrictions on such operations;
- in order to separate the performance of critical functions from other functions, changing legal or operational structure of the firm or a subsidiary;
- establishment of a financial holding company which is not a subsidiary of an institution, another financial holding company, or a mixed financial holding company;
- requirement to maintain a minimum requirement for own funds and eligible liabilities expressed as a percentage of the total own funds and liabilities of the relevant person, to maintain particular kinds of eligible liabilities, or to issue particular kinds of eligible liabilities or take other specified steps;
- Directing a relevant person to endeavour to re-negotiate any eligible liability or relevant capital instruments issued by that person, for the purpose of ensuring that any decision by the Bank of England to write down or convert the liability or instrument concerned would have effect under the law which governs that liability or instrument.

13.11 Other important pre-resolution powers are contained in Article 17 of the BRRD. These are summarized in Table 13.1.

13.12 The United Kingdom has implemented this requirement through a wide-ranging power vested in the Bank of England as resolution authority to give directions to banks, holding companies, and group members established in the United Kingdom.[15]

13.13 It should be noted that the effect of this provision is to give resolution authorities powers over firms which are potentially greater than those possessed by the regulators of those firms. The potential for effective dual-regulation is therefore present.

Recovery plans

13.14 The BA as originally drafted provided that it was the responsibility of UK banks and building societies to draw up recovery plans. The BRRD requires any group which is subject to consolidated supervision in the European Union to draw

---

[15] BA, s 3A.

Table 13.1 Pre-resolution powers in Article 17 of the BRRD

Structural	Art 17(5)(a)	Requiring the institution to revise any intra-group financing arrangements or review the absence thereof, or draw up service agreements (whether intra-group or with third parties) to cover the provision of critical functions
	Art 17(5)(g)	Requiring changes to legal or operational structures of the institution or group entity so as to reduce complexity in order to ensure that critical functions may be legally and economically separated from other functions through the application of the resolution tools
	Art 17(5)(h)	Requiring a parent undertaking to set up a parent financial holding company in a member state or a Union parent financial holding company
	Art 17(5)(k)	Where an institution is the subsidiary of a mixed-activity holding company, requiring that the mixed-activity holding company set up a separate financial holding company to control the institution, if this is necessary in order to facilitate the resolution of the institution and to avoid the application of the resolution tools and powers specified in Title IV having an adverse effect on the non-financial part of the group
Financial	Art 17(5)(b)	Requiring the institution to limit its maximum individual and aggregate exposures
	Art 17(5)(d)	Requiring the institution to divest specific assets
	Art 17(5)(e)	Requiring the institution to limit or cease specific existing or proposed activities
	Art 17(5)(f)	Restricting or preventing the development or sale of new or existing business lines or products
	Art 17(5)(i)	Requiring an institution or parent undertaking to issue liabilities eligible for bail-in
	Art 17(5)(j)	Require an institution, or an entity referred to in points (b), (c), or (d) of Article 1, to take other steps to meet the minimum requirement for own funds and eligible liabilities under Article 39, including in particular to attempt to renegotiate any eligible liability, additional Tier 1 instrument or Tier 2 instrument it has issued, with a view to ensuring that any decision of the resolution authority to write down or convert that liability or instrument would be effected under the law of the jurisdiction governing that liability or instrument
Information	Art 17(5)(c)	Impose specific or additional information requirements relevant for resolution purposes

(*Source*: Transposition of the Bank Recovery and Resolution Directive, Her Majesty's Treasury, July 2014)

up a recovery plan.[16] This means that regulators must have powers to compel unregulated group entities to compile such plans. It is also technically possible for a group to have a UK parent but to be subject to consolidated supervision elsewhere in the European Union[17] —in such a case, the United Kingdom has powers to require the UK parent to create a recovery plan and deliver it to the relevant EU-consolidating supervisor.

---

[16] Art 5.
[17] See Art 111 of the EU Capital Requirements Directive (CRD) 2013/36/EU.

13.15 It is also interesting to note that the old UK 'resolution plan' provisions,[18] now repealed, in fact imposed a requirement on UK banks to compile and provide the information that resolution authorities would require to implement a resolution strategy (known as a 'resolution pack'). This requirement continues, but the power to require it is no longer within the scope of the resolution plan requirements.

13.16 Separately, it has been necessary to introduce provisions requiring the Bank of England (as resolution authority) to assess the 'resolvability' of institutions and group entities,[19] and communicate the results of this finding to the European Banking Authority.

13.17 Article 17 of the BRRD provides that a resolution authority may order a firm to restructure itself in order to make itself more resolvable. These powers may be grouped into three broad classes: powers to change the structure of the group concerned,[20] powers to restrict financial exposures of members of the group,[21] and powers to impose information requirements.[22] One of the interesting issues that arose in the UK implementation of this requirement is that resolution authorities are generally not structured as regulators, and as such do not have enforcement powers. Thus the question arises of what happens if a resolution authority imposes a requirement on a firm but is not happy with the firm's implementation of that requirement. The default setting would be that enforcement would be the responsibility of the competent supervisory authority, leading to the situation where one authority imposes a requirement and a different authority enforces it—a potentially undesirable position. One way to address this would be to give the resolution authority enforcement powers in respect of these matters. However, this in turn leads to the resolution authority coming to look increasingly like a supervisor, and faces the relevant firm with the prospect of multiple—potentially conflicting—supervisory requirements being imposed as to its structure. The United Kingdom has implemented this requirement by giving the Bank of England, as resolution authority, draconian powers to give instructions to UK-authorized institutions and any parent or subsidiary of such an institution which is established in the United Kingdom.[23] The power, which is set out in s 3A of the BA, is presented as an absolute power to give instructions. The safeguards provided[24] are an appeal to the bank itself, with appeal from that decision lying to the Upper Tribunal.

13.18 It is expected that the requirement on UK banks to issue minimum requirement for eligible liabilities (MREL)[25] will be imposed through an instruction under s 3A.

---

[18] BA, s 137K, now repealed.
[19] See part VI (ss 59–82) of the Bank Recovery and Resolution (No 2) Order 2014 (2014/3348).
[20] Art 17(5)(a), (g), (h), and (k).
[21] Art 17(5)(b), (d), (e), (f), (i), and (j).
[22] Art 17(5)(c).
[23] BA, s 3A.
[24] BA, s 3B.
[25] See above, paras 10.48 et seq.

C. Triggering Resolution

The BRRD effected an interesting change in the UK architecture of bank resolu- **13.19**
tion. In the original BA, the determination as to whether resolution should be
commenced was left entirely to the regulator (then the Financial Services Authority
(FSA)), which was responsible for determining both whether the bank was failing,
or was likely to fail, to satisfy its regulatory threshold conditions (as provided in the
FSMA, Sch 6—the 'Threshold Conditions') ('General Condition 1'),[26] and also
that it was not reasonably likely that action would be taken by or in respect of the
bank that would enable the bank to satisfy the Threshold Conditions, having regard
to timing and other relevant circumstances ('General Condition 2').[27] The FSA
(then the supervisory authority) gave guidance on the Threshold Conditions in the
Threshold Conditions chapter of the FSA Handbook of Rules and Guidance, which
was in turn relevant to assessing General Condition 1[28] and guidance in Chapter 3
of the Financial Stability and Market Confidence Sourcebook (FINMAR) to assessing General Condition 2.[29]

However, the BRRD reallocated responsibility for assessing Condition 2 from **13.20**
the regulator to the resolution authority. Thus the current position is that the
PRA (or possibly the FCA, where it is the appropriate regulator) is responsible
for determining whether Condition 1 has been breached, whilst responsibility for
determining whether Condition 2 has been breached now rests with the Bank as
resolution authority.

The conditions

There are now four conditions for resolution under the BA. They are as follows. **13.21**

- Condition 1 is that the bank is failing or is likely to fail.[30]
- Condition 2 is that it is not reasonably likely that action other than resolution
  will be taken that will result in Condition 1 ceasing to be met.[31]
- Condition 3 is that the exercise of a Stabilization Power is necessary having
  regard to the public interest.[32]
- Condition 4 is that placing the bank in liquidation would not achieve all of the
  special resolution objectives.[33]

---

[26] BA, s 7(2).
[27] BA, s 7(3).
[28] See FINMAR 3.2.4.
[29] See FINMAR 3.1.2.
[30] BA, s 7(2).
[31] BA, s 7(3).
[32] BA, s 7(4).
[33] BA, s 7(5).

D. Factors Common
to Assessing General Conditions 1 and 2

13.22 In determining whether General Condition 1 is satisfied, the PRA must discount any financial assistance provided by the Treasury or the Bank of England
(disregarding ordinary market assistance offered by the bank on its usual
terms),[34] and the Bank of England must equally disregard these considerations in determining whether Condition 2 is satisfied.[35] The Treasury takes the
view that the concept of 'ordinary market assistance' does not create a new
'hard-edged' legal definition and whether or not financial assistance from the
bank constitutes 'ordinary market assistance...on its usual terms' will depend
on a combination of factors including the terms of the bank's operation, the
circumstances of the bank receiving liquidity from the bank, and conditions
in the relevant markets in which the firm was or would otherwise be seeking to
access funding.[36]

13.23 The special resolution objectives set out in BA, s 4 are not applicable to the decision
on whether a bank meets General Condition 2.[37] The purpose of this limitation is
to make clear that that, in making its assessment, the authorities are not considering whether the Stabilization Powers could successfully resolve the situation which
the troubled bank faces, but is considering whether alternative measures, such as
use of the PRA powers, to set individual requirements on its own initiative, might
provide for this instead.[38]

E. Assessing General Condition 1

13.24 FSMA, Sch 6 contains five Threshold Conditions which must be satisfied before
a firm is authorized to conduct investment or banking business in the United
Kingdom under the FSMA. These conditions are elaborated on in the FCA and
PRA Handbook on Conditions for Authorisation (COND). This sets out guidance in COND 2.1 to COND 2.7 on whether a firm, such as a bank satisfies and
continues to satisfy the Threshold Condition, and these criteria will be applied in
determining whether the firm is likely to fail to meet the threshold conditions.
These conditions are as follows.

---

[34] BA, s 7(5A).
[35] BA, s 7(5B).
[36] See further the SRR Code, para 6.16.
[37] BA, s 7(6).
[38] This was set out in the FSA guidance FINMAR 3.2.5.

Legal status

This requires a firm carrying on or seeking to carry on certain PRA-regulated activ- **13.25**
ities to have a specific legal form. For example, a firm that wishes to carry on the
regulated activity of accepting deposits or issuing electronic money must be a body
corporate or partnership.[39]

Location of offices

This imposes requirements with respect to the place where a firm's offices must be **13.26**
located. For example, where a firm is a body corporate constituted under the laws of
any part of the United Kingdom, it must have both its head office and its registered
office in the United Kingdom.[40]

Business conducted in a prudent manner, including appropriate resources

The relevant regulator (i.e. the PRA or FSA) must be satisfied that a firm has resources **13.27**
which are adequate in relation to the activities which the firm seeks to carry on or
carries on. The regulator may take into account the firm's membership of a group
and the provisions which the firm makes or which the group makes in respect of
liabilities and the means by which both the firm and the group manages risk in connection with the firm's business.[41] The appropriate resources Threshold Condition
is perhaps the most important in relation to the exercise of the Stabilization Powers
insofar it is the most closely connected Threshold Condition to the FSA's financial stability objective. The term 'appropriate' means sufficient in terms of quality, quantity, and availability and 'resources' as including all financial resources,
non-financial resources, and means of managing resources giving capital, provisions against liabilities, holdings of or access to cash and other liquid assets, human
resources, and the effective means by which to manage risk. PRA (but not FCA)
firms are also required to conduct their business 'in a prudent manner'.[42]

Effective supervision

The regulator will have regard to the way in which the relevant business, and the **13.28**
group of which it is a part, is structured, and will also consider any person in a
relevant relationship with the firm, for example, a firm's controllers, directors, or
partners, those with close links and those that may exert influence on a firm which
might pose a risk to the firm's satisfaction of the Threshold Conditions.[43]

---

[39] FSMA, Sch 6, para 5B. See COND 2.1.
[40] FSMA, Sch 6, para 5C as regards PRA firms, and 2B as regards FCA firms. See COND 2.2.
[41] FSMA, Sch 6, para 4D as regards PRA firms, and 2D as regards FCA firms. See COND 2.4
generally and COND 2.4.3(2)(b) for guidance on the impact of a group.
[42] FSMA Sch 6 5D. See COND 2.4.2.
[43] FSMA Sch 6 5F for PRA firms, and 2C for FCA firms. See COND 2.4.3(a).

Suitability

13.29 The regulator must be satisfied that the firm is fit and proper having regard to all circumstances, and in particular that it has management of appropriate skill and experience and can be expected to act with probity.[44]

F. Assessing General Condition 2

Timing

13.30 In assessing General Condition 2, it will be important to consider the timeframe during which any actions taken by or in relation to the bank are likely to be available and to have effect. For the Bank of England, the purpose of the reference to timing in General Condition 2 is to require it to consider whether a return to full compliance is likely to occur within a reasonable period of time. In making its determination regarding timing, the Bank of England may consider various factors, including but not limited to: the extent of any loss, or risk of loss, or other adverse effect on consumers; the seriousness of any suspected breach of the requirements of the FSMA or PRA Handbook, and the steps that need to be taken to correct that breach; the risk of the bank's conduct of business presents to the stability of the UK financial system, and to confidence in that system; the likelihood that remedial action could be taken by or in relation to the bank will take effect before consumers, market confidence, or financial stability suffers significant detriment. The FSA, when Condition 2 was within its remit, had indicated that if it was satisfied that a bank's breach of the Threshold Conditions was likely to be temporary and to be rectified within a reasonable time, it would have been unlikely to conclude that General Condition 2 has been met, and this is probably still accurate.[45]

Consultation with Bank and Treasury

13.31 Before confirming that General Condition 2 is met the bank must consult the PRA, the FCA, and the Treasury.[46]

Write-down powers and Condition 2

13.32 The power to write down capital instruments is an anomalous one within the BRRD, since it can be used either as a resolution measure or as a free-standing measure

---

[44] FSMA, Sch 6, para 5E for PRA firms and 2E for FCA firms.
[45] FINMAR 3.2.7.
[46] BA, s 7(5G).

outside resolution.[47] This is given effect within the BA by s 6A, which specifies six cases in which the write-down power can be used. These are:

1. The stabilization conditions are met, and a bail-in has not been selected as the stabilization tool.[48]
2. The stabilization conditions are met, and will continue to be met unless a write-down order is made.[49]
3. The stabilization conditions will be met if a write-down order is made, but not otherwise.[50]
4. The bank is a parent undertaking, and the group will not be viable unless a write-down order is made.[51]
5. Extraordinary public support is required by the bank, and the Bank of England is satisfied that in order for it to meet its capital requirements a write-down order must be made.[52]

The first of these illustrates the somewhat complex interaction of the bail-in and write-down powers. In effect bail-in subsumes write-down, in that where a bail-in is effected, the principles which govern bail-in (in particular the no-creditor-worse-off-than-in-liquidation (NCWOL) protection) will apply to all creditors bailed in, including holders of capital instruments.[53] However, the write-down power, when used outside bail-in, is covered by no such safeguards.[54] This creates difficulties for holders of capital instruments in terms of predicting the likely impact on them of bank resolution, in that it would be theoretically possible for a resolution authority to exercise a write-down power outside resolution, eliminating the claims of capital holders, before declaring resolution and conducting a bail-in, thereby maximizing recoveries for senior creditors. The United Kingdom has addressed this issue through ss 6A(2)(c) and 12AA of the BA, which effectively prohibit this approach. The cumulative effect of these provisions is that if the authorities wish to conduct a bail-in, they are required to write down holders of capital instruments in accordance with the bail-in regime, and not the write-down regime. The final step in this dance (in the United Kingdom) is provided by the Bank of England's statement in its 'approach to resolution' document that: **13.33**

> The second condition is that it must not be reasonably likely that action will be taken—outside the resolution regime—that will result in the firm no longer failing or likely to fail. This assessment is made by the Bank as resolution authority, having consulted the PRA or FCA, and [Her Majesty's Treasury] HMT. When making

---

[47] Art 59(1).
[48] BA, s 6A(2).
[49] BA, 6A(3).
[50] BA, 6A(4).
[51] BA, s 6A(5).
[52] BA, s 6A(6).
[53] Art 48 of the BRRD.
[54] BRRD Art 60(2)(c).

this determination, the Bank must take into account the requirement, introduced through the BRRD, that any remaining regulatory capital must be written down or converted once the firm is no longer viable (that is, once it is failing or likely to fail) before stabilisation tools can be used. In practice, this is likely to occur as the firm enters resolution, since the write-down or conversion is unlikely to be sufficient in itself to resolve the difficulties of the failing firm.[55]

13.34 This constitutes, in practice, a declaration that by the time a firm has reached the stage where write-down could be justified, it is likely that bail-in rather than write-down will be justified.

G. Assessing General Conditions 3 and 4

13.35 General Condition 3 is that the exercise of the powers is necessary having regard to the public interest in the advancement of one or more of the specified resolution objectives, and General Condition 4 is that one or more of the special resolution objectives would not be met to the same extent by a winding up of the bank. These two conditions both tend towards the same point, that the exercise of special resolution tools should be an exceptional remedy, and that these tools should not be used unless there is a significant public interest in their being so used.

13.36 The decision to put a firm into resolution does not, on its own, directly allow use of resolution tools. By BA, s 7, no Stabilization Power can be exercised unless the bank is satisfied that the exercise of the power is necessary to achieve one of the specified resolution objectives set out in BA, s 4. Further, ss 8–9 of the BA set out further conditions which must be satisfied before specific powers may be used. It is therefore in theory possible for the bank to conclude that an institution satisfies the threshold conditions to be placed in resolution, but that there is no ground for exercising any special resolution power. In such a case the bank will apply for the institution to be place in bank Insolvency through the bank insolvency procedure.[56]

H. Valuation Mechanisms and Creditor Safeguards

Valuation

13.37 The BRRD provides for two valuations to be undertaken. The Article 36 valuation determines the extent to which bail-in can be effected at all—Article 36(4)(d). The

---

[55] 'Approach to Resolution', p. 10, para 24.

[56] BA, Part 2. Note that an application for Bank Administration under Part 3 could not be made in this case, since Bank Administration is only available where a property transfer order has been made by the Bank, and a property transfer is a 'Stabilization Power' which can only be exercised in pursuit of a 'stabilization option' (BA, s 1(4)). It would presumably still be possible to apply to place such a bank in ordinary Insolvency Act insolvency.

Article 74 valuation determines what the position would have been had the institution concerned been placed in insolvency rather than resolution. Article 74 then provides that the insolvency valuation must be compared with 'the actual treatment that shareholders and creditors have received'. The question is as to how this latter figure is to be obtained. It would be somewhat odd to use the figure derived from the Article 36 valuation, since this is by definition a pre-estimate of the effect of action rather than a measure of the outcome of that action. Thus in order to apply Article 74, the independent valuer will need to make two determinations—one under Article 74(2)(a) of the position that would have obtained on insolvency and one under Article 74(2)(b) of the actual economic outcome of the measure.

This follows logically from the function performed by Article 74 as regards bail-in. If a proposed bail-in were to result in a situation where some creditors were left worse off than they would have been on insolvency, it would be prohibited by Article 34 (as set out above). Thus, the only way a bailed-in creditor is entitled to compensation under Article 73 is if the bail-in was, at the time it was undertaken, permissible under Article 34, but the outcome of the bail-in has been to leave the creditor worse off than he would have been under insolvency. In this case it would be a nonsense to use the Article 34 valuation as the basis for compensation, since it is the inaccuracy of the Article 34 valuation, which has given rise to the necessity for the valuation in the first place, and using the Article 34 number would always give a compensation value of zero. **13.38**

Valuations are critical for any resolution. However, a resolution valuation must satisfy two competing requirements, being both rapid and accurate. The BRRD complicates this further by adding a third requirement that the valuation be independent. The tension between these three requirements will be a major cause of difficulty in any future resolution. **13.39**

Valuations perform a number of functions, including: **13.40**

- providing an up-to-date estimate of the financial position of the firm,
- allowing the authorities to quantify future expected losses that should be addressed through resolution,
- providing an estimate of the value of the firm after resolution has taken place, and
- informing the extent to which losses will fall on different shareholders and unsecured creditors, and quantifying the size of any compensation that may be due to those shareholders and creditors.

Prior to resolution

The requirement that the decision to take resolution action must be based on an independent valuation[57] necessarily means that a valuer will have to be appointed **13.41**

---

[57] BRRD Art 36(1).

in advance of the taking of resolution action. This raises a logical difficulty, in that since in the run-up to resolution the only people who will know that resolution is a prospect are the resolution authority and the bank itself, the valuer must necessarily be appointed by one or other (or both) of them, and that in itself may be sufficient to compromise its independence. Such a valuation is likely to be a rushed affair, and the Bank of England suggests that it will be based on the firm's updated accounting balance sheet with appropriate regulatory capital adjustments.[58] At the same time, the independent valuer is likely to be required to prepare indicative estimates of the other resolution valuations.

During resolution

13.42 During resolution, the authorities will require a valuation of the firm's assets and liabilities to estimate the scale of the losses of the firm that need to be addressed. This valuation will not be based solely on accounting data since it is required to be forward-looking. It must therefore take into account the nature of the resolution tool that will be used, the losses expected; the plans to restructure the firm once it has been stabilized (e.g. following bail-in), and the costs of this restructuring.

13.43 This valuation may or may not feed through into the other requirement: a valuation of the firm's equity after resolution. This valuation is likely to be based to a large extent on the commercial position of the firm, which in turn will be driven by factors such as profitability.

13.44 It is important to note at this point that the valuation of equity resulting from an assets-minus-liabilities calculation may well be very different from the valuation of that equity on a market basis. If the institution placed in resolution had a stable and profitable business model, but failed because of unwise expansion into ultimately unprofitable areas of business, it is likely that the value of the new equity, stripped of the unprofitable activities and assets, may be well in excess of the book value of that equity. Conversely, if the failure of the institution was caused by a fundamentally flawed business model which turned out to be structurally loss making, it is possible that the market value of the new equity could be significantly below its book value.

13.45 This market value will represent the value available to authorities to compensate investors, and will therefore determine their freedom of movement to act without breaching NCWOL safeguards.

Post-resolution

13.46 Once the firm has left resolution, two further independent valuations will be commissioned by the Treasury where a stabilization tool has been used. The purpose of

---

[58] Approach, Annex 2 p. 25.

these valuations is to protect the interests of the shareholders and creditors affected by the resolution, by ensuring that no relevant creditor is worse off (NCWOL) than they would have been if the whole firm had entered insolvency.

The Treasury will therefore appoint an independent expert to prepare: **13.47**

(i) an estimate of the financial outcome for each class of creditor based on a hypothetical insolvency of the whole firm at the date of resolution, and
(ii) an assessment of the actual financial outcome for each class of shareholder and creditor as a result of the resolution.

If the independent expert concludes that a relevant creditor would have received a better outcome from insolvency than they actually received from resolution, that creditor would be entitled to compensation.

Valuation work will need to be coordinated across jurisdictions, to support **13.48** the resolution of the largest global firms. These firms will have a home author-ity (where the firm is head-quartered) and host authorities (where a firm has subsidiaries). The valuation work required to resolve these firms is expected to be more complex, since it will involve different accounting, capital and regula-tory requirements.

NCWOL and valuations

In the broadest terms, both the BA and the BRRD approach resolution on the basis **13.49** that resolution should only be effected if the result of the intervention is to produce a better outcome than would have been achieved had the firm concerned been placed into insolvency. However, the mechanisms which are used to produce this result are very different, and the task of reconciling the two for the purposes of UK implementation is not straightforward.

The basis of the safeguards set out within the BA is the idea of compensation. **13.50** The basis of calculation of the entitlement to compensation is that no creditor should be left, as a result of the resolution action, in a position where he is financially worse off than he would have been had the resolution action not been taken and the institution placed in the appropriate insolvency proceeding (the NCWOL safeguard).

There are two ways in which a NCWOL safeguard can operate. The existing BA **13.51** mechanism is quite clear that the requirement is an after the event compensation calculation, and does not limit the freedom of the resolution authority to take resolution actions. The BRRD, by contrast, sets out the NCWOL safeguard as an explicit limitation on the resolution authority's freedom of action. The question is therefore as to the scope of this limitation.

It is quite clear that some parts of the BRRD text are intended to place express limi- **13.52** tations on the powers of resolution authorities (see, e.g. recital 95). Article 34(1) also makes clear that member states are required to ensure that their resolution authorities act in accordance with the principles set out in that article, including the NCWOL principle (34(1)(g)). This is, however, qualified by the reference to Articles 73–75. The effect of this is that member states must prohibit resolution authorities from acting in a way which is contrary to Articles 73–75. The question is therefore as to what these articles require.

13.53 Article 73 contains two safeguards, one as regards partial property transfers (PPTs) and another as regards bail-in. The revised language on the partial property transfer safeguard Article 73(a) makes clear that the obligation imposed is to compensate— that is, to ensure that those affected by a PPT 'receive at least as much' as they would have done under insolvency. Section 73(b), however, makes no reference to property being 'received', but states that:

> where resolution authorities apply the bail-in tool, the shareholders and creditors whose claims have been written down or converted to equity do not incur greater losses than they would have incurred if the institution under resolution had been wound up under normal insolvency proceedings immediately at the time when the decision referred to in Article 82 was taken.

13.54 It seems clear that 'do not incur greater losses' means 'do not incur greater losses as a result of the bail-in'. It is very hard to see how this requirement could be said to be satisfied by inflicting a loss on an investor through a bail-in and compensating him afterwards. In this regard it is critical that the two safeguards are expressed in different ways. If it had been intended that the s 73(b) requirement could be satisfied by compensating over-bailed-in creditors after the event, there would have been no reason to divide s 73(a) and (b) into different safeguards.

13.55 Consequently, it seems that the effect of Article 34 is to require member states to prohibit their domestic resolution authorities from 'over-bailing-in' senior creditors beyond the NCWOL level and compensating them afterwards. This does not appear to be currently reflected in UK legislation.

I. Variation of Contractual Protections

13.56 There are a number of provisions within the BA which permit the resolution authority to interfere with or vary the terms of a contract entered into by the institution in resolution. However, the most important of these are set out in s 70A–70C, which enable the resolution authority to disapply or vary the rights and obligations of a firm in resolution.

Suspension of obligations

13.57 The bank may suspend obligations to make a payment, or delivery, under a contract where one of the parties to the contract is a bank in respect of which it[59] is exercising a Stabilization Power. This power is bilateral. However, it does not apply to:

(a) payments of deposits or claims covered by any deposit protection or compensation scheme, or

(b) payments or deliveries to payment and clearing systems and central banks.[60]

This suspension must end no later than midnight at the end of the first business day following the day on which the instrument providing for the suspension is published.

Where a payment or delivery under the contract concerned falls due within the **13.58** period of the suspension, that payment or delivery is treated as being due immediately on the expiry of the suspension.[61]

It should be noted that there is no automatic obligation on the bank to impose this stay, **13.59** and it must have regard to the impact a suspension might have on the orderly functioning of the financial markets before exercising the power to declare such a suspension.

Suspension of security rights

Where a Stabilization Power is being exercised, the Bank may suspend the rights **13.60** of a secured creditor of the bank to enforce any security interest[62] the creditor has in relation to any assets of the bank. That suspension must end no later than midnight at the end of the first business day following the day on which the instrument institution the suspension was published.[63] This disapplication does not apply to securities granted to payment and clearing systems and central banks as collateral or as cover for margin.

Again, there is no obligation to impose a suspension of security rights, and the Bank **13.61** must have regard to the impact a suspension might have on the orderly functioning of the financial markets before exercising this power.

Suspension of termination rights

The bank may suspend the termination right of any party to a qualifying con- **13.62** tract (other than a party who is an excluded person). This provision applies

---

[59] BA 70A(1).

[60] These are set out in BA 70D(1), and include systems designated under either Reg 4 of the Financial Markets and Insolvency (Settlement Finality) Regulations 1999 or under Art 2(a) of the Settlement Finality Directive, a recognized central counterparties, EEA, or third-country central counterparties, or central banks.

[61] BA, s 70A(4).

[62] For the purposes of this section, a 'security interest' means an interest or right held for the purpose of securing the payment of money or the performance of any other obligation—BA, s 70B(7).

[63] BA, s 70B(2).

to all contracts to which the bank in resolution is itself a party. However, it also potentially applies to contracts entered into by subsidiaries of the bank, provided that:

(a) the obligations of the subsidiary undertaking are guaranteed or otherwise supported by the bank under resolution,

(b) the termination rights under the contract are triggered by the insolvency or the financial condition of the bank under resolution, and

(c) if a property transfer instrument has been made in relation to the bank under resolution:

    (i) all the assets and liabilities relating to the contract have been or are being transferred to, or assumed by, a single transferee, or

    (ii) the bank is providing adequate protection for the performance of the obligations of the subsidiary undertaking under the contract in any other way.

13.63 Such a suspension should only be imposed having regard to the impact a suspension might have on the orderly functioning of the financial markets before exercising the power in subsection.

13.64 This suspension must end no later than midnight at the end of the first business day following the day on which that instrument is published. Where the suspension is imposed in relation to a subsidiary undertaking of a bank under resolution, 'midnight' means midnight in the EEA state in which the subsidiary undertaking is established.

13.65 If the bank decides that the relevant contract will not be transferred or bailed in, and gives notice of that determination to the counterparty to the contract, this suspension is automatically lifted, and the counterpart may then terminate in accordance with the provisions of the contract.[64]

13.66 Finally, where a contract which contains an automatic termination provision is transferred to a new entity, in circumstances where the automatic termination has been triggered, the contract is to be treated as not being terminated as regards the new entity unless the event giving rise to the termination right has been triggered by that entity.

13.67 For this purpose, 'termination right' means a right to terminate a contract, and also a right to accelerate, close out, set-off, or net obligations, or any similar provision that suspends, modifies, or extinguishes an obligation of a party to the contract. It also includes any provision that prevents an obligation from arising under the contract.[65]

---

[64] BA, s 70C(7).
[65] BA, s 70C(10).

Permanent suspension of termination rights

BA s 48Z sets out the provisions of the BA which permanently extinguish certain **13.68** contractual termination rights. It implements Article 68 of the BRRD. The termination rights which arise under s 48Z apply to contracts with the bank in resolution, its subsidiaries and members of its group.[66]

The approach is based on a classification of rights. A Type 1 default event provision **13.69** is a provision of a contract or other agreement that has the effect that if a specified event occurs or situation arises:

(a) the agreement is terminated, modified or replaced,
(b) rights or duties under the agreement are terminated, modified or replaced,
(c) a right accrues to terminate, modify or replace the agreement,
(d) a right accrues to terminate, modify or replace rights or duties under the agreement,
(e) a sum becomes payable or ceases to be payable,
(f) delivery of anything becomes due or ceases to be due,
(g) a right to claim a payment or delivery accrues, changes or lapses,
(h) any other right accrues, changes or lapses, or
(i) an interest is created, changes or lapses.

A Type 2 default event provision is a provision of a contract or other agreement that **13.70** has the effect that a provision of the contract or agreement:

(a) takes effect only if a specified event occurs or does not occur,
(b) takes effect only if a specified situation arises or does not arise,
(c) has effect only for so long as a specified event does not occur,
(d) has effect only while a specified situation lasts,
(e) applies differently if a specified event occurs,
(f) applies differently if a specified situation arises, or
(g) applies differently while a specified situation lasts.

In both of these cases, a crisis prevention measure, crisis management measure, or **13.71** recognized third-country resolution action taken in relation to the bank, third-country institution, or a member of the same group as the bank or third country institution, is to be disregarded in determining whether the termination right created by the provision has in fact been triggered, provided—importantly—that substantive obligations provided for in the contract or agreement (including payment and delivery obligations and provision of collateral) continue to be performed. An event which is not itself a crisis prevention measure, but is directly linked to such a measure, must also be disregarded.[67]

---

[66] BA, s 48Z(5).
[67] BA, s 48Z(6).

13.72 Separately from this, an order made by the bank under any part of the Special Resolution Regime may specify that the disapplication of termination rights shall apply, either in whole or in part, to that order and to anything done in connection with that order.

J. Other Resolution Powers

Intra-group financial support

13.73 These provisions of the BRRD are not easy to understand in isolation. Intra-group support is common within financial groups,[68] and the difficulty is to identify which particular arrangements fall within the scope of these requirements. To complicate the picture, national legal systems within Europe vary widely in their approach to group support arrangements. At one extreme, the French and German systems permit companies within a group to act for the good of the group as a whole, on the basis of the indirect interest that each entity affiliated to a group has in the prosperity of the group as a whole.[69] However many other systems give primacy to the rights of creditors of individual legal entities, and provide that those entities must be run by their directors and managers in their own best interests. This gives rise to a series of issues:

- Under banking law, intra-group transfers may trigger supervisory action to defend the financial soundness of banks subject to that supervisor's jurisdiction. This may result in ring fencing of a local bank's assets. An intra-group transfer of assets is also normally considered to be a transaction with a connected party which may be subject to additional regulatory conditions (such as a requirement for arm's length pricing).
- Under company law, the influence and liability of a parent company over its subsidiary is usually limited, and the board of directors' fiduciary duties and duty of loyalty are usually to the individual company, rather than the group as a whole.
- Adverse tax implications can be expected in many cases —intra-group transfers of funds may not be tax-deductible.
- Under insolvency law, transfers of assets executed in a suspect period before the opening of the insolvency proceedings of the transferor might be latter found retroactively void or ineffective vis-à-vis other creditors.

13.74 The initial idea behind the BRRD proposal was therefore to create a permissive regime, under which a bank group could obtain advance consent for a particular arrangement which would be upheld within resolution.

---

[68] There is a useful overview in The Joint Forum Report on intra-group support measures February 2012: <http://www.bis.org/publ/joint28.pdf> (accessed 26 October 2015).
[69] For example, see for France, Cour de Cassation Criminelle 4 fèv. 1985, Rozenblum, Rev. Soc. 1985, p. 665, and for Germany the German Companies Act (Aktiengesetz) of 6 September 1965.

The idea of this regime as a pure privilege was thoughtful and effective, and is still **13.75** in the directive—Article 19(4) provides that 'Member States shall remove any legal impediment in national law to intra-group financial support transactions that are undertaken in accordance with this Chapter'. However, almost as soon as this was proposed it was hedged about with requirements that the various supervisors of the group should be granted the right to review and ultimately veto the provision of such support.

The reason that this creates difficulty is that most financial groups already have **13.76** relatively significant arrangements for intra-group support. These are generally specific to the tax, corporate, and financial requirements to which different members of the group are subject. The issue which arises is as to how to distinguish between the 'directive' intra-group support arrangements—which require regulatory consent and are subject to regulatory control—and 'non-directive' intra-group support arrangements, which do not. This distinction is acknowledged—but not clarified—by recital 38 to the BRRD, which provides that '[t]he provisions regarding intra-group financial support in this Directive do not affect contractual or statutory liability arrangements between institutions which protect the participating institutions through cross-guarantees and equivalent arrangements'.

The United Kingdom has implemented these parts of the BRRD by transcription,[70] **13.77** and appears to take the view that 'intra-group financial support arrangements' are narrowly confined to the partial definition set out in Article 19, which refers to 'an agreement to provide financial support to any other party to the agreement that meets the conditions for early intervention pursuant to Article 27'. This approach would mean that the regulatory power of control would be applied only to arrangements which are specifically triggered by the occurrence of one or more of the triggers set out in Article 27. If this approach is adopted, ordinary intra-group arrangements will be unaffected.

Administrators in recovery

Another innovation in the BRRD is the provision under Article 29 for the competent authority to appoint a 'temporary administrator' during the early intervention phase whose function will be 'either to replace the management body of the institution temporarily or to work temporarily with the management body of the institution', and the provision under Article 35 to appoint a 'special manager' to replace the management of the institution under resolution. This function is created by s 62B–62E, is referred to in the BA as the 'Resolution Administrator', and replaces the old 'bail-in administrator'.

---

[70] See Part VII (Arts 83–106) of the Bank Recovery and Resolution (No. 2) Order 2014, 2014/3348.

Powers to make regulations about tax

13.79   The BA empowers the Treasury to make regulations including provision in relation to tax, such as capital gains, corporation, and income tax, in connection with the exercise of a Stabilization Power. The BA sets out the effects which the regulations governing tax may have, gives.[71]

The power to change law

13.80   The BA, s 75 gives the Treasury the power to modify, by order:

- primary and secondary legislation, excluding the provisions of the BA itself and secondary legislation to be made under the BA, other than instruments and orders made in exercise of any Stabilization Power, and
- the provisions of common law

for the purpose of enabling the effective exercise of any Stabilization Power having regard to the Special Resolution Regime (SRR) objectives.[72] A modifying order may make provision which has retrospective effect, although the Treasury must have regard to the fact that it is in the public interest to avoid retrospective legislation.[73]

13.81   Section 75 is an example of a delegation of power by parliament to amend its own Acts, also known as a 'Henry VIII clause' because '[Henry the VIII] is regarded popularly as the impersonation of executive autocracy'.[74] Traditionally, this type of clause has been criticized but, as Wade and Forsyth put it, 'as the intricacy of legislation grows steadily more formidable, some power to adjust or reconcile statutory provisions has to be tolerated. If there is to be delegated legislation at all, it is inevitable that it should affect statute law as well as common law'.[75]

13.82   In light of the exceptional amount of power which the BA, s 75 places in the Treasury's hands, the internal qualifiers are unsurprising: the type of instrument which the Treasury may modify relying on s 75 does not include the BA itself; the Treasury may only justify its exercise of the power under s 75 by reference to the SRR objectives; where the Treasury seeks to amend any instrument retrospectively in reliance on s 75, it must further demonstrate that it has given sufficient weight to the fact that it is in the public interest to avoid retrospective legislation; the Treasury will also necessarily need to have regard to existing public law restrictions, in particular the requirement to have respect for the rule of law, legal certainty and

---

[71] See BA, s 74. The Treasury has yet to make regulations under this section.

[72] BA, ss 75(1), (2), (4), (5), and (6). The power is subject to the affirmative procedure but in cases of necessity (in practice, where the power needed to be exercised urgently), the section makes provision for the Treasury to make the order immediately, following which there are twenty-eight days for both Houses of Parliament to approve the order, failing which, the order would lapse (BA, s 75(7)). The lapse of an order does not prevent another order being made in new terms (BA, s 75(8)).

[73] BA, s 75(3). For guidance on the exercise of the s 75 power, see the SRR Code paras 6.18 et seq.

[74] See William Wade and Christopher Forsyth, *Administrative Law* (Oxford University Press 2009) (10th edn), 734.

[75] Ibid. See the other examples of such clauses at 734 to 737.

Convention Rights and ensure that it does not use the s 75 power for purposes unconnected with the use of the powers under the BA, for example, to change the law for wider public policy objectives.[76]

The Treasury's exercise of any power under the BA, s 75 is subject to judicial review **13.83** and, as Wade and Forsyth point out, the courts, in reviewing the exercise of the type of power in s 75, have insisted upon a narrow and strict construction and any doubts about such a clause's scope are resolved by a restrictive approach.[77]

Miscellaneous obligations on Bank and Treasury

The Treasury has the power to require the bank not to exercise a Stabilization Power **13.84** where that exercise would be likely to contravene an international obligation of the United Kingdom in which case the bank must consider alternative actions, which both pursue the SRR objectives and avoid the objections on which Treasury's notice or refusal was based.[78]

The bank may not exercise a Stabilization Power without the Treasury's consent if **13.85** the exercise would be likely to have implications for public funds. The Treasury may specify considerations that should or should not be taken into account in determining whether action has implications for public funds. The bank must consider another exercise of the Stabilization Powers if the Treasury has refused consent and must pursue the SRR objectives and avoid the objections that the Treasury first made.[79]

---

[76] See the SRR Code, para 6.20.
[77] Ibid, 737 citing *R v Secretary of State for the Environment ex p Spath Holme Ltd.* [2001] 2 AC 349.
[78] See further BA, s 76.
[79] See further BA, s 78.

14

PROPERTY TRANSFERS AND BAIL-IN UNDER THE BANKING ACT

A. Powers

14.01 Once a bank has been placed in resolution, the next question is what the resolution authority is permitted to do. The powers set out in the Bank Recovery and Resolution Directive (BRRD) and the UK Banking Act (BA) may be compared as shown in Table 14.1.

14.02 The Banking Act 2009 ('BA') provides five stabilization options for dealing with the situation where all or part of the business of a bank[1] has encountered, or is likely to encounter, financial difficulties:

- Transfer to a private sector purchaser.[2] This permits the sale of all or part of a bank's business to a commercial purchaser. It can be achieved by (a) one or more share transfer instruments or (b) one or more property transfer instruments. The bank is responsible for the exercise of a private sector transfer power.[3]
- Transfer to a bridge bank.[4] This permits the transfer of all or part of the business to a bridge bank—a company that is wholly owned by the bank. It can only be achieved by one or more property transfer instruments. The bank is responsible for the exercise of a bridge bank transfer power.[5]
- Transfer to an asset management company.[6] This permits the transfer of all or part of the business to a bridge bank—a company that is wholly owned by the bank. It can only be achieved by one or more property transfer instruments. The bank is responsible for the exercise of a bridge bank transfer power.[7]

---

[1] For discussion of what is meant by a 'bank' in this context, see Chapter 13.
[2] BA, s 1(3)(a).
[3] BA, s 11.
[4] BA, s 1(3)(b).
[5] BA, s 12.
[6] BA, s 1(3)(ba).
[7] BA, s 12ZA.

Table 14.1 Comparison of powers set out in the BRRD and the UK BA

UK BA	BRRD
Transfer to private sector purchaser	Sale of business tool
Transfer to a resolution company[a]	Bridge institution tool Asset separation tool
Bail-in[b]	Bail-in
Transfer to temporary public ownership	Government financial stabilization tools

[a] BA, s 29A.

[b] The bail-in provisions of the BA are inserted by the Financial Services (Banking Reform) Act 2013.

- Bail-in.[8] This permits the writing down of creditors of the institution. It is achieved by the making of a resolution instrument, which can only be made by the bank.[9]
- Transfer to temporary public ownership.[10] This can be achieved by one or more share transfer orders in which the transferee is (a) a nominee of the Treasury, or (b) a company wholly owned by the Treasury. The Treasury is responsible for the exercise of a temporary public ownership power.[11]

To give effect to the stabilization options, the BA identifies four basic powers ('sta-   **14.03** bilization powers'):

- the power to make a share transfer instrument;[12]
- the power to make a share transfer order;[13]
- the power to make a property transfer instrument;[14] and
- the power to make a resolution instrument.[15]

To supplement these basic powers, the BA gives the power to make a compensation   **14.04** scheme order,[16] a resolution fund order,[17] or a third-party compensation order.[18] In addition, the BA contains provisions governing the continuity of services and facilities provided to a bank by members of its group.[19] The BA also provides various other supplementary powers described as 'incidental functions', the most noteworthy of which is the power which the BA gives to the Treasury to change the law—a

---

[8] BA, 1(3)(c).

[9] BA, s 12ZA.

[10] BA, s 1(3)(d).

[11] BA, s 13.

[12] BA, s 15.

[13] BA, s 16.

[14] BA, s 33.

[15] BA, s 12A(2).

[16] See para 14.125.

[17] See para 14.130.

[18] See para 14.141.

[19] BA, ss 63–70. These are discussed at para 14.62.

so-called 'Henry VIII clause'.[20] Although the Bank and Treasury are responsible for the exercise of the stabilization powers, the exercise of the powers is contingent on the Financial Services Authority (FSA) being satisfied that certain general conditions apply.[21] In exercising the stabilization powers, the Bank and the Treasury must adhere to the *Banking Act 2009: Special Resolution Regime Code of Practice* issued by the Treasury for the use of the stabilization powers ('SRR Code').

The stabilization powers and interference with contractual rights and expectations

14.05 Amongst the more controversial areas of the stabilization powers are those relating to the primacy of share and property transfers which, under the BA, take effect despite any legislative restrictions, in effect giving the Bank of England and Treasury the power to override contractual provisions, the power to override the provisions in a contract that allow a party to terminate that contract where, for example, the other party commits an 'act of default',[22] the power for an transfer instrument or order to remove or alter the terms of a trust on which shares or property to be transferred are held,[23] and the power given to the Bank and Treasury, in imposing continuity obligations, to cancel or modify contractual obligations between a group company and a residual bank or transferred bank, as the case may be.[24]

14.06 The powers to make instruments or orders which, for example, specify that default event provisions are not to be disapplied, are significant because their exercise may alter the contractual expectations of the parties to contract or agreement containing the default event provisions. It also means that it may not be possible to enforce certain contractual provisions, such as those governing change of control events or covenants restricting property disposal, in so far as they are triggered by transfers made pursuant to a share transfer instrument or order ('disapplication powers'). The introduction of the disapplication powers has resulted in changed attitudes under English law about the effectiveness of early termination and close out netting provisions, such as that contained in section 6 of the International Swaps and Derivatives Association Master Agreement ('Netting Provisions'). Where a party to a contract containing Netting Provisions is a bank or other entity in respect of which the Bank or Treasury could exercise a stabilization power, it has become difficult for English lawyers to provide legal opinions, without making reference to the BA, as to the effectiveness of Netting Provisions in, for example, setting-off balances for regulatory capital purposes.[25]

---

[20] BA, s 75 discussed together with other supplementary powers at para13.82.
[21] See BA, s 7 discussed at 13.23 above.
[22] See BA, s 48Z.
[23] See BA, ss 17(5) and 34(7).
[24] See BA, ss 64(2) and 67(2).
[25] For discussion of legal opinions in the context of netting exposures see Simon Gleeson *International Regulation of Banking* (Oxford University Press 2010), para 9.04.

The potential interference with contractual rights and expectations created by **14.07** the disapplication powers is mitigated through the restrictions on partial property transfer orders, ie, where some, but not all, of the assets of a bank are transferred ('partial property transfer').[26] Under the powers governing the restrictions on Partial Property Transfer Orders, the Treasury has made the BA (Restrictions of Partial Transfers) Order 2009 ('Transfers Order').[27] The Transfers Order sets out various restrictions on Partial Property Transfers and the remedies for contravening the restrictions. These include set-off and netting restrictions designed to protect provisions, such as Netting Provisions.[28] The difficulty, however, is that the protections in the Transfers Order are limited to Partial Property Transfer Orders only and do not, as matter of law, extend to the exercise of the disapplication powers.[29]

Dunfermline Building Society

The stabilization powers were first used in relation to Dunfermline Building Society **14.08** ('DBS') which announced in March 2009 that it was expected to make loss of £24m in 2008. In 2002 DBS created its commercial real estate lending operation, which expanded significantly in the years 2004–2007, when property prices were rising. When commercial property prices collapsed, this caused a significant loss to the portfolio. As well as pursuing growth in new business areas, DBS also engaged in an aggressive business acquisition strategy, acquiring mortgage loans from other lenders, principally of buy-to-let and self-certified mortgage portfolios, just before the global market for such loans collapsed. The FSA argued that the problems which led to the failure of DBS were 'almost entirely related to its commercial property loans and to the mortgages which it bought from other mortgage originators, including buy-to-let mortgages'.[30]

The steps leading up to and the use of the stabilization included the following:[31] **14.09**

- On 28 March 2009, the FSA determined that DBS was encountering financial difficulties and failing to meet the requisite threshold conditions.
- On 30 March 2009, DBS's core business (retail and wholesale deposits, branches, head office, and originated residential mortgages and staff) was transferred to Nationwide Building Society under the Dunfermline Building Society Property Transfer Instrument 2009 and the Amendments to Law (Resolution of Dunfermline Building Society) Order 2009.
- DBS's social housing loans were transferred to a bridge bank ('DBS Bridge Bank Ltd'), owned by the Bank of England also under the Dunfermline Building

---

[26] See BA, ss 47 and 48 discussed.
[27] SI 2009/322.
[28] The restriction on Partial Property Transfers is discussed at para 14.108.
[29] These are discussed at para 14.87.
[30] Letter of 17 April from Lord Turner (Chairman of the FSA) to the Chancellor, Alistair Darling.
[31] Ibid.

Society Property Transfer Instrument 2009 ('DBS Transfer Instrument') and the Amendments to Law (Resolution of Dunfermline Building Society) Order 2009.

- The power to disregard termination rights and other contractual provisions was applied to the transfer of the DBS's business to Nationwide but was expressly disapplied 'to the extent that it would be incompatible with' Article 9 of the Transfers Order thereby applying the set-off and netting arrangements to the transfer.[32]
- No share transfer orders were made.
- As DBS was the first building society for which the powers under the BA were used, two statutory instruments (The Building Societies (Insolvency and Special Administration) Order 2009 and The Building Society Special Administration (Scotland) Rules 2009) were made on 29 March 2009 and laid before Parliament on 30 March 2009. These the regimes in the BA, Parts Two and Three to building societies and set out the procedure for the building society special administration process under Part 3 of the Banking Act 2009 in Scotland.
- A court order was made on 30 March 2009 to place the remainder of DBS's business into the Building Society Special Administration Process. KPMG was appointed as building society special administrator. Amongst other things, the administration process included: DBS's 6 per cent. subordinated notes due 2015; medium-term notes and residential mortgage-backed securities held by DBS as treasury assets.
- The administration process also included any property, rights, or liabilities the transfer of which would contravene the Transfers Order.
- On 1 July 2009, the further assets were transferred to Nationwide from DBS and certain assets onward transferred from DBS Bridge Bank Ltd by virtue of the DBS Bridge Bank Limited Supplemental and Onward Property Transfer Instrument 2009.

There is no guarantee that the manner of any future exercise of the stabilization powers would be consistent with that in the case of DBS. However, DBS is useful in illustrating many of the issues discussed below.

Sale of business/transfer to private sector purchaser

14.10 These are broadly equivalent tools, which allow resolution authorities to change the legal ownership of an entity itself (i.e. a share sale) by a transfer of equity to a third party or private sector purchaser. As an alternative to a share sale, the tool can also be used to effect a business sale, by mandatory transfer of the assets, and/or liabilities of an institution. Whether the share sale or business sale route is taken, there is no requirement to obtain the consent of the institution's shareholders or any third

---

[32] See the DBS Transfer Instrument, Clause 6(2).

party other than the transferee. Transfers are required to be made on commercial terms and in accordance with EU state aid rules.

Bridge bank/bridge institution and asset separation tools

The reason that the single UK tool is reflected in two separate tools in the BRRD is **14.11** that the UK regime imposes no significant restrictions on the entity to which the assets are transferred—a 'bridge bank', in the United Kingdom, is simply a transferee of the assets of a bank in resolution. The BRRD, however, subdivided this tool into two separate tools, which are distinguished primarily by the restrictions placed on the recipient in each case.

The essence of a UK bridge bank structure is that the resolution authority may **14.12** transfer property to a bridge institution owned by the Bank of England. Bridge banks must be (in effect) time-limited entities, subject to particular requirements as to management, reporting, and eventual disposal, and the relevant provisions are contained in the code of practice created under s 5 of the Act. It is notable that there is no restriction on the way in which a bridge bank may be used—the resolution authority may transfer good assets to a bridge bank with the intention of selling it as a going concern, but may also transfer bad assets to the bridge bank with the aim of returning the transferee bank to financial health. In the latter case the bridge bank is not sold, but wound up.

The BRRD, by contrast, draws a clear distinction between asset management vehi- **14.13** cles and bridge banks. Under the BRRD schema, a bridge bank is intended to transform into a solvent authorized institution or to be wound down within a period of two years,[33] whereas an asset management vehicle is subject to no such time limit, and can therefore be used as a repository for the working-out over a long term of bad assets.

A BRRD bridge institution is subject to normal prudential requirements under the **14.14** Capital Requirements Regulation (although it can be established and authorized subject to a short exemption from usual prudential requirements at the beginning of its operation, where necessary to meet resolution objectives). The Directive makes provision requiring member states to ensure that the bridge institution enjoys continued access to financial market infrastructure and to deposit guarantee schemes in which the institution under resolution participated.

The BRRD asset separation tool must be used in conjunction with other tools. **14.15** It allows resolution authorities to remove assets (and potentially accompanying liabilities) off the balance sheet of a failing bank and into a run-off vehicle. The

---

[33] Another possibility is that the vehicle is sold to a private purchaser. At that point it ceases to be an asset management vehicle (since such a vehicle is defined in the BRRD as 'wholly or partially owned by one or more public authorities') and becomes a normal company.

run-off vehicle is not authorized as a bank, but is not time-limited, and may take as long as it wishes to realize the portfolio of assets transferred to it.

Transfer to Public Ownership

14.16 The Transfer to Public Ownership tool is classed in the BRRD as a resolution tool, and is governed by Articles 56–58, which deal with government financial support. Although transfer to public ownership is treated as something that should only be capable of happening after resolution, it is arguably not strictly speaking a resolution tool since it is not a power which can be exercised by the resolution authority, but only by the government concerned.

14.17 Since neither the UK BA nor the BRRD prohibit direct government aid, it is necessary to address the position which arises if it is sought to combine government support with resolution. This can appear to be an either/or situation—if the treasury concerned appears to be backing the bank, it is difficult to argue that the bank satisfies the normal conditions for resolution. Under the BA, a carve-out is provided whose effect is that where the Treasury both provides financial support to the institution concerned and recommends that the relevant stabilization power be used, the resolution authority may exercise that power in that way if it feels that such exercise is appropriate. The test for the application of the bail-in power is the same, save that there is no ability to exercise this power after a treasury bail-out unless the conditions are then satisfied. In practice this means that if treasury does decide to make public funding available to a bank, the resolution authority can only exercise the power to bail-in if it is satisfied that the bank would otherwise fail or threaten public confidence in the banking system, and this in turn could only happen if the amount of funding provided by the Treasury had proved to be insufficient to stop the bank from collapsing.

B. Private Sector Transfers

14.18 The BA empowers the Bank of England to make:

- one or more share transfer instruments, or
- one or more property transfer instruments

to give effect to the sale of all or part of the business of a bank to a commercial purchaser ('private sector transfer powers').[34]

The decision to exercise the private sector transfer powers

14.19 The SSR Code sets out various considerations which the Bank may take into account in deciding whether to exercise the private sector transfer powers stating

---

[34] BA, s 11(2).

that transfer to a private sector purchaser is generally likely to be the stabilization option that best meets the SRR objectives if it can be effected in a cost-effective way.[35] This suggests that exercise of the private sector transfer powers should be the first-choice stabilization option.

Special conditions for exercising the private sector transfer powers

The Bank may exercise a private sector transfer power if it is satisfied that the general **14.20** conditions are satisfied. However, where an institution has received financial assistance from the Treasury for the purpose of resolving or reducing a serious threat to the stability of the United Kingdom, it may only be transferred to the private sector in this way with the consent of the Treasury.[36]

C. Transfer to a Bridge Bank

The BA empowers the Bank to make one or more property transfer instruments **14.21** to give effect to the transfer of all or part of the business of a bank to a 'bridge bank'—a company which the Bank wholly or partially[37] owns ('bridge bank transfer power').[38] A bridge bank is intended to be a short-term operation, until appropriate private sector solutions can be arranged and implemented and the primary bridge bank objective is to facilitate the sale of the bridge bank—in whole or in part—to one or more private sector purchasers or a sale to the public through one or more public offerings.[39] The bridge bank's objectives are subordinate to the SSR objectives, and where there is a conflict between the two, the SRR objectives take precedence.[40]

The key phases for a bridge bank as (a) the stabilization phase, immediately follow- **14.22** ing the transfer; and (b) the sale/purchase phase, where the Bank works with one or more private sector purchaser to transfer the business while managing the bridge bank on a conservative basis.[41]

The decision to exercise the bridge bank transfer powers

The SSR Code sets out various considerations which the Bank may take into **14.23** account in deciding whether to exercise the bridge bank transfer power stating that transfer to a bridge bank may be appropriate where an immediate private sector

---

[35] See further the SRR Code, para 5.19.
[36] BA, s 8.
[37] The old UK legislation required that a bridge bank be wholly owned by the Bank of England, but the BRRD permits it to be only partially owned.
[38] BA, s 12(2).
[39] See the SSR Code, para 9.1.
[40] See the SRR Code, para 9.6.
[41] See the SRR Code, para 9.25.

is not possible and where a stable platform is needed to prepare for and effect the onward sale of all or part of the bank to a private sector purchaser.[42] This suggests that exercise of the private sector transfer powers should be the second-choice stabilization option.

14.24 Where the Bank exercises a bridge bank transfer power it must comply with any notice provided by the Treasury, for the purpose of ensuring compliance by the United Kingdom with its international obligations, to take or not to take specified action in respect of a bridge bank and not take any action in respect of the bridge bank without the Treasury's consent if the action would be likely to have implications for public funds.[43]

14.25 Where the Treasury has provided financial assistance to an institution, for the purpose of resolving or reducing a serious threat to the stability of the United Kingdom, a bridge bank transfer may only be made with the consent of the Treasury.[44]

Establishing and governing bridge banks

14.26 The SSR Code sets out guidance on the establishment and governance of bridge banks. Insofar as the pursuance of the objective to facilitate sale of the bridge bank is not compromised, the Bank must take steps to manage its relationship with the bridge bank at an arm's length although a more in this may not be appropriate if a bridge bank is only in existence for a short period of time.[45]

14.27 The Bank must establish or acquire an incorporated company to which property, rights and liabilities will be transferred and is required to work with the FSA to arrange appropriate authorizations where necessary to carry on the relevant regulated activities. The bridge bank must be a company limited by shares that is wholly owned by the Bank and its articles of association must provide for the company regulations governing the relationship between the Bank and the bridge bank's directors.[46]

14.28 The Bank of England must take steps to put in place appropriate arrangements for the management of the bridge bank with the structure depending on the particular circumstances of the bridge bank and, in particular, whether the bridge bank is, as intended, only in existence for a short or a longer period of time. The composition of the board of a bridge bank will be decided by the Bank on a case-by-case basis and may or may not include employees of the Bank of England.[47]

---

[42] See further the SRR Code, para 9.36.
[43] BA, s 78.
[44] BA, s 8
[45] See the SSR Code, para 9.3 and paras 9.14–9.18, which provide guidance on when an 'arm's length' arrangement is appropriate.
[46] See the SSR Code, paras 9.13–9.18.
[47] See the SSR Code, paras 9.19–9.24.

A bridge bank's operating strategy must be decided by what best meets the objective **14.29**
to facilitate sale of the bridge bank. It is likely to involve the bridge bank operating
on a conservative basis, to protect the franchise value of the business, and provide
continuity of banking services. The Bank must work with the bridge bank's board
of directors to decide on how the bridge bank should be operated and, where appropriate, the bridge bank's board must produce a business plan setting out how the
directors intend to operate the bridge bank.[48]

The Bank must report to the Treasury on the activities of a bridge bank as soon **14.30**
as is reasonably practicable after the end of one year and each subsequent year
and the Chancellor of the Exchequer must lay a copy of the reports before parliament (a 'bridge bank report').[49] A bridge bank report is not, therefore, required
where a bridge bank is intended to exist for less than a year, the Bank must report
appropriately about the resolution to the Chancellor. Where the Bank makes a
bridge bank report, it must contain: an account of the activities of the bridge
bank over the year; and how the Bank is intending to achieve the objective set
for the bridge bank.[50]

D. Transfer to an Asset Management Vehicle

The BA empowers the Bank to make one or more property transfer instruments to **14.31**
give effect to the transfer of all or part of the business of a bank to an asset management vehicle 'bridge bank'—a company which the Bank wholly or partially owns
('Asset Management Vehicle Transfer Power').[51] An Asset Management Vehicle is
intended to hold assets for the medium term, with the aim of eventual sale or
orderly wind down.[52] The Asset Management Vehicle objectives are subordinate to
the SSR objectives and where there is a conflict between the two, the SRR objectives
take precedence.[53]

The Asset Management Vehicle Transfer Power may not be used in isolation, but **14.32**
only as part of a package of measures including at least one other stabilization
power.[54]

---

[48] See the SRR Code, paras 9.25–9.27.
[49] See further BA, s 80.
[50] See the SRR Code, paras 9.28 et seq. When compiling a bridge bank report, the Bank may
choose to not reveal market-sensitive information. Bridge bank reports are supplementary to the
reporting arrangements that the Bank in its role as shareholder in a bridge bank must put in place to
ensure it receives appropriate management information from the bridge bank.
[51] BA, s 12ZA.
[52] BA 12ZA(4), SSR 6.47–6.50.
[53] See the SRR Code, para 9.49.
[54] BA 8ZA(2).

The decision to exercise the Asset Management Vehicle Transfer Powers

14.33 The SSR Code sets out various considerations which the Bank may take into account in deciding whether to exercise the Asset Management Vehicle Transfer Power stating that transfer to an Asset Management Vehicle may be appropriate where either:

(a) the situation of the market for the assets which it is proposed to transfer by the exercise of the stabilization power is of such a nature that the liquidation of those assets under normal insolvency proceedings could have an adverse effect on one or more financial markets,

(b) the transfer is necessary to ensure the proper functioning of the bank or bridge bank from which the transfer is to be made, or

(c) the transfer is necessary to maximise the proceeds available for distribution.[55]

14.34 Where the Bank exercises an Asset Management Vehicle Transfer Power it must comply with any notice provided by the Treasury, for the purpose of ensuring compliance by the United Kingdom with its international obligations,[56] to take or not to take specified action in respect of an Asset Management Vehicle and not take any action in respect of the Asset Management Vehicle without the Treasury's consent if the action would be likely to have implications for public funds.[57]

14.35 Where the Treasury has provided financial assistance to an institution, for the purpose of resolving or reducing a serious threat to the stability of the United Kingdom, an Asset Management Vehicle transfer may only be made with the consent of the Treasury.[58]

Establishing and governing Asset Management Vehicles

14.36 The SSR Code sets out guidance on the establishment and governance of Asset Management Vehicles. Asset Management Vehicles are likely to exist for some time, but have a clearly defined mandate, and its management is directly controlled by the Bank for the duration of that life.[59] However, the Code does provide that if it appears to the Treasury that the vehicle is likely to exist for an extended period of time, it may impose on the Bank, as manager, an obligation to ensure that the vehicle is managed in a way that minimizes costs.[60] The Asset Management Vehicle may be a company or a limited liability partnership (LLP).[61]

---

[55] SRR Code, para 6.47 and BA, s 8ZA(3).
[56] BA, s 77.
[57] BA, s 78.
[58] BA, s 8.
[59] SRR Code, para 9.60.
[60] SRR Code, para 9.56.
[61] SRR Code, para 9.60.

The reporting obligations for an Asset Management Vehicle are the same as those **14.37**
for a bridge bank.[62]

E. Temporary Public Ownership Transfers

The BA empowers the Treasury to make one or more share transfer orders in which **14.38**
the transferee is:

- a nominee of the Treasury, or
- a company wholly owned by the Treasury

in order to take a bank into temporary public ownership ('Temporary Public
Ownership Transfer Power').[63]

Exercise of the Temporary Public Ownership Transfer Power is the only stabiliz- **14.39**
ation option which may be exercised with respect to bank holding companies.[64]

Special conditions for exercising the Temporary Public Ownership Transfer Power

The Treasury may only exercise the Temporary Public Ownership Transfer Power if: **14.40**

- the FSA is satisfied that General Conditions have been met;[65] and
- the Treasury is satisfied that the exercise of the Temporary Public Ownership
  Transfer Power is necessary to resolve or reduce a serious threat to the stability
  of the financial systems of the United Kingdom ('Public Ownership Transfer
  Condition A');[66] or
- the Treasury is satisfied that the exercise of the Temporary Public Ownership
  Transfer Power is necessary to protect the public interest, where the Treasury
  has provided financial assistance in respect of the bank for the purposes of
  resolving or reducing a serious threat to the stability of the UK's financial systems ('Public Ownership Transfer Condition B').[67]

The Treasury must consult the Prudential Regulation Authority (PRA), the **14.41**
Financial Conduct Authority (FCA), and the Bank before determining whether
either Public Ownership Transfer Condition A or Public Ownership Transfer
Condition B is met.[68]

---

[62] SRR Code, para 9.70.
[63] BA, s 13(2).
[64] BA, ss 82 and 83.
[65] BA, s 9(5).
[66] BA, s 9(2).
[67] BA, s 9(3). See also SRR Code, para 5.26.
[68] BA, s 9(4).

14.42 The Treasury must lay before parliament an annual report about banks in temporary public ownership.[69]

Bank Holding Companies

14.43 The Treasury may exercise the Temporary Public Ownership Transfer Power with respect to a parent undertaking of a bank ('Bank Holding Company'), that is, take the Bank Holding Company into temporary public ownership.[70]

In order for the Treasury to exercise the Temporary Public Ownership Transfer Power with respect to a Bank Holding Company, the following conditions must apply:

- the General Conditions have been met;[71]
- the Treasury is satisfied that Public Ownership Transfer Conditions A and B apply;[72] and
- the Bank Holding Company is an undertaking incorporated in, or formed under the law of any part of the United Kingdom.[73]

14.44 The Treasury must consult the PRA, the FCA, and the Bank before determining whether either Public Ownership Transfer Condition A or Public Ownership Transfer Condition B is met with respect to a Bank Holding Company.[74]

14.45 The BA, s 83 sets out the manner in which various provisions of the BA governing the Temporary Public Ownership Transfer Power apply to Bank Holding Companies.

Governing institutions in temporary public ownership

14.46 The SRR Code sets out guidance on the governance arrangements for institutions in temporary public ownership. Immediately following the exercise of the Temporary Public Ownership Transfer Power and for the initial period of stabilization, the Treasury may take a 'hands-on' role in managing the affairs of the bank. However, once stabilized, the Treasury must seek to introduce corporate governance arrangements in line with best practice, as soon as is reasonably practicable. The nature of these arrangements will depend on how likely the bank is to remain in public ownership.[75]

14.47 If a bank is likely to remain in public ownership for longer than a short period, the Treasury must set out for the directors' objectives as to how the bank should be operated. Based on these objectives, the board must produce a business plan

---

[69] See further BA, s 81.

[70] This is the only stabilization option in relation to a Bank Holding Company. (See the SRR Code, para 7.11.)

[71] BA, s 82(2).

[72] BA, s 82(3).

[73] BA, s 82(4). See also SRR Code, para 5.26.

[74] BA, s 82(5).

[75] See the SSR Code, para 9.87.

containing (a) a commercial strategy, (b) a funding plan, including arrangements for repaying any public money that has been provided, (c) a risk management strategy, and (d) an approach for complying with competition issues, state aid and regulatory requirements.[76]

In circumstances where an institution is likely to remain in public ownership for longer than a short period, the Treasury may seek to put in place arrangements to operate the bank at arm's length and set out objectives for the directors as to how the bank should be operated. It is likely that these objectives would include protecting and creating value with due regard to the special resolution objectives, and maintaining and promoting competition in the banking sector. Where an institution in temporary public ownership is being managed at arm's length by a separate body, it will be the responsibility of the arm's-length body, with appropriate consultation with the Treasury, to develop and execute an investment strategy for disposing of the investments in an orderly and active way.[77]   **14.48**

The Treasury must make arrangements to ensure that a bank in temporary public ownership reports on a similar basis to other commercial banks, including regulatory reporting appropriate to the activities undertaken by the bank.[78]   **14.49**

F. Transfers of Securities

The BRRD sets out an explicit group of powers that resolution authorities should be given in order to do specific acts. The UK resolution authority has these powers, but rather than being made explicit on the face of the BA, they are left implicit in the scope of the 'share transfer instrument (or resolution instrument) which is expected to me made in respect of any resolution.   **14.50**

'Securities'

The private sector transfer powers include the power to make a share transfer instrument, while the temporary public ownership transfer power is the power to make a share transfer order. The use of the term 'share' is inaccurate because the type of financial instruments which may be transferred via a share transfer instrument or share transfer order is not limited to a share but extends to the securities listed in the BA, s 14. These are: **14.51**

- shares and stock;
- debentures, the definition of which includes debenture stock, loan stock, bonds, certificates of deposit and any other instrument creating or acknowledging a debt;

---

[76] See the SSR Code, paras 9.7–9.12.
[77] See the SSR Code, paras 9.93–9.96.
[78] See the SSR Code, para 9.98.

- warrants or other instruments that entitle the holder to acquire share and stock or debentures; and
- other rights granted by a deposit taker which form part of its own funds for the purposes of Title 1 of Part 2 of the Capital Requirements Regulation.[79]

14.52 The definition in this section ensures that share transfer powers can be exercised to transfer complete control of a bank. But it also means that if a share transfer power is exercised in relation to a bank or its UK-incorporated holding company, not only will shareholders and holders of equivalent equity be affected, but also, holders of any debt issued by the company in the form of bonds or loan stock, etc, or warrants. Therefore, a holder of bonds or other securities could have them transferred out of its ownership by virtue of a share transfer order.

General effect of a share transfer instrument and share transfer order

14.53 Any transfer provided for by a share transfer instrument or order takes effect by virtue of any the instrument or order and in accordance with its provisions as to timing or other ancillary matters.[80] Therefore, any transfer of securities under a share transfer instrument or order takes place by operation of law.[81] Any transfer provided for by a share transfer instrument or order takes effect regardless of any restriction, including restrictions arising by contract or legislation.[82] This includes any restriction relating to non-assignment and to a requirement for consent.[83] A share transfer instrument or order may provide for a transfer to be carried out free from any encumbrances, such as a trust, which may be extinguished under the instrument or order and may extinguish rights to acquire shares and stock or debentures within the meaning of BA, s 14.[84] Share options are an example of such rights.

14.54 As mentioned above, the primacy of the provisions of a share transfer instrument or order which means that, in effect, the Bank or Treasury can override contractual provisions is significant because, inter alia, the inclusion of such provisions in a share transfer instrument or order could result in the alteration of contractual expectations of the parties to contract or agreement containing the default event provisions.[85]

14.55 It should also be noted that Part 17 and Schedule 4 of the Bank Recovery and Resolution (No 2) Order (2014/38) disapply a number of shareholder protections in respect of banks in resolution. Thus shareholders in banks placed in

---

[79] Capital Requirements Regulation 575/2013.
[80] BA, a 17(2).
[81] See BA, Explanatory Notes.
[82] BA, s 17(3).
[83] BA, s 17(4).
[84] BA, ss 17(5) and (6).
[85] See 14.05 above.

resolution have fewer protections than ordinary shareholders even if their shares are not transferred.

Specified effects of a share transfer instrument and share transfer order

In addition to the general effects described above, the BA empowers the Bank or **14.56** Treasury to make various provisions in a share transfer instrument or order which have the effects described below.

Continuity

A share transfer instrument or order may provide for the continuity of arrange- **14.57** ments operating in respect of the bank, the securities of which are transferred and may: include provision that the transferee can be treated as the same person as the transferor for any purpose connected with the transfer,[86] or include provision that agreements made or other things done by or in relation to a transferor are treated as made or done by or in relation to the transferee.[87] This would enable for example, the transferred deposit taker to continue to benefit from arrangements entered into by the transferors, notwithstanding any rights triggered on the transfer.[88] The share transfer instrument or order may also allow for transitional provision about things transferred to be continued, modify references to the transferor in instruments or documents, and provide for information to be required or permitted between the transferor and the transferee.[89]

Conversion and delisting

A share transfer instrument or order may provide for: the conversion and delist- **14.58** ing of securities (the power applies to all of a specified bank's securities, whether transferred or not), and discontinuing the listing of securities issued by the speci- fied bank on a UK-regulated market.[90] A share transfer instrument or order may make provision, for example, for the conversion of securities from one form to another to deal, for example, with the conversion of uncertificated or bearer securities into certificated securities or the conversion of a special class of shares into ordinary shares.

Powers of governing directors

A share transfer instrument and order may contain provisions enabling the Bank **14.59** and Treasury to exercise various powers regarding directors, including appointment and removal, termination, and variation of service contracts.[91] These powers may

---

[86] BA, s 18(1).
[87] BA, s 18(2).
[88] See BA Explanatory Notes.
[89] BA, ss 18(3), (4), and (5).
[90] BA, s 19.
[91] BA, s 201(1). 'Service contract' has the meaning given by the Companies Act 2006, s 227. (See BA, s 32.)

be exercised in respect of both bank and group directors.[92] The appointments contained in a share transfer instrument and order may be made on terms and conditions agreed by the Bank and Treasury.[93]

Ancillary instrument

14.60 A share transfer instrument or order may contain provisions concerning ancillary share transfer instruments or registration requirements to ensure that effect is given to a transfer. In particular, it may permit or require the execution, issue, or delivery of an instrument; have immediate effect, regardless of registration of the share transfer instrument or order or the status of an instrument; make provision for the effect of an instrument executed or issued in accordance with the provision of the share transfer instrument or order; modify or annul the effect of an instrument; and entitle a transferee to be registered or require a person to effect registration in respect of the transferred securities of the specified bank.[94]

Other provisions

14.61 A share transfer instrument or order may include incidental, consequential, or transitional provision made generally or for a specified purpose or purposes.[95] In addition, the BA gives:

- the Bank, with the consent of the Treasury, or the Treasury the power to make provision in a share instrument or order relating to pensions.[96]
- The Bank or the Treasury the power to make provision in a share instrument or order relating to the resolution of disputes.[97]

Continuity of services and facilities by group companies

General continuity obligations

14.62 The BA imposes a general continuity obligation on any entity which was a group undertaking in relation to a bank, the securities of which have been transferred ('transferred bank') immediately before the transfer ('former group company'). In terms of the general continuity obligation, a former group company must provide the services and facilities required to enable the transferred bank to operate effectively.[98] The general continuity obligation may be enforced as if created by a

---

[92] BA, s 20(1A).
[93] BA, s 20(2).
[94] BA, s 21.
[95] BA, s 23.
[96] See BA, s 71. The need to make such provision could arise when the pension schemes of employees who are subject to the transfer form part of the pension scheme of a wider corporate group. (See BA, Explanatory Notes.)
[97] See BA, s 73.
[98] BA, s 66(2).

contact between the former group company and the transferee but is not limited to the provision of services and facilities directly to the transferee.[99] The Bank or Treasury may, by notice to the former group company, state that specific activities on specific terms should be undertaken in accordance with the general continuity obligation.[100] In performing any general continuity obligation, the former group company has a right to reasonable consideration.[101]

A continuity obligation continues to apply to a group company even if it becomes **14.63** insolvent.[102]

Special continuity obligations

In addition to the general continuity obligation, the Bank (with the Treasury's **14.64** consent) or Treasury may, by way of a share transfer instrument or order where they think it is necessary to enable the transferred bank to operate effectively, cancel, impose or impose continuity obligations or confer rights on a former group company or transferred bank ('special continuity obligations').[103] When imposing special continuity obligations, the Bank or Treasury must aim, so far as is reasonably practicable, to preserve or include provision for reasonable consideration and other provisions that would be expected in arrangements concluded between parties operating at arm's length.[104]

As mentioned above, this power to impose continuity obligations is significant **14.65** because, inter alia, its exercise may alter the contractual expectations of the parties to contract or agreement between a bank and a former group company or transferred bank.[105]

Continuity obligations and onward share transfers

The BA also makes provision for continuity obligations in the case of an onward **14.66** share transfer.[106] In this case, the Bank (with the Treasury's consent) or Treasury may impose the general continuity obligation and special continuity obligations on a bank, anything which is or was a group undertaking of the bank, anything which

---

[99] BA, s 66(3) and (5).

[100] See further BA, s 66(7), (8), and (9). The BA also gives the Bank and Treasury the power to terminate a General Continuity Obligation by notice. (See BA, s 70.)

[101] BA, s 66(4). The Treasury has the power, by order, to specify matters which are to be or not to be considered in determining what amounts to reasonable consideration and secondary legislation may specify matters which are to be or not to be considered in determining what provisions would be expected in arrangements concluded between parties dealing at arm's length. (See BA, s 69.)

[102] BA, s 66 (3A).

[103] BA, s 67(2) and 67(4).

[104] BA, s 67(3). See also BA, s 69 discussed in n 107 above.

[105] See [*] above.

[106] See further BA, ss 68(1) (which sets out the meaning of an 'onward transfer' for these purposes), 68(2), and 68(8). The powers are exercisable by giving notice and various provisions of the BA, s 66 apply to onward share transfers. (BA, s 68(6) and (7).)

is or was a group undertaking of a residual bank, or any combination.[107] These extended obligations may be in addition to, or replace, any initial obligations.[108]

Share transfer instruments

Characteristics

14.67 The Bank may make a share transfer instrument in the exercise of the private sector transfer powers.[109] A share transfer instrument is an instrument which:

- provides for securities issued by a bank specified in the instrument to be transferred;
- makes other provision for the purposes of, or in connection with, the transfer of securities issued by the bank, whether or not the transfer has been or is to be effected by that instrument, by another share transfer instrument or otherwise.[110]

14.68 A share transfer instrument may relate to specified securities or securities of a specified description.[111] This means that the share instrument could provide for the transfer of, for example: all of the shares, debentures, warrants, and other securities issued by a bank to a particular entity; or all of the shares issued by the bank.

Supplemental share transfer instruments

14.69 The BA empowers the Bank to make supplemental share transfer instruments which may provide for anything that a share transfer instrument may generally provide for, including a further transfer of securities which were issued before the original instrument but not transferred under the original or any other instrument. The general conditions contained in the BA, s 7 and specific conditions contained in BA, s 8 do not apply to supplemental share transfer instruments but the Bank must consult the FSA and the Treasury before making the instrument.[112]

Resolution company share transfer and reverse share transfer instruments

14.70 The BA empowers the Bank to make a resolution company share transfer instrument where the Bank has made a property transfer instrument in the exercise of a resolution company transfer power.[113] A resolution company share transfer instrument may provide for: securities issued by the resolution company to be transferred; and other provision in relation to the securities of the resolution company.[114] The BA, therefore, empowers the Bank to transfer the securities of a resolution company.

---

[107] See further BA, s 68(4).
[108] See BA, s 68(5).
[109] BA, s 24 sets out the procedure for making share transfer instruments.
[110] BA, s 15(1).
[111] BA, s 15(2).
[112] BA, s 26. See the SRR Code, paras 6.2–6.7.
[113] BA, ss 30(1) and (2). See also the SRR Code, paras 6.2–6.7.
[114] BA, s 30(3).

The general conditions contained in the BA, s 7 and specific conditions contained in BA, s 8 do not apply to a resolution company share transfer instrument but the Bank must consult the FSA and the Treasury before making the instrument.[115] The Bank may make a supplemental share transfer instrument following the making of a resolution company share transfer instrument.[116] Like supplemental share transfer instrument and reverse share transfer instruments discussed above and below, the making of a resolution company share transfer may become necessary, for example, if additional details come to light about the nature of transferred securities after the initial transfer, which would have an effect on the saleability of the resolution company or the achievement of the SRR objectives more widely.[117]

The Bank may make a resolution company reverse share transfer instrument where **14.71** the Bank has made a resolution company share transfer instrument ('original instrument') to a company wholly owned by the Bank, the Treasury, or a nominee of the Treasury ('original transferee').[118] A resolution company reverse share transfer instrument provides for the transfer of securities of a resolution company to be transferred back from an original transferee to the transferor under the original instrument or makes other provision for the purposes of or in connection with such a transfer.[119] The general conditions contained in the BA, s 7, the specific conditions contained in BA, s 8, and the compensation order requirements in BA, s 51, do not apply to a resolution company share transfer instrument but the Bank must consult the FSA and the Treasury before making the instrument.[120] The Bank may make a supplemental share transfer instrument following the making of a resolution company reverse share transfer instrument.[121]

Share transfer orders

Characteristics

The Treasury may make a share transfer order in the exercise of the Temporary **14.72** Public Ownership Transfer Power.[122] A share transfer order is an order which:

- provides for securities issued by a bank specified in the order to be transferred;
- makes other provision for the purposes of, or in connection with, the transfer of securities issued by the bank, whether or not the transfer has been or is to be effected by that order, by another share transfer order or otherwise.[123]

---

[115] BA, s 30(4) and (5).
[116] BA, s 30(6).
[117] See SRR Code, para 6.3.
[118] BA, s 31(1) and (2). See also the SRR Code, paras 6.2–6.7.
[119] BA, s 31(3).
[120] BA, s 31(4) and (5).
[121] BA, s 31(6).
[122] BA, s 25 sets out the procedure for making a share transfer order.
[123] BA, s 16(1).

14.73 As is the case with a share transfer instrument, a share transfer order may relate to specified securities or securities of a specified description.[124] This means that the share instrument could provide for the transfer of, for example: all of the shares, debentures, warrants, and other securities issued by a bank to a particular entity; or all of the shares issued by the bank.

Supplemental share transfer orders

14.74 The BA empowers the Treasury to make supplemental share transfer orders which may provide for anything that a share transfer order may generally provide for, including a further transfer of securities which were issued before the original order but not transferred under the original or any other order. The general conditions contained in the BA, s 7 and specific conditions contained in BA, s 9 do not apply to supplemental share orders instruments but the Treasury must consult the FSA and the Bank before making the instrument.[125]

Onward share transfer orders and reverse share transfer orders

14.75 The BA empowers the Treasury to make an onward share transfer order where the Treasury has made a transfer order in the exercise of the Temporary Public Ownership Transfer Power ('original order').[126] An onward share transfer order may provide for: securities issued by the bank before the original order and transferred by the original or a supplementary order or after the original order; and other provision in relation to the transfer of the securities issued by the bank.[127] The transferee under an onward share transfer order may not be the transferor under the original order.[128] The general conditions contained in the BA, s 7 and specific conditions contained in BA, s 9 do not apply to an onward share transfer order but the Treasury must consult the FSA and the Bank before making the instrument.[129] The Treasury may make a supplemental share transfer order following the making of an onward share transfer instrument.[130]

14.76 The Treasury may make two types of reverse share transfer orders. The first is where an original order has transferred securities issued by a bank which a person ('original transferee') holds.[131] Here the reverse share transfer order may provide for the transfer of securities of a bank to be transferred back from an original transferee to the transferor under the original instrument or make other provision for the purposes of or in connection with such a transfer.[132] The second is where an onward

---

[124] BA, s 16(2).
[125] See BA, s 26. See also the SRR Code, paras 6.8–6.10.
[126] BA, s 28(1) and (2). See also the SRR Code, paras 6.8–6.10.
[127] BA, s 28(3).
[128] BA, s 28(4).
[129] BA, s 28(5) and (6).
[130] BA, s 28(7).
[131] BA, s 29(1) and (2). See also the SRR Code, paras 6.8–6.10.
[132] BA, s 29(4)(a) and (c).

share transfer instrument has transferred securities issued by a bank which a company wholly owned by the Bank, a company wholly owned by the Treasury or a nominee of the Treasury and no other person, such a private sector company ('onward share transferee') holds. Here the reverse share transfer order may provide for the transfer of securities of a bank to be transferred back from onward share transferee to the original transferee or make other provision for the purposes of or in connection with such a transfer.[133] The limitation on the use of the reverse share transfer order to transfers back from an onward share transferee is to prevent the reverse share transfer powers from being exercisable in relation to an onward transfer to a person, such as a private sector company, who wished to acquire the bank from temporary public ownership.[134] A reverse share transfer order provides for the transfer of securities of a bank to be transferred back from an original transferee to the transferor under the original Instrument or makes other provision for the purposes of or in connection with such a transfer.[135] The general conditions contained in the BA, s 7, the specific conditions contained in BA, s 9, and the compensation order requirements in BA, s 51 do not apply to a reverse share transfer order but the Treasury must consult the FSA and the Bank before making the instrument.[136] The Treasury may make a supplemental share transfer order following the making of a reverse share transfer order.[137]

G. Transfers of Property

The private sector transfer powers and the resolution company transfer power include the power of the Bank to make a property transfer instrument.[138] The BA also empowers the Treasury to make property transfer and reverse property transfer orders where it has exercised a temporary public ownership power, although the BA, s 13 does not identify this as a temporary public ownership power as such.[139] **14.77**

Property transfer instruments

Characteristics

A property transfer instrument is an instrument which: **14.78**

- provides for property, rights and liabilities ('property') of a bank specified in the instrument to be transferred;

---

[133] BA, s 29(4)(b) and (c).
[134] See BA, Explanatory Notes.
[135] BA, s 29(4).
[136] BA, s 29(5) and (6).
[137] BA, s 29(7).
[138] See, for example, the DBS Transfer Instrument 2009. BA, s 41 sets out the procedure for making Property Transfer Instruments.
[139] A property transfer order is to be treated as in the same way as a share transfer order for the procedural purposes of BA, s 25 but as a Property Transfer Instrument for all other purposes. (BA, s 45(5).)

- makes other provision for the purposes of, or in connection with, the transfer of property of a bank, whether or not the transfer has been or is to be effected by that instrument, by another property transfer instrument or otherwise.[140]

14.79 A share transfer instrument may transfer some or all of the property and may relate to specified combinations of the property specified in the instrument.[141]

Supplemental property transfer instruments

14.80 The BA empowers the Bank to make supplemental property transfer instruments which may provide for anything that a property transfer instrument may generally provide for, including a further transfer of property which were issued before the original instrument but not transferred under the original or any other instrument. The general conditions contained in the BA, s 7 and specific conditions contained in BA, s 8 do not apply to supplemental property transfer instruments but the Bank must consult the FSA and the Treasury before making the instrument.[142]

Resolution company onward property transfer instruments and reverse property transfer instruments

14.81 The BA empowers the Bank to make an onward property transfer instrument where the Bank has made a property transfer instrument in the exercise of a resolution company transfer power ('original property instrument').[143] An onward property transfer instrument may provide for property of the resolution company whether accruing or arising before the original property instrument and other provision in relation to the transfer of the property of the resolution company.[144] An onward property transfer instrument may relate to property whether or not transferred under the original property instrument but may not transfer property under the original property instrument.[145] The general conditions contained in the BA, s 7 and specific conditions contained in BA, s 8 and the resolution fund order requirements in BA, s 52 do not apply to an onward property transfer instrument but the Bank must consult the FSA and the Treasury before making the instrument.[146] The Bank may make a supplemental property transfer instrument following the making of an onward property transfer instrument.[147]

---

[140] BA, s 33(1).

[141] BA, s 33(2). This is subject to restrictions which may be imposed by the Restriction of Partial Property Transfers Order made under BA, s 47. These are discussed at 14.99 et seq below.

[142] BA, s 42. See, for example, the DBS Bridge Bank Limited Supplemental and Onward Property Transfer Instrument 2009.

[143] BA, ss 43(1) and (2). See, for example, the DBS Bridge Bank Limited Supplemental and Onward Property Transfer Instrument 2009.

[144] BA, s 43(3).

[145] BA, s 43(4) and (5).

[146] BA, s 43(6) and (7).

[147] BA, s 43(8).

The Bank may make two types of reverse property transfer instruments. The first **14.82** is where an original property instrument has transferred property which a person ('original property transferee') holds.[148] Here the reverse property transfer instrument may provide for the transfer of property of a bank to be transferred back from an original property transferee to the transferor under the original property instrument or make other provision for the purposes of or in connection with such a transfer.[149] The second is where an onward property transfer instrument has transferred property of a bank which a company wholly owned by the Bank, a company wholly owned by the Bank or a nominee of the Bank and no other person, such as a private sector company ('onward property transferee') holds.[150] This limitation is to prevent the reverse property transfer powers from being exercisable following an onward transfer to a private sector party who wished to acquire the business of a resolution company.[151] Here the reverse property transfer instrument may provide for the transfer of property of a bank to be transferred back from onward property transferee to the original property transferee or make other provision for the purposes of or in connection with such a transfer.[152] The general conditions contained in the BA, s 7, the specific conditions contained in BA, s 9 and the resolution fund order requirements in BA, s 52 do not apply to a reverse property transfer instrument but the Bank must consult the FSA and the Bank before making the instrument.[153] The Bank may make a supplemental property transfer instrument following the making of a reverse property transfer instrument.[154]

Temporary Public Ownership Property Transfer Orders and Reverse Property Transfer Orders

The BA empowers the Treasury to make a property transfer order where the Treasury **14.83** has made a share transfer order in the exercise of the Temporary Public Ownership Transfer Power ('Original Property Transfer Order').[155] A property transfer order may provide for property of the bank transferred before or after the Original Property Transfer Order and other provision in relation to the transfer of the property of the bank.[156] The general conditions contained in the BA, s 7 and specific conditions contained in BA, ss 8 and 9 do not apply to a property transfer order but the Treasury must consult the FSA and the Bank before making the order.[157] The

---

[148] BA, s 44(1) and (2). There are special restrictions on any Partial Property Transfer Order made under a reverse Property Transfer Instrument. These are discussed at 10.85 below.
[149] BA, s 44(4)(a) and (c).
[150] BA, s 44(3).
[151] See BA, Explanatory Notes.
[152] BA, s 44(4)(b) and (c).
[153] BA, s 44(5) and (6).
[154] BA, s 44(7).
[155] BA, s 45(1) and (2).
[156] BA, s 45(3).
[157] BA, s 45(4) and (8).

Treasury may make a supplemental property transfer order following the making of a property transfer order.[158]

14.84 The Treasury may make a reverse property transfer order where an Original Property Transfer Order has transferred property of a bank to a company wholly owned by the Bank, a company wholly owned by the Treasury or a nominee of the Treasury.[159] The reverse property order may provide for property of the bank transferred before or after the Original Property Transfer Order and other provision in relation to the transfer of the property of the bank.[160] The general conditions contained in the BA, s 7 and specific conditions contained in BA, ss 8 and 9 do not apply to a reverse property transfer order but the Treasury must consult the FSA and the Bank before making the order.[161] The Treasury may make a supplemental reverse property transfer order following the making of a reverse property transfer order.[162]

'Transferable property'

14.85 A property transfer instrument or order may transfer any property, rights, or liabilities, including rights and liabilities:

- arising between the making of the instrument and the transfer date;
- arising on or after the transfer date in respect of matters occurring before that date;
- under the law of a country or territory outside the United Kingdom;
- under an enactment, including legislation of the European Union.[163]

14.86 Where the property is (a) property outside the United Kingdom or (b) rights and liabilities under the law of a country or territory outside the United Kingdom ('foreign property'), both the transferor and the transferee must take any necessary steps to ensure that the transfer of foreign property is effective as a matter of the law of the country or territory outside the United Kingdom ('foreign law').[164] For the period before a transfer, the transferor must act on behalf of the transferee by holding any property or right for its benefit and discharging any liability on its behalf.[165] The transferee must meet any expenses of the transferor in relation to any transfer.[166] Any obligations imposed with respect to the transfer of foreign

---

[158] BA, s 45(7).
[159] BA, s 46(1) and (2). A reverse property transfer order is to be treated as in the same way as a share transfer order for the procedural purposes of BA, s 25 but as a property transfer instrument for all other purposes. (BA, s 46(5).) There are special restrictions on any Partial Property Transfer Order made under a reverse property transfer order.
[160] BA, s 46(3).
[161] BA, s 46(4) and (7).
[162] BA, s 46(8).
[163] BA, s 35.
[164] BA, s 39(2) and (3).
[165] BA, s 39(4).
[166] BA, s 39(5).

property are enforceable as contracts and the Bank, in the case of a transfer of foreign property by means of a property transfer instrument, or the Treasury, in the case of a transfer by means of a property transfer order or reverse property transfer order, may give directions in relation to those obligations, with which the transferor must comply.[167]

General effect of a property transfer instrument or order

Any transfer provided for by a property transfer instrument or order takes effect **14.87** by virtue of any the instrument or order and in accordance with its provisions as to timing or other ancillary matters.[168] Any transfer provided for by a property transfer instrument or order takes effect regardless of any restriction, including restrictions arising by contract or legislation.[169] This includes any restriction relating to non-assignment and to a requirement for consent.[170] Any transfer provided for by a property transfer may be made conditional on events occurring or arising or not occurring or arising.[171] It may provide for the consequences should such a condition be breached.[172] Where a property transfer instrument makes provision in respect of property held on trust, it may also make provision about the terms on which the property is to be held after the instrument takes effect and how the powers, provisions, and liabilities in respect of the property are to be exercisable or have effect after the instrument takes effect.[173]

As mentioned above, the powers to make a property transfer instrument or order **14.88** which specifies that default event provisions or trust arrangements are to be disapplied or disregarded are significant because, inter alia, their exercise may alter the contractual expectations of the parties to contract or agreement containing the default event provisions.[174]

Specified effect of a property transfer instrument or order

Continuity

A property transfer or order may contain provisions to ensure the continuity of **14.89** arrangements operating in respect of a bank.[175] This may include provision that the transferee can be treated as the same person as the transferor for any purpose connected with the transfer and for the transfer to be treated as a succession,[176]

---

[167] BA, s 39(6) and (7) and s 45(6) and 46(6).
[168] BA, s 34(2).
[169] BA, s 34(3).
[170] BA, s 34(4).
[171] BA, s 34(5).
[172] See further BA, s 34(6).
[173] BA, s 34(7).
[174] See [*] above.
[175] See, for example, the DBS Transfer Instrument 2009.
[176] BA, s 36(1).

provision that agreements made or other things done by or in relation to a transferor are treated as made or done by or in relation to the transferee,[177] provision that anything, such as legal proceedings, relating to the Property transferred to be continued,[178] provisions about continuity of employment,[179] the modification of references to the transferor in instruments or documents,[180] provision that, in so far as rights and liabilities in respect of anything transferred are enforceable after a transfer date, a property transfer instrument can apportion them as between the transferor and the transferee.[181] Modifications to a provision of the instrument or order although the modification must achieve a result that could have been achieved by the instrument or order and may not transfer or arrange the transfer of property, rights, or liabilities;[182] requirements or permissions relating to information and assistance by the transferor to the transferee, and vice versa.[183]

Licences

14.90 The general rule is that any permission and approval and any other permissive document in respect of anything transferred ('licence') in respect of property transferred by a property transfer instrument shall continue to have effect despite the transfer.[184] The Bank may disapply this general rule so that a licence may be discontinued.[185] Where a licence imposes rights or obligations, a property transfer instrument may apportion responsibility for exercise or compliances between the transferor and transferee.[186]

Trusts

14.91 By s 34(7) of the BA, a property transfer order may be made in respect of property which is held on trust, and the terms of the trust may be varied by that order. BA, s 34(8) provides that such an order may only vary the terms of such a trust to the extent that the Bank considers necessary or expedient for the purpose of transferring the legal or beneficial interest of the transferor in the property, or any powers, rights, or obligations of the transferor in respect of the property. The Code also provides that the authorities will generally seek to ensure that wherever possible all property held subject to any particular trust will be transferred together.[187]

---

[177] BA, s 36(2). This would enable, for example, the transferred deposit taker to continue to benefit from arrangements entered into by the transferor, notwithstanding any rights triggered on the transfer. (See BA, Explanatory Notes.)
[178] BA, s 36(3).
[179] BA, s 36(4).
[180] BA, s 36(5).
[181] BA, s 36(6).
[182] BA, s 36(7).
[183] BA, s 36(7).
[184] BA, s 37(1) and (4).
[185] BA, s 37(2).
[186] BA, s 37(3).
[187] SRR Code, para 7.37.

Incidental provisions

A property transfer instrument or order may include incidental, consequential, or **14.92** transitional provision made generally or for a specified purpose or purposes.[188] In addition, the BA gives:

- the Bank, with the consent of the Treasury, or the Treasury the power to make provision in a property instrument or order relating to pensions.[189]
- the Bank or the Treasury the power to make provision in a property instrument or order relating to the resolution of disputes.[190]

Continuity of services and facilities by group companies

General continuity obligations

As is the case with share transfers, the BA imposes a general continuity obligation **14.93** on a bank (a 'residual bank') and any entity which is or was a group undertaking in relation to the residual bank in relation to all or part of a bank's property transferred ('transferred business') to a commercial purchaser or resolution company ('transferee'). In terms of the general continuity obligation, a residual bank and group undertaking must provide the services and facilities to the transferee required to enable the transferee to operate all or part of the transferred business effectively.[191] The general continuity obligation may be enforced as if created by a contact between the former group company and the transferee but is not limited to the provision of services and facilities directly to the transferee.[192] The Bank or Treasury may, by notice to the residual bank or group undertaking, state that specific activities on specific terms should be undertaken in accordance with the general continuity obligation.[193] In performing any general continuity obligation, the residual bank or group undertaking has a right to reasonable consideration.[194]

Special continuity obligations

In addition to the general continuity obligation, the Bank (with the Treasury's con- **14.94** sent) or Treasury may, by way of a property transfer instrument where they think it is necessary to enable a transferee to operate a transferred business effectively, cancel or impose continuity obligations, add or substitute a transferee, or confer rights on a group undertaking or residual bank ('special continuity obligations').[195] When imposing special continuity obligations, the Bank or Treasury must aim, so

---

[188] BA, s 40.
[189] See BA, s 71.
[190] See BA, s 73.
[191] BA, s 63(2).
[192] BA, s 63(3) and (5).
[193] See further BA, s 63(6) and (7). The BA also gives the Bank and Treasury the power to terminate a General Continuity Obligation by notice. (See BA, s 70.)
[194] BA, s 63(4). See also BA, s 69 discussed in n 107 above.
[195] BA, ss 64(2) and 67(4).

far as is reasonably practicable, to preserve or include provision for reasonable consideration and other provisions that would be expected in arrangements concluded between parties operating at arm's length.[196] The continuity obligation resulting from a property transfer continues despite the insolvency of the entity concerned, and may not be disclaimed by a liquidator.[197]

14.95 As mentioned above, this power to impose continuity obligations is significant because, inter alia, its exercise may alter the contractual expectations of the parties to contract or agreement between a bank and a group undertaking.

Continuity obligations and onward property transfers

14.96 The BA also makes provision for continuity obligations in the case of an onward property transfer.[198] In this case, the Bank (with the Treasury's consent) or Treasury may impose the general continuity obligation and special continuity obligations on an original transferee, residual bank, bank, anything which is or was a group undertaking of the bank, anything which is or was a group undertaking of an original transferee, bank, residual bank, or any combination.[199] These extended obligations may be in addition to, or replace, any initial obligations.[200]

Further powers

14.97 The BA grants further powers with respect to continuity obligations which are relevant both in the case of share transfers and property transfers.

H. Restrictions of Partial Property Transfers

14.98 A property transfer instrument may transfer (a) all or (b) some, but not all, of the property of a bank ('Partial Property Transfer Order').[201] This means that Bank, in its exercise of the private sector transfer powers and the resolution company transfer power, or the Treasury, in its exercise of the Temporary Public Ownership Power, may transfer the 'good assets' to a new 'good bank', either a private sector purchaser or a bridge bank, leaving behind the 'bad assets' in a 'bad bank' which may be insolvent or the Bank or Treasury may need to place in administration.[202]

14.99 The power to make Partial Property Transfer Orders has implications for transactions which a bank, which may later be subject to the exercise of a stabilization

---

[196] BA, s 64(3). See also BA, s 69 discussed in n 107 above.

[197] BA, s 63(3A).

[198] See further BA, s 65(1) (which sets out the meaning of an 'onward transfer' for these purposes), 65(2) and 65(8). The powers are exercisable by giving notice and various provisions of the BA, ss 63 and 64 apply to onward property transfers. (BA, ss 65(6) and (7).)

[199] See further BA, ss 65(4) and (8).

[200] See BA, s 65(5).

[201] BA, ss 33(2) and 47.

[202] Bank insolvency and bank administration under the BA are discussed in Chapter 12.

power, enters into where the commercial rationale for that transaction derives from a group of assets and liabilities held by the bank. The power of a public authority, which was not a party to the transaction, to split some assets and liabilities from other assets and liabilities has the potential to interfere with the interests of the parties to the transaction and frustrate the commercial intention of the parties. This is particularly relevant with respect to early termination, netting and set-off arrangements and security interests where the rights and expectations of the counterparties to transactions with a bank and the bank's other creditors.

In order to safeguard the interests of bank counterparties and creditors of, the BA **14.100** gives the Treasury the power to make secondary legislation restricting the making of Partial Property Transfer Orders.[203] In particular, the BA gives the Treasury the power to restrict the making of Partial Property Transfer Orders which might affect security interests, title transfer collateral arrangements, set-off arrangements, and netting arrangements, defined collectively as 'protected arrangements'.[204]

As mentioned above, in reliance on the power in BA, ss 47 and 48, the Treasury **14.101** made the Transfers Order setting out various restrictions on Partial Property Transfer Orders and the remedies for contravening the restrictions.[205]

The Transfers Order

The general provisions

Application   The Transfers Order applies where: **14.102**

- the Bank in the exercise of a private sector transfer power, or resolution company transfer power, or a resolution instrument has: made a Partial Property Transfer Order; or made a property transfer instrument (whether or not that instrument is a Partial Property Transfer Order) and a Partial Property Transfer Order under a supplemental property transfer instrument, resolution company onward property transfer instrument or reverse property transfer instrument;[206]
- the Treasury, in the exercise of a Temporary Public Ownership Transfer Power, has made a share transfer order and a property transfer under a property transfer order and reverse property transfer orders which is to be treated as a Partial Property Transfer Order.

Protected arrangements   Protected arrangements are set-off arrangement, netting arrangement, or title transfer financial collateral arrangement. 'Title transfer

---

[203] See further BA, ss 47, 48, and 48A.
[204] See further BA, s 48 which also defines each of the 'protected arrangements'.
[205] The Treasury has indicated that it will keep the safeguards under review. (See the SSR Code, para 7.11 and paras 7.11–7.14 for discussion of the Transfers Order generally.)
[206] Transfers Order, Arts 2(2) and (3).

financial collateral arrangement' has the meaning given by regulation 3 of the Financial Collateral Arrangements (No 2) Regulations 2003, SI 2003/3226.[207]

14.103 **Effect of transfers of foreign property or rights or liabilities relating to foreign property** Under the Transfers Order, a property transfer instrument or order which purports to transfer all of the property of a bank is to be treated as having done so effectively despite the possibility that any of the property is foreign property and may not have been effectively transferred in accordance with BA, s 39. Therefore, any property transfer under the instrument or order will not be treated as a Partial Property Transfer Order.[208]

14.104 Similar provisions with respect to the effectiveness of transfers of foreign property or rights and liabilities relating to Foreign Property are contained in the parts of the Transfers Order dealing with the set-off and netting restrictions,[209] secured liabilities restrictions,[210] and capital market arrangements restrictions.[211]

14.105 **Consequences for breach of the Transfers Order: Article 12** Articles 10–12 of the Transfers Order set out the consequences of and remedies for breach of the Order. The Treasury indicates that the Articles 10–12 exist to provide certainty to the market as to the outcome should the restrictions in the Transfers Order be inadvertently contravened which is necessary for the achievement of special resolution objectives, 1, 2, and 5.[212]

14.106 Article 10 deals with the consequences of a breach of the Transfers Order by the Treasury or Bank in the exercise of the powers under the BA, ss 64(2) and 67(2) to ensure the continuity of services ('continuity powers')[213] and breach of the financial markets restrictions and restrictions on termination rights. Article 11 deals with a breach of the set-off and netting restrictions and aspects of the Community law restrictions. The Article 10 and Article 11 consequences are discussed below with the relevant restrictions.

14.107 Article 12 applies where Articles 10 or 11 do not.[214] It provides that where any person ('P') considers that a Partial Property Transfer Order has been made in

---

[207] Transfers Order, Art 1. Under the Financial Collateral Arrangements (No 2) Regulations 2003, Art 3 a title transfer financial collateral arrangement is an agreement or arrangement, including a repurchase agreement, evidenced in writing, where: (a) the purpose of the agreement or arrangement is to secure or otherwise cover the relevant financial obligations owed to the collateral taker; (b) the collateral-provider transfers legal and beneficial ownership in financial collateral to a collateral-taker on terms that when the relevant financial obligations are discharged the collateral-taker must transfer legal and beneficial ownership of equivalent financial collateral to the collateral-provider; and (c) the collateral-provider and collateral-taker and both non-natural persons.

[208] Transfers Order, Art 2(5). See para 14.103 for discussion of foreign property.

[209] See Transfers Order, Art 3(4).

[210] See Transfers Order, Art 5(6).

[211] See Transfers Order, Art 6(4).

[212] See SRR Code, paras 8.13–8.14. The special resolution objectives are discussed at 13.23 above.

[213] See para 14.89.

[214] Transfers Order, Art 12(2).

contravention of the Transfers Order and as a result the P's property, rights, or liabilities have been affected, P may give notice to the Bank, in the case of an exercise of a private sector or resolution company transfer power, or the Treasury, in the case of an exercise of the temporary public ownership power, of the alleged contravention of the Transfers Order.[215] The Bank or Treasury must, within sixty days of receipt of the notice:[216]

- if it agrees that the Transfers Order been contravened in the manner specified in the notice, take the steps to remedy the contravention by transferring property, rights, or liabilities to the transferee or the transferor under the Partial Property Transfer Order;[217] or
- if it does not agree that a provision of the Transfers Order has been contravened in the manner specified in the notice, give reasons to P as to why it considers that, no provision of this Order has been contravened in the manner specified in the notice[218] ('Article 12 consequences').

The restrictions in the Transfers Order

The set-off and netting restrictions   There are two set-off and netting restrictions: **14.108**

- A Partial Property Transfer Order instrument or order may not provide for the transfer of some but not all of the protected rights and liabilities between a particular person ('P') and a bank under a particular Protected Arrangement.[219] Where a Partial Property Transfer Order is made in contravention of this restriction, under Article 11 the transfer will not affect the exercise of any right to set-off or net.
- A Partial Property Transfer Order instrument or order may not include any provision which empowers the Bank, in the exercise of the Continuity Powers to terminate or modify any protected rights or liabilities between P and a bank.[220] Where a Partial Property Transfer Order is made in contravention of this restriction, the transfer will be void under Article 10.

---

[215] Transfers Order, Arts 12(1) and (3). The notice must: be given within sixty days of the day on which the Partial Property Transfer Order took effect; be in writing; specify the provision of the Transfers Order which is alleged to have been contravened and the manner in which that contravention has occurred; identify the property, rights, or liabilities to which the alleged contravention relates; and contain or be accompanied by such information as the Bank or Treasury may reasonably require. (See Transfers Order, Art 12(4).)

[216] The Bank or Treasury may extend this period. (See Transfers Order, Art 12(8).)

[217] Transfers Order, Arts 12(5)(a) and 12(6). The property, rights, or liabilities which are transferred under Art 12(6) may be the same property, rights, or liabilities which were, in contravention of the Transfers Order, transferred or not transferred or, if the transfer of the property, rights, or liabilities is not practicable, property, rights, or liabilities which, in the opinion of the Bank or treasury, are equivalent to that property, or those rights or liabilities. (See Transfers Order, Art 12(9).)

[218] Transfers Order, Arts 12(5)(b) and 12(7).

[219] Transfers Order, Art 3(1).

[220] Transfers Order, Art 3(2).

14.109 For the purpose of the application of the set-off and netting restrictions, 'protected rights' and 'protected liabilities' are 'rights and liabilities which either P is entitled to set-off or net under a Protected Arrangement which P has entered into with the bank so long as they are not excluded rights or excluded liabilities.[221] The Transfers Order amplifies the definition of protected rights and protected liabilities as follows:

- It is immaterial whether (a) the arrangements which permits P or the bank to set-off or net rights and liabilities also permits P or the bank to set-off or net rights and liabilities with another person or (b) the right of P or the bank to set-off or net is exercisable only on the occurrence of a particular event.[222]

- 'Excluded rights' or 'excluded liabilities' are rights or liabilities relating to (a) a retail deposit made with a bank,[223] (b) a retail liability owed to a bank,[224] (c) a contract entered into by or on behalf of a bank otherwise, than in the course of carrying on of an activity which relates a to relevant financial instruments[225] or an activity referred to in Annex I to the CRD,[226] (d) a claim for damages, an award of damages, or a claim under an indemnity which arose in connection with the carrying on by a bank of an activity which relates to relevant financial instruments or an activity referred to in Annex I to the Banking Consolidation Directive; (e) which relate to subordinated debt issued by P or the bank; or (f) which relate to transferable securities issued by P or the bank (other than transferable securities referred to or described in a set-off arrangement, netting

---

[221] Transfers Order, Art 3(3).

[222] Transfers Order, Art 3(5).

[223] The Transfers Order, Art 1 defines a retail deposit as 'a deposit in relation to which the condition in (a) or (b) is satisfied: (a) the depositor is an eligible claimant; or (b) the deposit is held in an account of a particular class or brand provided by a particular banking institution which either (i) is mainly used by eligible claimants; or (ii) has been mainly marketed by the banking institution to, eligible claimants.' For these purposes, an 'eligible claimant' has the meaning given by rules of the FCA or the PRA respectively under s.213 of the FSMA. (See Transfers Order, Art 1.)

[224] The Transfers Order, Art 1 defines a retail liability as a 'liability which is owed by a [bank] to an eligible claimant'. As is the case with the definition of a retail deposit, for these purposes an 'eligible claimant' has the meaning given in rules made by the PRA or the FCA under s.213 of the FSMA (See Transfers Order, Art 1.)

[225] The Transfers Order, Art 1 defines a 'relevant financial instrument' as '(a) a financial instrument [, that is (A) any instrument listed in Section C of Annex I to the Markets in Financial Instruments Directive, read with Chapter VI of the Commission Regulation 1287/2006/EC; (B) any option, future, swap, forward, contract, for differences or other derivative contract not falling within paragraph (A); and (C) any combination of any of the foregoing]; (b) a deposit; (c) a loan; (d) a [debenture within the meaning of] Art 77 of the FSMA (Regulated Activities Order) 2001 (disregarding the exclusions in Art 77(2)(b) to (d)); or (e) any contract for the sale, purchase or delivery of (i) transferable securities [within the meaning of Art 4(18) of the Markets in Financial Instruments Directive]; (ii) the currency of the United Kingdom or any other country, territory or monetary union; (iii) palladium; platinum, gold, silver, or any other precious metal; or (iv) any other commodity.

[226] Directive 2013/36/EU of the European Parliament and of the Council relating to the taking up and pursuit of the business of credit institutions. These include: acceptance of deposits and other repayable funds; lending; financial leasing; payment services; issuing and administering other means of payment; guarantees and commitments; trading for own account or for account of customers in money market instruments, foreign exchange, financial futures and options, exchange,

arrangement, or title transfer financial collateral arrangement referred to in the set-off and netting restrictions.[227]

The community law restrictions   There are two community law restrictions: **14.110**

- A Partial Property Transfer Order instrument or order may not transfer property to the extent that to do so would contravene community law.[228] Where a Partial Property Transfer Order is made in contravention of this restriction and relates to protected arrangements, under Article 11 the transfer will not affect the exercise of the right to set-off or net. Where the contravention does not relate to protected arrangements, the Article 12 consequences will apply.
- A Partial Property Transfer Order instrument or order may not include any provision which empowers the Bank, in the exercise of the continuity powers to terminate or modify any protected rights or liabilities between P and a bank.[229] Where a Partial Property Transfer Order is made in contravention of this restriction, the transfer will be void under Article 10.

The secured liabilities restrictions   There are four secured liabilities restrictions:

- A Partial Property Transfer Order instrument or order may not transfer the property or rights against which the liability is secured unless that liability and the benefit of the security are also transferred.[230] Where a Partial Property Transfer Order is made in contravention of this restriction, the Article 12 consequences will apply.
- A Partial Property Transfer Order instrument or order may not transfer the benefit of the security unless the liability which is secured is also transferred.[231] Where a Partial Property Transfer Order is made in contravention of this restriction, the Article 12 consequences will apply.
- A Partial Property Transfer Order instrument or order may not transfer the liability unless the benefit of the security is also transferred.[232] Where a Partial Property Transfer Order is made in contravention of this restriction the Article 12 consequences will apply.
- A Partial Property Transfer Order instrument or order may not include any provision which empowers the Bank, in the exercise of the continuity powers to terminate or modify any security arrangement if the effect of that provision is to provide that the liability is no longer secured against the property or

---

and interest-rate instruments or transferable securities; participation in securities issues and related services; corporate finance advice; money brokering; portfolio management and advice; safekeeping and administering securities; credit reference services; safe custody services; issuing electronic money.

[227] Transfers Order, Arts 1 and 3(6).
[228] Transfers Order, Art 4.
[229] Transfers Order, Art 4.
[230] Transfers Order, Art 5(2).
[231] Transfers Order, Art 5(2A).
[232] Transfers Order, Art 5(3).

right.[233] Where a Partial Property Transfer Order is made in contravention of this restriction, the transfer will be void under Article 11.

14.111 These secured liabilities restrictions apply where an arrangement has been entered into under which one party owes a liability to the other and that liability is secured against property or rights. In this respect, it is immaterial that (a) the liability is secured against all or substantially all of the property or rights of a person, (b) the liability is secured against specified property or rights, or (c) the property or rights against which the liability is secured are not owned by the person who owes the liability.[234]

14.112 The secured liabilities restrictions do not apply if the bank has entered into the secured liabilities arrangement in contravention of a rule prohibiting such arrangements made under the Financial Services and Markets Act 2000 (FSMA) or in breach of the bank's FSMA Part IV permission.[235]

14.113 **The capital market arrangements restrictions** An arrangement is a 'capital market arrangement' if it involves a grant of security to (a) a person holding it as trustee for a person who holds a capital market investment issued by a party to the arrangement, or (b) a party to the arrangement who issues a capital market investment or a person who holds the security as trustee for a party to the arrangement in connection with the issue of a capital market investment, (c) it involves a grant of security to a person who holds the security as trustee for a party to the arrangement who agrees to provide finance to another party, or (d) at least one party guarantees the performance of obligations of another party, or at least one party provides security in respect of the performance of obligations of another party, or the arrangement involves options, futures, and contracts for differences within the meaning of FSMA (Regulated Activities) Order 2001, Articles 83–85.[236]

14.114 There are two capital market arrangement restrictions:

- A Partial Property Transfer Order instrument or order may not provide for the transfer of some, but not all, of the Property which is or forms part of a capital market arrangement to which a bank is a party.[237] Where a Partial Property

---

[233] Transfers Order, Art 5(4).
[234] Transfers Order, Art 5(1).
[235] Transfers Order, Art 5(5).
[236] Transfer Order, Art 6(5) which takes the definition from the Insolvency Act 1986, sch 2A, para 1. For these purposes: (a) a reference to holding as trustee includes a reference to holding as nominee or agent, (b) a reference to holding for a person who holds a capital market investment includes a reference to holding for a number of persons at least one of whom holds a capital market investment, a person holds a capital market investment if he has a legal or beneficial interest in it and the reference to the provision of finance includes the provisions of an indemnity. A 'party' to an arrangement includes a party to an agreement which forms part of the arrangement, provides for the raising of finance as part of the arrangement, or is necessary for the purposes of implementing the arrangement.
[237] Transfers Order, Art 6(1).

Transfer Order is made in contravention of this restriction, the Article 12 consequences will apply.

- A Partial Property Transfer Order instrument or order may not include any provision which empowers the Bank, in the exercise of the continuity powers to terminate or modify any property which are or form part of a capital market arrangement to which the bank is a party.[238] Where a Partial Property Transfer Order is made in contravention of this restriction, the transfer will be void under Article 11.

The capital markets restrictions do not apply where the only property transferred or not transferred, or terminated or modified is property which relate to deposits.[239]   **14.115**

The capital market restrictions are designed to save securitizations from the effects of Partial Property Transfer Orders, with the objective of attempting to ensure that any capital market arrangement remains intact and thereby protects investors' rights.   **14.116**

The financial markets restrictions   The financial markets provide protection for the following: **14.117**

- Contracts entered into by a Recognized Investment Exchange (RIE) or Recognized Clearing House (RCH) with members to settle their transactions, contracts entered into by a member of a RIE with a person other than that UK RIE made on, or subject to the rules of the RIE, contracts entered into by a designated non-member of a RIE with a person other than that UK RIE made on, or subject to the rules of the RIE ('market contracts');[240]
- the rules of a RIE or RCH which provide for the taking of action in the event of a person, including another RIE or RCH, appearing to be unable or likely to become unable, to meet its obligations in respect of one or more market contracts connected with the RIE or RCH ('RIE and RCH Default Rule');[241] and
- the rules of a RIE or RCH as to the settlement of market contracts not dealt with under the relevant RIE or RCH Default Rule ('RIE and RCH Rule').

There are two financial markets restrictions: **14.118**

- A Partial Property Transfer Order instrument or order may not transfer property to the extent that to do so would have the effect of modifying, modifying the operation of or rendering unenforceable any market contract, RIE or RCH Default Rule, or RIE and RCH Rule.[242]

---

[238] Transfers Order, Art 6(2).
[239] Transfers Order, Art 6(3).
[240] Transfers Order, Art 7(2); see further the definition of market contract in the Companies Act 1989, s 155 which Art 7(2) incorporates into the Transfers Order.
[241] Ibid. See further the Companies Act 1989, s 188.
[242] Transfers Order, Art 7(1).

- A Partial Property Transfer Order instrument or order may not include any provision which empowers the Bank, in the exercise of the continuity powers to modify, modify the operation of or render unenforceable any market contract, RIE or RCH Default Rule, or RIE and RCH Rule.[243]

14.119 Where a Partial Property Transfer Order is made in contravention of either of the financial markets restrictions, the transfer will be void under Article 10.

14.120 **The trusts restriction** In terms of the trusts restriction, a Partial Property Transfer Order instrument or order provision which makes provisions about the terms on which Property is to be held on trust after the instrument or order takes effect may remove or alter the terms of the relevant trust only to the extent necessary or expedient for the purpose of transferring from the bank to the transferee: (a) the legal or beneficial interest of the banking institution in the property held on trust; (b) any powers, rights or obligations of the banking institution in respect of the property held on trust.[244] Where a Partial Property Transfer Order is made in contravention of the trusts restriction, the Article 12 consequences will apply.

Additional restrictions on reverse transfers A Partial Property Transfer Order made by (a) the Bank under a reverse property transfer instrument under the BA, s 44 or (b) the Treasury under a reverse property transfer order under the BA, s 46 may not provide for the transfer of:

- any property, rights, or liabilities which were not transferred under the original instrument or order;
- any liability which was not, at the time immediately before the original instrument or order was made, a liability owed by the bank institution; or
- rights or liabilities under a relevant financial instrument.[245]

14.121 The additional restrictions on reverse transfers does not apply to: (a) a transfer of property, rights, or liabilities which have accrued, become or ceased to become payable, changed, or lapsed as a result of the application, of a default event provision which applies by virtue of the original instrument or order; (b) a transfer of property, rights, or liabilities to which consent has been given by the transferee, the transferor and any other person whose consent for the transfer would be required were the transfer not being effected by a property transfer instrument or order; (c) a transfer of a claim for damages or an award of damages against the banking institution which was in existence immediately before the original instrument or order was made; (d) a transfer to an undertaking which has not entered insolvency; or a transfer under Article 12(6) of the Transfers Order.[246]

---

[243] Transfers Order, Art 7(1).
[244] Transfers Order, Art 7A.
[245] Transfers Order, Arts 8(1) and (2).
[246] Transfers Order, Art 7(3). The reference to insolvency includes a reference to liquidation, bank insolvency, administration, bank administration, receivership, a composition with creditors, and a scheme of arrangement. (Transfers Order, Art 7(4).)

I. Compensation Orders

The BA requires the Bank, in its exercise of a private sector transfer power or the **14.122**
resolution company transfer power, and the Treasury, in its exercise of the temporary public ownership transfer power, to provide compensation for the purpose
of protecting financial interests of transferors.[247] The identity of the transferor or
transferors will depend on the stabilization power exercised. In the case of a share
transfer instrument or order, the transferors will be the holders of the securities
transferred under the instrument order. In the case of a property transfer instrument or order, the transferor will be the bank from whom property, rights or liabilities were transferred.[248]

The BA provides for four types of compensation order.[249] It makes special provi- **14.123**
sion for third-party compensation in the case of partial property transfer orders
and empowers the Treasury, the Financial Services Compensation Scheme or
any other person to make an order or regulations dealing with the sources of
compensation.[250]

The BA gives the Bank and Treasury the power to provide compensation to persons **14.124**
who are not transferors—'third parties'.[251] In the case of Partial Property Transfer
Orders, requires the BA requires the Bank, in the exercise of a private sector transfer
power or resolution company transfer power to compensate persons who are not
transferors.[252]

Compensation scheme orders

Characteristics

A compensation scheme order is an order: **14.125**

- determining whether transferors should be paid compensation; or
- providing for transferors to be paid compensation; and
- establishing a scheme for paying any compensation.[253]

Circumstances for making compensation scheme orders

Private sector transfers   The Bank must make a compensation scheme order in **14.126**
the exercise of a private sector transfer power.[254]

---

[247] See BA, ss 49(1), 50(2), 51(2) and 52(2) discussed further below. The BA, s 62 sets out the
procedure for the making of compensation orders.
[248] See BA, Explanatory Notes.
[249] See BA, ss 49(2), (3), and (4).
[250] BA, s 61. The relevant regulations or order have yet to be made.
[251] See BA, ss 49(1), 50(3), 51(3), and 52(3) discussed further below.
[252] See BA, ss 50(4) and 51(4) discussed further below.
[253] BA, s 49(2).
[254] BA, s 50(2).

14.127 Resolution company transfers The Bank may make a compensation scheme order as part of a resolution fund order in the exercise of a resolution company transfer power.[255]

14.128 Temporary public ownership transfers The Treasury must make a compensation scheme order or a resolution fund order in the exercise of a temporary public ownership transfer power.[256]

14.129 Bail-in option The Treasury must make a bail-in compensation order in the exercise of a resolution instrument.[257]

Resolution fund orders

Characteristics

14.130 A resolution fund order is an order establishing a scheme under which transferors become entitled to the proceeds of the disposal of things transferred in specified circumstances and to a specified extent, for example, the full or partial sale of a bridge bank company, whether through business or share transfer.[258]

14.131 A resolution fund order must contain provisions governing how proceeds and shares are to be calculated.[259] The order may allow for any payments to be net of resolution costs, which include public financial assistance or administrative expenses; include provisions for arranging to appoint an independent valuer and to apply the valuation principles; confer discretion on a minister of the Crown, Treasury, Bank, or another person; include provision for the determination of disputes about the application of its provisions; place a management duty on the Bank or Treasury in managing a resolution company or bank in temporary public ownership and set out how the Bank and Treasury are to meet these duties; and provide that any duties are only to be complied with to the extent that this is compatible with the pursuit of the SSR objectives and compliance with the SSR Code.[260]

Circumstances for making resolution fund orders

14.132 Private sector transfers The BA gives no powers to the Bank in the exercise of a private sector transfer power to make a resolution fund order.

---

[255] BA, s 52(3)(a). The Treasury may make a compensation scheme order where the Bank has made onward share, reverse share, onward property or reverse property instruments or orders in the exercise of a bridge bank transfer power (BA, s 53).

[256] BA, s 51(2). The Treasury may make a compensation scheme order where the Bank has made onward share, reverse share, onward property, or reverse property instruments or orders in the exercise of a temporary public ownership transfer power (BA, s 53).

[257] BA, s 52A.

[258] BA, s 49(3). See also BA, Explanatory Notes.

[259] BA, s 58(1).

[260] See BA, s 58(2)–(8).

Resolution company transfers The Bank must make a resolution fund order in **14.133**
the exercise of a resolution company transfer power.[261]

Temporary public ownership transfers The Treasury must make a resolution **14.134**
fund order or a compensation scheme order in the exercise of a temporary public
ownership transfer power.[262]

Third-party compensation orders

Characteristics

A third-party compensation order is an order establishing a scheme for pay- **14.135**
ing compensation to persons who are not transferors.[263] These persons would
include, for example, counterparties of a bank whose property rights are interfered with in a manner which requires them to be compensated under Article 1
of the First Protocol to the European Convention on Human Rights as a result
of the transfer.[264]

A third-party compensation order can be a part of a compensation scheme order or **14.136**
a resolution fund order or may be separate and may include provisions for arranging to appoint an independent valuer and to apply the valuation principles.[265]

Circumstances for third-party compensation orders

Private sector transfers The Bank may make a third-party compensation order **14.137**
as part of a compensation scheme order made in the exercise of a private sector
transfer power.[266]

Resolution company transfers The Bank may make a third-party compensa- **14.138**
tion order as part of a resolution fund order made in the exercise of a resolution
company transfer power.[267]

Temporary public ownership transfers The Treasury may make a third party **14.139**
compensation order as part of a resolution fund order made in the exercise of a
Temporary Public Ownership Transfer Power.[268]

---

[261] BA, s 52(2).
[262] BA, s 51(2).
[263] BA, ss 49(4) and 59(1).
[264] See BA, Explanatory Notes.
[265] See BA, ss 59(2) and (3).
[266] BA, s 50(3).
[267] BA, s 52(3)(b). The Treasury may make a third party compensation order where the Bank has
made onward share, reverse share, onward property or reverse property instruments or orders in the
exercise of a bridge bank transfer power (BA, s 53).
[268] BA, s 51(3)(b). This power does not extend to compensation scheme orders made in the
exercise of a temporary public ownership transfer power. The Treasury may make a third-party
compensation order where the Bank has made onward share, reverse share, onward property, or
reverse property instruments or orders in the exercise of a temporary public ownership transfer
power (BA, s 53).

14.140 **Resolution instrument** The Treasury must make a third-party compensation order as part of a bail-in resolution instrument.[269]

Third-party compensation orders: partial property transfers

14.141 In a similar way that the BA, ss 47 and 48 empower the Treasury to make an order protecting various interests in the cases of Partial Property Transfer Orders, ss 59 and 60 empower the Treasury to make regulations governing the treatment of third-party compensation payments in the case of Partial Property Transfer Orders of the property of a failed bank. The basic principle underlying these regulations is that where a residual bank enters an insolvency procedure following a Partial Property Transfer Order, pre-transfer creditors should not receive less favourable treatment than they would have received than had the bank entered an insolvency procedure prior to the partial transfer.[270] In essence, a creditor must be no worse off than it would have been in the event that the bank had entered into insolvency proceedings.[271] The BA, s 60 sets out various other mandatory requirements for the regulations.[272]

14.142 In reliance on the powers in BA, ss 59 and 60, the Treasury has made the BA (Third Party Compensation Arrangements for Partial Transfers) Order 2009 (the 'Compensation Regulations')[273] setting out the provisions which must or which may be included in a third-party compensation order in the case of a Partial Property Transfer Order.[274]

The Compensation Regulations

Mandatory provisions

14.143 A third-party compensation order in relation to a Partial Property Transfer Order ('Partial Property Compensation Order') must include the provisions which have the following effect:

14.144 **Appointment of independent valuer** The Bank or Treasury must appoint an independent valuer who is responsible for (i) determining whether all pre-transfer creditors, a class of pre-transfer creditors or a particular pre-transfer creditor should be paid compensation, and (ii) if compensation should be paid, what amount is to be paid.[275]

---

[269] BA, s 52A.

[270] BA, s 60(2).

[271] This does not extend to the shareholders of the bank.

[272] BA, s 259 governs the procedure for making the regulations under BA, s 60.

[273] 2009 SI 322/2009.

[274] The SSR Code does not contain any specific provisions dealing with third party compensation in the case of Partial Property Transfer Orders.

[275] See the Compensation Regulations, r 4 which also provide that the BA provisions governing independent valuers apply to an independent valuer appointed under a Partial Property Compensation Order.

The assessment of process   An independent valuer must assess: (i) which pre- **14.145**
transfer creditors would have received had the bank in relation to which or in
connection with which the Partial Property Transfer Order has been made entered
insolvency immediately before a Partial Property Transfer Order took effect
('insolvency treatment'), and (ii) the treatment which pre-transfer creditors have
received, are receiving or are likely to receive (as specified in the order) if no (or
no further) compensation is paid ('actual treatment').[276]

If the independent valuer considers that, in relation to any pre-transfer creditor, **14.146**
the actual treatment is less favourable than the insolvency treatment assessed under
paragraph, he must determine that compensation be paid to that pre-transfer
creditor. The independent valuer must determine the amount of compensation
payable by reference to (i) the difference between the insolvency treatment and the
actual treatment and on the basis of the fair and equitable value of that difference
in treatment.[277]

Choice of insolvency process   The independent valuer must (i) assess the insolv- **14.147**
ency treatment as required under the assessment process on the basis that the
bank had entered a particular insolvency process specified in the Partial Property
Compensation Order, or (ii) determine what insolvency process it is likely that
the bank would have entered had the Bank or Treasury made the relevant share or
property instrument or order, as the case may be.[278]

Valuation principles   In making the assessment of the insolvency treatment **14.148**
under the assessment process, the independent valuer must determine the amount
of compensation in accordance with the following principles:

- that the relevant bank has been made would have entered insolvency immediately before the relevant time;
- that the Partial Property Transfer Order has not been made and that no other
  order or instrument would have been made in relation to or in connection with
  the bank (or, in appropriate cases, any of the banks);
- that no financial assistance would have, after the relevant time, been provided
  by the Bank or the Treasury.[279]

Interim payments

The independent valuer may determine that payments should be made to a pre- **14.149**
transfer creditor, a class of pre-transfer creditors, or all pre-transfer creditors on
account of compensation to be payable under the third-party compensation order

---

[276] See the Compensation Regulations, rr 5(2) and (3).
[277] See the Compensation Regulations, rr 5(4) and (5).
[278] See the Compensation Regulations, r 6.
[279] See the Compensation Regulations, r 7. These are in addition to the valuation principles discussed at para 14.160.

('Payments on Account'). The independent valuer may make this determination at any time before the determination required under the assessment process and once that determination has been made, the independent valuer must determine what balancing payments are appropriate to ensure that the pre-transfer creditor receives the amount of compensation determined under the assessment process (and no more than that amount).[280]

14.150 The independent valuer may make such provision as to Payments on Account as he thinks fit, including a requirement that payments be made in instalments, subject to the following conditions: (i) the acceptance of such a payment by the pre-transfer creditor reduces any obligation, whether in existence at the time of the payment or not, on the Treasury, the Financial Services Compensation Scheme (FSCS), or any other person (as the case may be) to pay compensation to the pre-transfer creditor by the amount of the Payment on Account; (ii) where the independent valuer determines that the pre-transfer creditor should make a balancing payment to the Treasury, the FSCS, or any other person, the pre-transfer creditor is liable to pay that amount.[281]

14.151 In considering whether to require a payment on account, the independent valuer must have regard to the merits of ensuring that pre-transfer creditors receive compensation in a timely manner.[282]

Valuations provided by creditors

14.152 A Partial Property Compensation Order transfer must make provision requiring the independent valuer to have regard to any information provided by a pre-transfer creditor which is relevant to the exercise of the independent valuer's functions under the order; in particular, the independent valuer must have regard to any information which relates to the assessment of the insolvency treatment required under the assessment process.[283]

Optional provisions

14.153 A Partial Property Compensation Order may make any of the following provisions which have the following effect:

14.154 **Assumptions regarding price** In making the assessment of the insolvency treatment under the assessment process, the independent valuer must assume that property specified in the order or property of a class specified in the order would have been sold for the price specified in the order or calculated by reference to criteria specified in the order.[284]

---

[280] See the Compensation Regulations, rr 8(2), (3), and (4).
[281] See the Compensation Regulations, rr 8(5) and (6).
[282] See the Compensation Regulations, r 8(7).
[283] See the Compensation Regulations, r 9.
[284] See the Compensation Regulations, r 10(2).

Assumptions regarding treatment   In making the assessment of the insolvency   **14.155**
treatment under the assessment process, the independent valuer must assume that
property specified in the order or property of a class specified in the order would
have been treated in the manner specified in the order.[285]

*Effect of transfers of foreign property or rights or liabilities relating
to foreign property*

As is the case with the Transfers Order, under the Compensation Regulations a   **14.156**
property transfer instrument or order which purports to transfer all of the property
of a bank is to be treated as having done so effectively despite the possibility that any
of the property is foreign property and may not have been effectively transferred in
accordance with BA, s 39. Therefore, any property transfer under the instrument or
order will not be treated as a Partial Property Transfer Order.[286]

Independent valuers

Appointment and removal

A compensation scheme order and a third-party compensation order may include   **14.157**
provision for the amount of compensation to be determined by an independent
valuer appointed by a person appointed by the Treasury. The BA provides two
different methods for appointing the valuer: the Treasury may arrange to identify
candidates or provide that another person will arrange to appoint a valuer. The
independent valuer can be removed only on grounds of incapacity or serious
misconduct. The removal must be made by a person specified by the Treasury
in accordance with the relevant order which must also include provision for
resignation.[287]

Powers, functions, and records

The BA empowers an independent valuer to do anything necessary or desirable   **14.158**
in relation to the performance of his functions and enables the Treasury by
order to make provision to assist the independent valuer in the discharge of his
functions; for example, by providing him with certain powers. These include
the power to appoint staff. The relevant order must provide for the reconsid-
eration of the decisions of the valuer, and for onward rights of appeal from
the valuer to a court or tribunal. The BA specifies that the independent valuer
and his staff are not servants of the Crown but provides that the records of the
independent valuer are public records for the purposes of the Public Records
Act 1958.[288]

---

[285] See the Compensation Regulations, r 10(3).
[286] Compensation Regulations, r 2(5). See para 14.103 above for discussion of foreign property.
[287] See BA, s 54. See also SSR Code, paras 10.11–10.12.
[288] See BA, s 55 and the Dunfermline Building Society Independent Valuer Order 2009 SI 2009/1810.

Remuneration and allowances

14.159 A compensation scheme order or third-party compensation order may provide for
the remuneration and allowances of the independent valuer, his staff, appointing
persons, or monitors. Although such payments will be made by the Treasury, the
order may require the Treasury to appoint a person to monitor the arrangements
made for the remuneration and allowances. An order may confer further functions
on the monitor, such as requiring his approval to certain actions and may include
provision in the order about records, accounts and staff resources. The BA makes
it clear that the independent valuer and his staff are not liable for damages for
anything done in good faith when undertaking their respective roles in relation to
independent valuation, except for awards of damages for unlawful actions under
the Human Rights Act 1998.[289]

Valuation principles

14.160 The BA allows a compensation scheme order and a third-party compensation
order to specify valuation principles to be applied during the determination of
the amount of compensation. The valuation principles may require an independent valuer to apply specific methods of valuation, assess values at specified dates
or periods, take specified matters into account, or not take specified matters into
account. The valuer may disregard actual or potential financial assistance provided by the Bank or Treasury, other than ordinary market assistance offered
by the Bank on its usual terms. A valuer may be required or permitted make
certain assumptions about a bank, including that the FSA has varied or cancelled
a permission under FSMA, Part 4 of the FSMA, it is unable to continue as a
going concern, that it is in administration, or that it is being wound up. There is
nothing to prevent the application of valuation principles from resulting in no
compensation being payable.[290]

J. Bail-in and the Banking Act

14.161 The core provisions of the Banking Act relating to Bail-in powers are in sections
48B–48Y. Bail-in is implemented through a resolution instrument which contains
special bail-in provisions[291] and associated provisions.[292]

14.162 The essence of a bail-in resolution instrument is that it may (a) cancel a liability
owed by the bank, (b) modify or change the form of a liability owed by the bank,
or (c) provide that a contract under which the bank has a liability is to have effect as

---

[289] See BA, s 56. See also SSR Code, paras 10.13–10.14 and the Dunfermline Building Society
Independent Valuer Order 2009 SI 2009/1810.
[290] See BA, s 57. See also SSR Code, para 10.15.
[291] BA, s 48B(1).
[292] BA, s 48B(3).

if a specified right had been exercised under it. 'Associated provisions' for this purpose are provisions cancelling or modifying a contract under which a bank group company has a liability.

Certain liabilities are exempt from bail-in under the BA. There are two classes of **14.163** these. One is the list prescribed in Article 44(2) of the BRRD—that is:

(a) liabilities representing protected deposits;
(b) any liability, so far as it is secured;
(c) liabilities that the bank has by virtue of holding client assets;
(d) liabilities with an original maturity of less than seven days owed by the bank to a credit institution or investment firm;
(e) liabilities [with a remaining maturity of less than seven days] arising from participation in designated settlement systems and owed to such systems or to operators of, or participants in, such systems;
(f) liabilities owed to an employee or former employee in relation to salary or other remuneration, except variable remuneration that is not regulated by a collective bargaining agreement, and variable remuneration of material risk takers as referred to in Article 92(2) of the CRD;
(g) liabilities owed to a pension scheme, except for liabilities owed in connection with variable remuneration;
(h) liabilities owed to creditors arising from the provision to the bank of goods or services (other than financial services) that are critical to the daily functioning of the bank's operations;
(i) liabilities owed by the bank to the scheme manager of the Financial Services Compensation Scheme[293] in relation to levies imposed by the scheme manager for the purpose of meeting expenses in relation to payments required to be made by Deposit Guarantee Schemes Directive.[294]

All of these are excluded by s 48B(8) BA. However, s 48B(1) also provides that the **14.164** Bank may, in a resolution instrument, exclude any other eligible liability if it is satisfied that the exclusion is justifiable under Article 44(3) of the BRRD and it gives the European Commission notice of the proposed exclusion prior to making the instrument. The criteria which must be satisfied before a liability may be excluded from bail-in are:

(a) that it is not reasonably possible to give effect to special bail-in provision in relation to the liability or class within a reasonable time;
(b) that the exclusion is necessary and proportionate to achieve the continuity of critical functions and core business lines in a manner that maintains the ability of the bank to continue key operations, services, and transactions;

---

[293] Established under Part 15 of the Financial Services and Markets Act 2000.
[294] 2014/49/EU.

(c) that the exclusion is necessary and proportionate to avoid giving rise to widespread contagion, in particular as regards protected deposits held by natural persons or micro-enterprises, small or medium-sized enterprises, which would severely disrupt the functioning of financial markets, including financial market infrastructures, in a manner that could cause a serious disturbance to the economy of a European Economic Area state;

(d) that the making of special bail-in provision in relation to the liability would cause a reduction in value such that the losses borne by other creditors would be higher than if the liability were excluded.

14.165 In principle, all creditors of a bank should be treated equally, and it is certainly the express policy of the BRRD[295] that a bail-in instrument should be applied to all non-excluded exposures equally unless exclusion is required or justified. It is therefore surprising that there is no explicit reference to do this placed in the Bank. The closest that the BA gets in this regard is the requirement in BA, s 48B(13) that in deciding which exposures to exclude in this way, the bank 'should give due consideration' to (a) the principle that all the liabilities of the bank ought to be treated in accordance with the priority they would enjoy on a liquidation, and (b) the principle that any creditors who would have equal priority on a liquidation ought to bear losses on an equal footing with each other, However these principles are to be weighed alongside (c) the level of loss absorbing capacity that would remain in the bank if the liability or liabilities of a class were wholly or partly excluded, and (d) the need to maintain adequate resources to deal with the implications for public funds of anything done, in future, in connection with the exercise of one or more of the stabilization powers. Thus, as a result, the bank is in fact under no positive statutory obligation to reduce creditors' claims equally. Interestingly, by BA, s 48G, the Treasury is given power to correct this, since it may 'for the purpose of ensuring that the treatment of liabilities in any instrument that contains special bail-in provision is aligned to an appropriate degree with the treatment of liabilities on an insolvency, by order specify matters or principles to which the Bank of England is to be required to have regard in making any such instrument'. However, no such order has been made.

14.166 A resolution instrument is more than merely a bail-in instrument. A resolution instrument may:

(a) cancel, modify or convert any stocks and shares issued by the bank,[296] require such securities to be listed or delisted;[297]

(b) remove a director or senior manager of the bank, or vary or terminate the contract of such a director;[298]

---

[295] Art 44(1).
[296] BA, s 48L(1).
[297] BA, s 48L(3).
[298] BA, s 48M(1).

(c) give directions to any director, or to the directors as a whole, or enable the Bank to give such directions;[299]

(d) impose continuity requirements in respect of anything (including legal proceedings) on foot prior to the making of the order;[300]

(e) permit or require the execution of documents.[301]

In addition, provisions made in a resolution instrument are deemed to top take effect despite any restrictions arising by contract, under legislation or in any other way.[302] **14.167**

The Bank also has similar powers to those which arise in the context of property transfers to make further instruments—this once a resolution instrument is made, the bank may make supplementary resolution instruments,[303] and where the resolution instrument provides for the transfer of securities, it may make an onward transfer resolution instrument which has the effect of transferring those securities again (although an onward transfer resolution instrument may not be used to reverse the original transfer by transferring securities to the transferor under the original instrument.[304] This must be done through a reverse transfer instrument.[305] **14.168**

What the bail-in provisions do necessitate, however, is a set of protections for claims which would otherwise be disturbed by a reduction. This protection is created in a similar way to the protections in respect of partial property transfers, with BA, s 48P providing for the making of an order protecting certain arrangements from being affected by a bail-in. The arrangements to be protected are netting arrangements, security interests, set-off arrangements, and title transfer collateral arrangements. The relevant order (the Banking Act 2009 (Restriction of Special Bail-in Provision, etc) Order 2014[306] gives effect to these protections. **14.169**

Set-off and netting

The Order prohibits a resolution instrument from making special bail-in provision in respect of liabilities which are owed by the bank to a particular person in circumstances where either the person or the bank is entitled to set-off or net under particular set-off arrangements, netting arrangements or title transfer collateral arrangements into which the person has entered.[307] Where the liability relates to a derivative, financial contract, or qualifying master agreement, this protection is only available prior to the agreement's being closed out—when the claim arising **14.170**

---

[299] BA, s 48O(1).
[300] BA, s 48Q.
[301] BA, s 48R.
[302] BA, s 48S.
[303] BA, s 48U.
[304] BA, s 48V(4).
[305] BA, s 48W.
[306] SI 2014/3350.
[307] BIO, Art 4.

under the agreement has been converted into a net debt, claim or obligation, that claim may be bailed in. Such conversion may of course be effected by the resolution instrument itself,[308] but it remains the case that netting under un-closed-out masters will be respected. Where the liability relates to any other type of contract, the same principal applies—it remains protected until it is converted into a net debt claim or obligation.

14.171 Certain liabilities are explicitly excluded from this protection. These include:

(a) any liabilities arising out of an unsecured debt instrument which is a transferable security issued by the bank;[309]

(b) liabilities in relation to a capital instrument issued by the bank;

(c) liabilities owed in relation to subordinated debt;

(d) unsecured liabilities in relation to any instrument or contract (other than a derivative, financial contract or master agreement) which had an original maturity on creation of twelve months or more; and

(e) unsecured liabilities owed to another member of the same group[310] except for those owed in relation to derivatives, financial contracts or qualifying master agreements;

(f) liabilities which relate to a claim for damages or an award of damages or a claim under an indemnity.

14.172 For these purposes, 'derivative' has the same meaning as in the European Markets Infrastructure Regulation,[311] 'financial contract' means any or any combination of the following (other than a derivative):

(a) a contract for the purchase, sale, transfer, or loan of a transferable security, a group of transferable securities, or index of transferable securities;

(b) a repurchase or reverse repurchase transaction on any transferable security, group of transferable securities or index of transferable securities;

(c) a commodities contract of a financial nature, including:

(i) a contract for the purchase, sale, transfer, or loan of a commodity, a group of commodities, or an index of commodities for future delivery;

(ii) a swap or option on a commodity, a group of commodities, or an index of commodities;

(iii) a repurchase or reverse repurchase transaction on any such commodity, group, or index;

(d) a futures contract, including a contract (other than a commodities contract) for the purchase, sale or transfer of property of any description under which

---

[308] BIO 4(6).

[309] BIO 4(3)(a). for these purposes a 'debt instrument' is any instrument falling within Art 77 of the Financial Services and Markets Act 2000 (Regulated Activities) Order 2001.

[310] 'Group' for this purpose has the meaning given in s1161(5) of the Companies Act 2006.

[311] No 648/2012.

delivery is to be made at a future date and at a price agreed when the contract is made.

A 'qualifying master agreement' means a master agreement in so far as it relates to: **14.173**

(a) a derivative;

(b) a financial contract; or

(c) a contract for the sale, purchase or delivery of the currency of the United Kingdom or any other country, territory or monetary union.

Remedy

Where a resolution instrument is made which has the effect of contravening the   **14.174** order, the validity of the instrument is not affected. The remedy of a person who is affected by an instrument made in breach of the order is to apply to the Bank within sixty days of the date of the instrument. If the Bank accepts that the instrument contravened the Bail-in Order (BIO), it must arrange for the complainant to be compensated. Where the instrument is not made as part of a resolution involving a bridge bank (i.e. where the resolution is effected solely by a write-down of claims on the institution concerned), the bank must require the institution to issue securities, or transfer securities issued by it, or to pay cash, to the value of the loss suffered. Where the resolution involves both a bail-in and a bridge bank, either the bailed-in bank or the bridge bank may be required to issue securities, or to pay cash, to the value of the loss suffered.

INDEX